THE EU LAW OF INVESTMENT

Over the past decade, Europe's traditionally open investment landscape has shifted towards a more protectionist stance due to evolving geopolitical factors. This open access book delves into the emerging challenges within the EU legal order related to this shift. Featuring contributions from leading scholars, civil servants and practitioners, it offers a comprehensive analysis through four key themes: investment frameworks, arbitration, sustainability, and future developments. With its expert insights and broad scope, this collection is an invaluable resource for investment lawyers both within and beyond the European Union.

The EU Law of Investment: Past, Present, and Future

Swedish Studies in European Law

Volume 20

Edited by
Xavier Groussot
Marja-Liisa Öberg
and
Graham Butler

•HART•
OXFORD • LONDON • NEW YORK • NEW DELHI • SYDNEY

HART PUBLISHING

Bloomsbury Publishing Plc

Kemp House, Chawley Park, Cumnor Hill, Oxford, OX2 9PH, UK

1385 Broadway, New York, NY 10018, USA

Bloomsbury Publishing Ireland Limited, 29 Earlsfort Terrace, Dublin 2, D02 AY28, Ireland

HART PUBLISHING, the Hart/Stag logo, BLOOMSBURY and the Diana logo are trademarks of Bloomsbury Publishing Plc

First published in Great Britain 2025

A catalogue record for this book is available from the British Library.

A catalogue record for this book is available from the Library of Congress.

ISBN: HB: 978-1-50996-585-4
ePDF: 978-1-50996-587-8
ePub: 978-1-50996-586-1

Typeset by Compuscript Ltd, Shannon

Contents

Contributors

EDITORS

Xavier Groussot
Professor of Law, Lund University, Sweden.

Marja-Liisa Öberg
Associate Professor of Law, Lund University, Sweden.

Graham Butler
Full Professor of Law, Linnaeus University, Sweden.

AUTHORS

Laurens Ankersmit
Assistant Professor of European Law, University of Amsterdam, Amsterdam, the Netherlands.

Anatole Boute
Professor of Law, Chinese University of Hong Kong, Hong Kong.

Colin M Brown
Head of Unit, Legal Aspects of Trade and Sustainable Development and Investment, Directorate-General for Trade, European Commission, Brussels, Belgium; Head of the Delegation of the European Union to UNCITRAL Working Group III; Guest Lecturer, Edinburgh Law School, University of Edinburgh, Edinburgh, Scotland, United Kingdom.

Graham Butler
Full Professor of Law, Linnaeus University, Sweden.

Ivana Damjanovic
Senior Lecturer, Canberra Law School, University of Canberra, Australia.

Nicolas de Sadeleer
Professor of Law and Jean Monnet Chair, Saint-Louis University, Brussels, Belgium; Senior Researcher, METRO, Maastricht University, Maastricht, the Netherlands.

Maria Fanou
Legal Secretary (*Référendaire*), Court of Justice, Court of Justice of the European Union, Luxembourg.

Szilárd Gáspár-Szilágyi
Researcher, Department of Public and International Law, Faculty of Law, University of Oslo, Norway; Managing Editor, *European Investment Law and Arbitration Review*.

Claes Granmar
Associate Professor of Law, Stockholm University, Sweden.

Steffen Hindelang
Professor of International Investment and Trade Law, Uppsala University, Sweden.

Gesa Kübek
Assistant Professor of European Law, University of Groningen, the Netherlands.

Hannes Lenk
Legal Advisor, National Board of Trade, Stockholm, Sweden.

Relja Radović
Senior Associate, BDK Serbia Law Firm, Belgrade, Serbia.

Sara Soini
Project Development Manager, Ren-Gas, Espoo, Finland.

Konstanze von Papp
Professor of Public Law, Hamburg University of Applied Sciences, Hamburg, Germany.

Abbreviations

AA	Association Agreements
BIT	Bilateral Investment Treaty
CAI	Comprehensive Agreement on Investment
CCP	Common Commercial Policy
CEE	Central and Eastern European
CETA	Comprehensive Economic and Trade Agreement
CFR	Charter of Fundamental Rights of the European Union
CFSP	Common Foreign and Security Policy
CJEU	Court of Justice of the European Union
ECHR	European Convention on Human Rights
ECtHR	European Court of Human Rights
ECT	Energy Charter Treaty
EEA	European Economic Area
EFTA	European Free Trade Association
EMD	Electricity Market Directive
EPA	Economic Partnership Agreement
EU	European Union
EUVIPA	EU-Vietnam Investment Protection Agreement
EUSIPA	EU-Singapore Investment Protection Agreement
EUVFTA	EU-Vietnam Free Trade Agreement
EWHC	High Court of Justice in England and Wales
FDI	Foreign Direct Investment
FET	Fair and Equitable Treatment
FPS	Full Protection and Security

FTA	Free Trade Agreement
GATT	General Agreement on Tariffs and Trade
GC	General Court of the European Union
ICS	Investment Court System
ICSID	International Centre for Settlement of Investment Disputes
IIL	International Investment Law
ILO	International Labour Organization
IPA	Investor Protection Agreement
ISDS	Investor-State Dispute Settlement
ITA	Investment Treaty Arbitration
JHA	Justice and Home Affairs
MFN	Most-Favoured-Nation
MIC	Multilateral Investment Court
NYC	Convention on Recognition and Enforcement of Foreign Arbitral Awards
OJ	Official Journal of the European Union
PCA	Permanent Court of Arbitration
PTA	Preferential Trade Agreements
REIO	Regional Economic International Organisations
SDG	Sustainable Development Goals
SDI	Sovereign-driven investment
SNEF	Swedish Network for European Legal Studies (*Svenska nätverket för Europarättsforskning*)
SWF	Sovereign wealth fund
TBT	Technical barriers to trade
TEU	Treaty on European Union
TFEU	Treaty on the Functioning of the European Union
TRIPS	Agreement on Trade-Related Aspects of Intellectual Property Rights

TSD	Trade and Sustainable Development
UKSC	Supreme Court of the United Kingdom
UNCTAD	United Nations Conference on Trade and Development
UNCITRAL	United Nations Commission on International Trade Law
VCLT	Vienna Convention on the Law of Treaties
WTO	World Trade Organization

1

Investment in the EU Legal Order

GRAHAM BUTLER

1.1. INTRODUCTION

AT A VERY basic level, when it comes to investment and EU law, it will be the EU free movement lawyer who says, 'investment relates to the free movement of capital'. However, as much such a statement that might be true, it must be specified further that merely looking at or examining the issue of 'investment' through the lens of free movement, or the internal market more generally, would not be paying heed to the wider issue of how investment intersects so many different areas of law today, be it national law, EU law, public international law, or private international law.

Text in primary law can be deceiving. Upon inspection of the EU Treaties, the term 'investment' does not appear very often, which might give the impression that rights conferred by EU law concerning it are confined to the free movement of capital, and appears as otherwise limited. It is referred to in the free movement of capital provision of Article 64 TFEU that distinguishes direct investments and indirect investments as regards third countries,[1] and Article 65 TFEU on written potential grounds of exception to the free movement of capital.[2] It is also mentioned in passing as regards competition law and policy in Article 101 TFEU, on the Union's association with overseas countries and territories (OCTs) in Article 199 TFEU, the common commercial policy (CCP) in the context of foreign direct investment (FDI) in Articles 206–207 TFEU, and at various instances regarding the European Investment Bank (EIB), *inter alia*.

These explicit references, however important they may be, give anything but a complete picture as to the nature of investment in EU law, and the way in

[1] For more, see Steffen Hindelang, *The Free Movement of Capital and Foreign Direct Investment: The Scope of Protection in EU Law* (Oxford University Press, 2009).

[2] For more, see Graham Butler, 'Free Movement of Capital: General Rules and Exceptions' in Robert Schütze and Takis Tridimas (eds), *Oxford Principles of European Union Law: Volume II: The Internal Market* (Oxford University Press, 2026).

which investment is embedded within the EU legal order more generally. It is this contradiction between the text of investment, and the reality of investment, that this book intends to explore, against a very particular backdrop of how investment has arisen in the past decade.

1.2. INVESTMENT: THE ISSUE OF INTERNATIONAL AGREEMENTS OF THE MEMBER STATES

There is increased tension in the air within the EU's system of governance.[3] On the one hand, there is free (internal) movement and open (though regulated) international trade, and on the other hand a new instinctive reactiveness towards making it more difficult and/or closing the door to greater movement and trade across international borders, between the EU and the rest of the world. This is dominated by legal, political and economic developments. Legally, and most importantly, there have been judgments of the Court of Justice of the European Union (CJEU or the Court) that, to some, were something of a surprise.

Take *Achmea* as a case in point.[4] There, the Court was faced with the question of the lawfulness of a bilateral investment agreement (treaty) – a BIT – between two Member States: an intra-EU situation. At the time of the conclusion of that BIT, only one of the two parties was a Member State (the Netherlands), with the other being a third state (Slovakia). Did the accession of that latter third state to the EU have implications for the relevance of the BIT? For the Court, it most certainly did. Given that the BIT in question provided for an arbitral tribunal to settle disputes under it, and that such an arbitral tribunal would indeed be called upon to interpret EU law in the course of deciding on whether an arbitral award was appropriate or not, the Court ruled that Article 267 TFEU and Article 344 TFEU excluded the possibility of such an arbitral tribunal between two EU Member States under a BIT.

Through a thorough reading of the Court's judgment, it is evident that the Court viewed BITs – a common feature of international agreements made by many Member States to protect investments made by legal persons within them in Central and Eastern Europe (CEE) after the fall of communism – as a threat to the autonomy of the EU legal order. This was because, for the Court, what was at stake was essentially fundamental market freedoms, as

[3] See, *inter alia*, Antonina Bakardjieva Engelbrekt and Xavier Groussot (eds), *The Future of Europe: Political and Legal Integration Beyond Brexit* (Hart Publishing, 2019); Antonina Bakardjieva Engelbrekt, Andreas Moberg and Joakim Nergelius (eds), *Rule of Law in the EU: 30 Years After the Fall of the Berlin Wall* (Hart Publishing, 2021).

[4] Case C-284/16 *Slowakische Republik v Achmea BV* ECLI:EU:C:2018:158. See also Xavier Groussot and Marja-Liisa Öberg, 'The Web of Autonomy of the EU Legal Order: Achmea' in Graham Butler and Ramses A Wessel (eds), *EU External Relations Law: The Cases in Context* (Hart Publishing, 2022).

provided under the EU Treaties (in particular, the freedom of establishment and the free movement of capital, but also others), and given that such an arbitral tribunal was not part of the national judicial systems of either of the two Member States, the full effectiveness of EU law could not be guaranteed. In other words, it was national courts of Member States that are entrusted with such tasks of deciding disputes (that are, importantly, within the EU judicial architecture), and not arbitral tribunals (that are not part of the EU judicial architecture).

The *Achmea* judgment went down in many quarters like a bombshell. In the years since its delivery, *Achmea* has become one of the most frequently analysed cases within EU legal scholarship, largely criticised, and a judgment that few have defended. Private commercial arbitrators at first worried about the wide ramifications that *Achmea* could have on their legal practice. For many years prior to this, they had been operating under the *Eco Swiss* approach,[5] a Court-sanctioned approach which states the principle that private arbitral tribunals must apply EU law in their rulings, even if the parties to such arbitration have not raised it, with the aim in mind that EU law and the EU legal order is not undermined by private legal arrangements, and private law more generally. According to the Court in *Eco Swiss*, a failure of arbitral tribunals to account for EU law would result in national courts having the possibility to set any arbitral awards aside. As such, *Achmea* placed a new demand on private arbitration: how to handle disputes that could potentially threaten the autonomy of the EU legal order. The full effects of the *Achmea* judgment on arbitration will take some time to play out in real terms.

Notwithstanding the criticism of *Achmea*, the Court has been unwavering in retaining *Achmea* as the new law of the land. The judgments that the Court subsequently delivered in *Komstroy*[6] and *PL Holdings*[7] amongst others have shown that the Court has been resolute, and its *Achmea* judgment stands firm. Whilst *Achmea* eliminated intra-EU BITs and their arbitration, the *Komstroy* judgment of the Court eliminated intra-EU cases under the Energy Charter Treaty (ECT), the only investment agreement that the EU ratified alongside its Member States before the Treaty of Lisbon was ratified. The actual dispute in *Komstroy* was an extra-EU dispute involving an investor in Ukraine and the state of Moldova, and, remarkably, the issue of intra-EU aspects of the ECT did not explicitly arise. Yet the Court seized the opportunity to pronounce on Article 26 ECT which was the arbitration clause in the agreements, and its relevance on an intra-EU basis.[8] This was strongly criticised, both on the issue of the Court

[5] Case C-126/97 *Eco Swiss China Time Ltd v Benetton International NV* ECLI:EU:C:1999:269. See also Case C-168/05 *Elisa María Mostaza Claro v Centro Móvil Milenium SL* ECLI:EU:C:2006:675.

[6] Case C-741/19 *Republic of Moldova v Komstroy* ECLI:EU:C:2021:655.

[7] Case C-109/20 *Republic of Poland v PL Holdings Sàrl* ECLI:EU:C:2021:321.

[8] This issue of delivering judgments on matters not immediately before the referring court has received little scholarly attention. Typically, the Court confines itself to the issues of EU law necessary for the referring court to decide on the matter before it. A related (though different) consideration is

pronouncing on the non-issue before the referring court, but also on the wider ramifications of what the Court in *Komstroy* did as regards investment and legal protection more generally.[9]

Thereafter, in *PL Holdings*, a case referred by the Supreme Court of Sweden (*Högsta domstolen*), the Court ruled that ad hoc *investor-state* arbitration, in lieu of the fact that arbitration under intra-EU investment agreements was no longer possible under *Achmea*, was also caught under the logic of *Achmea*. This is because the way in which the case transpired was seen to be a circumvention of the *Achmea* judgment, which the Court was unwilling to tolerate. Whilst ad hoc *commercial* arbitration is still possible under the logic of *Eco Swiss*, it is only for now that it appears to escape the Court's broadening case law.

For all that this investment-related case law has done, it is also important to note what it has *not* done. So far, it has not sought to eliminate extra-EU investment arbitration. Individual Member States continue to have BITs in place with third states,[10] though the Commission would certainly be licking its lips over the possibilities that it might affect the EU's CCP, and seize an opportunity to initiate infringement proceedings. Therefore, whilst Member States may have extra-EU BITs in place, at the same time, they must be compatible with EU law as regards their BITs in place prior to their accession,[11] or risk being chased by the Commission.[12] For now, however, the logic of this case law, affirmatively within the field of investment, is beginning to have wider implications into other fields.

1.3. INVESTMENT: LOGIC, AND THE WIDER AUTONOMY OF THE EU LEGAL ORDER

In 2023, during the Court's annual judgment-dumping on the last sitting day of a calendar year, the Court delivered its judgment in *International Skating Union*

where the Court answers questions where EU law does not apply. See, eg, Morten Broberg and Niels Fenger, 'Should the Court of Justice Give Preliminary Rulings in Cases Where EU Law Does Not Apply?' (2023) 29 *European Public Law* 27.

[9] See, Alan Dashwood, 'Republic of Moldova v Komstroy LCC: Arbitration under Article 26 ECT Outlawed in Intra-EU Disputes by Obiter Dictum' (2022) 47 *European Law Review* 127; Alan Dashwood, 'Komstroy and Opinion 1/20 – Curious and Curiouser' (2022) 59 *Common Market Law Review* 51; Alan Dashwood, 'Article 26 ECT and Intra-EU Disputes – the Case Against an Expansive Reading of Achmea' (2021) 46 *European Law Review* 415.

[10] For example, through the International Centre for Settlement of Investment Disputes (ICSID), *inter alia*.

[11] Article 351 TFEU.

[12] As the 1990s acceders to the EU found out the hard way. See Case C-205/06 *Commission v Austria* ECLI:EU:C:2009:118; Case C-249/06 *Commission v Sweden* ECLI:EU:C:2009:119; and Case C-118/07 *Commission v Finland* ECLI:EU:C:2009:715. Further, see Luigi Lonardo, 'Potential Incompatibility of International Agreements Concluded by Member States before Accession: Commission v Austria, Commission v Sweden, and Commission v Finland' in Graham Butler and Ramses A Wessel (eds), *EU External Relations Law: The Cases in Context* (Hart Publishing, 2022).

v Commission.[13] There, in what was either an off-the-cuff remark (or a deliberate swipe), the Court stated that

> rules such as the prior authorisation and eligibility rules must be subject to effective judicial review ... [and that such] ... requirement ... means that, in the event that such rules [of an international sports body] contain provisions conferring mandatory and exclusive jurisdiction on an arbitration body [(the Court of Arbitration for Sport, the CAS)], the court having jurisdiction to review the awards [(the Federal Supreme Court, Switzerland)] made by that [arbitration] body may confirm that those awards comply with Articles 101 and 102 TFEU.[14]

However, it is apparent in practice that the Federal Supreme Court of Switzerland merely confines its review of CAS's decisions to public policy issues like procedural matters, rather than matters of substance. In other words, it does not check whether EU competition law, emanating from Articles 101 and 102 TFEU, is correctly applied or not. Because of this, the Court in *International Skating Union v Commission* continued that, as a result, it is necessary that such court

> [satisfies] all the requirements under Article 267 TFEU, so that it is entitled, or, as the case may be, required, to refer a question to the Court of Justice where it considers that a decision of the Court is necessary concerning a matter of EU law raised in a case pending before it.[15]

The Federal Supreme Court of Switzerland is not a court or tribunal within the meaning of the reference for a preliminary ruling procedure in Article 267 TFEU, as it is evidently a court in a third state. Therefore, decisions rendered under CAS, whilst it sits in Switzerland, are decisions that cannot be referred to the Court through the reference for a preliminary ruling procedure. It is thus conceivable that the current setup of CAS, in Switzerland, as a mandatory location for sports arbitration, is incompatible with EU law and the EU legal order.

That is where the *Royal Football Club Seraing* case comes in.[16] The referring national court asked for clarity on, *inter alia*, the lawfulness of particular national law relating to the treatment of an arbitral award – the conformity of which with EU law has been reviewed by a court of a state that is not a Member State of the European Union, which is not permitted to refer a question to the Court for a preliminary ruling under Article 267 TFEU – and its compatiblity with EU primary law, namely, Article 19(1) TEU, Article 267 TFEU and Article 47 of the Charter of Fundamental Rights. Framed as a matter of EU law,

[13] Case C-124/21 P *International Skating Union v Commission* ECLI:EU:C:2023:1012. It should be noted that the judgment in *International Skating Union v Commission* was delivered alongside two other sports-related judgments the same day in Case C-680/21 *Royal Antwerp Football Club* ECLI:EU:C:2023:1010; and Case C-333/21 *European Superleague Company* ECLI:EU:C:2023:1011.

[14] Case C-124/21 P *International Skating Union v Commission* (n 13) paras 198–199.

[15] ibid para 199.

[16] Case C-600/23 *Royal Football Club Seraing v Fédération Internationale de Football Association (FIFA), Union Royale Belge des Sociétés de Football Association ASBL (URBSFA), Union européenne des Sociétés de Football Association (UEFA), and Doyen Sports Investment Ltd*, pending.

the Advocate General in the case was of the view that there is a clash between the system of dispute resolution in certain sports before CAS, and the principle of effective judicial protection that is guaranteed within the EU legal order.[17] She came to the conclusion that national courts, when having to deal with arbitral awards issued by CAS, in which there is no recourse to the Court, is precluded by EU law. If the Court arrives at a similar conclusion, the seat of CAS and its arbitral awards may have to move inside the EU, to ensure their capture by the EU judicial architecture.

Whilst no explicit reference was made to the *Achmea* judgment by the Court in *International Skating Union v Commission*, or its ensuing line of investment case law that followed it, the logic of *Achmea* is very strongly evident: any sort of dispute settlement that has intra-EU effects that has no possible direct line of judicial dialogue to the Court is an inherent problem, whether this is for investor-state arbitration (as seen in *Achmea*), or private arbitration between athletes and international sports bodies (as seen in *International Skating Union v Commission*, or in *Royal Football Club Seraing*, pending). In other words, the logic of *Achmea* has now been transplanted from the investment arena to the sports arena. What arena is next is anyone's guess, but the Court is demonstrating that it is absolutely unwilling to let anything go from its immediate grasp, despite the maturity of the EU legal order.

It should also be noted that before the *Achmea* judgment was delivered, though less of a surprise, there was also the Opinion of the Court in *Opinion 2/15 (EU-Singapore FTA)*.[18] This pre-ratification judicial review mechanism[19] – the Opinion procedure in Article 218(11) TFEU – has proved itself to be extremely useful for the Commission in determining the extent of the Union's exclusive competence post-Lisbon.

In terms of investment in this case, two matters arose. First, the Court established that insofar as non-foreign direct investment is concerned, it was a shared competence of the EU and its Member States. That is because, for the Court, insufficient secondary law had been adopted on the basis of the free movement of capital provisions in the EU Treaties for non-direct investment to come within the scope of the *ERTA* doctrine[20] – the doctrine of implied exclusive competence

[17] See Opinion of Advocate General Ćapeta, Case C-600/23, *Royal Football Club Seraing v Fédération Internationale de Football Association (FIFA), Union Royale Belge des Sociétés de Football Association ASBL (URBSFA), Union européenne des Sociétés de Football Association (UEFA), and Doyen Sports Investment Ltd* ECLI:EU:C:2025:24.

[18] *Opinion 2/15* ECLI:EU:C:2017:376 (*EU-Singapore FTA*). See Christine Kaddous, 'The EU Competence to Conclude the New Generation of Free Trade Agreements: Opinion 2/15 (EU–Singapore FTA)' in Graham Butler and Ramses A Wessel (eds), *EU External Relations Law: The Cases in Context* (Hart Publishing, 2022).

[19] See Graham Butler, 'Pre-Ratification Judicial Review of International Agreements to be Concluded by the European Union' in Mattias Derlén and Johan Lindholm (eds), *The Court of Justice of the European Union: Multidisciplinary Perspectives* (Hart Publishing, 2018).

[20] Case 22/70 *Commission v Council* ECLI:EU:C:1971:32 (*ERTA*). See Graham Butler and Ramses A Wessel, 'EU External Relations Law and Navigating the Case Law of the Court of Justice of the

of the EU in external relations. Second, the Court stated that investor-state dispute settlement (ISDS) was also a shared competence.[21] Thus, exclusive competence of the EU in external relations, whilst broadening over time, was not confirmed, and the Court was of the view that there are some areas of EU law in which competence is still shared, including certain aspects of investment.

1.4. INVESTMENT: THE ISSUE OF EU SECONDARY LAW

Investment, as an area of the EU legal order, has in recent times also seen developments as regards EU secondary law. Numerous instruments have been adopted by the EU legislature, on proposals from the Commission, which will have both direct and indirect ramifications. There are now various instruments on investment screening (already undergoing its first review, and potential revision), foreign subsidies, and anti-dumping, *inter alia*. Under the Foreign Subsidies Regulation,[22] if the Commission finds that such financial contributions to undertakings in third states constitute distortive subsidies, it has the ability to impose measures to redress their distortive effects when it comes to economic activity within the EU. The rationale for the introduction of this Regulation is that subsidies (state aid) granted by non-EU Member States to undertakings in third states were, up until now, unchecked at EU level, while similar subsidies granted by EU Member States to undertakings within the EU had long been subject to close scrutiny by the Commission under EU state aid law.

There has even been a byproduct of the Foreign Subsidies Regulation in a Nordic context, and the wider European Economic Area (EEA). The Regulation is *not* a 'Text of EEA Relevance', despite one of the Regulation's legal bases being Article 114 TFEU (the internal market harmonisation legal basis). The Regulation is based on Article 114 TFEU *and* Article 207 TFEU (CCP). The CCP is not a part of the EEA Agreement.[23] Therefore, in addition to Iceland's

European Union' in Graham Butler and Ramses A Wessel (eds), *EU External Relations Law: The Cases in Context* (Hart Publishing, 2022); Inge Govaere, 'Implied EU Powers, Limits to Political Expediency, and Internationally Inspired Pragmatism: ERTA' in Graham Butler and Ramses A Wessel (eds), *EU External Relations Law: The Cases in Context* (Hart Publishing, 2022).

[21] Contrary to the Advocate General, who viewed ISDS as an exclusive competence of the EU. Opinion of Advocate General Sharpston, *Opinion 2/15* ECLI:EU:C:2016:992 (*EU-Singapore FTA*). See Panos Koutrakos, 'EU Competence to Conclude Trade Agreements: Opinion of Advocate General Sharpston in Opinion 2/15' in Graham Butler and Adam Łazowski (eds), *Shaping EU Law the British Way: UK Advocates General at the Court of Justice of the European Union* (Hart Publishing, 2022).

[22] Regulation (EU) 2022/2560 of the European Parliament and of the Council of 14 December 2022 on Foreign Subsidies Distorting the Internal Market [2022] OJ L330/1.

[23] Case E-2/97 *Mag Instruments v California Trading Company Norway, Ulsteen*, Advisory Opinion (Judgment) of the EFTA Court, 3 December 1997 (*Mag Lite*), para 27; and, Joined Cases E-9/07 and E-10/07 *L'Oréal and Aarskog*, Judgment of the EFTA Court, 8 July 2008, para 30. See, for a comprehensive study of the substantive law of the EEA, Graham Butler (ed), *Research Handbook on EEA Internal Market Law* (Edward Elgar Publishing, 2025).

and Norway's requirement to notify state aid measures to the EFTA Surveillance Authority (ESA), this means there is now the possibility that Icelandic and Norwegian aid would *also* have to be notified to the European Commission, to ensure there is no distortion of the internal market.

This might appear unusual, given that the internal market and state aid measures are ordinarily within the scope of the EEA Agreement. But it is true, and the Commission has confirmed that '[a]ll foreign financial contribution granted by [states] that are not EU Member States (thus including those granted by [EFTA-EEA states] count' for determining whether state aid granted by Iceland and Norway is distorting the internal market. The effect, in a Nordic setting, is that it potentially puts Icelandic/Norwegian undertakings operating in the internal market at a potential disadvantage compared to Danish, Finnish and Swedish undertakings, and is a conundrum that will have to be played out. Again, however, investment and its ties to the internal market are all the more evident in being a prevailing theme of EU law of late.

These developments have in some way forced scholars of EU law, more generally beyond its silos, who have not thus far taken a keen interest in EU investment law, to begin to consider it more thoroughly, given it is more evident now than ever before. This once sub-field of EU law, in reality, actually intertwines with many of the basic principles of the EU legal order, and the more mainstream fields of EU law such as EU constitutional law, EU internal market law, and EU external relations law, and others.

1.5. INVESTMENT: THIS BOOK

As will be seen from the chapters that are included in this book, they collectively offer a panorama of different views upon which issues of investment and EU law are intertwined, one way or another. With each author coming with their own perspective on how 'investment' sits across these fields and areas within EU law, a more coherent face to investment can be drawn, and what it means for the EU legal order.

Part I (Investment and Primary/Secondary Law) commences with chapter 2, '*The Freedom to Invest in the EU's Internal Market from Third States*' by Steffen Hindelang, which sets the scene for the way in which investment is now a more entrenched area of the EU legal order, and that, in recent years, the EU has put in place 'intervention-intensive, far-reaching instruments, capable of restricting cross-border capital inflows significantly, directed at preventing threats to "security and public order"'. He comes to a rather grim conclusion for non-EU investors seeking to be active in the EU's internal market, in that the days of freedom to freely invest for non-EU investors are over.

Continuing onwards in chapter 3, '*Screening of Foreign Direct Investment in EU Law: Frameworks, Non-EU Investors, and Security Considerations*', Graham Butler analyses the way in which pan-EU investment screening has now come into place for foreign direct investment (FDI) coming into the EU from the outside. Yet, as noted, FDI is now under the auspices of the exclusive competence of the EU since the adoption of the Treaty of Lisbon in 2009, and thus there is a problem therein for the uniformity of the 'EU' screening mechanism given that, in reality, it is merely 27 Member States each having their own screening mechanism, with each of them taking their own decisions, in the name of security and public order. As he argues, the new FDI Screening Regulation in its present form will not last too long, and it will only be a matter of time before a more comprehensive, second-generation FDI screening mechanism will be put in place.

Concluding Part I is chapter 4, '*Investment and EU International Agreements*' by Ivana Damjanovic, where she examines the post-*Opinion 2/15* landscape that applies on division of competence in the EU legal order. In doing so, she highlights how the EU's own internal legal order counterintuitively impinges upon a fully coherent and consistent external relations policy on investment. Thus, different to the seen practice of facultative mixity – a phenomenon whereby mixed agreements are chosen as a form of political preference over EU-only agreements, rather than legal obligation – it is evident that investment matters still remain, to some yet-to-be-fully-defined extent, a place whereby Member States still have powers. In portraying a broader outlook, she considers the various ways in which EU international agreements – covering trade or investment, or both – will have an impact on EU external relations practice in the years ahead.

Part II (Investment and Arbitration) commences with chapter 5, '*Arbitration, Investment, and the EU Legal Order*', by Konstanze von Papp. She highlights that in light of the case law of the Court over the past decade, with intra-EU arbitration under BITs now no longer possible, a huge amount of responsibility will now fall on the shoulders of national courts and tribunals of Member States, who in turn will need to be more engaged with the law of arbitration. Her approach underlines that whilst arbitration is based on the time-honoured approach of contractual freedom, which Member States respect, those same Member States have a higher obligation, which is to respect EU law, and that contractual freedom cannot impinge on essential requirements of the EU legal order, which is to ensure that national courts and tribunals (and, thus, the Court of Justice) are within the realm of being able to adjudicate in cases. In conclusion, she argues that the logic of *PL Holdings*, with ad hoc arbitration in investor-state situations, should not be transposed to ad hoc arbitration in commercial situations.

In chapter 6, '*National Courts and Tribunals in Investor-State Disputes*', Relja Radović analyses the changing role for national courts in Member States in the future, given the Court of Justice's recent post-*Achmea* jurisprudence. He begins by noting that national courts have historically not been deeply vested in ensuring investment rules and policies function, as it is ordinarily the case that this role is best charged with executive and legislative institutions; but, at the same time, they are deeply empowered actors in investment issues, as they are asked to ensure the enforcement of arbitral awards rendered by arbitral bodies.

With the line of recent case law, he argues that national courts and tribunals are now going to have to take on an additional role that arbitrators in intra-EU situations are used to having in investor-state situations, by ensuring that both parties have their rights protected. His analysis points to examples where, post-*Achmea*, the precise reach of that judgment has been unclear, with national courts in different Member States arriving at different conclusions. The chapter also analyses the approach of national courts in third states to issues of investment that are essentially intra-EU in nature. By way of conclusion, he promotes the need for a future research agenda on the need to more closely scrutinise the role of national courts replacing arbitrators in intra-EU situations, to see the impact that it will have on investment protection, and the EU law of investment more generally.

In chapter 7, '*The Incompatibility of the ISDS Mechanism in the Energy Charter Treaty with EU Law: Nothing New Under the Sun*', Nicolas de Sadeleer examines the state of the case law, the ECT, and what it all means for EU law in terms of its adaptation towards ensuring climate change is addressed in a facilitative manner. He notes that when the ECT was adopted, the differentiation amongst different sources of energy (and the differing environmental impact they have) was not duly considered. Given that the ECT still applies, though its intra-EU dynamics are uncertain given the *Komstroy* judgment, the EU will nevertheless be proceeding with adapting its internal legislative framework to bring about further decarbonising methods of energy production, and to eventually eliminate fossil fuel-sourced energy as a source. However, he cautions that the full effect the ECT will have on internal EU policies cannot be realised until a reformed or modernised ECT is agreed to, which, at the time of writing, remains uncertain.

In chapter 8, '*State Compliance with Intra-EU Investment Awards or the EU "Elephant" in the Investment "Porcelain Shop"*', Szilárd Gáspár-Szilágyi illustrates the fragility of international investment law, notwithstanding the EU's entry into the field. Whilst he leaves the full analysis of *Achmea* and post-*Achmea* cases to the other preceding and succeeding chapters, he notes the by-product of this line of case law: the increased complexity of this area of the EU law for everyone, be it investors, Member States, the Commission, and third states. In that vein, this in turn, contributes, in the author's view, to greater uncertainty, and will contribute to greater doubt surrounding compliance with EU law, and the enforcement thereof. He takes issue, also, with the length of proceedings that some investment cases take. He points to the never-ending *Micula* litigation, whereby disputes in various Member States and third states, as well as other proceedings, put into jeopardy the notion that disputes should be settled within a reasonable timeframe. This vivid chapter, full of graphic illustrations (of a written kind), lays bare what happens when an inexperienced actor – the EU – with ambitious internal institutions, enters a field in which it has no serious prior experience.

In chapter 9, '*State-to-State Arbitration in EU Investment Protection Agreements*', Gesa Kübek considers another form of dispute resolution in investment matters that receives less attention than others – state-to-state arbitration – despite the fact that nearly all BITs in force contain such a form of arbitration. In her analysis, she looks at EU international agreements in the form of free trade agreements (FTAs) and investor protection agreements (IPAs), and how state-to-state arbitration can coincide or not with investor-state arbitration. The chapter highlights how the EU's recent IPAs with states like Canada, Singapore and Vietnam include both state-to-state and investor-state arbitration (despite no provisions on potential overlap of parallel proceedings), whilst, in a back-to-the-future narrative, demonstrates how future EU international agreements, such as those proposed with China as an IPA, have much in common with older international agreements of Member States, which envisage state-to-state arbitration on investment matters *only*, like that of Germany and Pakistan from 1959, and not investor-state arbitration. She argues that state-to-state arbitration in EU international agreements in the future can fulfil the function that investor-state arbitration plays, if it is carefully designed.

The concluding chapter in Part II is chapter 10, '*Investor-State Dispute Settlement from the Perspective of EU Law*' by Claes Granmar, who provides a panoramic view of the investment issues currently facing the EU legal order. Contrary to much scholarship, however, he is sympathetic to the dilemmas that the EU is currently facing, that are largely being left on the doorstep of the Court to resolve in the absence of any legislative developments. He argues that the Court's recent jurisprudence can be seen through the need to balance many competing interests: ensuring the internal consistency of EU law within the EU legal order; ensuring that the autonomy of the EU legal order is protected; promoting the Union's external objectives with third states; as well as trying to ensure the internal and external aspects of the EU are promoted in conformity with one another. In this sense, he argues in favour of a permanent investment court that could be established internationally, ensuring that investments are protected under a rules-based system as opposed to a power-based system.

Part III (Investment and Sustainability) begins with chapter 11, '*Sustainable Development in EU Trade and Investment Agreements*' by Hannes Lenk, who explores the integration of sustainable development objectives into EU trade and investment policies. The chapter begins by discussing the concept of sustainable development and its application in EU trade policy, highlighting the EU's strategic use of this concept to legitimise its free trade and investment agenda. It then delves into the structure and content of Trade and Sustainable Development (TSD) chapters in EU international agreements, noting significant variations in their scope, bindingness, and enforceability. It emphasises that while environmental and labour standards are included, they are often limited to trade-related aspects, reflecting the EU's primary focus on economic growth. The chapter also examines the implementation and enforcement mechanisms of TSD chapters, pointing out that most international agreements rely on cooperative approaches rather than sanctions, which has been criticised for its limited effectiveness. It highlights the EU's recent review of TSD policy, which suggests a more assertive enforcement approach, including the possibility of temporary trade sanctions in certain circumstances.

Chapter 12, '*The EU's Powers to Green International Investment Law*' by Laurens Ankersmit, examines the EU's capacity to reform investment agreements to align with climate goals. It highlights the EU's commitment to net-zero emissions by 2050 and the challenges posed by existing and new fossil fuel investments, which are often protected under investment agreements. These agreements, which include ISDS mechanisms, can lead to significant financial liabilities for governments attempting to phase out fossil fuels, thereby creating a 'regulatory chill' that hinders climate action. He further discusses the EU's limited ability to compel Member States to reform some of their existing BITs with third states. The chapter also explores the division of competences between the EU and Member States, noting that while the EU has exclusive competence over FDI, portfolio investments and ISDS remain shared competences, and that this division complicates the EU's ability to implement comprehensive reforms. In conclusion, the chapter argues that while the EU can negotiate new investment agreements that align with climate goals, the process is cumbersome and limited by the need for Member State cooperation.

In chapter 13, '*Coal Phase-out and Investment Law: Navigating the Arbitration Barrier Through Market Forces*', Sara Soini and Anatole Boute investigate the challenges and strategies for phasing out coal-fired power plants within the EU while navigating the complexities of international investment law. They highlight the significant greenhouse gas emissions from coal power and the urgent need for its phase-out to meet climate goals. They further discuss the effectiveness of direct regulatory measures, such as coal bans, which provide certainty and coordination but face potential legal challenges from investors under international arbitration, particularly through the ECT. Whilst it is argued that market mechanisms can reduce legal risks and have initially succeeded in reducing coal power, they are vulnerable to geopolitical and economic disruptions. Together they suggest that aligning market-based approaches with regulatory measures, such as adjusting the ETS cap to account for coal phase-outs, could enhance effectiveness.

Penultimately in chapter 14, '*EU International Investment Agreements with Third States: A "New" Paradigm and the EU Constitutional Framework Challenge*', Maria Fanou examines the evolution of the EU's approach to investment agreements and its efforts to redefine substantive investment standards and balance them with the right to regulate, marking a departure from traditional BITs. A significant focus of the chapter is on the establishment of a permanent Investment Court System (ICS) to replace the traditional ISDS mechanisms. She notes that while the idea of a permanent court is not new, the EU's branding and timing have brought it to the forefront of global debates. That said, the EU's interest here has to consider the ever-present principle of autonomy of the EU legal order as interpreted by the Court. She warns, however, that the EU must consider constitutional constraints on its ambitious plans for any permanent international court to ensure compliance with the Court's requirements.

To see out the book, chapter 15, '*Towards a Multilateral Investment Court*' by Colin Brown, outlines the EU's efforts to establish a multilateral investment court to enhance the rule of law in the field of investment protection. He argues that the current system of ISDS fails to meet the challenges of the present, and that a common international approach, as a matter of public law, is preferable. He suggests that a permanent court, with full-time adjudicators and an appellate mechanism, would address the well-known issues of ISDS by providing greater consistency, predictability and independence. The EU's proposal for such a body includes features such as long, non-renewable terms for adjudicators, expertise in public international law, and mechanisms to ensure gender and regional diversity. Conclusively, the chapter asserts that a multilateral investment court stands to benefit states, investors and other stakeholders by providing a clearer and more reliable legal framework for international investment, at a time when investment rights are under increased scrutiny.

1.6. GRATITUDE

There are three groups of people that deserve special mention in the coming about of this volume: the network, the publisher, and the authors.

The bringing together of this book would not have been possible without the support of the Swedish Network for Euröpean Legal Studies (*Svenska nätverket för Europarättsforskning* (SNEF)). For this, thanks is owed to its chairperson, Professor Björn Lundqvist, and chairperson emerita, Professor Antonina Bakardjieva Engelbrekt, both of whom are at Stockholm University, for their work in steering the network.

At the publisher, Hart Publishing/Bloomsbury, its long-standing editor for all things European law, Sinead Moloney, has been on hand for all matters as always, as has Sasha Jawed, ensuring that everything ran into production in a smooth fashion. Their endeavours behind the scenes in ensuring there is space for qualitative outputs in European law should not be underestimated, and for which the legal community is deeply appreciative. A note of thanks is also owed to David Stott for his brilliant copy-editing skills.

Most of all, however, thank you to the authors who contributed to the colloquium hosted at the Faculty of Law, Lund University, that preceded this volume's publication, and for putting all their thoughts down in writing. Tack så mycket.

Part I

Investment and Primary/Secondary Law

2

The Freedom to Invest in the EU's Internal Market from Third States

STEFFEN HINDELANG

2.1. INTRODUCTION

IT APPEARS PARADOXICAL considering the current zeitgeist: the free movement of capital in Article 63(1) TFEU, as one of the key provisions governing investment from non-European Union (EU) states into the internal market, declares rather unmistakably: 'all restrictions on the movement of capital … between Member States and third countries shall be prohibited.' Yet, while Article 63(1) TFEU calls for open doors to capital, including foreign investments, the said zeitgeist clearly bears restrictive traits. A partial turn away from (neo)liberalism towards what is often termed as geoeconomic[1] competition is now beginning to be seen.

After the end of the Cold War, (neo)liberalism, underpinned in particular by distributed private ownership and separation, or at least larger distance, between the state and private enterprise, gained track in the 1990s, and continued to flourish until the current twenty-first century. The period was characterised by multipolarity, the win-win proposition of free trade, and international cooperation.[2] Yet, other economic governance models have gained more and more significance with the rise of China, resembling some type of state capitalism.[3] They depart from the aforesaid characteristics of a liberal

[1] This manuscript was finalised in 2022; developments after that date could only be taken into account in a few instances during production. Although there is no singular definition of the term 'geoeconomics', it can be approached as 'the use of economic instruments to promote and defend national interests, and to produce beneficial geopolitical results; and the effects of other nations' economic actions on a country's geopolitical goals.' (B Constant, 'What is Geoeconomics?' in R Blackwill and J Harris (eds), *War by Other Means: Geoeconomics and Statecraft* (The Belknap Press of Harvard University Press, 2016) 19, 20.

[2] N Crafts, 'The world economy in the 1990s: a long-run perspective' in PW Rohde and G Toniolo (eds), *The Global Economy in the 1990s* (Cambridge University Press, 2010) 21–22.

[3] Y Zhang, *China's Economic Reform* (Routledge, 2017) 1–74; X Hou, *Community Capitalism in China* (Cambridge University Press, 2013) 121–34.

market order by relying on considerations of a 'zero-sum game' of international politics,[4] strategic competition, and economic statecraft.[5]

States around the world, not just China, increasingly rediscover economic policy as a tool to unilaterally pursue national security and other non-economic interests. Instead of choosing to maximise global growth and with it absolute gains, such (neo)mercantilist approaches aim for 'relative gains', focusing on increasing the (economic) power of one state, relative to its partners and rivals. In the area of cross-border capital movements, geoeconomic competition has manifested itself most obviously through the rise of sovereign-driven investment (SDI), ie, investments by sovereign wealth funds (SWFs) and state-owned enterprises, as well as 'strategic' investments that are otherwise enjoying state support from their states of origin, for example, by way of state aid.[6]

While SDI is no new phenomenon – recalling the debate on the activities of SWFs on the internal market a decade ago,[7] which led to some – in retrospect – cautious tightening of market access rules in some Member States,[8] today, SDI

[4] The term 'zero-sum-game' in international politics describes a situation which involves two sides where the result is an advantage for one side and an equivalent loss for the other. Cf S Bowles, *Microeconomics: behaviour, institutions and evolution* (Princeton University Press, 2006) 33–36; *Cambridge Business English Dictionary* (Cambridge University Press, 2011).

[5] The term 'economic statecraft' describes the use of economic means to pursue national policy goals. In particular the use of foreign aid, trade and the governing of the flows of capital is considered the most common form of economic statecraft. DA Baldwin, 'economic statecraft' (*Encyclopaedia Britannica*, 21 January 2016); DA Baldwin, *Economic Statecraft* (Princeton University Press, 1985) 29–51.

[6] The EU has responded by adopting the Regulation 2019/452 of the European Parliament and of the Council of 19 March 2019 establishing a framework for the screening of foreign direct investments into the Union [2019] OJ L79I/1 most recently 'Proposal for a regulation of the European Parliament and of the Council on the screening of foreign investments in the Union and repealing Regulation (EU) 2019/452 of the European Parliament and of the Council' COM(2024) 23 final; see also Regulation (EU) 2022/2560 of the European Parliament and of the Council of 14 December 2022 on foreign subsidies distorting the internal market [2022] OJ L330/1, as well as Regulation (EU) 2023/2675 of the European Parliament and of the Council of 22 November 2023 on the protection of the Union and its Member States from economic coercion by third countries [2023] OJ L2675/1.

[7] cf R Koch, 'Wir sind die Dummen' (*Frankfurter Allgemeine Sonntagszeitung*, Frankfurt, 9 September 2007); see also P Steinbrück, 'Schlüsselindustrien und ausländische Staatsfonds – die Sicht der Bundesregierung' [2008] 1 *Kreditwesen* 11; More differentiated: European Commission, 'A Common European Approach to Sovereign Wealth Funds' COM (2008) 115 final. More recent accounts of SWFs include I Liu and A Dixon, 'SWF in-depth. The great experiment: China investment corporation in Europe and beyond' in Center for the Governance of Change (*Sovereign Wealth Funds Report*, 2020) 42–49; P Schena and J Capapé, 'Toward a new normal? Sovereign Wealth Fund Direct Investments 2020–2021' in Center for the Governance of Change (*Sovereign Wealth Funds Report*, 2021) 22–30; V Fotak, X Gao and WL Megginson, 'A Financial Force to be Reckoned With? An Overview of Sovereign Wealth Funds' in D Cumming and others (eds), *The Oxford Handbook on Sovereign Wealth Funds* (OUP, 2017) 16–62; K Lavelle, 'Sovereign Wealth Funds and Foreign Policy' in D Cumming and others (eds), *The Oxford Handbook on Sovereign Wealth Funds* (OUP, 2017) 182–207; J Chaisse, 'The Regulation of Sovereign Wealth Funds in the European Union: Can the Supranational Level Limit the Rise of National Protectionism?' (*Sovereign Investment: Concerns and Policy Reactions*, New York, 2012; online edn, Oxford, 20 April 2015).

[8] See for example: Décret n° 2005-1739 réglementant les relations financières avec l'étranger et portant application de l'article L 151-3 du code monétaire et financier, JO n° 304 du 31 décembre 2005,

from certain regions of the world is not just subject to political enquiry, but intense regulatory scrutiny. Third state investments stirring controversies archetypically share three common characteristics.

First, target companies operate in 'politically sensitive areas'. In Europe, these 'sensitivities' are rapidly growing, and include areas such as transport or energy infrastructure, high-tech, research and innovation, software and cryptography, or manufacturing. Some goods/products in these areas are not only eligible for civilian use, but possibly also military use. Second, it is not always clear who ultimately controls the company in a third state acting as immediate buyer, and whether such ultimate owner operates according to market principles only. Obfuscation strategies feed the allegation of strategically oriented investment activities. Third, the ultimate foreign purchaser may attempt to circumvent rules for non-EU investors through an intermediary company resident in the EU.[9]

Later than the United States,[10] as well as other major economies, the EU and its Member States reacted to the changing political landscape with a series of legislative measures and initiatives that have become part of EU secondary law. Particularly noteworthy in this context is Regulation 2019/452 establishing a framework for the screening of foreign direct investments into the Union (Screening Regulation),[11] which concerns the review of inward foreign, ie, third state direct investment (FDI) on the grounds of security and public order. It essentially provides a framework for administrative cooperation in the field, and has arguably established a nascent EU screening mechanism, albeit a well-camouflaged one.[12] Its adoption may indeed mark an important step in the establishment of FDI screening as a new EU regulatory field.[13]

20779 et seq. And Federal Ministry of Economics and Technology, 'Thirteenth Act Amending the Foreign Trade and Payments Act and the Foreign Trade and Payments Ordinance', 18 April 2009.

[9] S Hindelang and A Moberg, 'The art of casting political dissent in law: The EU's framework for the screening of foreign direct investment' (2020) 57(5) *CMLR* 1427, 1451; S Hindelang and TM Hagemeyer, 'Enemy at the Gates?' (2017) *EuZW* 882, 884; on the diving lines of capital and establishment, see S Hindelang, *The Free Movement of Capital and Foreign Direct Investment: The Scope of Protection in EU Law* (OUP, 2009) 81–115.

[10] See the Foreign Investment Risk Review Modernization Act of 2018 (FIRRMA), revising section 721 of the Defense Production Act of 1950. Section 721 of the Defense Production Act of 1950, as amended, is codified at 50 USC 4565.

[11] Regulation (EU) 2019/452 establishing a framework for the screening of foreign direct investments into the Union [2019] OJ L79I/1. See further ch 3.

[12] S Hindelang and A Moberg, 'The art of casting political dissent in law: The EU's framework for the screening of foreign direct investment' (2020) 57(5) *CMLR* 1427, 1460.

[13] 'Proposal for a regulation of the European Parliament and of the Council on the screening of foreign investments in the Union and repealing Regulation (EU) 2019/452 of the European Parliament and of the Council' COM(2024) 23 final; European Parliament, Draft Report on the proposal for a regulation of the European Parliament and of the Council on the screening of foreign investments in the Union and repealing Regulation (EU) 2019/452 of the European Parliament and of the Council (COM(2024)0023 – C9-0011/2024 – 2024/0017(COD)).

At Member State level, the number of national investment screening mechanisms increased significantly from around a dozen to 23 as of May 2025,[14] with several more on the way. Even Member States traditionally favouring liberal trade regimes, such as Germany and Sweden, significantly broadened the scope of the respective mechanism,[15] or are about to introduce such.[16] While any attempt to depart from what has traditionally been a liberal foreign trade regime was at least controversial in the past, for example in the aftermath of the 2007 financial crisis,[17] more recent restrictions have hardly been criticised, but rather embraced as an expression of increased 'resilience' and strategic autonomy of the EU.[18]

The EU and its Member States have been creating intervention-intensive, far-reaching instruments, capable of restricting cross-border capital inflows significantly, directed at preventing threats to 'security and public order'.[19] While tying screening to threats to 'security and public order' should arguably discourage Member States from pursuing industrial policy in the name of 'investment screening', significant differences can be seen between them in terms of intended use of such instruments.[20] The question of whether, when, and to what degree third

[14] List of screening mechanisms notified by Member States of the EU, available from the European Commission (Last update: 8 January 2025).

[15] Germany intensified the screening of foreign investments under the Foreign Trade and Payments Act (*Außenwirtschaftsgesetz – AWG*) and the Foreign Trade Ordinance (*Außenwirtschaftsverordnung – AWV*) by passing several amendments in 2020, 2021 and 2022. In particular, the 17th Amendment to the AWV, which came into force on 1 May 2021, expanded the list of critical sectors to 27 and implemented a more resilient (protectionist) policy.

[16] See Act (2023:560) on Screening of Foreign Direct Investments (Lag (2023:560) om granskning av utländska direktinvesteringar); Direct Investment Inquiry, 'Review of Foreign Direct Investment' (*Direktinvesteringsutredningen, 'Granskning av utländska direktinvesteringar'*) (2021) SOU 2021:87, 59–70.

[17] For an early assessment of the impact of the financial crisis on global FDI flows, see KP Sauvant, 'The FDI Recession Has Begun' (The Vale Columbia Center on Sustainable International Investment, 2008). In retrospective: Simon J Evenett, 'Protectionism, State Discrimination, and International Business since the Onset of the Global Financial Crisis' (2019) 2 *J Int Bus Policy* 9.

[18] See, eg, Business Europe, 'Foreign investment screening: responsible investing and democratic resilience' in BusinessEurope Headlines No 2022-19; but see also BDI, Press release, *'AWG amendment: BDI against stricter investment controls'* (AWG-Novelle: BDI gegen schärfere Investitionskontrollen) (17 March 2020).

[19] cf Article 1(1) of the EU Screening Regulation.

[20] Sweden, for example, understands itself as 'a modern economy, an attractive country for [foreign] investments and as a place where professionals with particularly sought-after skills can work' (Government Offices of Sweden, 'Sweden's Trade and Investment Strategy'). Even if Sweden is now implementing an FDI screening mechanism in regard to 'security-sensitive activities or assets', it 'remains a country that recognizes the beneficial effects of [FDI] and ownership on the Swedish economy and on consumers' (Direct Investment Inquiry, 'Review of Foreign Direct Investment' (*Direktinvesteringsutredningen, 'Granskning av utländska direktinvesteringar'*) (2021) SOU 2021:87, 59–70). The French FDI screening mechanism, in contrast, seems to be focused on protecting French interests in general, strengthening the Ministry of Economics' (MOE) (ie, the Minister's) power to intervene: 'Indeed, from 2014, which marks the beginning of the political realisation that national assets and knowledge should be kept within national folds, the FFIR [French Foreign Investment Regime] has continued to expand, leading to a strengthening of the intervention powers of the MOE. … The revamped FFIR notably involves strengthened enforcement powers for the MOE and a larger scope of review thanks to lower review thresholds and a larger list of covered strategical sectors. … Even though prohibition decisions remain rare, in the past few months a number of deals

states behind SDI can or want to exert the apparently feared political pressure on the respective host Member State through their holdings in strategically important companies in the EU, or gain access to know-how and technology, is still one which is difficult to answer across the board. Ex ante, it has to be judged against the background of an ever-changing geopolitical landscape.

In light of such rampant security thinking, it appears that a fresh look should be taken on the question of what remains of the 'freedom to invest' into the EU from third states, as enshrined in Article 63(1) TFEU in the age of geoeconomic powerplays. More specifically, for the limited purposes of this chapter, the attempt shall be made to assess whether the EU's Screening Regulation increases the Member States' leeway to interfere with third state investment beyond the limits stipulated by the fundamental freedoms.

2.2. HARMONISATION AND ARTICLE 4 OF THE SCREENING REGULATION

Article 4 of the EU Screening Regulation is of particular interest. It constitutes a non-exhaustive list[21] of factors that Member States and the Commission 'may consider' in determining whether a foreign direct investment 'is likely to affect security or public order'.[22] In doing so, the Member States, as well as the Commission, may consider factors linked to the foreign investment itself,[23] as well as factors linked to the investor.[24] According to Article 4(1) of the EU Screening Regulation, Member States and the Commission may take into consideration, *inter alia*, an FDI's 'potential effect' on critical infrastructure and related real estate, critical technology and dual-use items, the supply of critical inputs, food security, access to and control of sensitive information, as well as on freedom and pluralism of the media. Regarding the foreign investor, the Member States

have been blocked by the MOE, sending a clear message that the MOE is not averse to using its new-found discretionary powers to ensure the protection of French national interests. Citing as reasons the protection of industrial and food sovereignty, the French Minister of the Economy, Bruno Le Maire, prevented two potential transactions without even having opened a formal review.' Jérôme Philippe and Aude Guyon, 'The Foreign Investment Regulation Review: France' (*The Law Reviews*, 17 October 2021).

[21] cf Article 4(1): 'inter alia', and Article 4(2): 'in particular'. See also recital 12 of the EU Screening Regulation.

[22] Although the discussion of potential future disputes under international trade law as a consequence of restrictive measures taken following decisions by screening mechanisms acting on the basis of the EU Screening Regulation falls outside the main remit of this contribution, it is important to emphasise that the terminology chosen ('security and public order') is consistent with the language used in WTO/GATS. Cf recitals 3 and 35 of the preamble to the EU Screening Regulation as well as European Parliament Report on the proposal for a regulation of the European Parliament and of the Council establishing a framework for screening of foreign direct investments into the European Union, A8-0198/2018, p 49. It would seem that the EU is not expecting investment screening carried out by the Member States to conflict with WTO law, since the invocation of the national security interest has been consistently accepted in dispute settlement under the WTO.

[23] Article 4(1) of the EU Screening Regulation.

[24] Article 4(2) of the EU Screening Regulation. See also recital 13 of the EU Screening Regulation.

and the Commission may also 'take into account' control or funding by non-EU states, previous involvement in activities affecting security and public order, as well as the serious risk of engagement in illegal or criminal activities.[25]

What is already clear from the language is that Article 4 of the EU Screening Regulation does *not* harmonise the material scope of the Member States' screening mechanisms. As it merely enumerates factors which may be relevant for the determination of whether or not an FDI 'is likely to affect security or public order', the EU Screening Regulation leaves the decision on what the factors actually are to the Member States' discretion. The Member States 'may consider', 'inter alia', the factors relating to the particular FDI mentioned in Article 4(1), and 'may also' take into consideration 'in particular' the factors listed in Article 4(2) in respect of the non-EU investor.[26] By suggesting a number of factors that the Member States 'may consider' when determining whether or not an FDI is likely to affect security or public order, the EU Screening Regulation initiates a collective process, aimed at a converging interpretation and application of those legal terms across the Member States: in other words a 'rough consensus'. As a 'harmonising' measure, this rough consensus approach still has to prove, in practice, whether it can bring together the diverging interests and needs of the Member States when it comes to 'security' and 'public order'.[27]

Besides informing, but without prejudicing, the Commission's and Member States' assessments of likely effects of a particular FDI on security and public order within the cooperation mechanism,[28] the further effects of Article 4 of the

[25] Article 4(2) of the EU Screening Regulation.

[26] The European Parliament proposed that some of these factors should in fact be made compulsory, by switching 'may' to 'shall'. However, this was not accepted in the final version of the EU Screening Regulation. See J Warchol, 'The birth of the EU screening regulation' in S Hindelang and A Moberg (eds), *A Common European Law on Investment Screening (CELIS), Yearbook of Socio-Economic Constitutions* (Springer, 2021) 53–75; see also A Neergaard, 'The adoption of the regulation establishing a framework for screening of foreign direct investment into the European Union' in J Bourgeois (ed), *EU Framework for Foreign Direct Investment Control* (Kluwer Law International, 2020) 151–167, 155.

[27] The empowerment of the Member States by the EU in the area of the Common Commercial Policy can also be found – taking various forms and different scopes – in other regulatory areas. Cf eg Article 10 of Regulation (EU) 2015/479 of the European Parliament and of the Council on common rules for exports [2015] OJ L83/34 ('*Without prejudice to other Union provisions*, this Regulation shall not preclude the adoption or application by a Member State of quantitative restrictions on exports on grounds of … *public policy or public security* …' (emphasis added)); similar also in Article 24(2)(a) of Regulation (EU) 2015/478 of the European Parliament and of the Council on common rules for imports (codification) [2015] OJ L83/16; Article 9(1) of Regulation (EU) 2021/821 of the European Parliament and of the Council of 20 May 2021 setting up a Union regime for the control of exports, brokering, technical assistance, transit and transfer of dual-use items (recast) [2021] OJ L206/1 ('A Member State may prohibit or impose an authorisation requirement on the export of dual-use items not listed in Annex I *for reasons of public security*, including the prevention of acts of terrorism, or for human rights considerations.') (emphasis added).

[28] cf eg Article 6(1) of the EU Screening Regulation: 'The notification may include a list of Member States whose security or public order *is deemed likely to be affected*.'; Article 6(2) of the EU Screening Regulation: 'Where a Member State considers that a foreign direct investment undergoing screening in another Member State *is likely to affect* its security or public order …'; Article 6(3) of the EU Screening Regulation: 'Where the Commission considers that a foreign direct investment undergoing screening is likely to affect security or public order in more than one Member

EU Screening Regulation are uncertain. In particular, the question arises whether Article 4 increases the Member States' leeway to interfere with third state direct investment *beyond* the limits stipulated essentially by the strict interpretation by the Court of Justice of the public policy exception in the third clause of Article 65(1)(b) TFEU.[29] In the absence of EU harmonisation, the regulation of third state investment (ie, investment into the EU from a non-EU investor) by a Member State is, in principle, controlled by that freedom, and its narrow range of potential exceptions.

2.3. FREE MOVEMENT OF CAPITAL AND THE FREEDOM OF ESTABLISHMENT

The scope of application of Article 63(1) TFEU, however, is also, in a third state context, significantly determined by the relationship between the freedom of capital movements, and the freedom of establishment, the latter of which the Court of Justice perceives as competing and largely prevailing.[30] Consequently, even before the question arises of whether 'Article 4 factors' have any harmonising or concretising effect with regard to the public policy exception in the context of free movement of capital and, consequently, may broaden the Member States' leeway, that freedom must be applicable to the situation.

Free movement of capital in Article 63(1) TFEU is the only freedom whose scope of application extends, by its clear and unmistakable wording, to the third state context. However, as far as direct investment as a subcategory of capital movement is concerned,[31] there has been an ongoing debate on the scope of this freedom, which the Court of Justice determines by its relationship to the freedom of establishment. Although the freedom of establishment is clearly not applicable to third state scenarios, the Court of Justice nonetheless perceives it as competing and largely prevailing. In *Kronos*,[32] the Court of Justice summarised its controversial view on the relationship between the two freedoms in a textbook-like fashion.[33]

State …'; Article 7(1) of the EU Screening Regulation: 'Where a Member State considers that a foreign direct investment planned or completed in another Member State which is not undergoing screening in that Member State *is likely to affect* its security or public order …'; Article 7(2) of the EU Screening Regulation: 'Where the Commission considers that a foreign direct investment … *is likely to affect* security or public order in more than one Member State …'; Article 8(1) of the EU Screening Regulation: 'Where the Commission considers that a foreign direct investment *is likely to affect* projects or programmes of Union interest on grounds of security or public order …' (emphasis added).

[29] There are certain exceptional cases where the rules relating to the freedom of establishment may be applicable. cf *infra*.

[30] cf, *inter alia*, Case C-47/12 *Kronos International* ECLI:EU:C:2014:2200, paras 30–43.

[31] S Hindelang, *The Free Movement of Capital and Foreign Direct Investment: The Scope of Protection in EU Law* (OUP, 2009) 63–64.

[32] cf eg Case C-47/12 *Kronos International* (n 31) paras 30–43.

[33] For a critical appraisal of the CJEU's case law, see S Hindelang, *The Free Movement of Capital and Foreign Direct Investment: The Scope of Protection in EU Law* (OUP, 2009) 329; S Hindelang,

Essentially, the Court of Justice applied a three-step test. The Court of Justice held that, first, as

> regards the question whether national legislation falls within the scope … [of free movement of capital or the freedom of establishment,] … *the purpose of the legislation* concerned [, ie, its scope of application,] must be taken into consideration. … National legislation intended to apply *only* to those shareholdings which *enable the holder to exert a definite influence* on a company's decisions and to determine its activities falls within the scope of Article 49 of the TFEU on freedom of establishment. … On the other hand, national provisions which apply to shareholdings acquired *solely with the intention of making a financial investment without any intention to influence the management and control of the undertaking* must be examined exclusively in light of the free movement of capital.[34]

Second, if the national legislation at issue applies to such shareholdings which *enable or do not enable* the holder to exert a definite influence over the undertaking, it cannot be determined from the purpose of the legislation, ie, its scope of application, 'whether it falls predominantly within the scope of Article 49 TFEU or Article 63 TFEU'.[35] In such a situation, *in an intra-EU context*, 'account should be taken of the facts of the case in point in order to determine whether the situation to which the dispute in the main proceedings relates falls within the scope of Article 49 TFEU or of Article 63 TFEU.'[36]

Lastly, in a third country context, however,

> it is sufficient to examine the purpose of national legislation [, ie, its scope of application,] in order to determine whether … [the national legislation] falls within the scope of the provisions of the [T]FEU … on the free movement of capital, as national legislation relating to … third countries is not capable of falling within the scope of Article 49 TFEU.[37]

Thus, if the scope of application of national legislation is to regulate shareholdings which enable or do not enable the holder to exert a definite influence over the undertaking, the respective legislation is subject to Article 63(1) TFEU in a third state context. In such a situation, it does not matter, according to the facts of the actual case, that 'a company that is resident in a Member State and has a shareholding in a company resident in a third country giving it definite influence over the decisions of the latter company and enabling it to determine its

Kommentierung der Vorschriften zum Kapital- und Zahlungsverkehr im AEUV (WHI Paper 02/2014) 'Artikel 63 AEUV', paras 176 et seq; see also S Hindelang, 'Die steuerliche Behandlung drittstaatlicher Dividenden und die europäischen Grundfreiheiten – Die teilweise (Wieder-)Eröffnung des Schutzbereiches der Kapitalverkehrsfreiheit für Dividenden aus drittstaatlichen Direktinvestitionen – zugleich eine Besprechung des Urteils in der Rechtssache Test Claimants in the FII Group Litigation II' (2013) *IStR* 77.

[34] Case C-47/12 *Kronos International* (n 31) paras 30–32 (emphasis added, in-text citations omitted).

[35] ibid para 37.

[36] ibid.

[37] ibid para 38.

activities'.[38] However, if the purpose of the national legislation is to regulate only such shareholdings which enable the holder to exert a definite influence over the undertaking, it is not covered by Article 63(1) TFEU; as a matter of fact, not by any freedom.[39]

The question of whether the 'Article 4 factors' have any harmonising or concretising effect with regard to the public policy exception in Article 65(1)(b) of the TFEU is thus only relevant with regard to the scenario in which the national screening legislation covers both foreign direct and portfolio investments.[40]

Moreover, in some cases, *EU resident* investors will also be subjected to a Member State's investment screening mechanisms on foot of the EU Screening Regulation. This is the case, for example, when an EU-based undertaking is used by nationals of a third state as a vehicle to circumvent investment screening. Article 3(6) of the EU Screening Regulation explicitly tasks the 'Member States which have a screening mechanism in place [to] … maintain, amend or adopt measures necessary to identify and prevent circumvention of the screening mechanisms and screening decisions'. Some Member States' legislation actually already provides for anti-circumvention, such as the respective German legislation in Section 55(2) of the Außenwirtschaftsverordnung – AWV (Foreign Trade and Payments Ordinance).[41] In such a situation, Union citizens and legal persons resident in a Member State can, in principle,[42] rely on both the freedom

[38] ibid para 39.

[39] From a dogmatic point of view, the Court of Justice has yet to answer the question of how a freedom that is *not* factually applicable to third state situations can nevertheless be primarily affected in the case of norms that only apply to foreign direct investment, and, consequently, displace the free movement of capital. See J Snell, 'Free Movement of Capital: Evolution as a Non-Linear Process' in P Craig and G de Búrca (eds), *The Evolution of EU Law*, 3rd edn (OUP, 2021) 603–04.

[40] Since the EU Screening Regulation is only applicably to FDI, the question of a broader leeway for the Member States only arises with regard to direct investment. For portfolio investments, the CJEU's strict standard for restricting their free flow on the basis of the first clause of Article 65(1)(b) of the TFEU would apply even if the 'Article 4 factors' had any harmonising or concretising effect.

[41] Available at the website of the Federal Office for Justice. Note that the CJEU ruled that the EU Foreign Direct Investment Screening Regulation does not apply except in cases of circumvention. Case C-106/22 *Xella Magyarország* ECLI:EU:C:2023:568, para 32 et seq.

[42] While the CJEU has recognised in principle that economic activities can be excluded from benefiting from the protection of the fundamental freedoms if they constitute an abusive or fraudulent exploitation of the fundamental freedoms (cf Case C-196/04 *Cadbury Schweppes* ECLI:EU:C:2006:544, para 34 et seq), the Court seems to assign the problem of the abusive exploitation of the fundamental freedoms predominantly to the level of justification. In the area of the free movement of capital, there is an explicit provision in Article 65(1)(b) TFEU, first clause; in the areas of the other fundamental freedoms, the CJEU falls back on unwritten grounds of justification. S Hindelang, *Kommentierung der Vorschriften zum Kapital- und Zahlungsverkehr im AEUV* (WHI Paper 02/2014) 'Artikel 65 AEUV', para 14 et seq, 19. See also G Butler, 'Free Movement of Capital: General Rules and Exceptions' in R Schütze and T Tridimas (eds), *Oxford Principles of European Union Law: Volume II: The Internal Market* (OUP, 2026). Addressing cases of abuse at the level of justification is also the more convincing solution overall. It enables the State measure to be examined on the basis of the principle of proportionality to determine whether it merely accompanies a protectionist Member State regulation or whether it follows legitimate interests. Finally, it should be remembered that it is precisely the full exercise of fundamental freedoms by those entitled to them that Union law wishes to see. S Hindelang and M Hagemeyer, 'Enemy at the Gates?

of establishment and the free movement of capital,[43] and, thus, the question of whether the 'Article 4 factors' have any harmonising or concretising effect with regard to the public policy exception becomes relevant here as well.

All in all, there seem to be constellations in which someone affected by Member State investment screening legislation, may, in principle, rely on fundamental freedoms. For example, a third state investor making an FDI into the EU is protected by Article 63(1) TFEU if the screening legislation of the Member State in question applies to both portfolio and direct investment. In an intra-EU context, the freedom of establishment or free movement of capital may be applicable. This, in turn, would mean that the Member States may not restrict (foreign) direct investment with reference to public policy or public security enshrined in Article 65(1)(b), 3rd clause TFEU, or Article 52(2) TFEU, unless they are addressing 'a genuine and sufficiently serious threat to a fundamental interest of society'.[44]

2.4. ARTICLE 4 OF THE SCREENING REGULATION, AND HARMONISING AND CONCRETISING EFFECTS OF EU SECONDARY LAW ON EU PRIMARY LAW

Some scholarship points to the fact that EU secondary law can have a concretising effect on EU primary law, which can diminish the protective scope of the fundamental freedoms, and thus broaden Member States' leeway to interfere with FDI. In enacting such EU secondary law, the EU institutions may also deviate from the requirements set by case law, for example, relating to the protective scope of fundamental freedoms. The harmonisation competences of the EU also regularly allow the EU to enact secondary law restricting the fundamental freedoms to a degree which the Member States could not justify by reference to the exceptions to the fundamental freedoms if they sought to enact restrictive legislation themselves.[45] However, while the *description* of the possibility of harmonising and concretising effects of EU secondary law on EU primary law, *as such*, is correct, the EU Screening Regulation does not have such effects. By its clear and unmistakable wording, Article 4, with its illustrative, non-exhaustive list of factors potentially affecting security and public order, simply does *not* harmonise.

Die aktuellen Änderungen der Investitionsprüfvorschriften in der Außenwirtschaftsverordnung im Lichte des Unionsrechts' (2017) *EuZW,* 882–89, 886; see also G Ress and J Ukrow, 'Artikel 65 AEUV' in E Grabitz, M Hilf and M Nettesheim (eds), *Das Recht der Europäischen Union* (CH Beck, 2022) para 45 with further references.

[43] In an intra-EU scenario, the above-mentioned problem of delineation of fundamental freedoms is only of secondary importance.

[44] Case C-54/99 *Scientologie* ECLI:EU:C:2000:124, para 17; cf also S Hindelang, *The Free Movement of Capital and Foreign Direct Investment: The Scope of Protection in EU Law* (OUP, 2009) 226.

[45] C Herrmann, 'Europarechtliche Fragen der deutschen Investitionskontrolle' (2019) 22(3) *ZeuS* 429, 465.

Since the EU Screening Regulation does not harmonise, and does not further define the level of protection of security and public order, the Member States are 'still, in principle, free to determine the requirements of public order and public security in the light of their national needs'.[46] They must, therefore, justify any restriction of the fundamental freedoms with reference to the public policy clause, ie first and foremost, Article 65(1)(b) TFEU, 3rd clause.[47] A permissible restriction requires 'a genuine and sufficiently serious threat to a fundamental interest of society',[48] and in accordance with the principle of proportionality.

2.5. ARTICLE 4 OF THE SCREENING REGULATION AS A SOURCE OF 'INSPIRATION' FOR THE INTERPRETATION OF EU PRIMARY LAW

Even if the Court of Justice were to seek 'inspiration' in Article 4 of the EU Screening Regulation in the context of assessing a Member State's restrictions on FDI in light of Article 65(1)(b) TFEU, 3rd clause, or Article 52(2) TFEU with a view to identifying and specifying legitimate public interests capable of justifying a restriction on free movement of capital or the freedom of establishment, this does not mean that the Member States have received *carte blanche* in Article 4 of the EU Screening Regulation.[49]

Rather, the Court of Justice in *Commission v Portugal (Energias de Portugal)* made it clear that, absent harmonisation and despite the

> *importance attached by … the European Union* to the protection of a secure energy supply *[reflected in some EU secondary legislation,]* … it is undisputed that requirements of public security must, in particular as a derogation from the fundamental principle of the free movement of capital, be interpreted strictly, so that their scope cannot be determined unilaterally by each Member State without any control by the institutions of the European Union. Thus, *public security may be relied on only if there is a genuine and sufficiently serious threat to a fundamental interest of society*'.[50]

Thus, Article 4 of the EU Screening Regulation does not seem to broaden Member States' powers to interfere with FDI. This, however, does not rule out that the Court of Justice may further develop its case law on the notion of

[46] Case C-54/99 *Scientologie* (n 45) para 17.

[47] In this way one must understand recital 4 of the EU Screening Regulation which reads: 'This Regulation is without prejudice to the right of Member States to derogate from the free movement of capital as provided for in point (b) of Article 65(1) TFEU.'

[48] Case C-54/99 *Scientologie* (n 45) para 17; S Hindelang, *The Free Movement of Capital and Foreign Direct Investment: The Scope of Protection in EU Law* (OUP, 2009) 226.

[49] Possibly of a different view is C Herrmann, 'Europarechtliche Fragen der deutschen Investitionskontrolle' (2019) 22(3) *ZeuS* 429, 465–66, which seems, however, not to find strong support in the judgment cited in support of his opinion.

[50] Case C-543/08 *Commission v Portugal* ECLI:EU:C:2010:669, paras 84–85 (emphasis added). In para 89, the CJEU also stated that '[e]ven were it accepted that, pursuant to provisions of European Union secondary legislation, a Member State has an obligation to guarantee the supply of energy within its territory, as is claimed by the Portuguese Republic, compliance with such an obligation cannot be relied on to justify any measure which is contrary in principle to a fundamental freedom'.

'genuine and sufficiently serious threat to a fundamental interest of society', in light of technological advancement and changing political landscapes.

Furthermore, and needless to say, a national measure of a Member State restricting FDI must be proportionate. Thus, when a Member State finds, is inspired by, or even exclusively using the factors mentioned in Article 4 of the EU Screening Regulation, that 'a foreign direct investment *is likely to affect* security or public order', this does not automatically mean that the said Member State may restrict fundamental freedoms by 'conditioning, prohibiting, or unwinding foreign direct investment', as Article 4 does not set the threshold, or 'risk level', for permissible government intervention of such severity. Rather, and at most, in the event of a '*likely effect*' on security and public order, the Member State may have recourse to the EU Screening Regulation's coordination mechanism. More severe interferences with an FDI, therefore, still require a more specific and more concrete risk to security and public order.

By way of example, the German Foreign Trade and Payments Act (AWG)[51] adopted the language of the EU Screening Regulation when setting the threshold for intervention. Section 5(2) of the AWG reads as follows:

> Restrictions or obligations to act … can particularly be imposed with reference to the acquisition of domestic companies or shares in such companies by non-EU residents if the acquisition is *likely to impair* the public order or security of the Federal Republic of Germany or of another Member State of the European Union ….[52]

In light of the above, one may wonder whether legislation actually is not overshooting the mark. Moreover, while Article 4 of the EU Screening Regulation may be read as also relating to the empowerment of the Member States to act within an area of exclusive competence of the EU according to Article 2(1) TFEU in connection with Article 3(1) of the EU Screening Regulation,[53] at the same time, it does not in any way further specify (or restrict) such empowerment beyond the point that screening must be 'on the grounds of security or public order'.

The Member States may also refer to any other possible factor not listed, as long as it relates to the screening of FDI on the grounds of security or public order. Article 4 of the EU Screening Regulation, therefore, serves as a source of inspiration only. At any rate, when exercising such empowerment, the Member States are

[51] Außenwirtschaftsgesetz – AWG of 6 June 2013, BGBl (Federal Law Gazette) I, 1482; last amended 20 December 2022, BGBl (Federal Law Gazette) I, 2752.

[52] (Emphasis added). The German original reads as follows 'Beschränkungen oder Handlungspflichten … können insbesondere angeordnet werden in Bezug auf den Erwerb inländischer Unternehmen oder von Anteilen an solchen Unternehmen durch unionsfremde Erwerber, wenn infolge des Erwerbs die öffentliche Ordnung oder Sicherheit der Bundesrepublik Deutschland oder eines anderen Mitgliedstaates der Europäischen Union … *voraussichtlich beeinträchtigt* wird ….' (emphasis added).

[53] Since the EU based the EU Screening Regulation on its exclusive competence under Article 207(2) of the TFEU, it is only consistent that it empowers (cf Article 2(1) of the TFEU) the Member States in Article 3(1) of the EU Screening Regulation to 'maintain, amend or adopt mechanisms to screen foreign direct investments in their territory on the grounds of security or public order'. At the same time, this also means that the Member States may not screen FDI for any grounds other than security and public order.

not exempted from observing other EU law, especially fundamental rights, such as the freedom to conduct a business or the right to property in Article 16 and Article 17 of the Charter of Fundamental Rights of the EU respectively, and fundamental freedoms.[54]

2.6. CONCLUSION

While political and economic fundamentals, and with it the perception of foreign investments, have changed significantly over the course of the past years, the provisions in EU primary law covering free movement of capital between the EU and third states have remained, essentially,[55] unchanged since they were last significantly altered by the Treaty of Maastricht in the early 1990s.[56] Article 63(1) TFEU unilaterally liberalised third state capital movements, and is a prominent expression of an EU based on a non-protectionist economic order with an open market.[57] The current restrictive legislative activities of the EU and its Member States may, therefore, potentially lead to tensions with the fundamental freedom contained in Article 63(1) TFEU.

However, and apart from the exceptions contained in the chapter on free movement of capital, the case law of the Court of Justice on the freedom has traditionally followed the prevailing political views in the EU on the 'acceptable' degree of openness with regards to third state capital movements, considering the freedom's potential impact on exchange rates,[58] taxation,[59] and now 'economic resilience' in the 'age of geoeconomic struggle'. In other words, the Court of Justice's case law can be sketched as essentially 'sovereignty-preserving',[60] and it can be expected that this will not change significantly when, eventually, a Member State investment screening mechanism finds its way to the Court of Justice.

[54] cf TM Hagemeyer, 'Access to legal redress in an EU investment screening mechanism' in S Hindelang and A Moberg (eds), *A Common European Law on Investment Screening (CELIS), Yearbook of Socio-Economic Constitutions* (Springer, 2021) 795–833.

[55] The Treaty of Lisbon of 2009 brought some minor changes to the provisions on free movement of capital, most notably the newly phrased Article 75 TFEU, and a new Article 65(4) of the TFEU.

[56] For more details, see M Sedlaczek and M Züger, 'Artikel 63 AEUV' in R Streinz (ed), *Beck'scher Kurzkommentar EUV/AEUV*, 3rd edn (CH Beck, 2018) para 7.

[57] Article 119(1) TFEU and Article 127(1) TFEU.

[58] AFP Bakker, 'The Political Economy of Capital Controls and Lateralisation in the European Union' in S Hindelang and A Moberg (eds), *YSEC Yearbook of Socio-Economic Constitutions* (Springer, 2021) 11–28, 14–15; see also AFP Bakker, *The Liberalisation of Capital Movements in Europe* (Springer, 1996) 191.

[59] cf Case C-279/93 *Finanzamt Köln-Altstadt v Schumacker* ECLI:EU:C:1995:31; note that the *Schumacker* case was decided on the basis of free movement of workers. In Case C-80/94 *Wielockx v Inspecteur de Directe Belastingen* ECLI:EU:C:1995:271, the doctrine was held to apply also under the freedom of establishment. See also, for example, for the application of the '*Schumacker* doctrine' in the ambit of free movement of capital: Case C-376/03 *D (Opinion of AG Colomer)* ECLI:EU:C:2004:663; S Hindelang, *Kommentierung der Vorschriften zum Kapital- und Zahlungsverkehr im AEUV* (WHI Paper 02/2014) 'Artikel 63 AEUV', para 110.

[60] S Hindelang, *The Free Movement of Capital and Foreign Direct Investment: The Scope of Protection in EU Law* (OUP, 2009) 329; Hindelang, *Kommentierung der Vorschriften zum Kapital- und Zahlungsverkehr im AEUV* (n 60) paras 176 et seq.

3

Screening of Foreign Direct Investment in EU Law: Frameworks, Non-EU Investors, and Security Considerations

GRAHAM BUTLER

3.1. INTRODUCTION

THE EU POSSESSES the extensive right to regulate its internal economic affairs. This internal area – the internal market – is theoretically open to external commercial actors, in that few hindrances and restrictions, in recent decades, have been imposed at EU level on non-EU investment (capital) entering the internal market. Foreign direct investment (FDI) into the EU has come in waves, and from different regions of the world, from North America in particular. However, FDI is now entering the EU from other places around the world, such as Asia and the Middle East. This non-North American investment is, at some level, not as welcome as North American investment. Accordingly, the EU and its Member States have been rethinking the very open approach to FDI seen in recent decades, and have begun to question, in the form of concrete actions, whether *all* forms of inward FDI into the EU are indeed in the interest of the EU and its Member States, or not. In other words, the EU has been on an intellectual journey as regards its position on inward FDI from non-EU investors.

There have been many different ways that the EU has gone about more closely scrutinising the ways in which non-EU investment is entering the EU, with non-EU investors being active in the internal market,[1] particularly regarding the ownership of certain types of assets, which has become a highly salient issue. Distinctions have been and can be drawn between welcome, genuine FDI from non-EU investors that pose no majority security problems; and unwelcome, potentially harmful, FDI from non-EU investors. The EU legislature has thus

[1] See further ch 1.

taken a firmer grip, in certain terms, on inward-bound FDI from non-EU investors in the name of security and public order. One such concrete initiative has been, in 2019, the adoption of the FDI Screening Regulation (the Regulation).[2] This demonstrates that the EU has gone beyond mere thoughts and formally, amongst other instruments, abandoned its very open approach to attracting inward FDI.

FDI, as a phenomenon, has a special place in Europe. It, through its Member States and all the commercial undertakings therein, is a source of FDI into wider global markets (outward FDI); but similarly, the EU is a host to extensive FDI from non-EU investors (inward FDI). The Union is committed, at least legally as per the EU Treaties, in the common interest, to the 'progressive abolition of restrictions on international trade and on foreign direct investment'.[3] On the other hand, the EU Treaties only state that its Common Commercial Policy (CCP), its external trade policy, 'shall be conducted in the context of the principles and objectives of the Union's external action'.[4]

The EU Treaties also refer, however, to 'free and *fair* trade'.[5] This *fair* element can be seen as a form of potential reticence, given it is located in the initial provisions, and omitted from both the external objectives of the Union contained within Article 21 TEU, and the more specific aims of external trade policy within the CCP contained within Article 207 TFEU, or the general treaty power within Article 216 TFEU. Therefore, notwithstanding the ideology of the EU in its primary law, there are open political choices for which this EU trade mandate can be used, in that FDI can either be permitted, restricted, discouraged or prohibited.

From the outset, it is necessary to note that there is a sharp distinction to be drawn between *intra*-EU investment (within the EU) and *extra*-EU investment (from outside-to-inside the EU), given that the Regulation only concerns the latter extra-EU investment. This is particularly notable given that, under free movement law, such as the free movement of capital, it does not allow for Member States to engage in 'arbitrary discrimination or a disguised restriction'[6] on intra-EU investment.

The Regulation is a clear affirmation that the EU's openness to trade with third states – non-EU investors – is being counterbalanced with control mechanisms to wall off certain types and kinds of investment. It is as much about the restriction of EU trade with third states, as it is to improve the effectiveness of FDI screening within the EU. This is given that prior to the Regulation's

[2] Regulation (EU) 2019/452 of the European Parliament and of the Council of 19 March 2019 establishing a Framework for the screening of foreign direct investments into the Union [2019] OJ L79I/1.

[3] Article 206 TFEU.

[4] Article 207(1) TFEU.

[5] Article 3(5) TEU, emphasis added.

[6] Article 65(3) TFEU.

adoption, some Member States had FDI screening for investments from non-EU investors already in place (particularly for sensitive sectors of national economics), and some Member States had no FDI screening mechanisms whatsoever.

This chapter, examining the screening of foreign direct investment in EU law, is structured as follows. Section 3.2 begins by examining the background to the new Regulation, by analysing the concept of investment, and its place within the EU legal order. It accounts for the different types of investment that are regulated, how and at what level such regulation occurs, and considers the legal basis for such secondary law that is now in place at EU level. From there, section 3.3 moves onto the foreground, the Regulation itself, by analysing the common framework of the screening done by Member States, the different types of non-EU investors which it seeks to include, what information sharing and related practices are envisaged between the Member States and the Commission, what might constitute a security concern for European security, as well as grounds for judicial review of screening decisions that are taken. Following this background and foreground, and by way of conclusion, section 3.4 brings the context back in, and considers the future of FDI screening in the EU.

3.2. BACKGROUND: INVESTMENT, THE REGULATION, AND THE EU LEGAL ORDER

3.2.1. Direct Investment and Portfolio Investment as FDI

Direct investment is covered by two areas of the EU Treaties – internally within the Union within the meaning of the free movement of capital,[7] and externally within the CCP. Internally, direct investment within the EU is *not* FDI, given that it is merely an intra-EU capital movement. Consequently, it is evident that in EU law, 'FDI' is a term used to cover extra-EU capital movements, with capital coming into the EU from outside the EU. Moreover, the free movement of capital is a pre-determined policy choice placed within the EU Treaties, and ruled by a relatively strict framework.[8] By contrast, the CCP is much more open in terms of evolving political choices, and is not predetermined by the EU Treaties. Put another way, the governing logic of the free movement of capital, and of the CCP, are very different.

The EU legal order makes a distinction too between direct investment and portfolio investment. In particular, *Opinion 2/15* confirmed what whilst direct

[7] Articles 63–66 TFEU.

[8] See Graham Butler, 'Free Movement of Capital: General Rules and Exceptions' in Robert Schütze and Takis Tridimas (eds), *Oxford Principles of European Union Law: Volume II: The Internal Market* (Oxford University Press, 2026).

investment, externally, is a matter of exclusive competence of the EU, by contrast, portfolio investment continues to be a matter of shared competence of the EU and its Member States.[9] It is thus necessary to be able to draw the distinction between *direct* investment and *portfolio* investment.

The state of the case law of the Court was neatly summarised in *Test Claimants I*, by noting that direct investment entails investments 'of any kind made by natural or legal persons which serve to establish or maintain *lasting and direct links* between the persons providing the capital and the undertakings to which that capital is made available in order to carry out an economic activity',[10] and that presupposes that 'the shares held by the shareholder enable him, either pursuant to the provisions of the national laws relating to companies limited by shares or otherwise, to participate effectively in the management of that company or in its control'.[11]

By contrast, portfolio investment has been described by the Court, in the same *Test Claimants I* case, as 'non-direct foreign investment', and that that may occur 'in the form of the acquisition of company securities with the intention of making a financial investment without any intention to influence the management and control of the undertaking'.[12] For the Court, such portfolio investment, non-direct investment, is considered the free movement of capital within the meaning of Article 63 TFEU. Thus, portfolio investment is not within the scope of the Regulation.

The starting point for analysing FDI with regard to the external dimension of the internal market, therefore, are the amendments made to the CCP by the Treaty of Lisbon in 2009,[13] in particular in (now) Article 207(1) TFEU. This provided for the inclusion of FDI within the CCP, which it did not previously. Pre-Lisbon, when FDI was not *explicitly* within the CCP, it would not have been accepted by the Court that FDI was within the CCP in an implied manner.[14] With FDI therefore, post-2009, coming explicitly into the exclusive competence of the Union through the CCP, it has made the overall relationship between EU law and international investment law more complex.[15] But at the same time, today, investment goes hand-in-hand with external trade. For the sake of

[9] *Opinion 2/15* ECLI:EU:C:2017:376 (*EU-Singapore FTA*). See Christine Kaddous, 'The EU Competence to Conclude the New Generation of Free Trade Agreements: Opinion 2/15 (EU–Singapore FTA)' in Graham Butler and Ramses A Wessel (eds), *EU External Relations Law: The Cases in Context* (Hart Publishing, 2022).

[10] Case C-446/04 *Test Claimants in the FII Group Litigation v Commissioners of Inland Revenue* ECLI:EU:C:2006:774 (*Test Claimants I*), para 181 (emphasis added).

[11] ibid para 182. Moreover, see *Opinion 2/15* ECLI:EU:C:2017:376 (*Singapore*), para 80.

[12] *Opinion 2/15* (n 9) para 227.

[13] On the history of FDI and its inclusion in the CCP, see Sophie Meunier, 'Integration by Stealth: How the European Union Gained Competence over Foreign Direct Investment' (2017) 55 *Journal of Common Market Studies* 593, 598–603.

[14] See, for example, *Opinion 1/94* ECLI:EU:C:1994:384 and, *Opinion 2/92* ECLI:EU:C:1995:83.

[15] Panos Koutrakos, 'The Relevance of EU Law for Arbitral Tribunals: (Not) Managing the Lingering Tension' (2016) 17 *Journal of World Investment & Trade* 873, 873–74.

coherence and consistency of the EU's external relations, trade and investment ought to not develop on entirely separate trajectories, with different Member States having differing arrangements. Therefore, the EU having the exclusive competence for FDI has long made sense, even if getting to that point has been only progressively been achieved.

Many Member States have arms of the state, either ministries or agencies, that are specifically designed to attract FDI as a form of FDI *promotion*. Similarly, many Member States have had investment screening mechanisms – national mechanisms – to screen FDI in certain areas. Such unilateral approaches by Member States to screening FDI have obviously been to the detriment of the Union's CCP. Therefore, post-Lisbon, the Commission was not going to authorise Member States to introduce or amend existing national screening mechanisms unless there was going to be some level of a commonality in the way each Member State went about its activities.

3.2.2. Competence, Legal Basis, and Authorisation

The CCP has long been an exclusive competence of the EU.[16] Even so, exclusive competence of the EU can even be derived, implicitly, in areas in which internal competence has not been exercised.[17] In considering FDI screening, however, there have been two noted trends in the Court's case law that are relevant. First, the preference for a single legal basis for secondary law, and, second, to favour legal bases with explicit external competence, rather that implied external powers derived from internal powers.[18]

Article 207 TFEU is rarely used as a legal basis for matters that are not related to international agreements. In fact, Article 207(2) TFEU as a legal basis for the Regulation is only the third time where it has been utilised post-Lisbon.[19]

[16] Article 3(1)(e) TFEU. Though this was evident as far back as *Opinion 1/75* ECLI:EU:C:1975:145 (*Local Cost Standard*). See Marise Cremona and Jaka Kukavica, 'Common Commercial Policy and the Determination of Exclusivity: Opinion 1/75 (Local Cost Standard)' in Graham Butler and Ramses A Wessel (eds), *EU External Relations Law: The Cases in Context* (Hart Publishing, 2022).

[17] See, eg, *Opinion 1/76* ECLI:EU:C:1977:63. See Allan Rosas, 'EU External Competence in the Absence of Internal Rules, and the Sleeping Beauty: Opinion 1/76 (Laying Up Fund for Inland Waterway Vessels)' in Graham Butler and Ramses A Wessel (eds), *EU External Relations Law: The Cases in Context* (Hart Publishing, 2022).

[18] Marise Cremona, 'Regulating FDI in the EU Legal Framework' in Jacques HJ Bourgeois (ed), *EU Framework for Foreign Direct Investment Control* (Kluwer Law International, 2019), 33.

[19] The two other times were Regulation (EU) No 1219/2012 of the European Parliament and of the Council of 12 December 2012 establishing transitional arrangements for bilateral investment agreements between Member States and third countries [2012] OJ L351/40 (the 'Grandfathering Regulation') and Regulation (EU) No 912/2014 of the European Parliament and of the Council of 23 July 2014 establishing a framework for managing financial responsibility linked to investor-to-state dispute settlement tribunals established by international agreements to which the European Union is party [2014] OJ L257/121. There has also been one subsequently adopted, in part, on Article 207 TFEU: Council Decision (EU) 2022/438 of 14 March 2022 on the position to be adopted

Whilst Article 207 TFEU does not exclude harmonising measures for internal EU purposes, that said, Article 207(6) TFEU states that '[t]he exercise of the competences conferred by … Article [207 TFEU] in the field of the common commercial policy … shall not lead to harmonisation of legislative or regulatory provisions of the Member States in so far as the Treaties exclude such harmonisation'.[20]

Thus, Article 207(6) TFEU is to be read as that, although exclusive competence of the EU may be there, that exclusivity is external. Thus, that does not deprive Member States of adopting internally applicable measures. In other words, Article 207(6) TFEU preserves an internal right to regulate the internal market within the EU. That said, as best put, the Regulation in question 'may well turn out to be a "non-harmonizing measure" having significant "harmonising effects"'.[21] The legal basis of the Regulation, Article 207 TFEU, is therefore all the more curious when it is considered that in *Daiichi Sankyo*, the Court said that Article 207 TFEU is 'not [about] the harmonisation of the laws of the Member States' but, rather, is about 'the liberalisation of international trade'.[22]

The Regulation was adopted on this single legal basis. It could not have been adopted on a dual legal basis of both Article 207 TFEU and Article 64(2) TFEU, because the procedures that apply for these two legal bases are different. By being different, that is to say that the adoption of such procedurally different legal bases is procedural incompatibility. When legal bases are incompatible, the most appropriate legal basis must be utilised, even if one legal basis marginally impinges on the other. The Regulation potentially undercuts the potential of the free movement of capital provisions being the legal basis on treating all origins of capital equally, whether it be intra-EU investment, or inward investment from third states in the form of FDI. However, Article 63 TFEU's apparent equation of EU investors and non-EU investors is most deceiving. In real terms, despite Article 63 TFEU appearing to cover an external dimension, it does not fully equate the internal and the external.[23]

Since FDI became an exclusive competence of the Union with the Treaty of Lisbon, it is assumed that Member States are forbidden, unless expressly authorised to act otherwise in line with Article 2(1) TFEU, to adjust their national screening mechanisms already *in situ*, and for Member States which did not have screening mechanisms, to introduce their own mechanisms, given this

on behalf of the European Union within the Administrative Council of the International Centre for Settlement of Investment Disputes (ICSID) [2022] OJ L89/8.

[20] Article 207(6) TFEU (emphasis added).

[21] Andreas Moberg and Steffen Hindelang, 'The Art of Casting Political Dissent in Law: The EU's Framework for the Screening of Foreign Direct Investment' (2020) 57 *Common Market Law Review* 1427, 1460.

[22] Case C-414/11 *Daiichi Sankyo* ECLI:EU:C:2013:520, para 60. See Joris Larik, 'Intellectual Property and the Post-Lisbon Common Commercial Policy: Daiichi Sankyo' in Graham Butler and Ramses A Wessel (eds), *EU External Relations Law: The Cases in Context* (Hart Publishing, 2022).

[23] See, for a thorough an in-depth study, Steffen Hindelang, *The Free Movement of Capital and Foreign Direct Investment: The Scope of Protection in EU Law* (Oxford University Press, 2009).

would impinge upon exclusive competence of the Union. The likely view of the Commission, post-Lisbon, with the introduction of FDI into the CCP, was that existing Member States' screening mechanisms were not in compliance with EU law, because they were not authorised by the Union. The Commission therefore took the opportunity to use the Regulation in question as a chance to permit such screening retroactively.

Having exclusive competence of the Union exercised by Member States is certainly unusual. Therefore, the Regulation, first and foremost, must been seen as an authorising measure. That is despite the Regulation not specifically saying it empowers Member States. Furthermore, it should in no way be considered a 'returning' of any competence to the Member States, given no secondary law can repatriate exclusive competence of the Union as defined by the EU Treaties, of which the CCP certainly is explicitly so.

Long ago in *Donckerwolcke*, the Court stated that the 'full responsibility in the matter of commercial policy was transferred to the [Union] by means of [Article 207 TFEU]', and as such, 'measures of commercial policy of a national character are only permissible … by virtue of specific authori[s]ation by the [Union]'.[24] Thus, with Article 207 TFEU as its legal basis, the Regulation is an authorising act, though, as will be seen, it is not without its problems.

3.3. FOREGROUND: THE FOREIGN DIRECT INVESTMENT SCREENING REGULATION

3.3.1. Screening by the Member States

The Regulation is an internal legislative act of the EU and essentially regulates a part of the EU's CCP, with a 'screening' of investment coming into the EU from outside the EU. It does not concern investment between Member States,[25] which is otherwise regulated by the free movement of capital under Articles 63–66 TFEU, and/or the freedom of establishment in Articles 49–55 TFEU. Therefore, intra-EU cross-border capital movements and establishment rights under both primary and secondary establishment are not within the scope of the Regulation.

Amusingly, despite the Regulation being an EU legal act, it is not actually an *EU* screening mechanism, but rather a plethora of national screening mechanisms

[24] Case 41/76 *Suzanne Criel, née Donckerwolcke and Henri Schou v Procureur de la République au tribunal de grande instance de Lille and Director General of Customs* ECLI:EU:C:1976:182, para 32. Piet Eeckhout, 'Linking Internal and External Trade in a Perfect Customs Union: Donckerwolcke' in Graham Butler and Ramses A Wessel (eds), *EU External Relations Law: The Cases in Context* (Hart Publishing, 2022). See also Case 174/84 *Bulk Oil (Zug) AG v Sun International Limited and Sun Oil Trading Company* ECLI:EU:C:1986:60, para 31.

[25] Accordingly, the lawfulness of a Member State screening intra-EU investment (not regulated by the Regulation) in the same way as it does extra-EU investment (regulated by the Regulation) is highly questionable.

in the Member States, subject to a basic framework brought in by the Regulation that Member States apply. Beyond the basic framework, some nuances are left for the Member States to decide that are in line with broader Union law, making for numerous frameworks. Thus, the Regulation does not provide for FDI screening at EU level, nor mandate an evenly-applied and absolutely consistent FDI screening mechanism across the EU. Rather, the Regulation's objective is much more minimal, whereby it can be considered a first-generation screening mechanism, potentially subject to future reforms and improvements.

Whilst the Regulation is the first broad attempt to screen inward investment into the EU *at EU level*, specific sectoral mechanisms for screening investment have long existed in certain fields. For example, for air carriers to operate and be based within the Union, secondary law demands that ownership of such air carriers must be primarily in the hands of nationals of Member States, and not third country nationals (TCNs).[26] Furthermore, under the electricity and natural gas directives, various notification requirements are in place for transmission system operators from third states.[27] In the hydrocarbon sector, entities in third states and TCNs may also be excluded from the market on national security grounds.[28] For these sectors subject to specific screenings and like mechanisms, the Regulation does not replace them, but merely complements them. Similarly, but different, another comparator to the effects of the Regulation at hand is the Merger Regulation in matters of competition law.[29] Article 21(4) of the Merger Regulation allows for the possibility of Member States, on narrow grounds, to 'take appropriate measures to protect legitimate interests', such as creating restrictions that may be potentially justified, if acted on proportionately, in the name of public security.

3.3.2. Strategic Sectors

Strategically important sectoral areas to the Union and its Member States can be numerous. The Regulation is not just concerned with certain types of FDI

[26] See Regulation (EC) No 1008/2008 of the European Parliament and of the Council of 24 September 2008 on Common Rules for the Operation of Air Services in the Community (Recast) (Text with EEA Relevance) [2008] OJ L293/3.

[27] See Directive 2009/72/EC of the European Parliament and of the Council of 13 July 2009 concerning common rules for the internal market in electricity and repealing Directive 2003/54/EC (Text with EEA Relevance) [2009] OJ L211/55 and Directive 2009/73/EC of the European Parliament and of the Council of 13 July 2009 concerning common rules for the internal market in natural gas and repealing Directive 2003/55/EC (Text with EEA Relevance) [2009] OJ L211/94, in particular Article 11, otherwise known as the 'Gazprom clause'.

[28] See Directive 94/22/EC of the European Parliament and of the Council of 30 May 1994 on the conditions for granting and using authorizations for the prospection, exploration and production of hydrocarbons [1994] OJ L164/3, in particular Article 2(2), second para.

[29] Council Regulation (EC) No 139/2004 of 20 January 2004 on the control of concentrations between undertakings (the EC Merger Regulation) (Text with EEA Relevance) [2004] OJ L24/1.

however. Theoretically, the Regulation applies to all sector areas, but it is obviously of most concern to sectoral areas that are considered strategic, or sensitive.

Article 4(1) of the Regulation mentions certain sectors that are singled out as being of particular concern regarding non-EU investment. This includes 'critical infrastructure, whether physical or virtual, including energy, transport, water, health, communications, media, data processing or storage, aerospace, defence, electoral or financial infrastructure, and sensitive facilities, as well as land and real estate crucial for the use of such infrastructure',[30] critical technologies and dual use items,[31] supply of critical inputs, including energy or raw materials, as well as food security,[32] sensitive information, including personal data, or the ability to control such information,[33] and the media.[34]

This list is merely indicative, and non-exhaustive, but it covers quite an expansive array of sectors and industries. Given that Member States may consider other areas as being strategic or sensitive, how this is reconciled with the premise that the Regulation is adopted on the legal basis of Article 207 TFEU – exclusive competence of the EU – is quite the mystery. Therefore, the Regulation is certainly a risky regulatory manoeuvre by the EU by delegating some unilateral decisions to the Member States in what is essentially an exclusive competence of the EU.

3.3.3. A Common Framework, but No Harmonisation

FDI screening processes by some Member States have long been in place, as various types of frameworks. Thus, prior to the Regulation coming into force, FDI screening amongst the Member States was a complete patchwork. Despite FDI screening now being imposed at EU level, the Regulation does *not* actually harmonise investments. Rather, its anticipated achievement is much more meagre, by simply ensuring that Member States put *a common framework* in place.

Instead, the Regulation is about trying to achieve substantive conformity, in line with what the Regulation sets out. Whilst substantive, this common framework can also be understood as a procedural standard which must be followed. This minimum common framework is not to be understood as a form of minimum harmonisation, despite the factors to be considered by Member States being non-exhaustive. Existing FDI screening mechanisms by Member States just have to be brought into line with the Regulation.

The fact that it is merely a common framework does not exactly square with the stated aim of the CCP, which 'shall be based on *uniform* principles'.[35] Such

[30] Article 4(1)(a) of the Regulation.
[31] Article 4(1)(b) of the Regulation.
[32] Article 4(1)(c) of the Regulation.
[33] Article 4(1)(d) of the Regulation.
[34] Article 4(1)(e) of the Regulation.
[35] Article 207(1) TFEU (emphasis added).

uniform principles for the Court in *Diamantarbeiders* meant '*the elimination of national disparities* … affecting trade with third [states]'.[36] Allowing but a common framework in place, but letting Member States decide other criteria over and above the Regulation, would therefore appear to deviate from the uniformity of any legislative measure that has Article 207 TFEU as its legal basis. In fact, vague authorisation grounds for the Member States to act are, in principle, not allowed.[37]

Article 3(1) of Regulation provides that Member States '*may maintain, amend or adopt* mechanisms to screen foreign direct investments'.[38] The Regulation could be read as a *de facto* obligation upon Member States, who have never exercised investment screening, to establish an FDI screening mechanism, given that, read as a whole, it weighs heavily in favour of FDI screening being undertaken in all Member States.[39] The articulation of this mandate within the Regulation is poor,[40] but the Regulation amounts to implied obligation for Member States to have FDI screening mechanisms in place. After all, the notification requirements that Member States must make to the Commission for non-EU investments made would be impossible to comply with if no FDI screening mechanism was in place.

3.3.4. Types of Non-EU Investors

The Regulation is not targeted against specific third states given it applies irrespective of the non-EU origin of the investment. In other words, it is to be applied in a non-discriminatory manner vis-à-vis third states. Article 2(2) of the Regulation states that 'foreign investment' applies to both natural and legal persons, assuming they would be private actors.

[36] Joined Cases 37/73 and 38/73 *Sociaal Fonds voor de Diamantarbeiders v NV Indiamex and Feitelijke Vereniging De Belder* ECLI:EU:C:1973:165, para 16 (emphasis added).

[37] For criticism on how the Regulation is problematic, as there are no limits to the authorisation, see Stefan Korte, 'Exploring the Possibilities and Limits of the EU and Member States to Set Up an Investment Screening Mechanism in the Light of Union Law' in Steffen Hindelang and Andreas Moberg (eds), *A Common European Law on Investment Screening (CELIS)* (Springer, 2021), 442–43.

[38] Emphasis added.

[39] For example, in Sweden, a public authority, the National Inspectorate of Strategic Products (*Inspektionen för strategiska produkter*) (ISP), has been dealing with authorisation and clearances regarding export controls for military and dual-use (civil-military) products, even when Sweden had no general national investment screening in place. That authority, typically orientating around goods imports, has been designated the national competent authority (NCA) under the Regulation, since 1 December 2023, is now handling the screening of inward investment, now that Sweden has put in place a general national investment screening mechanism under the Regulation.

[40] There is even the view that the Regulation is 'integration by stealth'. See Thomas Verellen, 'When Integration by Stealth Meets Public Security: The EU Foreign Direct Investment Screening Regulation' (2021) 48 *Legal Issues of Economic Integration* 19.

There is a hidden aspect, however, of such private investment, as it can be undertaken by private firms who, in some cases, are state backed, supported, or owned by a third state. Because a definition of 'foreign investor' (ie, non-EU investor) is included in the Regulation, it ensures that non-EU investors provide the necessary information as to whom is the ultimate or true investor. That said, the extent of third state influence in FDI is not extensively addressed in the Regulation.

One of the factors to be considered is if a third state investor is in fact a state-controlled body under the arm of a government of a third state. Investment into Europe has been seen from certain investors in third states with close links to the third states themselves, which in turn raises particular motivational questions about such investments. Third state-backed non-EU investors can sometimes have more than a commercial interest, with, in some cases, the commercial interest seeking to mask a non-commercial interest. Furthermore, profit may not be the overarching motive of investors, who may rather have their eyes on the assets of a particular investment made in the EU. The Regulation does not specifically regulate (nor outright prohibit) government-backed FDI from non-EU investors, but it does provide that this be given consideration on grounds that the non-EU investor is 'directly or indirectly controlled … by state bodies or armed forces, of a third state, including through ownership structure or significant funding'.[41]

3.3.5. Information Sharing, Notification, and Cooperation

Information sharing, notification, and cooperation between various parties are an integral part of the Regulation. It includes both vertical and horizontal elements, with both the Commission and other Member States. In effect, the Regulation is designed for Member States to exert peer pressure on one another, in the name of each other's (and the Union's) interests. Such a cooperation mechanism provides a genuine channel for both the Commission and other Member States to obtain written views on the security arrangements of other Member States that can have a broader impact on European security. After all, a threat that is specific to one Member State only could also be construed as having an impact on European security.

Article 3 of the Regulation mandates procedural rules to be put in place by Member States,[42] with set timeframes,[43] with a guarantee for potential non-EU investors that information made available to Member States 'shall be protected' from public disclosure.[44] This is supplemented by the fact that

[41] Article 4(2)(a) of the Regulation.
[42] Article 3(2) of the Regulation.
[43] Article 3(3) of the Regulation. Though not exact timeframes according to EU law but, rather, set down by individual Member States.
[44] Article 3(4) of the Regulation.

Article 11 of the Regulation demands a 'secure and encrypted system' provided by the Commission to facilitate screening processes, which is coupled with the guarantee of confidentiality of transmitted information, where there is an obligation on both Member States and the Commission not to disclose such without consent.[45]

Article 6(9) of the Regulation provides that Member States doing the screening must give comments of other Member States and the opinion of the Commission 'due consideration'. This is light, non-binding language. It is very conceivable that, if Member States do not notify other Member States and the Commission in good time, when investments have already been made, the Commission would view this as a breach of their obligation under the Regulation to notify them 'as soon as possible',[46] so that they are all afforded good opportunity to comment or provide an opinion on the proposed FDI.

The information that must be handed over to Member States by non-EU investors seeking to make FDI includes, according to Article 9(2) of the Regulation, includes:

(a) the ownership structure of the foreign investor and of the undertaking in which the foreign direct investment is planned or has been completed, including information on the ultimate investor and participation in the capital;
(b) the approximate value of the foreign direct investment;
(c) the products, services and business operations of the foreign investor and of the undertaking in which the foreign direct investment is planned or has been completed;
(d) the Member States in which the foreign investor and the undertaking in which the foreign direct investment is planned or has been completed conduct relevant business operations;
(e) the funding of the investment and its source, on the basis of the best information available to the Member State;
(f) the date when the foreign direct investment is planned to be completed or has been completed.

The Regulation will only be successful in the longer term if Member States are forthcoming in a timely manner with their lodging of information with the Commission and other Member States. Whilst no specific timeline it set down, it must be done 'without undue delay'.[47] No penalties or sanctions for the Member States were specifically written into the Regulation itself for failing to properly notify the Commission and other Member States, or to take due regard of the comments/opinion made by such parties after the notification has been made. Instead, default enforcement mechanisms under EU primary law are available,

[45] Article 10 of the Regulation.
[46] Article 6(1) of the Regulation.
[47] Article 9(3) of the Regulation.

like the Commission's ordinary infringement procedure that it can utilise against Member States.[48]

The Regulation mainly concerns pre-investment screening, but it does contain some post-investment aspects. Practically speaking, screening should, in theory, take place *before* an investment is made. The Regulation makes clear, if a negative decision is rendered, that investments can be unwound,[49] so as to ensure there is no easy circumvention of the Regulation. This is somewhat at odds with a prior remark of the Court, as stated in the *Church of Scientology* case that, '[i]n the case of direct foreign investments, the difficulty in identifying and blocking capital once it has entered a Member State may make it necessary to prevent, at the outset, transactions which would adversely affect public policy or public security'.[50]

3.3.6. Security Concerns

Security concerns are no longer just individual Member States' concerns – they have Union-wide implications. The aim of the Regulation is to ensure there are legal grounds to scrutinise inward FDI that is likely to affect 'security or public order'.[51] In doing so, it ensures cooperation of the Member States both vertically with the Commission, and horizontally between Member States. More wide-rangingly, however, the Regulation seeks to balance the exclusive competence of the Union under the CCP on the one hand, with the issue of security and public order on the other hand, which is largely but not solely a matter for the Member States.

The terminology of 'security or public order' in the Regulation is nuanced, and consideration must be had as regards the precise choice of wording that appears and persistently reappears throughout. The concept of 'security' is not necessarily *national* security or *public* security,[52] but *security* more generally, including the encompassment of *European* security. This means that the concept of security in the Regulation has the potential to open up the possibility of allowing it to be construed quite broadly. Thus, the Regulation has an interest in the security interests of the *Union*, and not just individual Member States.

Yet there is room for the concept of security to begin to have common understanding, given that security interests are now beginning to come together under

[48] eg, Article 258 TFEU.

[49] Article 2 of the Regulation, which refers to an 'unwind[ing]' an investment.

[50] Case C-54/99 *Association Eglise de scientologie de Paris and Scientology International Reserves Trust v The Prime Minister* ECLI:EU:C:2000:124, para 20.

[51] For an unexplained reason, the Regulation varies between 'security *or* public order' and 'security *and* public order' (emphasis added).

[52] The concept of 'public security' is typically associated with a written ground of derogation from various market freedoms. See Panos Koutrakos, 'Public Security Exceptions and EU Free Movement Law' in Panos Koutrakos, Niamh Nic Shuibhne and Philip Syrpis (eds), *Exceptions from EU Free Movement Law: Derogation, Justification and Proportionality* (Hart Publishing, 2016).

this piece of secondary law. Historically within free movement law, which is primary law, the concepts of 'public security' and 'public order' have been hopelessly abstract. There has never been any real attempt as a matter of secondary law to provide for a fixed or workable definition of security in free movement, for that is typically context dependent, and evolves over time. As put by Advocate General Jacobs in *Werner*, 'each Member State may have specific security concerns, whether because of its location, because of its internal situation, or because of specific external threats'.[53] Furthermore, the EU has no security or intelligence services of its own and has to rely on its respective Member State bodies if such information is needed. With the Regulation therefore, security interests are now subject to the common framework, with the Commission empowered to input its view on screening decisions of Member States on foot of the Regulation. With *national* security, *public* security, and *European* security all having related (but different) matters in mind, the Regulation could, however, over time, lead to some convergence across the Union as to what is mean by *security*.

The Regulation is also, therefore, a huge point of entry for the Commission into the security domain, and curious given the Commission has no security apparatus in order to have a view of what constitutes a threat to European security. Accordingly, if the Commission has a view on particular investment that is being screened by a Member State, and the Commission wishes to offer an opinion, the Commission only has a basis to argue on policy grounds, with political considerations in mind, rather than clear evidential grounds to support its arguments.

Prerogatives on *national* security typically rest with the state,[54] yet in compliance with EU law. The Court has stated that Member States 'retain exclusive competence as regards the maintenance of public order and the safeguarding of internal security', and therefore 'unquestionably enjoy a margin of discretion' in that regard.[55] This margin is understandable. But moving away from *national* security towards considering *European* security is thus an inevitability if the Regulation is to function as it is envisaged.

Lastly, Article 346 TFEU provides that a Member State is not obligated, as a matter of EU law, to provide information to anyone which it considers 'contrary to the essential interests of its security', and that a Member State 'may take such measures as it considers necessary for the protection of the essential interests of its security' which includes trade defence measures. That said, Article 346 TFEU cannot be interpreted in an overly expansive way. As the Court stated in *Johnston*, that Article and other related provisions 'do not lend themselves to a wide interpretation and it is … not possible to infer from them that there is inherent in

[53] Opinion of AG Jacobs, Case C-70/94 *Fritz Werner Industrie-Ausrüstungen GmbH v Federal Republic of Germany* ECLI:EU:C:1995:151, para 43.

[54] Article 4(2) TEU: '… national security remains the sole responsibility of each Member State.'

[55] Case C-265/95 *Commission v France* ECLI:EU:C:1997:595 (*Spanish strawberries*), para 33.

the Treaty a general proviso covering all measures taken for reasons of public safety'.[56] In *Commission v Finland (Duty-free imports of military equipment)*, the Court said that any Member State wishing to rely upon Article 346 TFEU must 'prove that it is necessary to have recourse to that derogation in order to protect its essential security interest'.[57] Such measures taken by Member States, on grounds utilised under Article 346 TFEU, must be exercised in a proportionate manner.[58]

3.3.7. Judicial Review, and Ensuring No Misuse

There are safeguards built into the Regulation for non-EU investors. Review of FDI screening by Member States is specifically provided for in the Regulation, with Article 3(5) of the Regulation stating that there is 'possibility to seek recourse' against decisions of Member States. That does not necessarily set out that they have to be *judicial* recourses. This might, on some reading, leave open the possibility for mere *administrative* review to be in place, with no judicial remedy possible. That would be an incorrect reading, however.

The *Les Verts* judgment of the Court demands that the EU legal order, encompassing the Member States, is 'a complete system of legal remedies and procedures'.[59] Similarly as per the Court in *Johnston*, '[i]t is for the Member States to ensure effective judicial control as regards compliance with the applicable provisions of [Union] law'.[60] Not to mention that the attempted exclusion of potential judicial redress under the Regulation would also be suspect under Article 47 of the Charter of Fundamental Rights. Thus, there must ultimately be a judicial remedy against decisions of Member States regarding FDI screening under the Regulation.

Whilst there must be guaranteed availability of judicial review of screening decisions before national courts of the Member States, it is an open question whether the opinions of the Commission could be subject to an action for annulment under Article 263 TFEU before the Court given the influence they could have on the eventual screening decisions of the Member States. On the one hand, the Commission would likely take the view that its opinions are non-binding and would in any event be addressed to the Member State to whom

[56] Case 222/84 *Marguerite Johnston v Chief Constable of the Royal Ulster Constabulary* ECLI:EU:C:1986:206, para 26. Furthermore, Case C-414/97 *Commission v Spain* ECLI:EU:C:1999:417, para 21.

[57] Case C-284/05 *Commission v Finland*, ECLI:EU:C:2009:778 (*Duty-free imports of military equipment*), para 49. See also Case C-615/10, *Insinööritoimisto InsTiimi Oy* ECLI:EU:C:2012:324, para 35.

[58] Case C-474/12 *Schiebel Aircraft GmbH v Bundesminister für Wirtschaft, Familie und Jugend* ECLI:EU:C:2014:2139, para 38.

[59] Case 294/83 *Parti écologiste 'Les Verts' v European Parliament* ECLI:EU:C:1986:166, para 23.

[60] Case 222/84 *Marguerite Johnston v Chief Constable of the Royal Ulster Constabulary* ECLI:EU:C:1986:206, para 19.

it has issued an opinion, rather than the potential non-EU investor that had made the notification to the Member State. Consequently, this would mean that non-EU investors would lack the requisite legal standing to challenge the opinion of the Commission. And in any event, even if legal standing were established, in substance, the opinion would merely be a preparatory measure, and therefore not a challengeable measure. On the other hand, whilst opinions of the Commission under the Regulation are an 'opinion' within the meaning of Article 288 TFEU,[61] which non-exhaustively sets down the different types of EU legal acts, opinions can indeed have binding effects in some instances. Whilst they are not ordinarily (nor commonly) subject to judicial review under an action for annulment procedure, it is at least conceivable that they could be.[62] For example, it could be argued that the opinions of the Commission could amount to producing legal effects. However, since the Regulation only empowers the Member States to make formal screening decisions – at least under the Regulation as it currently stands – it is likely that challenging screening decisions ought to be made in the appropriate national courts concerned. If the opinion of the Commission is to be somehow challenged, the appropriate procedural route could be for a national court hearing a legal challenge to make a reference for a preliminary ruling to the Court under Article 267 TFEU.

Misuse of the Regulation has both intra-EU and extra-EU concerns. FDI screening is done, occasionally, in the name of protecting elements of general state interest, in other words, on the premise of state protectionism by Member States (and not of security or public order concerns). After all, Member States might, in some instances, protect the interests of a particular commercial undertaking in their state, in which the state might occasionally be a shareholder. The Regulation should not lead a drive towards new forms of protectionism by the Member States, and, thus, misuse of the Regulation by Member States has to be closely watched. The screening conducted under the new Regulation could lead to prejudice against non-EU investors who are seeking to genuinely invest in the EU, who do not pose a security or public order challenge. After all, not all inward FDI from third states should be categorised as unwelcome by Member States' mechanisms.

The Regulation is to preserve *Union* interests. No doubt, however, Member States may, over time, see it (and use it) to protect national interests beyond those permitted by the Regulation. It does not allow the Member States to pursue domestic industrial policy objectives, and should not be construed as a means to maintain the industrial competitiveness of select businesses. There is also an inherent risk that Member States might try operationalising the

[61] See recital 16 of the preamble to the Regulation.

[62] See, for example, on judicial review of recommendations, Case C-501/18 *BT v Balgarska Narodna Banka* ECLI:EU:C:2021:249, where the Court declared a recommendation of an EU agency, the European Banking Authority (EBA), invalid.

screening decisions under the Regulation for what could be, essentially, intra-EU investment.[63] This contamination of the free movement of capital and the freedom of establishment with the CCP by the Member States, if tried, should be condemned and rejected, whereby intra-EU investment should remain subject to the various free movement provisions.

Dividing issues between the freedoms is as much a challenge as it is deciphering the external dimension of the freedoms from Article 207 TFEU itself on the Union's CCP. But as the Court has long held, as it did in *Holböck*, the right of establishment in the EU 'does not include any provision extending its application to situations which involve the establishment in a non-member country of a Member State national or of a company incorporated under the legislation of a Member State'.[64] The Court has always been very conscious of ensuring that non-EU investors do not use the free movement of capital, which theoretically extends to third states, from making use of the other freedoms, which do not grant such a right. As illustrated in *Test Claimants II*, for example, the Court stated that '[s]ince the [EU] Treat[ies] do[] not extend freedom of establishment to third [states], it is important to ensure that the interpretation of Article 63(1) TFEU as regards relations with third [states] does not enable economic operators who do not fall within the limits of the territorial scope of freedom of establishment to profit from that freedom'.[65]

In mid-2022 came the Court's judgment in *Xella Magyarország*,[66] which was the first case in which the Regulation came before the Court since its adoption in 2019. The facts of the case concerned a complex structure of the investor's affairs, incorporated in many Member States, but whose parent group was domiciled outside the EU, albeit whose ultimate owner was a national of a Member State. The entity had sought to make an investment in a Member State but was rendered with a negative decision made under a national screening decision on foot of the Regulation. The Court ruled, quite surprisingly, that the issue did not come within the scope of the Regulation at all,[67] and, thus, the national measures had to be assessed under free movement law instead. It furthermore added that the applicable freedom that the national measures were to be scrutinised under was the freedom of establishment, and not the free movement of capital. Further cases brought to the Court under the Regulation, or restrictions on investments at Member State level, leading to negative decisions by national

[63] On the lack of intra-EU applicability of the Regulation, see Jochem de Kok, 'Towards a European Framework for Foreign Investment Reviews' (2019) 44 *European Law Review* 24, 44–45. It should be noted that the lack of intra-EU relevance is because the Regulation was based on Article 207 TFEU, and solely focused on the EU's *external* relations.

[64] Case C-157/05 *Winfried L Holböck v Finanzamt Salzburg-Land* ECLI:EU:C:2007:297, para 28.

[65] Case C-35/11 *Test Claimants in the FII Group Litigation v Commissioners of Inland Revenue and The Commissioners for Her Majesty's Revenue & Customs* ECLI:EU:C:2012:707, para 100.

[66] Case C-106/22 *Xella Magyarország* ECLI:EU:C:2023:568.

[67] For a different view compared to the judgment of the Court, see Opinion of Advocate General Ćapeta, Case C-106/22 *Xella Magyarország* ECLI:EU:C:2023:267.

authorities, will shed further light on the actual effectiveness of the Regulation, given that in this first case, it turned out to be not applicable at all.

3.4. CONCLUSION

The EU is an open federation, and a believer in the benefits of international economic law by having an extensive trade policy, demonstrated by its willingness to be bound by international agreements with third parties. The EU has every right, however, to ensure that such openness to third parties with whom it does and does not have such treaties is not abused, or where EU economic undertakings are being stonewalled in third states when they are trying to receive reciprocal treatment. Screening FDI is today a normal occurrence in most parts of the developed world, for states can afford to be selective about which forms of inward FDI they wish to see. The EU is now part of this club with its own particular form of screening under the Regulation.

The main theme of the Regulation is security and public order, but it must also be read in both its broader and specific context. Broadly, Europe is becoming a more geopolitical actor, and the Regulation is evidence of another trend in placing European security at the centre of EU external relations. Specifically, Member States have always fretted when sudden surges in FDI have entered their jurisdiction. But there is one underlying political reason that underpins why FDI screening is coming about now: the rise of China, and its growing presence on the global stage. The EU views China, depending on the policy domain in question, as being simultaneously a cooperation partner, a negotiation partner, an economic competitor.[68] In terms of investment, the EU is now treading with greater caution.

The introduction of FDI screening at European level, as a matter of EU law, could be seen as somewhat of a turn in the EU's open approach to international trade, with EU trade being less liberal. This is partially true but, in fact, could be distorting a bigger issue, which is the lack of reciprocal market access for EU investors in third states, who do not enjoy the same level of investment protection that non-EU investors do in the EU.

The EU's right to regulate is beginning to be utilised in a much more forceful way against non-EU investors, where its core interests are at stake. After all, the EU is permitted, according to its own internal law, not only to promote trade, but also to restrict it.[69] It is very difficult as a matter of law to distinguish between 'threatening', unwanted FDI, and 'non-threatening', welcome FDI. Thus, the

[68] See, eg, 'Joint Communication of the European Commission and the High Representative of the Union for Foreign Affairs and Security Policy to the European Parliament, the European Council and the Council: EU-China – A Strategic Outlook' (JOIN(2019) 5 Final).

[69] eg, Case 112/80 *Firma Anton Dürbeck v Hauptzollamt Frankfurt am Main-Flughafen* ECLI:EU:C:1981:94, para 44; Case 245/81 *Edeka Zentrale AG v Germany* ECLI:EU:C:1982:277, para 24; and Case C-150/94 *UK v Council* ECLI:EU:C:1998:547 (*Toys from China*), para 67.

Regulation leaves inherent discretion for the decision-maker, as a matter of law, for them to adapt to contemporary circumstances at the time that screening decisions are made. The EU's investment regime still encourages inward FDI, whilst ensuring, or at least trying to achieve, a pan-EU response to unwanted FDI. In this vein, the Regulation can be viewed as the Commission trying to hedge some of the potential negative by-products of globalisation, and understanding that certain sectors or industries may be directly or indirectly controlled by third states. Going forward, the openness of the EU internal market is, in future, conditional.

As identified in this chapter, the Regulation has curious regulatory techniques. After all, it demands that Member States exercise powers that are exclusive competence of the EU. Albeit a regulation (and not a directive), the Regulation is almost like a hidden directive, in that it demands Member States act by putting in place screening mechanisms. Most importantly, however, it lays bare that all Member States have a level of responsibility in the exercise of the EU's CCP. But it does not resolve the basic conundrum: there is still no single FDI screening mechanism for the EU. It is not an 'EU' screening mechanism, but rather authorises (and demands) that Member States have a common basis in place for *national* screening mechanisms under the auspices of the Regulation. Thus, considerable discretion is vested in the Member States frameworks, even with the Regulation providing the framework. For market actors, this has the potential to mean a lack of uniformity in the screening conducted. Compared to normal CCP matters, which is governed uniformly by the Commission, this represents a mismatch that at some point will have to be rectified.

In terms of the future direction of investment screening, first, at a very minimum, (national) law and policy convergence under secondary law, by doing away with national screening, in favour of an EU-wide FDI screening mechanism, should be the next step. Europe is eventually on the road to having a Committee on Foreign Investment, perhaps even modelled on something like the version in the United States of America.[70] A more integrated procedure could indeed be a future way of designing such a system. Second, given that FDI within the CCP is to be understood as both inward FDI (regulating FDI on entry into the EU) and outward FDI (securing the ability of EU investors to invest in third states through international agreements), the Regulation is about further controlling the former, in order to indirectly enhance the latter. Yet, naturally, a further step that could be taken at EU level, under the exclusive competence of the EU, would be for outbound screening of FDI from the EU to third states to be undertaken.

As the Regulation now approach five years since its initial adoption,[71] consideration will soon be given to what changes need to be made and a move towards a second generation Regulation. There are no shortages of issues with the Regulation that can be improved through a coalition of the willing.

[70] For example, the Committee on Foreign Investment in the United States (CFIUS).

[71] Article 15(1) of the Regulation stipulates that in 2023, and every five years thereafter, an evaluation on the 'functioning and effectiveness' of the Regulation must take place, with such a report presented to the two legislative institutions, the Parliament and the Council.

4

Investment and EU International Agreements

IVANA DAMJANOVIC

4.1. INTRODUCTION

FOLLOWING THE AMENDMENTS to EU primary law by the Treaty of Lisbon of 2009, foreign direct investment (FDI) has been included in the scope of the Common Commercial Policy (CCP).[1] Accordingly, the EU has gained competence for treaty-making in the area of foreign investment protections and dispute settlement, which previously fell within the scope of the Member States' treaty-making competence. However, the lack of clarity on the scope of the EU's foreign investment competence led to disagreements between the EU and the Member States. The ruling of the Court of Justice in *Opinion 2/15* clarified the vertical distribution of powers between the EU and Member States for external foreign investment,[2] and has consequently shaped the treaty-making policy choices of the EU regarding foreign investment.

This chapter analyses the EU legal framework and practice with respect to its international agreements in the field of foreign investment. It argues that competence for foreign investment, which is shared between the EU and its Member States, has placed a significant limitation on implementing EU international investment agenda through EU international agreements.[3] With more actors involved in the EU treaty-making process, it is more difficult for the EU to achieve its investment policy objectives and compete on the world stage. However, treaty-making procedure in the EU is not simply a matter of political preference, but is grounded in the delineation of competences

[1] Articles 206 and 207 TFEU.

[2] *Opinion 2/15* ECLI:EU:C:2017:376. See also Christine Kaddous, 'The EU Competence to Conclude the New Generation of Free Trade Agreements: Opinion 2/15 (EU–Singapore FTA)' in Graham Butler and Ramses A Wessel (eds), *EU External Relations Law: The Cases in Context* (Oxford, Hart Publishing, 2022) 891–906.

[3] See also ch 12.

in EU primary law. Treaty requirements thus cannot be relaxed for the sake of political expediency. In accommodating its constitutional constraints, the EU's approach to the regulation of foreign investment in EU international agreements has been pragmatic, and is reflected in different types of international agreements.

The analysis in this chapter proceeds in three steps. First, the chapter provides an overview of the EU institutional framework regarding competences and legal bases for the conclusion of EU international agreements in the field of foreign investment. This serves to explain the limited EU sovereignty in the field of foreign investment and the underlying rationale for the EU policy approach to treaty-making in this field. Second, the chapter analyses EU practice regarding regulation of foreign investment in different types of its international agreements. The emphasis is primarily placed on the scope rather than the content of investment provisions in EU agreements, with a view to illustrate the extent to which the EU legal framework has shaped and limited the EU treaty-making practice and policy outcomes in the field of foreign investment. Finally, the chapter places investment in the wider context of EU external trade and investment policy. It concludes by considering the EU's shift towards sustainability and its impact on future directions in EU treaty practice in the field of foreign investment. This chapter thus aims to provide the reader with an overview of the EU legal framework and practice regarding its international agreements with investment provisions.

4.2. EU LEGAL FRAMEWORK FOR THE CONCLUSION OF INTERNATIONAL AGREEMENTS IN THE FIELD OF INVESTMENT

Article 207 TFEU lists FDI as one of the key aspects of the CCP,[4] and thus provides an explicit legal basis for the EU's competence over foreign investment regulation, including the conclusion of international agreements.[5] Given the broad scope of investment in international agreements, the lack of clarity on the scope of the EU's foreign investment competence following the amendments brought by the Treaty of Lisbon was resolved by the Court of Justice in *Opinion 2/15*. This section first considers the scope of EU competence to conclude international agreements with investment provisions and its evolution in light of the interpretation provided by the Court of Justice. In the second part, different legal bases for the conclusion of EU international agreements in the field of foreign investment are considered. The competence and legal basis are important as they determine whether an agreement will be concluded as 'EU-only' or mixed agreement, with 'mixity' entailing an additional layer of

[4] See Article 207(1) TFEU.
[5] Article 207(3) and (4) TFEU.

complexity, and likely delays of the agreements' entry into force, with consequences for policy efficiency.

4.2.1. The Scope of EU Investment Competence in International Treaty-making

EU trade treaties with third states in pre-Lisbon times, building upon the GATS classification of services,[6] involved provisions on the admission of investment (investment liberalisation) and its related post-admission treatment, through provisions on establishment for supply of services and capital movements.[7] The main purpose of these provisions was to secure for EU investors market access to third states while granting to third countries' foreign investors access to the EU market in the course of trade exchange. These agreements, depending on the third states involved, provided for different levels of investment liberalisation and reciprocity, by including diverse market access restrictions in specific sectors or by providing different levels of accorded treatment – national treatment (NT) or most favoured nation treatment (MFN), or both. Establishment of legal persons under these pre-Lisbon GATS regulatory model treaties, although within the EU competence, did not fall within the scope of the CCP, or, to the extent that it fell under the CCP, it was subject to different qualifications and sectoral limitations.[8]

In addition, some EU agreements were inspired by EU primary law, and thus contain clauses on establishment, which mirror EU law provisions on freedom of establishment and free movement of capital.[9] By the same logic, while these provisions fall within EU competence as they concern internal market rules,

[6] Article I(2) General Agreement on Trade in Services, Marrakesh Agreement Establishing the World Trade Organization, Annex 1B (signed 15 April 1994, entered into force 1 January 1995) 1869 UNTS 183, 33 ILM 1167 (GATS). Most investments will fall into mode 3.

[7] Establishment refers to setting up and management of an undertaking or setting up a subsidiary or a branch of an undertaking, and impediments in national regulation which restrict market access by foreign investors. Capital movements concern the transfer of funds necessary to make an investment (to establish an undertaking): see A Dimopoulos, *EU Foreign Investment Law* (Oxford, Oxford University Press, 2011) 82.

[8] *Opinion 1/94* [1994] ECR I-5267, paras 43-47. The CJEU in *Opinion 1/08* confirmed that after Nice all four WTO modes of provision of services fall within the CCP, however subject to conditions laid down in Article 133(5) and (6) TEC (agreements in defined sectors to be concluded jointly by the Community and the Member States): Opinion 1/08 [2009] ECR I-11129. For a most comprehensive analysis of *Opinion 1/08*, see M Cremona, 'Balancing Union and Member State Interests: Opinion 1/2008, Choice of Legal Base and the Common Commercial Policy Under the Treaty of Lisbon' (2010) 35 *European Law Review* 678.

[9] See Articles 31–35 and 40–45, Agreement on European Economic Area and establishment clauses in Stabilisation and Associations Agreements with Western Balkans – for example, Article 53 Stabilisation and Association Agreement between the European Communities and their Member States of the one part, and the Republic of Montenegro, of the other part [2010] OJ L108/3.

they could not be considered to be a part of the CCP.[10] Finally, provisions on post-establishment treatment of investments, both the narrower post-admission treatment in GATS-style agreements, as well as broader investment protection standards of traditional bilateral investment treaties (BITs),[11] equally did not exclusively fall within the scope of the CCP pre-Lisbon. This fragmentation required the conclusion of EU international agreements concerning foreign investment jointly with the Member States.

In the Treaty of Lisbon, FDI has been included in the CCP, which is an EU exclusive competence listed in Article 3(1) TFEU. In the areas of exclusive competence, the EU is authorised to act alone, and Member States can neither legislate internally nor enter into international obligations externally, unless empowered by the EU.[12] In contrast, in the areas of shared competence, both the EU and its Member States may act to exercise their competence; however, Member States may exercise their competence to the extent that the EU has not exercised its own competence.[13] As this difference affects the vertical distribution of powers within the EU, the lack of clarity on the scope of the EU's foreign investment competence led to disagreements between the EU and Member States. The scope of the CCP, which was resolved by the Court of Justice in *Opinion 2/15*, is of relevance as it determines the scope of the exclusive EU treaty-making competence in the field of trade and investment. It thus determines whether an international agreement is to be concluded as 'EU-only' – if it falls within the scope of the CCP – or if it is outside of the CCP scope, as a mixed agreement, which must be ratified by the EU and all Member States.

In assessing the EU's foreign investment competence, the Court of Justice examined the EU competence with respect to the investment chapter of the EU-Singapore Free Trade Agreement (EUSFTA), which contained provisions on investment protection and ISDS, previously falling within the ambit of Member States' bilateral investment treaties (BITs).[14] The Court focused on two issues in determining the scope of EU competence: (i) the type of investment, and (ii) the phases of investment.

With respect to the first issue, the Court of Justice distinguished between two types of foreign investment: 'direct' and 'non-direct' or 'portfolio', concluding

[10] In *Opinion 1/94* (n 8) para 46.

[11] The Energy Charter Treaty (ECT) is the only such agreement that was concluded by the EU in the pre-Lisbon era.

[12] Article 2(1) TFEU. Member States can act only to the extent that the EU has empowered them or for the implementation of EU acts. This includes situations when the EU repeals the existing legislation without replacing it with new legislation or when the CJEU annuls the legislation: R van Ooik, 'The European Court of Justice and the Division of Competence in the EU' in D Obradovic and N Lavranos (eds), *Interface between EU Law and National Law* (Zupthen, Europa Law Publishing, 2007) 24.

[13] Article 2(2) TFEU. These are known as shared pre-emptive competences. In some areas shared competences are parallel: see Articles 4(3) and (4) TFEU.

[14] Following *Opinion 2/15*, what is now referred as the EU-Singapore FTA differs from the EUSFTA examined by the CJEU in *Opinion 2/15*, and is incapsulated in the Investment Protection Agreement (IPA) with Singapore (EUSIPA). See section 4.3.1 below.

that *only* FDI falls within the scope of the CCP and Article 207(1) TFEU.[15] Direct investment relates to investments which 'establish or maintain *lasting and direct links* between the persons providing the capital and the undertakings to which that capital is made available in order to carry out an economic activity'. Such links enable the shareholder 'to participate effectively in the *management* of [the] company or in its *control*'.[16] On the other hand, 'non-direct foreign investment', also known as portfolio investment, is made 'with the intention of making a financial investment without *any* intention to influence the management and control of the undertaking'.[17] Such investment thus constitutes free movement of capital for the purposes of Article 63 TFEU, which, unlike other EU freedoms, applies both between the Member States, as well as between Member States and third states.[18] Examples of portfolio investment include 'types of investment other than the acquisition of company securities, such as certain categories of real-estate investment or the use of loans'.[19]

With respect to the second issue relating to the phases of investment, the Court of Justice clarified that EU competence regarding FDI includes acts concerned with the *admission* as well as those concerned with the *protection* of FDI.[20] The Court of Justice thus rejected the argument of the Council and some Member States that the EUSFTA investment chapter concerned only protection of FDI.[21] The rationale of this argument can be traced to differentiation between investment liberalisation and investment protection, with the former concerning the (pre-) establishment phase – admission and post-admission treatment of the investment – and the latter the post-establishment phase – the protection of investment once the investment has been made. With the explicit inclusion of FDI into the CCP in the Treaty of Lisbon, all aspects of FDI – admission, post-admission treatment and protection – now fall within the CCP.

While finding that FDI falls within the scope of the CCP and thus within express exclusive EU competence, the Court of Justice also identified that the EU and Member States share competence with respect to non-FDI investment

[15] See *Opinion 2/15* (n 2) para 83 (emphasis added).

[16] ibid para 80, citing, *inter alia*, Case C-446/04 *Test Claimants in the FII Group Litigation* ECLI:EU:C:2006:774, paras 181 and 182; Case C-326/07 *Commission v Italy* ECLI:EU:C:2009:193, para 35; Case C-464/14 *SECIL* ECLI:EU:C:2016:896, paras 75 and 76 (emphasis added).

[17] ibid para 227, citing, *inter alia*, Joined Cases C-282/04 and C-283/04 *Commission v Netherlands* ECLI:EU:C:2006:208, para 19; Case C-81/09 *Idryma Typou* ECLI:EU:C:2010:622, para 48; Case C-212/09 *Commission v Portugal* ECLI:EU:C:2011:717, para 47.

[18] See Article 63 TFEU. Free movement of capital is not defined in the treaties and its meaning is determined by reference to the nomenclature in Annex I to Council Directive 88/361/EEC of 24 June 1988 for the implementation of Art 67 of the Treaty [1988] OJ L178/5. The nomenclature is not exhaustive: see Case C-222/97 *Trummer and Mayer* [1999] ECR I-1671, paras 7, 13. Free movement of capital is, however, subject to limitations in Arts 64 and 65 TFEU (national law provisions on tax treatment, national law infringements and public policy exceptions, subject to proportionality test).

[19] *Opinion 2/15* (n 2) para 228.

[20] ibid paras 87, 109.

[21] ibid para 85.

(portfolio investment) and ISDS. With respect to portfolio investment, the Court of Justice found that no secondary EU legislation has been adopted under Article 63(1) TFEU and Article 64(2) TFEU relating to any type of investment other than FDI,[22] and hence EU primary law cannot be subsumed under 'common rules' within the meaning of Article 3(2) TFEU, which would provide the EU with implied exclusive treaty-making competence.[23] Nevertheless, the conclusion of an international agreement, such as the EUSFTA, contributes to free movement of capital as one of the internal market freedoms, and is thus necessary for the achievement of the treaty objectives related to the internal market.[24] Hence, the Court of Justice classified this competence as shared.

For the Court of Justice, the EU also shares competence with the Member States for commitments regarding ISDS. The Court of Justice reasoned that ISDS, as a regime, which 'removes disputes from the jurisdiction of the courts of the Member States', must be considered an exclusive EU competence.[25] On the contrary, Advocate General Sharpston argued for EU exclusive competence on the basis of the ancillary nature of the dispute settlement provisions. In her view, based on the Opinions of the Court of Justice in *Opinion 1/91*, *Opinion 1/09*, and *Opinion 2/13*, the competence regarding substantive provisions of an international agreement also gives the EU the competence regarding a dispute settlement mechanism. ISDS is no exception in this regard, as it concerns the *manner* in which the competence is exercised, rather than the nature of the competence.[26] However, the Court of Justice did not accept this argument, reasoning that competence for ISDS must be shared, since the ISDS regime cannot be established without the Member States' consent.[27] In other words, the Court of Justice considered ISDS to be of an essential nature around which investment protections unfold, not the other way around. This view was further endorsed later in the *Achmea* judgment concerning intra-EU arbitration.[28] Finally, the Court of Justice also found that the institutional provisions relating to an area of shared competence in the investment chapter also fall within the competence shared between the EU and its Member States.[29]

[22] See *Opinion 2/15*, Opinion of AG Sharpston ECLI:EU:C:2016:992, para 360.

[23] *Opinion 2/15* (n 2) para 235–38.

[24] In particular, the objectives of Title IV ('Free movement of persons, services and capital') of Part III of the TFEU. Internal market falls within the scope of Article 4(2)(a) TFEU. Additionally, the EU and Member States also share objectives under Article 216(1), in relation to Article 4(1) TFEU: ibid paras 240–42.

[25] ibid para 292.

[26] Opinion of AG Sharpston (n 22), paras 525–27, 529. See also Panos Koutrakos, 'EU Competence to Conclude Trade Agreements: Opinion of Advocate General Sharpston in Opinion 2/15' in Graham Butler and Adam Łazowski (eds), *Shaping EU Law the British Way: UK Advocates General at the Court of Justice of the European Union* (Oxford, Hart Publishing, 2022) 509–18.

[27] *Opinion 2/15* (n 2) paras 292–93. See also section 4.3.2 below.

[28] Case C-284/16 *Slovakische Republik v Achmea* ECLI:EU:C:2018:15.

[29] *Opinion 2/15* (n 2) paras 278–79, 284. In particular, the areas of shared competence are the provisions of Chapter 1 (Objectives and General Definitions), Chapter 14 (Transparency), Chapter 15 (Dispute Settlement between the Parties), Chapter 16 (Mediation Mechanisms) and Chapter 17

With respect to all other areas of the EUSFTA, the Court of Justice found the EU exclusively competent, either on the basis of relevant provisions falling within the scope of the CCP (express EU competence), or implied exclusive EU competence, as a result of internal harmonisation through EU legislation, developed in line with the case law of the Court of Justice – the *ERTA* doctrine.[30] In addition, institutional provisions of the EUSFTA, including those relating to transparency, due to their ancillary nature, fall within the same exclusive EU competence as substantive provisions which they accompany.[31] The delineation of competences in the key FTA areas stemming from *Opinion 2/15* of the Court of Justice is outlined in the following table.

Table 4.1 EU competence for trade and investment international agreements

COMPETENCE AREA	EXTERNAL COMPETENCE (TREATY-MAKING)
Market access of goods	EU express exclusive • CCP – Art 3(1)(e) TFEU
Services (except transport)	EU express exclusive
Government procurement (except transport services)	EU express exclusive
Commercial aspects of intellectual property rights	EU express exclusive
Competition rules	EU express exclusive
Trade and sustainable development	EU express exclusive
Provisions related to FDI	**EU express exclusive**
Transport services	EU implied exclusive • AETR-ERTA principle – Art 3(2) TFEU
Government Procurement (transport services)	EU implied exclusive
Provisions related to non-FDI investments	***EU and Member States shared***
Investor-state dispute settlement	***EU and Member States shared***

In addition to the delineation of competences between the EU and its Member States for the conclusion of international agreements in the field of investment,

(Institutional, General and Final Provisions), insofar as they relate to provisions of Chapter 9 that fall within shared competence.

[30] Case 22-70 *Commission v Council* (European Road Transport Agreement) [1971] ECR 263, para 17, in which the CJEU stated: 'each time the Community, with a view to implementing a common policy envisaged by the Treaty, adopts provisions laying down common rules, whatever form these may take, the Member States no longer have the right, acting individually or even collectively, to undertake obligations with third countries which affect those rules.' See also Case C-467/98 *Commission v Denmark* ('Open Skies' Agreement) [2002] ECR I-9519, paras 77–80.

[31] *Opinion 2/15* (n 2) paras 276–77, 282–83.

the legal basis of an international agreement in the EU treaties is another important aspect determining the EU treaty-making processes and outcomes.

4.2.2. Constitutional Nature of Legal Bases for EU International Agreements

Every EU action – a particular EU act or an international agreement – must be founded on one or more legal bases set out in EU primary law. This substantive legal basis determines the procedure to be followed for the adoption of an act, including the conclusion of an international agreement. Institutional powers vary considerably depending on the procedure used, which is ultimately determined by the choice of the legal basis. However, the choice of legal basis is not really a 'choice', but is determined with reference to the 'centre of gravity' approach. 'Objective factors', in particular, the aim and the content of the measure, rather than its effects, determine the legal basis.[32] It therefore follows that the choice of legal basis cannot simply be a tributary of a political choice. If a measure has more than one aim or more than one component, the legal basis is determined with respect to the measure's predominant aim or component, if they can be established.[33] Accordingly, interpretation of the content and the aim of the measure, and thus the choice of the legal basis, can lead to contradictory preferences between EU institutions and Member States.[34]

International agreements can include a range of different commitments over different competence areas, and their conclusion often involves multiple legal bases. EU agreements with trade and investment components are not an exception in this regard. However, if a measure pursues several objectives which are 'inseparably linked', it can be founded on the corresponding bases,[35] as long as multiple legal bases are not procedurally incompatible or do not undermine the role of the European Parliament.[36] The Court of Justice will invalidate EU acts based on an inappropriate legal basis, and the EU consent to be bound by an international agreement signed on the basis of such acts may be vitiated.[37] Therefore, the choice of legal basis is of 'constitutional significance', with the Court of Justice playing an important role in EU external trade and investment

[32] *Opinion 2/00* [2001] ECR I-9713, para 22 and case law cited therein.

[33] ibid para 23 and case law cited therein.

[34] R Barents, 'The internal market unlimited: some observations on the legal basis of EU legislation' (1993) 30 *Common Market Law Review* 85; H Cullen and A Charlesworth, 'Diplomacy by Other Means: the Use of Legal Basis Litigation as a Political Strategy by the European Parliament and Member States' (1999) 36 *Common Market Law Review* 1243.

[35] *Opinion 2/00* (n 32) para 23 and case law cited therein. Such situations are considered exceptional, because, if the objectives can be separated, two separate legal acts on two different legal bases should be adopted.

[36] Case C-94/03 *Commission v Council* [2006] ECR I-1, para 52.

[37] *Opinion 1/08* (n 8) para 110.

relations through review of the legal bases of different international agreements for their compliance with EU primary law.[38]

Classical FTAs of the EU are largely based on Article 207 TFEU. Nevertheless, additional legal bases could be added when the scope of an international agreement is beyond the scope of the CCP, as long as the involved legal bases are not procedurally incompatible, or do not encroach on the Parliament's prerogatives. Further, trade and investment provisions regularly find their place in a range of EU international agreements concluded as Association Agreements (AAs), which are broader in their scope and cover both political and economic cooperation (legal basis of Article 217 TFEU), or Economic Partnership Agreements in the field of development cooperation (legal basis of Article 209 TFEU). The rules determining the conclusion of EU international agreements differ according to the substantive legal basis of each agreement, requiring different procedures and levels of involvement of EU institutions and the Member States.

General rules for the conclusion of all EU international agreements, including trade and investment agreements, are prescribed in Article 218 TFEU. This provision outlines the procedure for the participation of EU institutions in the different stages of the treaty-making process: negotiation, signature, and treaty ratification. Trade and investment treaty negotiations with third states are led by the European Commission;[39] however, its powers are confined by the roles played by the Council during the entire process, and by the Parliament, particularly at the end of the process. In particular, the Council has a leading role in authorising the Commission's actions at different stages of the procedure,[40] while the Parliament plays the key role in the ratification stage through its consent.[41] During the negotiating process, the Commission is in consultation with the Council via the Trade Policy Committee of the Council (TPC), and it also keeps the Parliament informed via the Parliament's International Trade Committee (INTA).[42] Every decision in the EU treaty-making procedure is also subject to judicial review at the CJEU.[43] After receiving the consent from the Parliament, the Council will adopt the decision to conclude the agreement, which completes the procedure under Article 218 TFEU for 'EU-only' agreements, which fall

[38] See P Koutrakos, 'Legal Basis and Delimitation of Competence in EU External Relations' in M Cremona (ed), *EU Foreign Relations Law* (Oxford, Hart Publishing, 2008) 171–98.

[39] Articles 218(3) TFEU; Article 207(3)(2) TFEU.

[40] Article 218(2) TFEU.

[41] The formal role of the Parliament is outlined in Articles 207(3), 218(6) and 218(10) TFEU.

[42] Article 207(3)(3) TFEU.

[43] Certain EU institutions or any Member State may also request (binding) Opinions on the compatibility of the proposed international agreement with EU primary law: see Article 218(11) TFEU. See, Graham Butler, 'Pre-Ratification Judicial Review of International Agreements to Be Concluded by the European Union' in Mattias Derlén and Johan Lindholm (eds), *The Court of Justice of the European Union: Multidisciplinary Perspectives* (Oxford, Hart Publishing, 2018) 53–77.

within the exclusive competence of the EU (for example, the CCP), and thus do not require ratification by Member States.[44]

Both the substantive legal basis of an international agreement, as well as the procedure in Article 218 TFEU, must be taken into account in determining institutional equilibrium in EU international investment treaty-making. With respect to the CCP as a substantive legal basis of an agreement, EU institutions alone will be competent to conclude international agreements, subject to the procedure in Article 218 TFEU. A substantive legal basis of an international agreement that, in addition to the CCP, involves competence shared between the EU and its Member States will involve the conclusion of a mixed agreement. The same will happen if an international agreement includes trade and investment provisions but finds its legal basis in a different Treaty provision, for example, if it is concluded as an association agreement on the basis of Article 217 TFEU. While most EU agreements are concluded as mixed agreements, there are no specific treaty provisions concerning mixed agreements. However, the procedure under Article 218 TFEU can be completed only after all Member States have ratified a mixed agreement in accordance with its own constitutional requirements. This is usually a politically complex and lengthy process.[45]

4.3. IMPLICATIONS OF OPINION 2/15 FOR EU TREATY-MAKING PRACTICE AND POLICY CHOICES IN THE FIELD OF INVESTMENT

Given the constitutional nature of legal bases, its choice for an EU international agreement has significant consequences for the EU's performance in international affairs. To cite Advocate General Kokott: 'the more players there are on the European side at international level, the more difficult it will be to represent effectively the interests of the Community and its Member States outwardly, in particular vis-à-vis significant trading partners'.[46] Post-Lisbon, *Opinion 2/15* and the generous application of the Court of Justice to the centre of gravity test and the *ERTA* doctrine streamlined EU exclusive competence in the field of trade and FDI. It has simplified the procedure for the conclusion of EU trade agreements with FDI liberalisation provisions, which are concluded as 'EU-only' agreements. Nevertheless, important aspects of EU international investment policy related to investment protection and dispute settlement have been left outside of the CCP. This has made the EU treaty-making choices difficult, and has consequently impacted the achievement of EU policy objectives in the field of investment.

[44] Article 218(6) TFEU. The Parliament gives its consent on the recommendation of its INTA Committee.

[45] See analysis in section 4.3.2 below.

[46] Case C-13/07 *Commission v Council*, Opinion of AG Kokott ECLI:EU:2009:190, para 72.

4.3.1. EU International Agreements with Investment Provisions

Opinion 2/15 of the Court of Justice has set the new direction for the EU trade policy, placing investment on a parallel track with trade, in order to enhance policy efficiency. Trade and investment have thus been split in two separate international agreements. Trade aspects and FDI liberalisation (market access) are included in an encompassing FTA, concluded as an 'EU-only' agreement, and thus ratified only by the EU (Japan, Singapore, Vietnam). Investment aspects, encompassing post-establishment protection of FDI and portfolio investment, and an ISDS mechanism, are included in an investment protection agreement (IPA) which is concluded as a mixed agreement, and thus ratified by both the EU and all its Member States. This approach seems pragmatic, given the comprehensive definition of 'investment' and ISDS provisions in modern international investment agreements (IIAs). In principle, an FTA and an IPA with a third state are negotiated in parallel (Singapore, Vietnam).[47] However, the 'split' approach, albeit pragmatic, has not yet significantly contributed to a more efficient EU treaty-making practice.

The EU has aimed at building partnerships through bilateral investment agreements, with a view to support its multilateral efforts to reform the ISDS system. In the Comprehensive Economic and Trade Agreement (CETA) with Canada, the IPAs with Singapore and Vietnam, and some but not all modernised association agreements (Mexico, Chile), a bilateral Investment Court System (ICS) is envisaged as an interim solution, to be replaced by a similarly conceived Multilateral Investment Court (MIC) at the multilateral level,[48] which is currently being negotiated in the UNCITRAL.[49] However, there are EU partners which do not support the idea of a new multilateral investment court of such a kind that would replace investment treaty arbitration, or which oppose ISDS on conceptual grounds. The stalemate in reaching trade agreements with these states (Japan, Australia, New Zealand) has been avoided by excluding investment protection and dispute settlement altogether from the scope of the negotiations, without envisaging a conclusion of an IPA.[50] These trade agreements instead build upon the existing international standards and the WTO-plus rules, with investment provisions focused on liberalisation of market access for FDI and services.

While EU IPAs address ISDS, substantively they do not include sustainable development commitments, beyond their preamble pledges.[51] They are

[47] Council of the EU, 'Draft Council conclusions on the negotiation and conclusion of EU trade agreements' (8 May 2018) 8622/18.

[48] See Article 8.29 CETA. For the EU proposal of a MIC, see UNCITRAL, 'Possible reform of ISDS, Submission from the EU and its Member States' (24 January 2019) UN Doc A/CN.9/WG.III/WP.159/Add.1.

[49] See the contribution by Colin Brown in ch 15.

[50] However, see European Parliament Resolution 2017/2192(INI) of 26 October 2017 containing the Parliament's recommendation to the Council on the proposed negotiating mandate for trade negotiations with Australia [2018] OJ C346/212, which leaves such possibility open.

[51] In this regard, new EU IPAs follow the general trend in international investment law. The absence of substantive obligations for foreign investors beyond obligations in domestic law and

instead focused on limiting discretion of new ICS tribunals when assessing the compatibility of national measures made in the public interest with international law, through a combination of elements, such as specific 'right to regulate' clauses, and more elaborate investment protection standards.[52] Sustainability has played a more significant role only in relation to the Comprehensive Agreement on Investment (CAI) with China and the Energy Charter Treaty (ECT).

The CAI with China is not a typical EU IPA aimed at the protection of investments in their post-establishment phase. It is instead focused on FDI liberalisation and competitiveness, which should be achieved not only through more 'traditional' means of improving market access for EU companies to the Chinese market, but also sustainable development clauses on corporate social responsibility (CSR), environment and climate change, and labour,[53] which are usually part of EU trade agreements. The implementation of these trade and sustainable development (TSD) commitments is subject to state-to-state consultations and the panel of experts recommendations, as in other EU FTAs, while ISDS has been completely excluded from the scope of the CAI.[54]

Another notable exception among EU investment agreements is the ECT,[55] which is the only EU agreement with traditional ISDS arbitration clauses. The ECT was concluded in the 1990s, and at that time, it was perceived as a geopolitically important multilateral treaty aimed at facilitating political and economic transition of energy markets in the countries of the former communist bloc. However, the ECT has remained a controversial tool for investor claims against states, in particular within the EU.[56] The process of its modernisation sought to align the ECT with the European Green Deal (EGD) and EU international investment policy,[57] particularly focusing on substantive issues rather than the dispute settlement mechanism. Importantly, the EU did not succeed in including the structural aspects of ISDS in negotiations, due to Japan's veto.[58] Hence, the modernised ECT retains ISDS without reference to a possible future MIC. However, the EU and Euratom notified their withdrawal from the ECT in

the lack of recourse for affected communities to submit claims before ISDS tribunals for foreign investors' breaches of labour and environmental standards is a significant aspect of the criticism of environmental researchers and civil society against ISDS. See, for example, '300+ Civil Society Organisations From 73 Countries Urge Real Reform at United Nations Discussions on Corporate Investor Rights' (*Center for International Environmental Law*, 30 October 2018).

[52] See *Opinion 1/17* ECLI:EU:C:2019:341. See ch 14.

[53] See Section IV, CAI.

[54] Given the current multilateral reform of ISDS, the parties have agreed to continue negotiations for an IPA: see Section VI, Sub-Section 2, Article 3. For state-to-state arbitral tribunals in EU international agreements, see also ch 9.

[55] 2080 UNTS 95 (adopted 17 December 1994, entered into force 16 April 1998).

[56] See also ch 7.

[57] See Council of the European Union, 'Negotiating Directives for the Modernisation of the Energy Charter Treaty – adoption' (2 July 2019) 10745/19.

[58] Japan was the main obstacle for the EU in the ECT negotiations, opposing the MIC, while proposing further liberalisation, by extending protections to investments in the pre-establishment phase: see Japan's comments in ECT Secretariat, 'Decision of the Energy Charter Conference: Adoption by Correspondence – Policy Options for Modernisation of the ECT' (6 October 2019) CCDEC 2019, 5.

June 2024, due to a failure to reach the internal consensus among Member States on the approval of the modernised ECT.[59]

In addition to these typically investment agreements, the EU has been concluding Deep and Comprehensive Free Trade Area (DCFTA) agreements with countries in the EU neighbourhood, which aim at harmonising trading rules and transferring EU acquis (Ukraine, Georgia, Moldova, and envisaged agreements with Morocco and Tunisia), as well as Economic Partnership Agreements (EPA) with African, Caribbean and Pacific countries, which focus on these countries' economic development. While these agreements do not qualify as investment agreements, they still include some albeit limited investment provisions, mostly focusing on existing WTO commitments and post-admission non-discriminatory treatment.

The EU's practice in concluding international agreements with investment provisions is accordingly pragmatic, with a range of different types of agreements, but it has so far had limited policy effects. An overview of legal bases and investment clauses in select EU trade and investment agreements is summarised in the following table.

Table 4.2 Overview of investment provisions in different types of EU trade and investment agreements

Agreement	Legal basis substance and procedure	Investment clauses
PRE-LISBON TRADE AND INVESTMENT AGREEMENTS		
General Agreement on Trade in Services (GATS) • Mixed • WTO • In force	Art. 43, 54, 57, 66, 75, 84(2), 99, 100, 100a, 113, 235 TEC Art. 228(3) second subparagraph TEC	• **Liberalisation of investment**: – Provision of services through 'commercial presence': includes establishment of a juridical person or branch/representative office (Art. I (2)(c)) – Market Access (Art. XVI), NT (Art. XVII), MFN (Art. II). – Capital movements: FDI (Art. XVI (1)) • **Treatment (post-admission)**: NT (Art. XVII), MFN (Art. II) • **Dispute settlement**: State-to-State arbitration (WTO DSU)

(continued)

[59] In June 2022, after 15 rounds of negotiations, the ECT parties reached an agreement in principle on the ECT amendments, which were approved by the Energy Charter Conference on 3 December 2024. These amendments will provisionally enter into force on 3 September 2025. The EU's withdrawal takes effect on 28 June 2025. The EU's withdrawal follows earlier unilateral withdrawals made by several key EU Member States, including Italy, France, Germany, Poland, Spain. The EU has left the possibility for Member States to continue being contracting parties to the ECT in their own capacity, and a number of them still are.

Table 4.2 *(Continued)*

Agreement	Legal basis substance and procedure	Investment clauses
Energy Charter Treaty and the Energy Charter Protocol • Mixed • IIA • In force	▪ Art. 95 ECSC; ▪ Art. 54(2), 57(2) last sentence, 66, 73c(2), 87, 99, 100a, 113, 130s(1), 235 TEC; ▪ Art. 101 second paragraph Euratom Art. 228(2) second sentence, 228(3) second subparagraph TEC	• **Definition** of investment: FDI + portfolio (Art. 1(6)) • **Pre-establishment**: *Endeavour* to accord NT/MFN (Art. 10(2), (3) (6)) • **Post-establishment**: old style protection (Part III): FET (Art. 10(1)); NT/MFN (Art. 10(7)); expropriation (Art. 13); freedom of transfer (Art. 14) • **Dispute settlement**: ISDS (for breaches of Part III) • **Modernisation amendments approved** – new style protections; ISDS; no commitment to MIC
ASSOCIATION AGREEMENTS		
Stabilisation and Association Agreements (SAAs) with countries of Western Balkans • Mixed • In force	▪ Art. 217 TFEU; ▪ Art. 101 second paragraph Euratom Art. 216(6)(a), 218(8) TFEU	• **Liberalisation of investment**: – Capital movements: FDI + portfolio investment – Establishment (limited in economic activity scope) of business undertakings or subsidiaries/branches: NT/MFN • **Treatment (post-admission)**: – NT/MFN – Endeavour to bring about favourable climate for private investment and improve legal framework for protection of investment • **Dispute settlement**: State-to-State arbitration
Association Agreement with Ukraine • Mixed • In force	▪ Art. 217 TFEU ▪ Art. 79(2)(b) TFEU Art. 218(6)(a), 218(8) second subparagraph, 218(7) TFEU	• **Liberalisation of investment**: – Capital movements: FDI + portfolio investment (Art. 145) – Establishment (limited in economic activity scope) of subsidiaries/branches/representative offices of legal persons: NT/MFN (Art. 88) • **Treatment (post-admission)**: – NT/MFN (Art. 88(1)(ii), (2)(ii)) – Existing MSts IIAs (Art. 90) – Endeavour to negotiate investment protection and investor-to-state dispute settlement procedures (Art. 89)

(continued)

Table 4.2 *(Continued)*

Agreement	Legal basis substance and procedure	Investment clauses
		• **Dispute settlement**: State-to-State arbitration/ interpretation of EU law by CJEU: Art. 322
EU-Mexico modern-ised Global Agreement • Mixed • Agreed in principle	▪ Art. 37, 31(1) TEU, ▪ Art. 217 TFEU Art. 218(5), 218(6)(a), 218(8) TFEU	• **Definition** of investment: FDI + portfolio • **Liberalisation of investment**: – Capital movements: FDI + portfolio investment – Establishment of investment (subject to economic sector limitations): Market Access/NT/MFN/ prohibition of Performance Requirements • **Post-establishment**: NT, MFN, improved protections: FET, freedom of transfer, expropriation • **Investment dispute settlement**: ICS; commitment to MIC
ECONOMIC PARTNERSHIP AGREEMENTS		
EU-Kazakhstan Enhanced Partnership and Cooperation Agreement • Mixed • Provisionally applied	▪ Art. 37, 31 TEU, ▪ Art. 91, 100(2), 207, 209 TFEU Art. 218(5), 218(8) TFEU	• **Liberalisation of investment**: – Capital movements: FDI + portfolio investment (Art. 58) – Establishment (all economic activities other than services) of juridical persons: MFN (Art. 45(1)); NT – includes branches of the EU (Art. 46(b)) • **Treatment (post-admission)**: – MFN (Art. 45(2)); MFN in strategic resources and objects for subsidiaries of juridical persons of the EU (Art. 45(5)) – NT (Art. 46(a)) – Endeavour to negotiate general principles of investment protection (Art. 56) • **Dispute settlement**: State-to-State arbitration
EU-SADC Economic Partnership Agreement • Mixed • Provisionally applied	Art. 209(2) TFEU Art. 207(3), 207(4), 218(5) TFEU	• **Liberalisation of investments**: no new provisions – Reaffirming commitments regarding liberalisation of services in accordance with GATS (Art. 72) – Guiding principles for future negotiation on trade in services: include market access/NT (Art. 73(2)(b))

(continued)

Table 4.2 *(Continued)*

Agreement	Legal basis substance and procedure	Investment clauses
		• **Treatment (post-admission)**: possibility of negotiating an agreement on investment in economic sectors other than services (Art. 74)
POST-LISBON TRADE AND INVESTMENT AGREEMENTS		
Comprehensive Economic and Trade Agreement with Canada (CETA) • Mixed • Provisionally applied • Investment chapter not in force	Art. 43(2), 91, 100(2), 153(2), 192(1) TFEU Art. 207(4) first subparagraph, 218(5) TFEU	• **Definition** of investment: FDI + portfolio (Art. 8.1) • **Liberalisation of investment**: – Capital movements: FDI + portfolio investment – Establishment or acquisition of investment (subject to economic sector limitations): Market Access/prohibition of Performance Requirement/NT/MFN (Art. 8.4-8.7) • **Post-establishment**: improved protections (Section D): FET (Art. 8.10); NT (Art. 8.6); MFN (Art. 8.7); expropriation (Art. 8.12); freedom of transfer (Art. 8.13) • **Investment dispute settlement**: ICS (Section F); commitment to MIC (Art. 8.29)
EU-Republic of Korea Free Trade Agreement • Mixed • In force	Art. 91, 100(2), 167(3), 207 TFEU Art. 218(5) TFEU, 218(6)(a)(v)	• **Liberalisation of investment**: – Capital movements: FDI + portfolio investment (Art. 8.2) – Establishment (subject to economic sector limitations) of juridical person or branch/representative office: Market Access/NT/MFN (Art. 7.11-7.14) • **Treatment (post-admission)**: – NT/MFN (Art. 7.12, 7.14) – Existing MSts IIAs (Art. 7.15) – Endeavour to negotiate general principles of investment protection (Art. 7.16(2)) • **Dispute settlement**: State-to-State arbitration
EU-Singapore Free Trade Agreement • EU-only • In force	Art. 91, 100(2) TFEU Art. 207(4) first subparagraph, 218(5), 218(6)(a)(v)	• **Liberalisation of investment**: – Capital movements: FDI (Art. 16.7) – Establishment (subject to economic sector limitations) of a juridical person or branch/representative office: Market Access (Art. 8.10)/NT (Art. 8.11)

(continued)

Table 4.2 *(Continued)*

Agreement	Legal basis substance and procedure	Investment clauses
		• **Treatment (post-admission)**: – NT (Art. 8.11) • **Dispute settlement**: State-to-State arbitration
EU-Singapore Investment Protection Agreement • Mixed • Signed • Not yet in force	Art. 207(4) TFEU Art. 207(4) first subparagraph, 218(5), 218(6)(a)(v) TFEU	• **Definition** of investment: FDI + portfolio (Art. 1.2) • **Post-establishment**: improved protections (Chapter II): – NT (Art. 2.3(1)) – including for Compensation for Losses (Art. 2.5); – FET (Art. 2.4); – Expropriation (Art. 2.6); – Freedom of transfer (Art. 2.7) • **Investment dispute settlement**: ICS (Chapter III); consideration of MIC (Art. 3.12) • **Dispute settlement** (interpretation and application of IPA): State-to-State arbitration

4.3.2. Implications for the EU International Investment Policy Agenda

The conclusion of mixed agreements is a politically complex process, which can have consequences for achieving EU policy objectives. This complexity is evident in the voting procedures in the Council, as well as the requirement of the mixed agreement's ratification in all Member States.

First, in accordance with Article 218 TFEU, most decisions in the Council regarding trade and investment agreements (opening of the negotiations, their signing, and concluding) can be adopted by qualified majority voting (QMV). However, the Council has discretion to act via the process of common accord – the agreement of all Member States – in approving the signature and conclusion of mixed agreements. Following *Opinion 2/15*, the Council has emphasised that it will 'continue endeavouring to obtain, to the greatest extent possible, a consensus', which should 'ensure that all Member States' interests and concerns are adequately respected in trade agreements', indicating the need for consensus in legitimising the conclusion of EU agreements.[60] While common accord is part of the Council's practice which is not regulated in Article 218 TFEU, the Court

[60] Council of the EU, Conclusions on the negotiation and conclusion of EU trade agreements 2018 (n 47) para 9.

of Justice has emphasised that this practice cannot be an additional procedural step which would make the conclusion of the international agreement *contingent* on the prior establishment of a common accord.[61] Unanimity is, in any event, required for the conclusion of association agreements,[62] which can, *inter alia*, include investment protection provisions.[63]

Secondly, the process of conclusion of a mixed agreement is additionally complex due to the requirement of ratification in all Member States. In case of an agreement with a broader scope, the provisions of the mixed agreement that fall within exclusive competence of the EU can enter into force in accordance with the Council's decision, on the recommendation from the Commission,[64] and after the Parliament has given its consent.[65] Provisional application of mixed agreements has become a rule, as the ratification process in the Member States can take a long time.[66] However, while it has positive effects on policy efficiency, provisional application can also present national parliaments with a *fait accompli*. While common with respect to other mixed agreements, provisional application of IPAs has not been proposed by the Commission,[67] perhaps due to limited practical impact of the provisional application of provisions related to FDI protection in the absence of dispute settlement available for breaches of these provisions.

An additional problem could arise if the ratification of a mixed agreement is rejected in one or more Member States. Member States do not have an obligation to conclude a mixed agreement, even when the EU intends to conclude such an agreement, as this approach would infringe the principle of division of competences in Article 4(1) TEU.[68] Therefore, failure to ratify the agreement in any Member State would likely require the EU to terminate the provisional application of the agreement, as well as the agreement, unless some kind of remedial action to remove the impediment to ratification could be taken.[69] While this has not yet happened in practice, it could have significant political consequences.

[61] *Opinion 1/19* ECLI:EU:C:2021:198, paras 249, 274 (emphasis added).

[62] Article 218(8)(2) TFEU.

[63] See, for example, chapter on Investment in the EU-Mexico Agreement in Principle (*European Commission*, 6 May 2020).

[64] Article 218(5) TFEU. This decision can be adopted in the decision on the signing of the agreement (eg in the case of the EU-Korea FTA), or in a separate decision before the agreement's entry into force (eg in the case of CETA).

[65] While under the Treaties, the consent of the European Parliament is not required for provisional application, this has generally been adopted as practice, and departed from only in cases of technical measures or situations requiring urgency. For example, this was the case regarding the EU-UK Trade and Cooperation Agreement.

[66] For example, while CETA provisionally entered into force in September 2017, the ratification of the agreement is still pending in 10 Member States: European Commission, *Overview of FTA and other trade negotiations* (September 2024). See Council Decision (EU) 2017/38 of 28 October 2016 on the provisional application of the CETA between Canada, of the one part, and the European Union and its Member States, of the other part [2017] OJ L11/1080.

[67] See for example, Article 4.15.4 EUSIPA.

[68] *Opinion 1/19*, Opinion of AG Hogan ECLI:EU:C:2021:198, para 203.

[69] See G Van Der Loo and RA Wessel, 'The Non-Ratification of Mixed Agreements: Legal Consequences and Solutions' (2017) 54(3) *Common Market Law Review* 735, 760–61; A Suse and

It has thus been argued that competence struggles between the EU and its Member States, more than competing societal interests, have played a significant role in slowing down the development of the EU international investment policy.[70] The total number of concluded EU international agreements which endorse the EU's reformed approach to investment protection and ISDS is low (CETA with Canada, Singapore, Vietnam, Mexico and Chile), and none of these investment agreements have yet entered into force. Accordingly, the conclusion of investment protection agreements, as opposed to trade agreements, has not been a policy priority for the EU.

In order to address the efficiency of EU international investment policy, the question is whether exclusive competence of the EU could extend to portfolio investment and ISDS in the future, or whether the IPAs could be concluded as 'EU-only' agreements on the basis of a political agreement among the Member States. The recent example of the EU-UK Trade and Cooperation Agreement (TCA), which is the first Association Agreement concluded as 'EU-only', demonstrates a more efficient treaty-making approach with a trading partner of 'exceptional and unique' character, although the constitutional compatibility of the political choice to conclude an 'EU-only' agreement in this case has been questioned.[71]

As the Court of Justice clarified in *Opinion 2/15*, however, the limited scope of EU investment competence is a consequence of the 'unequivocal expression' of the intention of Member States, which the Court of Justice refers to as 'framers of the TEU', not to include in the CCP types of foreign investment other than FDI.[72] Exclusive competence of the EU over all foreign investment would mean a significant loss of power for the Member States when creating their national investment protection policies.[73] However, the Court of Justice's classification of portfolio investment as shared competence allows for future expansion of the EU's exclusive competence through the exercise of internal powers and EU secondary legislation, without the need to amend the founding treaties. In other words, the Court of Justice's reasoning allows the EU to gain exclusive external competence by pre-empting the field through internal rules. However, since Article 63 TFEU relates to free movement of capital and liberalisation, as opposed

J Wouters, 'The Provisional Application of the EU's Mixed Trade and Investment Agreements' (2018) Working Paper No 201, 19–21, who remain sceptical of this argument. The impediments would need to be of a constitutional nature, while remedial action could take the form of a renegotiation to address the concerns of the Member State.

[70] R Basedow, 'The EU's International Investment Policy ten years on: the Policy-Making Implications of Unintended Competence Transfers' (2021) 59(3) *Journal of Common Market Studies* 643, claiming that this struggle stems from pre-Lisbon resistance of Member States to empower the EU in international investment.

[71] See C Eckes and P Leino-Sandberg, '"In view of the exceptional and unique" character of the EU-UK Trade and Cooperation Agreement – an Exception to Separation of Powers within the EU?', *European Law Blog* (15 April 2021).

[72] *Opinion 2/15* (n 2) para 83.

[73] This would particularly adversely affect the capital-exporting Member States (eg Germany), whose interest is to provide the best possible conditions for their investors in third countries through the conclusion of IIAs.

to its harmonisation, it is difficult to conceive how EU internal action could pre-empt Member States' external action with respect to portfolio investment.[74] The EU-UK TCA example suggests that simply a *potential* to expand EU powers through internal legislation in the areas of shared competence could justify the political choice of an 'EU-only' agreement even when the subject matter warrants 'mixity'.[75]

The situation with ISDS provisions is less clear. ISDS as a mechanism, which directly affects the jurisdiction of national courts, cannot be considered merely ancillary to investment protection provisions, and, therefore, cannot be established without the Member States' consent.[76] The Court of Justice has thus impliedly recognised the profound implications of ISDS for domestic judicial systems of the Member States – a view further endorsed in the *Achmea* judgment of the Court of Justice. Regardless of the shared competence, this leaves open the question whether it would be legally possible for any international agreement of the EU containing ISDS to be concluded as an 'EU-only' agreement, even if a political agreement could be reached in the Council. In situations when political agreement was reached in the Council, the EU and its Member States have acted jointly in the interest of the EU in the areas which fall within shared competence, while reiterating the Council's position that ISDS mechanisms cannot be established without the Member States' consent.[77]

With limited outcomes of the EU investment treaty-making processes, the investment treaty field within the EU remains dominated by nearly 1,300 Member States' BITs with third states in force, mostly concluded in the pre-Lisbon period. These BITs are largely inconsistent with the EU international investment policy, with respect to both broadly defined substantive standards and the traditional ISDS as the dispute settlement mechanism. New Member States' extra-EU BITs, which are being approved post-Lisbon in accordance with EU secondary legislation through the Grandfathering Regulation,[78] contain

[74] AG Sharpston in her Opinion (n 22) suggested that the legal basis for the EU's internal legislative powers would be Article 114, insofar as it concerns the approximation of laws governing internal markets, and Article 352 TFEU: see para 368.

[75] The Council clarified that the exercise of EU competence through the EU-UK TCA is without prejudice to the respective competences of the EU and Member States in ongoing or future negotiations: see Article 10, Council Decision (EU) 2021/689 of 29 April 2021 on the conclusion, on behalf of the Union, of the Trade and Cooperation Agreement between the European Union and the European Atomic Energy Community, of the one part, and the United Kingdom of Great Britain and Northern Ireland, of the other part, and of the Agreement between the European Union and the United Kingdom of Great Britain and Northern Ireland concerning security procedures for exchanging and protecting classified information [2021] OJ L149/2.

[76] *Opinion 2/15* (n 2) para 292.

[77] See Council Decision (EU) 2022/438 of 14 March 2022 on the position to be adopted on behalf of the EU within the Administrative Council of the ICSID, ST/6125/2022/INIT, [2022] OJ L89/8, and its recital (3). The legal bases of this Decision are Article 207(4), first paragraph and Article 218(9) TFEU.

[78] Regulation (EU) 1219/2012 of the European Parliament and of the Council of 12 December 2012 establishing transitional arrangements for bilateral investment agreements between Member States and third countries OJ L 351/40. See also ch 12.

improved substantive standards but retain arbitration as the ISDS mechanism. This fragmentation between different IIAs of the EU and its Member States raises questions about the coherence of the EU external investment regulatory framework, but ultimately also the future direction of the EU international investment agenda, to which we turn next.

4.4. NEW DIRECTIONS IN EU INTERNATIONAL INVESTMENT POLICY AND TREATY PRACTICE

With new trade policy, adopted in February 2021, sustainability has become the core of the EU's approach to trade.[79] The EU's focus has also been shifting from the conclusion of new agreements towards the implementation of the existing ones, with significant implications for new EU agreements. For example, a sanctions-based enforcement model is envisaged to align TSD chapters with the general state-to-state dispute settlement under EU FTAs.[80] A new policy approach also envisages a range of regulatory tools to support the implementation of bilateral FTAs, in particular, through autonomous instruments.[81]

With sustainability at the heart of the new EU trade strategy, the focus of EU international investment policy is also shifting from ISDS towards substantive provisions and their compatibility with the EU's climate, environmental, and human rights objectives. The Parliament has stressed the challenge of ensuring consistency between IIAs and the EGD, the Sustainable Development Goals (SDGs) and EU values.[82] On the one hand, Member States' environmental and climate measures can be undermined by their existing unreformed BITs, which extend protections for fossil fuels.[83] On the other hand, the asymmetry enshrined in the international investment regime undermines the efforts for bringing investors to account in ways that are envisaged for the accountability of economic operators in the new EU trade policy.[84] The Parliament has thus called for a more substantive reform of EU international investment policy, which would ensure

[79] European Commission, Trade Policy Review – An Open, Sustainable and Assertive Trade Policy', COM(2021) 66/2 final.

[80] In particular, trade sanctions would be applied in cases of failure to comply with obligations that 'materially defeat the object and purpose of the Paris Agreement' or 'in serious instances of non-compliance with the ILO fundamental principles and rights at work': see European Commission, 'The power of trade partnerships: together for green and just economic growth', COM (2022) 409 final, 11; see also TSD (Chapter 19) and Dispute settlement (Chapter 27) – chapters of the EU-New Zealand FTA. See ch 12.

[81] See ibid 3–4.

[82] See European Parliament Resolution of 23 June 2022 on the future of EU international investment policy, 2021/2176(INI).

[83] ibid paras 20, 36. See chs 12 and 13.

[84] See for example, Directive (EU) 2024/1760 of the European Parliament and of the Council of 13 June 2024 on corporate sustainability due diligence and amending Directive (EU) 2019/1937 and Regulation (EU) 2023/2859 OJ L 2024/1760, to be applied across EU operators' value chains.

the strict compliance of Member States' extra-EU BITs with EU law,[85] and the expansion of investor obligations and their enforcement in bilateral EU IIAs. Obligations for investors should also be implemented in separate international instruments and 'via domestic frameworks for human rights and environmental due diligence',[86] suggesting that autonomous measures should not be excluded as an option for EU international investment policy.

Beyond a MIC, modernisation of 'old' international agreements includes improved substantive and procedural provisions but retains the 'old' ISDS approach of *ad hoc* arbitral tribunals.[87] The reformed ECT will retain investment treaty arbitration, as a significant element likely to undermine substantive changes to the ECT. Any new standards will be interpreted by arbitral tribunals, which are likely to retain the legacy of the old system. Moreover, interpretations by arbitral tribunals are likely to set the direction of any jurisprudence stemming from new standards.[88] A system of *ad hoc* tribunals could thus ultimately undermine the coherence of new substantive standards in their implementation. Without reforming the ISDS mechanism, the EU's efforts will eventually achieve more or less substantial improvements of bilateral Member States' BITs – something that all other States have been doing for some time.

As outcomes of structural ISDS reform in UNCITRAL remain uncertain and ISDS continues to 'chill' climate regulation, the focus of EU policy is shifting towards investment governance beyond ISDS, with a view to align trade and investment efforts in promoting sustainable development. New bilateral agreements on investment facilitation with African states with state-to-state measures and dispute settlement, which exclude portfolio investment and ISDS, seem to be a step in that direction, envisaged to be supported by the existing Member States' BITs and autonomous measures.[89] Importantly, these agreements can be concluded as 'EU-only' and thus can serve as a more efficient instrument in providing a stable regulatory framework for EU investors in third countries,

[85] European Parliament Resolution on the future of EU international investment policy (n 82) para 37.

[86] ibid para 27.

[87] European Commission, Annotations to the Model Clauses for negotiation or re-negotiation of Member States' Bilateral Investment Agreements with third countries, non-paper, 21 September 2023.

[88] See W Alschner, *Investment Arbitration and State-Driven Reform* (Oxford, Oxford University Press, 2022). However, the author seeks solutions not in new dispute settlement bodies but in the modernisation of old treaties, including through the completion of incomplete old treaties through renegotiation, with the ECT as a case in point: see ch 8.

[89] See Council of the EU, 'Negotiating directives for the negotiation of an agreement on investment facilitation with the Republic of Angola', 8441/21 and the concluded Sustainable Investment Facilitation Agreement between the European Union and the Republic of Angola, ST/10941/2023/REV/1, OJ L, 2024/830, 8.3.2024; the proposal for a revised EU Regulation on the Generalised Scheme of Preferences (COM(2021) 579, although related to trade preferences, focuses on the promotion of sustainable development, and includes a possibility for the EU to withdraw GSP benefits for serious and systemic violations of conventions on climate change and environmental protection.

thus ultimately more successfully achieving EU policy objectives in the field of foreign investment.

4.5. CONCLUSION

Opinion 2/15 clarified the EU's exclusive competence for all aspects of FDI; however, the competence of the EU and its Member States remains shared with respect to portfolio investment and ISDS. Given that conventional IIAs regulate both FDI and portfolio investment in addition to ISDS as their crucial element, EU IIAs must be concluded as mixed agreements, leaving the Member States with an essential role in the investment treaty-making process.

Accordingly, *Opinion 2/15* has important implications for the efficiency of the EU investment treaty-making process and the implementation of its international investment agenda. On the one hand, the EU has retained a diverse range of international agreements with different scope of investment provisions – from traditional FTAs to association agreements and modernised IPAs. However, the EU has managed to conclude only a limited number of international agreements with its reformed investment protection standards and dispute settlement mechanism, none of which are yet in force. On the other hand, the field of international investment in the EU remains fragmented between a limited number of EU IIAs with the reformed ISDS approach and an overwhelmingly larger number of Member States' extra-EU BITs with 'old'-type protections and traditional ISDS. However, even limited investment sovereignty has given the EU control in setting the direction of EU policy and in achieving a relative coherence between investment policies of the EU and the Member States at the national level post-Lisbon.

While this chapter has focused on internal limitations for EU international investment policy, the EU is also facing significant external challenges. The retention of investment treaty arbitration in the modernised ECT – a plurilateral agreement in whose modernisation negotiations the EU actively participated but eventually decided to withdraw – is indicative of the difficulties that the EU continues to face in introducing a MIC. The creation of a MIC remains the core aspect of the EU policy, and an important part of the Commission's multilateral agenda.[90] However, if the efforts to create a MIC fail, the future of EU international investment policy remains less clear, in light of the dominant role of Member States' extra-EU BITs and shared investment competence within the EU. These agreements are largely inconsistent not only with the reformed EU approach to foreign investment dispute settlement but also the EU's sustainability agenda. At the same time, the overwhelming focus of EU reform

[90] European Commission, Trade Policy Review 2021 (n 79) 11.

on the ISDS mechanism indicates that the reform has not gone far enough to efficiently support the implementation of the EGD goals.

With sustainability at the core of EU external action, the focus of EU international agreements in the field of investment is shifting towards improving investment regulatory governance beyond ISDS. This is likely to be supplemented by the EU's insistence on the substantive compliance of Member States' BITs with EU climate objectives, and autonomous measures for promoting due diligence of EU traders and investors. The efficiency of these legal instruments will ultimately depend on the effective implementation of available coordination mechanisms, the Member States' compliance with their duty of sincere cooperation, and the overall success of the EU's ISDS reform in the longer term.

Part II

Investment and Arbitration

5

Arbitration, Investment, and the EU Legal Order

KONSTANZE VON PAPP

5.1. INTRODUCTION

THE APPROACH OF the European Union (EU) to international arbitration has been mixed.[1] Traditionally, there has been some leniency towards commercial arbitration, where the Court of Justice acknowledged the efficiency of international arbitration.[2] It remains to be seen whether the most recent case law will be the starting point for stricter scrutiny from an EU law perspective in this respect. Regarding international investment law and arbitration, the picture darkened long before the Court of Justice completely shut the door for intra-EU investment arbitration.[3] It was as early as 2009 that several bilateral investment treaties of Austria, Sweden and Finland with third states (Member States that acceded only in the 1990s) were held incompatible with EU law.[4] The sweeping protection of EU primacy, especially in the case against Finland, where steps had been taken to eradicate the risk of any future incompatibility with EU law, indicated a very firm stance.[5] This approach to somehow shield EU law

[1] For a particular view, see ch 8.

[2] See Cases C-126/97 *Eco Swiss* ECLI:EU:C:1999:269 and C-168/05 *Mostaza Claro* ECLI:EU:C:2006:675. An overall positive picture is still drawn by Assimakis P Komninos and Maria Kawysi, 'Arbitration & EU Competition Law: Latest Developments' in Christophe Lemaire and Francesco Martucci (eds), *Laurence Idot: Concurrence et Europe, Liber Amicorum* (Paris, Concurrences, 2022) Vol 1, 415. But see the discussion at 5.4.2 below.

[3] Case C-284/16 *Achmea* ECLI:EU:C:2018:158 (for arbitration based on a bilateral investment treaty between EU Member States) and Case C-741/19 *Komstroy* ECLI:EU:C:2021:655 (for *intra*-EU cases under the Energy Charter Treaty). See 5.2.2, 5.3.1 and 5.3.2 below.

[4] Cases C-205/06 *Commission v Austria* ECLI:EU:C:2009:118, C-269/06 *Commission v Sweden* ECLI:EU:C:2009:119, C-118/07 *Commission v Finland* ECLI:EU:C:2009:715.

[5] See the critique by Eileen Denza, 'Bilateral Investment Treaties and EU Rules on Free Transfer' (2010) *EL Rev* 263; Nikos Lavranos, 'Member States' Bilateral Investment Treaties (BITs): Lost in Transition' (2011) *Hague Yearbook of International Law* 281.

from international law foreshadowed the Court of Justice's more recent position regarding intra-EU investment arbitration and its eventual phase-out.[6]

Nevertheless, it generally takes two sides to make a relationship work. So any critical appraisal of the rift between EU and international investment law must include arbitral case law, and its own take on EU law issues. This chapter starts with explaining the nature of international arbitration and illustrates where this collides with the self-understanding of the EU. In light of the Court of Justice's strict position on investment arbitration, it concludes that there is an important role to be filled by the courts and tribunals of Member States. Prospectively, it is argued that the EU's focus on free markets is not easily squared with public distrust in global trade and investment protection, including arbitration under modern EU investment agreements with third states.

5.2. INTERNATIONAL ARBITRATION: INTERNAL AND EU PERSPECTIVE

Any constructive critique must ensure to take on board different points of view in order to be able to find some common ground. Arbitration as one means of settling commercial and investment disputes shares one important value with EU law: economic freedom. The problem starts when states – more precisely, EU Member States – enter the picture. This is because EU law is concerned about commercial freedom of private actors, while regulating economic activity of its Member States in order to achieve its overall integrative purpose.

5.2.1. An Internal Perspective: Arbitration as Consequence of Contractual Autonomy

Arbitration is based on party autonomy, which makes the agreement to arbitrate the essential basis for arbitral proceedings.[7] This is the case for both commercial and investment treaty arbitration.[8] From the perspective of a state as an actor in international arbitration, the difference is the following: in commercial arbitration, the state is acting much like any private actor on the basis of an individually negotiated contract and arbitration agreement with a private party (ad hoc arbitration). In investment treaty arbitration, the host state has concluded an international treaty with another state containing a standing offer to arbitrate with nationals of that other state (home state of investors). Arbitration

[6] Agreement for the termination of Bilateral Investment Treaties between the Member States of the European Union [2020] OJ L169/1.

[7] Roy Goode, Herbert Kronke and Ewan McKendrick, *Transnational Commercial Law: Text Cases and Materials*, 2nd edn (Oxford University Press, 2017) para 19.27.

[8] For details see Konstanze von Papp, *EU Law and International Arbitration: Managing Distrust through Dialogue* (Oxford, Hart Publishing, 2021) 9–10, 32–39.

proceedings are then started by an individual investor taking up the host state's arbitration offer (treaty-based arbitration). So, doctrinally, these forms of arbitration are distinct in the way the arbitration agreement is concluded. Nevertheless, they both remain based on party consensus, which is why commercial and investment treaty arbitration can overlap. An example is the *PL Holdings* case discussed below.[9] From an arbitration perspective, its consensual nature represents an important value in itself, which is contractual freedom. The practical consequence of this is that the law of international arbitration typically takes a pro-arbitration approach.[10] This is especially true for commercial arbitration, but has repercussions for investment treaty arbitration as well. The reason for this is that investment arbitration, although involving public law type disputes, uses the legal rules and procedures established for commercial arbitration.

However, an arbitration agreement has more than purely contractual effects vis-à-vis the other party. It also constitutes a waiver of the jurisdiction of the courts which would otherwise be competent to hear the dispute.[11] In this respect, the difference between ad hoc arbitration and treaty-based arbitration means that the jurisdictional waiver in one individual case can be contrasted against a more general or 'systemic'[12] waiver in a series of cases under one treaty. This is why the underlying value of contractual freedom needs to be balanced against the rule of law, with the latter being particularly strong in cases involving state action. In other words, the legal framework for investment treaty arbitration is necessarily more regulatory in nature than that for commercial arbitration between private parties.

This suggests that the focus must be on legal limits to state contracting rather than simply drawing a distinction between commercial and investment treaty arbitration. From the EU's perspective, the question then becomes which red lines EU law draws for Member States as contracting parties.

5.2.2. An EU Perspective: Commercial Freedom versus Member State Obligations

Initially, the Court of Justice's case law took on board the pro-arbitration approach for commercial arbitration.[13] This must be put in the context of EU

[9] Case C-109/20 *Republiken Polen v PL Holdings Sàrl* ECLI:EU:C:2021:875. See below 5.4.2.

[10] Gary B Born, *International Commercial Arbitration*, Vol I, 2nd edn (The Netherlands, Wolters Kluwer, 2014) § 4.04 [A][1][b][i].

[11] Under Article II of the New York Convention on Recognition and Enforcement of Foreign Arbitral Awards of 10 June 1958 (NYC), courts of all contracting states are generally obliged to refer to arbitration disputes which arise under a valid and enforceable arbitration agreement.

[12] Opinion of Advocate General Szpunar in Case C-741/19 *Komstroy* ECLI:EU:C:2021:164, para 61.

[13] Starting with the implicit acknowledgment of the arbitrability of competition law claims in Case C-126/97 *Eco Swiss* ECLI:EU:C:1999:269. This 'regulated' pro-arbitration approach is discussed in more detail by von Papp (n 8) 70 et seq.

law taking a tolerant position vis-à-vis private law matters in general.[14] The EU's latitude as regards commercial actors is also exemplified by the arbitration exception in the Brussels I Recast Regulation.[15] As to the latter, it should be noted that it provides a regulatory framework for the mutual recognition and enforcement of judgments within the EU, and is hence based on traditional EU values, fostering the functioning of the internal market. This has had the effect that even in commercial arbitration, the principle of mutual trust took priority over the pro-arbitration approach: it addressed courts and tribunals in Member States involved in arbitration, and strictly prohibited anti-suit injunctions within the reach of the Brussels Regulation.[16] It is the same principle of mutual trust which is at play in *Achmea* discussed below,[17] where it firmly enforces the duty of Member States to use courts and tribunals in the EU, including Member State courts and tribunals, with access to the Court of Justice via the preliminary reference procedure in Article 267 TFEU ('the EU judiciary') for all EU law-related disputes.

From an EU perspective, contractual freedom ends where state obligations under EU law begin. The problem is that international arbitration works the other way round: international treaties oblige states to respect arbitration agreements – in particular Article 2 of the New York Convention (NYC), but also investment treaties binding contracting states to their own offer to arbitrate – and to enforce arbitral awards.[18] The issue hence becomes which one of two (or more) colliding international law obligations takes precedence over the other(s). As mentioned above,[19] the case law of the Court of Justice holds a bold stance on this, essentially exporting the concept of EU primacy with no further qualifications to the realm of external relations. This must be seen critically, even from an EU law perspective: the collision rule in Article 351 TFEU would allow for an interpretation which leaves more room for international law treaties, in particular in areas where Member State competences are later absorbed by the EU.[20]

[14] Von Papp, *EU Law and International Arbitration* (n 8) 54 et seq.

[15] Article 2(d) of Regulation (EU) No 1215/2012 of the European Parliament and of the Council of 12 December 2012 on jurisdiction and the recognition and enforcement of judgments in civil and commercial matters (recast) [2012] OJ L351/1.

[16] Case C-185/07 *West Tankers* ECLI:EU:C:2009:69.

[17] Case C-284/16 *Slovak Republic v Achmea BV* ECLI:EU:C:2018:158. See text accompanying nn 21–23.

[18] Article V NYC; see also Article 54 of the Convention on Settlement of Investment Disputes between States and Nationals of other States (ICSID).

[19] See text accompanying nn 4–5 above.

[20] See Konstanze von Papp, 'Solving Conflicts with International Investment Treaty Law from an EU Law Perspective: Article 351 TFEU Revisited' (2015) 42 *Legal Issues of Economic Integration* 325. Nevertheless, the Court has traditionally taken a robust stance here, as confirmed recently as part of the *Micula* saga (n 75 below) in Case C-516/22 *Commission v UK* ECLI:EU:C:2024:231 paras 58–88: the multilateral International Convention on the Settlement of Investment Disputes between States and Nationals of Other States (ICSID) can be divided up into bilateral rights and obligations. Accordingly, as between two EU Member States, it does not fall under the protection of international law treaties provided for by Article 351(1) TFEU. The enforcement of an *intra*-EU

For bilateral investment treaties (BITs) between EU Member States, the same effect, ie, an absolute and automatic prevalence of EU law obligations, is now achieved on the very formal basis of Article 267 TFEU and Article 344 TFEU. In the *Achmea* case, this is based on the following premises: (1) EU law is international law and at the same time part of domestic law, which makes a dispute under BITs a dispute involving EU law; (2) Article 344 TFEU forbids Member States from bringing EU law-related disputes to any other forum but the EU judiciary and, ultimately, the Court of Justice; (3) so Member States cannot agree in BITs to bypass the EU judiciary by offering investment arbitration, unless investment tribunals were part of the courts and tribunals with access to the Court of Justice; (4) which, according to the Court of Justice, they are not.[21] The underlying rationale here is the illusive concept of EU autonomy.[22] This allows the EU (through the Court of Justice) to define its own nature as a highly specialist regime, distinct from the overall international legal order on the basis of its own special rules and concepts. These include but are not limited to primacy, direct effect, and the principle of sincere cooperation (mutual trust), which are all ensured by the EU judiciary, on top of which the Court of Justice supervises uniform and effective application.[23] As a consequence of this focus on EU Member States' obligations as defined by the Court of Justice, *Achmea* shut the door for arbitration based on intra-EU BITs.

5.3. THE EU LEGAL ORDER

The outcome in *Achmea*, although a heavy blow for the international arbitration community, joins established case law by the Court of Justice, which found its most controversial point of culmination in *Opinion 2/13* on accession of the EU to the European Convention on Human Rights (ECHR).[24] It becomes understandable when considering the nature of the EU, which despite its high level of integration and increasing international presence, is no nation state. Therefore, the EU has a special need to ensure its own existence.

5.3.1. An Internal EU Perspective: EU Autonomy

Vis-à-vis its Member States (ie, internally), this has traditionally been done on the basis of EU principles such as direct effect and primacy of EU law. On the international law level (ie, externally), these internal concepts have been captured under

ICSID arbitration award therefore constituted a breach of the UK's EU law obligations (as per the Withdrawal Agreement).

[21] Case C-284/16 *Achmea* (n 17) paras 40 et seq.

[22] ibid para 33. EU autonomy is further discussed at 5.3.1 below.

[23] ibid paras 34 et seq.

[24] *Opinion 2/13* ECLI:EU:C:2014:2454 (*EU Accession to the ECHR II*).

the notion of 'essential characteristics'[25] of the EU's new legal order. In the aforementioned *Opinion 2/13*,[26] the Court of Justice then used these characteristics to build on the concept of EU autonomy, an increasingly used modern term, which essentially draws on the EU's 'independent' – *autonomous* – legal order in *Costa v ENEL*.[27] Much like the reasoning in *Van Gend en Loos* and *Costa v ENEL*,[28] the establishment of EU autonomy is based on an entirely self-referential argument:[29] The Member States have created a new legal order (says the Court of Justice based on the wording and the spirit of the EU Treaties). It follows from here that this new legal order must create direct rights for citizens in the Member States. And since it is an independent new legal order with direct effect, it must also prevail over the laws of the Member States. Furthermore, this autonomous legal order with direct effect and primacy must make sure that its internal division of competencies[30] is left intact by external irritations. This includes, first and foremost, the responsibility of the Court of Justice itself to interpret the EU Treaties under what is now Article 19 TEU.[31] This concludes the circle, and hence the operational closure of EU law, since it is the Court of Justice which in the first place determines whether the EU Treaties are engaged and, in the worst case, breached.[32]

In the investment arbitration context, the focus on EU autonomy is particularly problematic since it is linked solely to jurisdiction. In *Achmea*,[33] the compatibility with EU law hinged entirely upon the question of whether arbitral jurisdiction established under intra-EU treaties respects the CJEU's final authority on the reach of EU law. The answer given by the *Achmea* decision was negative: on the one hand, Article 344 TFEU[34] was interpreted broadly, with the consequence that disputes between investors and Member States under bilateral treaties must go before the EU courts, since they may raise EU law issues. On the other hand, Article 267 TFEU[35] is read relatively narrowly, meaning that investment arbitration tribunals cannot be understood as part of the EU judiciary. The construction

[25] *Opinion 1/91* ECLI:EU:C:1991:490 (*EEA I*), paras 21 and 30.

[26] *Opinion 2/13* (*EU Accession to the ECHR II*) (n 24).

[27] Case 6/64 *Costa v ENEL* ECLI:EU:C:1964:66.

[28] Case 26/62 *Van Gend on Loos* ECLI:EU:C:1963:1.

[29] For details see von Papp, *EU Law and International Arbitration* (n 8) 26 et seq. In systems theoretical terms, this is referred to as operational closure. Ibid 22.

[30] In its external relations case law, the Court refers to this as 'the allocation of responsibilities defined in the Treaties', *Opinion 1/91* (n 25) para 35.

[31] ibid.

[32] Critically, von Papp, *EU Law and International Arbitration* (n 8) 30–32.

[33] Case C-284/16 *Achmea* (n 17). See 5.2.2 above.

[34] Article 344 TFEU states: 'Member States undertake not to submit a dispute concerning the interpretation or application of the Treaties to any method of settlement other than those provided for therein.'

[35] Article 267 TFEU says: 'The Court of Justice of the European Union shall have jurisdiction to give preliminary rulings concerning: (a) the interpretation of the Treaties; (b) … Where such a question is raised before any court or tribunal of a Member State, that court or tribunal may, if it considers that a decision on the question is necessary to enable it to give judgment, request the Court to give a ruling thereon.' ….

of both provisions could well have been different.[36] *Achmea* ends the discussion. The CJEU, with the final authority as regards construing EU law, understands *inter se* treaties between Member States as automatically involving EU law, which in turn gives rise to a formal incompatibility with the dispute settlement provision of BITs.

5.3.2. Critique

The reasoning outlined above illustrates a somewhat circular approach by the CJEU, reminiscent of the establishment of EU primacy and direct effect and the implications drawn for EU external relations law.[37] This continuous self-referencing results in the EU's further detachment from general international law. And the wall which the Court of Justice builds around the EU and EU law does not stop in front of multilateral treaties to which the EU has signed up together with its Member States. The Court of Justice made clear that EU autonomy based on the reasoning of *Achmea* also applies to the EU Member States' obligations under the Energy Charter Treaty (ECT).[38] In the most recent *Opinion 1/20*, the Court confirmed that, as a matter of EU law, the dispute settlement provision (Article 26) of the ECT must be read as exempting intra-EU disputes from arbitration.[39] The problematic point from a jurisdiction angle in this line of cases is the Court of Justice's understanding that once an international agreement has been concluded by the EU, it becomes part of EU law and is, as such, again subject to the interpretive monopoly of the Court of Justice.[40] This last consequence is a bit of a stretch considering the fact that the EU itself is a contracting party to

[36] Before the *Achmea* judgment, the precise reach of Article 344 TFEU had been far from clear. Although *Opinion 2/13* (n 24) indicated a strict approach, the Court had not yet considered its application to the investment arbitration context, where the ultimate dispute is between a non-state entity (the investor) and a state. Regarding Article 267 TFEU, the case law had been more clear. It would have required a generous reading of this provision in order to bring arbitration tribunals established under investment treaties under the definition of a 'court or tribunal of a Member State' with access to the preliminary reference mechanism. Nevertheless, it would have been possible; and it would have cleared the path for a more fruitful interaction between EU and general international law (actors) than the current stalemate. For details see Konstanze von Papp, 'Clash of "Autonomous Legal Orders": Can EU Member State Courts Bridge the Jurisdictional Divide between Investment Tribunals and the ECJ? A Plea for Direct Referral from Investment Tribunals to the ECJ' (2013) 50 *Common Market Law Review* 1039.

[37] See text accompanying nn 28–35 above.

[38] Case C-741/19 *Republic of Moldova v Komstroy LLC* ECLI:EU:C:2021:655. For a critical discussion, see Bianca Böhme, 'The Future of the Energy Charter Treaty after *Moldova v Komstroy*' (2022) 59 *Common Market Law Review* 853.

[39] *Opinion 1/20* ECLI:EU:C:2022:485 (*Modernised Energy Charter Treaty*), para 47.

[40] Case C-741/19 *Komstroy* (n 38) para 23 with further references. The application of this rule to *Komstroy* has been rightly criticised since the case involved an *extra*-EU scenario and did as such not fall within the scope of EU law. See, eg, Böhme (n 38) 859–61, Nikos Lavranos, 'Regime Interaction in Investment Arbitration: EU Law; From Peaceful Co-Existence to Permanent Conflict', Kluwer Arbitration Blog (13 January 2022).

this international treaty: the CJEU may well be responsible for a uniform interpretation of the ECT as a matter of EU law, but as a matter of international law, the EU and its organs are still bound by the wording of the ECT. An EU-friendly interpretation of the ECT, even if desirable from an EU point of view, must therefore not go as far as breaching the EU's own commitments thereunder. The effect of *Komstroy* and *Opinion 1/20* is to read a disconnection clause for intra-EU disputes into Article 26 ECT, thus narrowing down the submission to international arbitration. Such a disconnection clause was not included in the ECT in 1994, in full knowledge of the Commission's wish to do so.[41] Still, the EU eventually signed up to the ECT and its – unqualified – dispute resolution clause. There is hence an argument that the EU at least silently accepted that it may become applicable in intra-EU disputes.[42]

From an international law perspective, the position of the Court of Justice in *Komstroy* seems to be backtracking from this promise, which is hardly tolerable.[43] The principle of *pacta sunt servanda*, which the EU enforces strictly when it comes to EU obligations of its Member States, also applies to the EU itself.[44] This has not only repercussions for the EU's own international law obligations, but also for the internal relationship between the EU and its Member States. In combination with the duty of loyalty,[45] it requires the EU to respect the international law obligations of its Member States to the extent possible.[46] After all, the EU principle of loyal cooperation can itself be understood as deriving from the international law concept of good faith.[47]

[41] See COM(93)542 final (4 November 1993), 'The European Energy Charter Treaty: Fresh Impetus from the European Community', at para 11 lit c).

[42] See also J Robert Basedow, 'The *Achmea* Judgment and the Applicability of the Energy Charter Treaty in Intra-EU Investment Arbitration' (2020) 23 *Journal of International Economic Law* 271.

[43] This is why arbitral tribunals constituted under the ECT continue to uphold their jurisdiction, including in *intra*-EU matters. See Böhme, 'The Future of the Energy Charter Treaty after *Moldova v Komstroy*' (n 38) 866 (with further references). See also the *Vattenfall* case at 5.4.1 below.

[44] See, eg, the robust position taken by Christian Tietje, 'The Applicability of the Energy Charter Treaty in ICSID Arbitration between EU Nationals vs EU Member States' (2008) 78 *Beiträge zum Transnationalen Wirtschaftsrecht*.

[45] The duty of loyal cooperation *mutually* binds the EU and its Member States, see, eg, Damien Gerard, 'Mutual Trust as Constitutionalism?' in Evelien Brouwer and Damien Gerard (eds), *Mapping Mutual Trust: Understanding and Framing the Role of Mutual Trust in EU Law* (European University Institute Working Papers, Max Weber Programme 2016/13) 69, 77 with further references.

[46] In the external relations literature, this is often referred to as respecting Member State (or shared) competencies in mixed EU-Member State agreements. See, eg, Christophe Hillion, 'Mixity and Coherence in EU External Relations: The Significance of the "Duty of Cooperation"' (Centre for the Law of EU External Relations, CLEER Working Papers 2009/1) 20 with further references. The CJEU case law is thin when it comes to the acknowledgment that mutual trust or the duty of loyalty also have tangible effects for the EU. In theory at least, this is accepted in Case 230/81 *Luxemburg v European Parliament* ECLI:EU:C:1983:32, para 38. For proposals how the EU's duty of loyalty could be made fruitful under Article 351 TFEU, see von Papp, 'Solving Conflicts with International Investment Treaty Law from an EU Law Perspective' (n 20) 347 et seq.

[47] See Geert de Baere and Timothy Roes, 'EU Loyalty as Good Faith' (2015) 64 *International and Comparative Law Quarterly* 829.

From an EU point of view, the EU's detachment from general international law is equally unfortunate. The sole focus on specific EU principles, especially such evasive ones as EU autonomy, creates communicative barriers between the Court of Justice and other international tribunals, which all have the same ultimate goal of fostering the rule of law as opposed to the rule of geopolitical power. A well-known instance is the *Kadi* case, where the Court of Justice held that EU fundamental rights review of a (then-) Community measure implementing UN sanctions was an essential part of EU autonomy and hence undisturbed by the UN Security Council's ultimate authority under Article 25 of the UN Charter.[48] Even if one were to agree with the result in the individual case, the reasoning lacks sensibility for a non-EU perspective on international law. The path chosen by the General Court, which was overruled by the Court of Justice on appeal, still holds the promise of a more responsive approach by relying on *ius cogens* as the (only) benchmark against which UN measures could effectively be judged by the EU judiciary. As an international law concept, this would have allowed for a broader debate and use of this one case, since in contrast to EU autonomy, *ius cogens* can be defined and further shaped not only by the Court of Justice, but by other international tribunals as well, taking ultimate guidance from the International Court of Justice (ICJ) and state practice. The case law of the Court of Justice dealing with international law and arbitration would benefit from a less EU-centric approach, which resembles that of a nation state insisting on its domestic law. It should be more open and international, akin to the reasoning of the General Court in *Kadi*.

The reasoning in *Achmea* was not the only available option for the Court of Justice to deal with international investment law.[49] One alternative would have been to accept that investment arbitration between a Member State and private parties is not necessarily a dispute falling under Article 344 TFEU, and therefore not automatically one that needs to be heard exclusively by the EU judiciary. Another alternative would have been to include investment arbitration tribunals within the definition of a 'court or tribunal' per Article 267 TFEU, hence allowing them to make use of the preliminary reference procedure and become part of the EU judiciary. The resolution of jurisdictional hurdles – which, to recall, the Court of Justice itself created in the first place by its construction of the above provisions – would then have allowed a focus on the substance of both EU and international economic law, in particular fundamental (market) freedoms and standards of protection under investment treaties. This would have raised issues such as whether foreign investors are equally well protected under EU law, or whether there are incompatibilities between ECT standards and EU fundamental freedoms. It is this kind of

[48] Joined Cases C-402/05 P and C-415/05 P *Kadi and Al Barakaat* ECLI:EU:C:2008:461, paras 281 et seq.

[49] See, in particular, Opinion of Advocate General Wathelet in Case C-284/16 *Achmea* ECLI:EU:C:2017:699, paras 84–131 and 132–228.

substantive analysis which would be very welcome, but is missing from the Court of Justice's analysis.[50]

5.4. LIMITS OF ECONOMIC FREEDOM IN THE PUBLIC INTEREST?

The above has shown that the EU is (necessarily) ensuring its own interests, and the Court of Justice does so in a way that forecloses discussion of substantive issues with other international tribunals. On the other hand, the question remains whether the actors in international arbitration are doing a better job regarding outside communication. The following example will illustrate that investment arbitration is not sufficiently open to deal with external challenges either.

5.4.1. Construing Consensus to Arbitrate under Article 26 ECT: *Vattenfall*

As seen above,[51] arbitration is firmly rooted in the agreement to arbitrate, which gives practical life to the value of contractual freedom in the form of party autonomy over dispute settlement proceedings outside public courts. This means that the finding and construction of a valid arbitration agreement is crucial. The agreement to arbitrate does not only enable arbitration proceedings. It also removes the dispute from the general jurisdiction of the courts and tribunals of Member States, and remains the point of reference for the arbitration proceedings going forward. This focus on the consensual nature of arbitration and party autonomy very much resembles the EU's self-referential approach and operational closure.[52]

This can be illustrated by an arbitral decision which was rendered as a response to the Court of Justice's judgment in *Achmea*. In the *Vattenfall* case, an intra-EU arbitration under the ECT, the tribunal faced the question of what *Achmea* meant for its own jurisdiction.[53] If *Achmea* were to be read broadly, Article 344 TFEU would not only lead to the unenforceability of arbitration clauses contained in bilateral agreements between EU Member States, but also question consensus established under Article 26 ECT, as between EU Member States. In an elaborate analysis, the tribunal explained that whether or not

[50] Compare the brief acknowledgment of the (future) necessity of such an analysis in the Opinion of Advocate General Szpunar in Case C-741/19 *Komstroy* (n 12) paras 93–97. This should be borne in mind given that disputes under the ECT may also go to national courts, not only to arbitration (see Article 26(2)(a) ECT).

[51] At 5.2.1.

[52] See 5.3.1 above at nn 29–32.

[53] This was before the CJEU confirmed in *Komstroy* (n 38) that the rationale of *Achmea* did not only cover bilateral investment treaties between EU Member States, but also extended to the arbitration clause of the ECT.

Achmea must be understood narrowly or broadly remains an issue to be resolved by the Court of Justice.[54] So it is not up to the arbitrators to extrapolate from *Achmea* and make inferences from the situation of intra-EU bilateral treaties for the ECT.[55] All the arbitral tribunal can do is interpret the international law agreement which defines the reach of their own competencies. According to the tribunal:

> It would have been a simple matter to draft the ECT so that Article 26 does not apply to disputes between an Investor of one EU Member State and another EU Member State as respondent. That was not done; and the Tribunal has been shown no indication in the language of the ECT that any such exclusion was intended. *The Tribunal's responsibility is to interpret and apply the ECT, which defines the Tribunal's jurisdiction.*[56]

This focus on a strictly grammatical interpretation of the relevant dispute resolution clause while ignoring any other law which may suggest a different reading has a very similar effect to that of the case law of the Court of Justice: it forecloses an engagement with substantive issues arising from an overlap of international treaties, making a discussion with other international courts or tribunals difficult. It is of course correct that Article 26 ECT is the sole basis for the arbitrators' jurisdiction in *Vattenfall*. Nevertheless, the fact that its wording suggests unconditional consent does not necessarily end the debate of how best to accommodate EU law as of today.

Put in historical context, intra-EU investment arbitration became a major problem only with the eastern enlargement of the EU.[57] Before then, a dispute, say, between a French investor and Poland would not have been intra-EU. The European Community which signed the ECT in 1994 looked very different from the EU today. Moreover, even after accession of the Central and Eastern European (CEE) states to the EU, it took many years for these legal issues to crystallise, and for the Court of Justice to eventually take the stand it took in *Achmea*. So the question of what the EU and its Member States as treaty parties to the ECT want to exclude from Article 26 ECT has only been emerging since *Achmea*, and cannot necessarily be inferred from the wording of the clause alone. If the wording were found to be so clear as to exclude a more dynamic interpretation, arbitrators would have to proceed to the question of how an ECT award rendered on this basis could be enforced in intra-EU cases, where EU Member States were bound to find, as a matter of EU law, that the arbitral tribunal lacked jurisdiction.

[54] *Vattenfall AB et al v Germany*, ICSID Case No ARB/12/12 (Decision on the *Achmea* Issue, 31 August 2018).

[55] ibid para 164.

[56] ibid para 187, emphasis added.

[57] See, eg, Berta Boknik, *Das Verhältnis von EuGH und Investitionsschiedsgerichten auf der Grundlage von* intra-*EU BIT: Eine Analyse anhand des Falls Achmea* (Baden-Baden, Nomos, 2020) 70 et seq

Be that as it may, what is interesting for the purpose of this chapter is that the tribunal in *Vattenfall*, when construing the ECT, used a mirror approach to that of the Court of Justice when construing the EU Treaties (even though the latter goes even further when claiming an interpretative monopoly). While the arbitrators can only look to the ECT and general international law, treating EU law as an external factor to be dealt with elsewhere,[58] the Court of Justice only looks to EU law and treats any other international law as an outside – negligible – irritation.

5.4.2. Court of Justice Oversight of Arbitration and the EU Judiciary: *PL Holdings*

Differences regarding the establishment of the consensus to arbitrate often end up before courts – and, as far as intra-EU arbitration is concerned, before the courts and tribunals of Member States. This could either be at the outset, or at the very end of arbitration proceedings.[59] So courts and tribunals of Member States play a decisive role when it comes to implementing the Court of Justice's reluctant stance vis-à-vis investment arbitration within the EU. In the already mentioned case of *PL Holdings*,[60] the Swedish courts had to consider the implications of *Achmea*. *PL Holdings* was a reference for a preliminary ruling to the CJEU from the Swedish Supreme Court. The Swedish courts had been asked to annul an arbitral award which was rendered on the basis of an intra-EU investment treaty[61] in arbitration proceedings conducted under the auspices of the Arbitration Institute of the Stockholm Chamber of Commerce. PL Holdings, a Luxembourg holding company, had acquired shares in two Polish banks, which it was later forced to sell by the Polish financial supervision authority. In November 2014, PL Holdings filed a request for arbitration. Poland replied promptly, including its intention to challenge consent to arbitrate. On this basis, the Polish Statement of Defence in November 2015 challenged jurisdiction of the arbitral tribunal, claiming that PL Holdings was not an 'investor' within the definition of the treaty. It did not, however, argue that the state's offer to arbitrate breached EU law, an argument which was added only in May 2016. In 2017, the tribunal rendered one partial and one final award in favour of PL Holdings, against which Poland brought challenges all the way up to the Swedish Supreme Court in order to have them set aside. In March 2018, when

[58] The *Vattenfall* tribunal in fact invited the CJEU to elaborate on the reasoning in *Achmea* and clarify the implications thereof for *intra*-EU arbitration under the ECT. The ball which was thus played back into the field of the EU was picked up by the Court in *Komstroy* (n 38).

[59] For details see von Papp, 'Clash of Autonomous Legal Orders' (n 36) 1044 et seq.

[60] Case C-109/20 *Republiken Polen v PL Holdings Sàrl* ECLI:EU:C:2021:875.

[61] Agreement between Belgium and Luxembourg, of the one part, and the Government of the People's Republic of Poland, of the other, concerning the reciprocal promotion and protection of investments of 19 May 1987.

the *Achmea* judgment of the Court of Justice was handed down, the question arose as to what the Court's prohibition of investment arbitration based on an intra-EU bilateral treaty implied for the survival of the awards in PL Holdings.

It seems difficult to argue that the arbitration based on an investment treaty between Belgium and Luxemburg on the one hand, and Poland on the other, should meet any other fate than the one in *Achmea*. Nevertheless, the Svea Court of Appeal understood the holding in *Achmea* narrowly, ie, confined to an arbitration agreement that came into existence by the investor's acceptance of the Member State's offer to arbitrate in an intra-EU bilateral investment treaty. It contrasted this with an ad hoc arbitration agreement which it found had been concluded here by way of preclusion: under Section 34(2) of the relevant Swedish law on arbitration proceedings, a party shall not be entitled to rely on a fact which, by participating in the proceedings without objection, or by any other conduct, it may be regarded as having refrained from raising. Under this rule, which follows the pro-arbitration approach[62] of the UNCITRAL Model law, a party who wishes to challenge the jurisdiction of the tribunal must do so by the latest in the Statement of Defence.[63] The Svea Court of Appeal was willing to construe such an ad hoc arbitration agreement on this basis, concluding that Poland had failed to raise the intra-EU arbitration objection in a timely manner.

This is noteworthy for two reasons. First, as matter of principle, it would mean that arbitration laws like Section 34(2) could outweigh EU principles. This is because, were it not for the specific construction of the arbitration agreement in this case, the reasoning underlying *Achmea* would have extended to the intra-EU scenario here. Second, as a matter of application of Section 34(2), there was no obvious failure to duly challenge jurisdiction in this case. In its Reply as well as in its Statement of Defence, Poland had in fact brought a jurisdictional challenge in time, albeit – from an EU law perspective – not on the correct point. However, the Svea Court of Appeal treated the precise reason given as constitutive for the objection on the EU law aspect. This is somewhat surprising, since the reasoning on any duly introduced issue can normally be refined and specified over time, as it was done in May 2016.

PL Holdings illustrates the self-referential logic of international arbitration – the pro-arbitration approach – which does not make the engagement with EU law any more likely than the Court of Justice's engagement with international law. Nevertheless, this does not mean that courts and tribunals of Member States involved in investment cases are restrained to give full effect to EU law. On the contrary, it is precisely the courts and tribunals of Member States, as part of the EU judiciary, to whom this task falls. In other words, it is much easier to forgive the tribunal in *Vattenfall* for leaving EU law aside and to be further clarified by the Court of Justice. For the Swedish courts, the matter is entirely different.

[62] See text accompanying n 10 above.
[63] Article 16(2) UNCITRAL Model Law on International Commercial Arbitration.

This is also the reason why the Supreme Court of Sweden eventually asked the CJEU whether the solution reached by the Svea Court of Appeal can be correct. Unsurprisingly, the Court of Justice held that this is not the case. In another rather bold holding, it concluded that *Achmea* extended to ad hoc arbitration agreements, which replaced consensus under an intra-EU investment treaty.[64] In this generality, this goes even further than the precise issue in *PL Holdings*, since this case was actually brought under an investment treaty.

The Court of Justice's answer to the Swedish Supreme Court opens up the possibility that *any* arbitration agreement concluded in an individual contract between an investor and an EU Member State might be caught, as long as this could be seen as a circumvention of the prohibition to arbitrate on the basis of a standing offer in an intra-EU treaty.[65] In other words, the judgment has the potential to become a new landmark in a downward spiral by reaching out to commercial arbitration. To be sure, the Court of Justice explains its intention to limit the scope of its judgment to the specific circumstances of the case.[66] Nevertheless, this boundary might well turn out a rather slippery slope for the following reasons. First, any ad hoc arbitration agreement between a state and an investor of a state with which the investor's home state is bound by an investment treaty could theoretically be construed as circumvention of the arbitral jurisdiction based on that treaty. Second, the Court of Justice itself questioned the construction of the ad hoc agreement to arbitrate in this case.[67] If it is correct to have doubts, then there is no circumvention – at least, no successful one. So limiting the holding to a factual scenario in which a rather cryptical circumvention of an international treaty might be at stake, is ultimately no limitation at all.

The courts and tribunals of Member States now face a delicate task. It was seen, above,[68] that the underlying value for a pro-arbitration approach is contractual freedom. It is the cornerstone of the New York Convention, and binds its contracting parties as a matter of international law. But as far as EU Member States are concerned, their obligations under EU law come first. It may be difficult to always align these with international law, but not impossible. And it should be done to the extent possible. The courts and tribunals of Member States are the only institutions which are apt to take on this juggling exercise. This is true for one structural and one practical reason. Structurally, the Member State courts are the basis of the EU judiciary.[69] Most cases start in the national courts and tribunals, and reach the Court of Justice upon referral. Practically, it is the Member States and their courts and tribunals which are eventually caught

[64] Case C-109/20 *PL Holdings* (n 60) paras 44–55.
[65] ibid paras 47, 65, 67.
[66] ibid para 67.
[67] ibid paras 41–43.
[68] See 5.2.1.
[69] See 5.2.2 and 5.3.1 above.

between the constraints of general international law on the one hand, and EU law on the other. It is ultimately up to them to resolve any remaining conflict.[70] Unlike the Court of Justice, which will follow the self-referential logic of EU law, and unlike arbitration tribunals, which will do the same *vice versa* regarding a pro-arbitration logic, courts and tribunals of Member States are less likely to automatically favour one over the other.

The facts underlying *PL Holdings* would have suggested one easy way out, even on the assumption that the application of *Achmea* was not as clear-cut as here suggested. As indicated before, there was in fact a jurisdictional challenge by Poland.[71] Although the relevant point of EU law was only delivered later, this could have easily been regarded as mere fleshing-out of an issue already – and timely – raised. At least, this could have been done on the basis that EU law may demand this (EU-conform interpretation), and any serious doubts could then still have led to a reference for a preliminary ruling. But, in any event, the question would have been whether EU demands such an interpretation of the national arbitration laws, ie, a refusal to apply the rule of preclusion. It would *not* have given rise to the much more sweeping pronouncement by the Court of Justice in *PL Holdings*.

5.4.3. Remaining Doubts on the EU's Suitability for Leadership as Regards Aligning Investment Law and Arbitration with the Public Interest

Investment law and arbitration has been under pressure for many years now.[72] Regarding the wider public, the level of distrust has become evident in the protests against the EU's new trade agenda under the proposed Transatlantic Trade and Investment Partnership (TTIP) as well as the Comprehensive Economic and Trade Agreement (CETA) with Canada. The responsibility for rectifying this now rests with the EU. This is true for various reasons. The first is the EU's increase in external competencies following the amendments to EU primary law by the Treaty of Lisbon.[73] The second is the EU's political will to make use of its new competency regarding foreign direct investment, and to do so through modern reforms which rehabilitate investment law and policy in the

[70] Even if this cannot be always done without breaching one of the colliding obligations, there is an argument from law and economics that the choice to breach an international law obligation could enhance overall efficiency. See, generally, Eric A Posner and Alan O Sykes, 'Efficient Breach of International Law: Optimal Remedies, "Legalized Noncompliance," and Related Issues' (2011–2012) 110 *Michigan Law Review* 243.

[71] This is also pointed out by the CJEU, see n 60 above.

[72] See, eg, Susan D Franck, 'The Legitimacy Crisis in Investment Treaty Arbitration: Privatizing Public International Law through Inconsistent Decisions' (2005) 73 *Fordham Law Review* 1521. For more details see von Papp, *EU Law and International Arbitration* (n 8) 89 et seq.

[73] With the addition of 'foreign direct investment' in Article 207 TFEU as discussed in detail by the Court of Justice in *Opinion 2/15* ECLI:EU.C: 2017:376 (*Singapore*).

eyes of the public.[74] The third is the Court of Justice's case law severely restricting EU Member States acting on the basis of existing *inter se* treaties,[75] which must be contrasted with a more lenient approach towards arbitration provisions under the modernised agreements with third states drafted under the auspices of the EU. This has become apparent in *Opinion 1/17*, where the Court of Justice, *inter alia*, upheld the dispute settlement mechanism in the CETA.[76]

The problem with this is that it might suggest a double standard in two respects. First, international treaties which the EU itself has drafted (as opposed to Member State bilateral agreements or the ECT) are looked upon with much more benevolence than all others. Second, the EU's trade agreements like CETA are favoured over non-trade agreements like the ECHR.[77] While the first concern can be addressed by stressing the reformed approach to investment arbitration under CETA's investment chapter,[78] the second is more difficult. After all, the EU is based on *economic* integration, and EU law focuses on the functioning of the internal market. It appears somewhat ironic when the EU as a trade organisation resolves to make the European public feel comfortable that its non-economic interests are well taken care of when it comes to attracting foreign investors. This is especially true when the EU is aiming for a higher level of public trust than the Member States previously achieved. This will be the future challenge for the EU. It needs to go beyond simply replacing its Member States as main international actors, ie, partners to investment treaties with the purpose of attracting foreign investment. The EU must also keep up its regulatory role, which in the intra-EU context led to the outright termination of bilateral treaties.[79] It will require some serious effort by the EU as a market organisation to square the balance between alleviating the public distrust in investment arbitration (including a more general anti-global trade sentiment) and protecting investment as an expression of economic freedom.

One obvious problem is to convince people that the public interest could be fully addressed by reforms of investment arbitration. It is questionable why the

[74] See Catherine Titi, 'International Investment Law and the European Union: Towards a New Generation of International Investment Agreements' (2015) 26 *European Journal of International Law* 639.

[75] See the case law regarding bilateral investment treaties (Case C-284/16 *Achmea* (n 17)) and the Energy Charter Treaty (Case C-741/19 *Komstroy* (n 38)) discussed above. The repercussions of *Achmea* can be severe for concluded arbitration cases as well, with no regard for *legal certainty* or *res iudicata*. This is illustrated by the *Micula* saga, where payment of an arbitration award based on an *intra*-EU BIT has been qualified as illegal state aid by the Commission, which after new litigation (Case C-638/19 P *European Food SA et al* ECLI:EU:C:2022:50) has eventually been confirmed as such by the General Court (Joined Cases T-624/15 RENV, T-694/15 RENV, T-704/15 RENV *European Food SA et al* ECLI:EU:T:2024:659.

[76] *Opinion 1/17* ECLI:EU:C:2019:341 (*EU-Canada CETA*). For details see von Papp, *EU Law and International Arbitration* (n 8) 79 et seq. Critically, also Böhme, 'The Future of the Energy Charter Treaty after *Moldova v Komstroy*' (n 38) 863 et seq.

[77] Compare the Court's controversial attitude in *Opinion 2/13* referred to at 5.3.1 above.

[78] See von Papp, *EU Law and International Arbitration* (n 8) 81 et seq.

[79] See n 6 above.

balance between economic and non-economic interests should be struck at the level of dispute resolution. The more straightforward and more efficient way to do so would be to regulate contracts between states and investors. But even if a more court-like form of dispute settlement were to do the trick, the question remains whether the safeguards in CETA, as addressed by the Court of Justice in *Opinion 1/17*, will live up to their promise.[80] There is also an argument that the EU's reform of investor-state arbitration is nothing more but a synopsis of the most recent features of other model investment treaties and older case law.[81] One would probably have to give some credit to the EU for structural changes such as the standing appellate mechanism and the proposal of an investment court in the longer run. Nevertheless, these proposals still need to fully materialise and have practical effect in future cases. For now, the main thrust appears to be that the main actor going forward will be the EU and no longer its Member States. Politically, the EU must make the call of whether it will side with economic interests in order to become attractive for foreign investors, or with the public interest in safeguarding non-economic values.

Legally, it was indicated before that the Court of Justice would be well advised to take a more international as opposed to an EU-centred approach which mirrors the acts of nation states.[82] Within broader Europe, the Court of Justice's case law might be stirring up issues such as whether the non-enforcement of arbitration awards can be reconciled with Protocol No 1 to the ECHR.[83] For the EU itself, the eradication of intra-EU investment arbitration as an alternative to litigation before the local courts and tribunals might raise problems from a rule of law perspective. This is especially true regarding investment in EU Member States in CEE, such as Poland or Hungary.[84] The argument that the EU is built on mutual trust is here thwarted by the Court of Justice's own case law holding these Member States liable for outright breach of the rule of law.[85] From the point of view of the Court of Justice, this tension can only be resolved by focusing on mutual trust and EU democratic values as ideals which bind all Member States. However, the principle of mutual trust as such does not mean that the

[80] For more detail see von Papp (n 8) 79 et seq.

[81] Martins Paparinskis, 'Investment Law and the European Union: A Reply to Catherine Titi' (2015) 26 *European Journal of International Law* 663.

[82] See 5.3.2 above.

[83] The European Court of Human Rights (ECtHR) has meanwhile opened the door to an argument that the failure of a contracting state to enforce an arbitration award – in that case, issued by a tribunal under the auspices of the International Chamber of Commerce (ICC) – might be considered arbitrary and hence constitute a deprivation of property prohibited under the ECHR. See *BTS Holding AS v Slovakia (Application no 556117/17)* ECtHR Judgment of 30 June 2022.

[84] Critically, Dimitry Kochenov and Nikos Lavranos, '*Achmea* versus the Rule of Law: CJEU's Dogmatic Dismissal of Investors' Rights in Backsliding Member States of the European Union' (2021) *Hague Journal on the Rule of Law*. See also Xavier Groussot and Marja-Liisa Öberg, 'The Web of Autonomy of the EU Legal Order: Achmea' in Graham Butler and Ramses A Wessel (eds), *EU External Relations Law: The Cases in Context* (Oxford, Hart Publishing, 2021) 927 (with further references at n 51).

[85] See, eg, Joined Cases C-585/18, C-624/18 and C-625/18 *A K et al* ECLI:EU:C:2019:982.

ideal is always fully achieved in practice. The Court of Justice's own case law accepts this and, if necessary, grants narrow exceptions from this principle.[86] If, in fact, adherence to EU values is not fulfilled in all Member States, there is no basis for unqualified mutual trust. So the logical consequence would have been similar to the one drawn in the asylum cases: where a clear breach of the legally required standards is established, the principle of mutual trust exceptionally does *not* apply.

5.5. CONCLUSION

The critical assessment of cases dividing EU law and investment arbitration has shown the same narrow-mindedness on both sides. This lies in the nature of specialised regimes of general international law. Nevertheless, for a fruitful dialogue to develop, it would be commendable to make more use of common concepts such as *legal certainty*, *res iudicata*, *ius cogens* or *good faith*, and less of self-referential notions like EU autonomy and mutual trust, or a pro-arbitration approach to consensual arbitration. Regarding intra-EU arbitration, it will be up to the Member States and their courts to implement the landmark decisions of the Court of Justice in *Achmea*, *Komstroy*, and *PL Holdings*. This should be done in an EU-conform way which at the same time respects international law obligations to the extent possible. Also, care should be taken not to use *PL Holdings* as a regular basis for subjecting commercial ad hoc arbitration to EU law scrutiny. Regarding extra-EU arbitration, time will tell whether reformed investor-state settlement provisions and other safeguards in modern EU agreements such as CETA can indeed become the stronghold for the EU's integrative principles as well as the public interest. Much of the success of the new investment chapters will depend on whether the public perceives the EU as doing a better job than its Member States in taking non-economic interests on board. Some scepticism is in order. The stage of dispute resolution is not the best point in time to find a balance between private and public interests; nor is social policy the EU's most prominent field of action.

[86] For the asylum context, see Joined Cases C-411/10 and C-493/10 *NS et al* ECLI:EU:C:2011:865 and their progeny, discussed by Georgios Anagnostaras, 'The Common European Asylum System: Balancing Mutual Trust Against Fundamental Rights Protection' (2020) 21 *German Law Journal* 1180. Concerning the European Arrest Warrant, see Joined Cases C-404 and 659/15 *Aranyosi et al* ECLI:EU:C:2016:198.

6

National Courts and Tribunals in Investor-State Disputes

RELJA RADOVIĆ

6.1. INTRODUCTION

NATIONAL COURTS HAVE maintained a marginal profile in investment treaty arbitration. This is a consequence of the fact that national courts do not provide direct protection of individual investor rights (like arbitral tribunals), nor do they create investment protection policies and rules (like state executives). However, such a modest profile is unjustified, because national courts exercise an important function in investment treaty arbitration by reviewing arbitral decisions rendered outside the framework of the International Centre for Settlement of Investment Disputes (ICSID), and by enforcing arbitral decisions in general. The footprint of national courts in the body of international investment law is not negligible either. They have engaged in discourses on the meaning of the term 'investment',[1] the foreign element in the scope of protected investors,[2] and the provisional application of investment treaties,[3] to name only a few examples.

The system of investment protection within the European Union (EU) has been restructured to the end of eliminating the applicability of international law and international dispute settlement means between EU investors and Member States. This is the result of several decisions of the Court of Justice within the Court of Justice of the EU (CJEU), which have already been covered in

[1] See eg *The Republic of Korea v Mohammad Reza Dayyani and others* [2019] EWHC 3580 (Comm), paras 57–59.

[2] See eg *Kingdom of Lesotho v Swissbourgh Diamond Mines (Pty) Limited and others* [2017] SGHC 195, paras 331–338.

[3] See The Hague District Court (Netherlands), ECLI:NL:RBDHA:2016:4230, Judgment of 20 April 2016, paras 5.6-95; The Hague Court of Appeal (Netherlands), ECLI:NL:GHDHA:2020:234, Judgment of 18 February 2020, ss 4.3-7; The Supreme Court of the Netherlands, ECLI:NL:HR:2021:1645, Judgment of 5 November 2021, paras 5.2.3-21.

scholarship,[4] and in this volume. The issues before the Court of Justice focused on the validity (colloquially speaking, not necessarily in terms of the law of treaties) of arbitration agreements in intra-EU investment disputes (disputes between EU investors and Member States) under EU law.[5] Oddly, the Court of Justice has not paid special attention, if any at all, to the future role of national courts in intra-EU disputes after its arbitration bans.[6] But the mere fact that intra-EU investment disputes cannot be resolved in arbitration anymore implies that national courts in Member States will play a stronger role in the protection of individual investor rights in the future.

This chapter first inquires what change in the role of national courts in intra-EU disputes results from the judgments of the Court of Justice on the validity of intra-EU arbitration agreements. The answer to this question is rather obvious: the role of national courts has been transformed from limited control of the protection of individual rights in international arbitration, to direct protection of individual rights in domestic adjudication. This means that the function of national courts in intra-EU disputes is now different from their traditional function, which continues to apply in extra-EU disputes (disputes where at least one disputing party is a non-EU investor or state). The chapter then goes further, and asks what was the attitude of national courts towards that change. The answer to this question, however, is surprising: it appears that national courts of Member States have been willing to preserve the traditional system involving the protection of individual rights in international arbitration, and a limited review of arbitral decisions in domestic adjudication. The same attitude is present in the practice of courts of third states acting in intra-EU cases, which implies a general adherence of national courts to the traditional system. Therefore, national courts seem to have

[4] See, among many others, Michael De Boeck, *EU Law and International Investment Arbitration: The Compatibility of ISDS in Bilateral Investment Treaties (BITs) and the Energy Charter Treaty (ECT) with the Autonomy of EU Law* (Brill, 2022); David Restrepo Amariles, Amir Ardelan Farhadi and Arnaud Van Waeyenberge, 'Reconciling International Investment Law and European Union Law in the Wake of *Achmea*' (2020) 69 *ICLQ* 907; Julian Scheu and Petyo Nikolov, 'The Setting Aside and Enforcement of Intra-EU Investment Arbitration Awards after Achmea' (2020) 36 *Arb Int'l* 253; J Robert Basedow, 'The *Achmea* Judgment and the Applicability of the Energy Charter Treaty in Intra-EU Investment Arbitration' (2020) 23 *J Int'l Econ L* 271; Panos Koutrakos, 'The Autonomy of EU Law and International Investment Arbitration' (2019) 88 *Nordic J Int'l L* 41.

[5] Case C-284/16 *Slovak Republic v Achmea BV* [2018] ECLI:EU:C:2018:158; Case C-741/19 *Republic of Moldova v Komstroy LLC* [2021] ECLI:EU:C:2021:655; Case C-109/20 *Polish Republic v PL Holdings Sàrl* [2021] ECLI:EU:C:2021:875.

[6] *Slovak Republic v Achmea BV* (n 5) paras 31–60; *Republic of Moldova v Komstroy LLC* (n 5) paras 39–66. The only mention of domestic courts in the context of the protection of existing rights under EU law appears in *Polish Republic v PL Holdings Sàrl* (n 5) para 68 ('the individual rights which PL Holdings derives from EU law must be protected within the framework of the judicial system of the Member States, namely, in the present case, the Polish judicial system. Consequently, even if it were established that there is a lacuna in the protection of those rights, as is alleged by PL Holdings, that lacuna would have to be filled within that system, if necessary with the cooperation of the Court in the context of its powers; however, such a lacuna cannot justify allowing a failure to comply with the provisions and fundamental principles …').

preferred to keep a marginal profile in the resolution of intra-EU investment disputes, which is a curious but important finding for the restructuring process of investment protection within the EU.

Section 6.2 examines the practice of national courts of Member States in relation to the three references for preliminary rulings to the CJEU regarding the compatibility of arbitration agreements with EU law. The three rulings concern bilateral investment treaties (BITs), the Energy Charter Treaty (ECT), and individual arbitration agreements. Section 6.3 turns to the practice of national courts of Member States in enforcement proceedings, not relating to the three referred cases. Section 6.4 observes the practice of national courts of third states in intra-EU matters. Section 6.5 concludes that the new role of national courts of Member States in intra-EU disputes requires further monitoring.

6.2. NATIONAL COURTS OF MEMBER STATES AND PRELIMINARY RULINGS

Between 2018 and 2021, the Court of Justice delivered three judgments dealing with the validity of arbitration agreements in intra-EU investment disputes through three separate jurisdictional channels, in response to references for preliminary rulings from national courts in Member States. This section examines the practice of domestic courts in relation to these preliminary reference proceedings.

6.2.1. BIT Arbitration Clauses

On 6 March 2018, the Grand Chamber of the Court of Justice ruled in *Slovakia v Achmea BV* that arbitration clauses contained in BITs between EU Member States are not compatible with EU law, because they infringe the principles of mutual trust, sincere cooperation, and the autonomy of EU law.[7] The judgment was rendered in response to a reference for a preliminary ruling made by the Federal Court of Justice of Germany (German FCJ) on 3 March 2016.[8] Section 6.2.1.1 analyses domestic court practice leading to that preliminary reference decision, while section 6.2.1.2 looks at domestic court practice afterwards.[9]

[7] *Slovak Republic v Achmea BV* (n 5) paras 58–60.

[8] Federal Court of Justice (Germany), Case No I ZB 2/15, Decision of 3 March 2016.

[9] This section observes only the occasions before domestic courts where the *Achmea* issue was raised. In some set aside proceedings before domestic courts, disputing parties simply chose not to plead an intra-EU objection on that account. See *GPF GP Sàrl v The Republic of Poland* [2018] EWHC 409 (Comm), para 3 ('The Respondent seeks to reserve any right to argue the compatibility of the BIT with EU law, and any rights it may have in the context of the pending decision of the

6.2.1.1. Slovakia v Achmea BV

The underlying arbitration was based on the Netherlands-Slovakia BIT, and it concerned a Dutch investment in the Slovak health insurance sector. The tribunal found that Slovakia violated the guarantees of fair and equitable treatment and free transfers, by introducing legislative bans on profits and transfers.[10] The tribunal issued two awards in the course of the proceedings: the 2010 Jurisdictional Award[11] and the 2012 Final Award.[12] The two awards were challenged separately by Slovakia in set aside proceedings before national courts in Germany, given that the arbitration was seated in Frankfurt am Main.

First, in 2012, the Higher Regional Court in Frankfurt am Main (Frankfurt HRC) dismissed Slovakia's attempt to set aside the 2010 Jurisdictional Award.[13] Slovakia put forward the well-known 'intra-EU objection'.[14] It argued that the tribunal lacked jurisdiction because the fact that both treaty parties are members of the EU rendered their BIT inapplicable, due to the primacy of EU law and the BIT's incompatibility with the autonomy of EU law, the prohibition of discrimination, and the principle of mutual trust.[15] The Frankfurt HRC disagreed, holding that arbitrating intra-EU disputes does not breach the autonomy of EU law. It contested the applicability of Article 344 TFEU, which prohibits Member States from submitting disputes concerning EU Treaties to any method that is not provided for in those treaties, to investor-state relations.[16] It also emphasised that arbitral awards are controlled by national courts, which can make

European Court of Justice in Case C-284/16 *Achmea v Slovakia*. I say nothing about whether the Respondent does or does not have any such rights. I have heard no argument on any such matters, and it is agreed that I should not address the same.'). Naturally, the intra-EU objection also does not appear in cases where investors were unsuccessful in arbitration, for some reasons unrelated to the intra-EU nature of the dispute, and then applied for set aside before local courts. Eg, the *Seventhsun Holdings Limited v Poland* case, see Svea Court of Appeal (Sweden), Department 02, Case No T 82-16, Decision of 18 May 2018.

[10] *Achmea BV (formerly known as 'Eureko BV') v The Slovak Republic*, PCA Case No 2008-13, Final Award (7 December 2012), para 352.

[11] *Eureko BV v The Slovak Republic*, PCA Case No 2008-13, Award on Jurisdiction, Arbitrability, and Suspension (26 October 2010).

[12] *Achmea BV v The Slovak Republic* (Final Award) (n 10).

[13] Higher Regional Court Frankfurt am Main (Germany), Case No 26 SchH 11/10, Decision of 10 May 2012.

[14] Besides the inapplicability of dispute settlement provisions in intra-EU investment treaties under EU law, which is the focus of this chapter, the intra-EU objection also comprises arguments about the inapplicability or invalidity of such treaties under public international law, most importantly the Vienna Convention on the Law of Treaties. See eg *Eureko BV v Slovakia* (Jurisdiction, Arbitrability, and Suspension) (n 11); *Jan Oostergetel and Theodora Laurentius v The Slovak Republic*, UNCITRAL ad hoc arbitration, Decision on Jurisdiction (30 April 2010), paras 72–109; *European American Investment Bank Ag (Austria) v The Slovak Republic*, PCA Case No 2010-17, Award on Jurisdiction (22 October 2012), paras 63–238.

[15] Higher Regional Court Frankfurt am Main (10 May 2012) (n 13) s I.

[16] Higher Regional Court Frankfurt am Main (10 May 2012) (n 13) s II.B.2; Consolidated Version of the Treaty on the Functioning of the European Union [2012] OJ C326/49 (TFEU), Article 344 ('Member States undertake not to submit a dispute concerning the interpretation or application of the Treaties to any method of settlement other than those provided for therein.').

references for preliminary rulings to the CJEU.[17] Furthermore, the prohibition of discrimination did not affect the validity of the arbitration clause, because it would be up to disadvantaged investors, who do not have access to international arbitration, to seek extension of such access.[18] As for the principle of mutual trust, because arbitration is a generally recognised means of legal protection, agreeing on arbitration for the settlement of disputes does not manifest distrust in national courts.[19] The Frankfurt HRC swiftly dismissed the argument that the 2010 Jurisdictional Award should be set aside due to the tribunal's inability to make a reference for a preliminary ruling to the CJEU on the ground that its review is limited to jurisdictional issues, not encompassing procedural economy.[20] Finally, the Frankfurt HRC analysed whether itself should refer to the CJEU questions about the validity of the BIT arbitration clause, concluding in the negative. It considered that the proposed questions were too specific, and that, in any event, there was no doubt about the meaning of Article 344 TFEU, rendering referral unnecessary.[21] The decision was appealed, but in 2013, the German FCJ opined that the need for legal protection no longer existed, given that the tribunal issued the 2012 Final Award in the meantime.[22]

Second, Slovakia moved to set aside the 2012 Final Award, but in 2014, the Frankfurt HRC dismissed that request too.[23] Slovakia repeated the arguments made in the earlier attempt at set aside,[24] but also challenged the reasoning of the 2012 Higher Regional Court's decision, arguing, among others, that the Frankfurt HRC was wrong in considering Article 344 TFEU inapplicable to investor-state relations, and that judicial review of arbitral decisions does not suffice to ensure compliance with EU law.[25] Furthermore, the fact that the tribunal could not make a reference for a preliminary ruling to the CJEU, as well as the failure to apply certain EU law provisions, rendered the award contrary to public policy.[26] The Frankfurt HRC once again did not follow Slovakia's arguments, and it repeated the main points made two years earlier: Article 344 TFEU does not apply to investor-state relations, arbitral awards are reviewable by national courts which ensures the observance of EU law, and the arbitration clause is not discriminatory and its extension to other EU investors would not be contrary to EU law.[27] Furthermore, the Frankfurt HRC did not find violation of public policy either in the tribunal's inability to make a reference for a

[17] Higher Regional Court Frankfurt am Main (10 May 2012) (n 13) s II.B.2.
[18] ibid s II.B.4.
[19] ibid s II.B.5.
[20] ibid s II.B.6.
[21] ibid s II.C.
[22] Federal Court of Justice (Germany), Case No III ZB 37/12, Decision of 19 September 2013.
[23] Higher Regional Court Frankfurt am Main (Germany), Case No 26 Sch 3/13, Decision of 18 December 2014.
[24] ibid para 29.
[25] ibid paras 30–31.
[26] ibid para 34.
[27] ibid paras 50–57.

preliminary ruling to the CJEU, or in the substance of its award.[28] The Frankfurt HRC saw no reason for making a reference for a preliminary ruling to the CJEU on this occasion either.[29]

The 2014 decision of the Frankfurt HRC was then appealed further, and this time, the German FCJ did refer questions about the validity of intra-EU BIT arbitration clauses to the CJEU. It posed three alternative questions, namely whether Article 344 TFEU (the prohibition of the use of non-EU dispute settlement means) precluded the applicability of intra-EU BIT arbitration clauses; if no, whether Article 267 TFEU (the power of the CJEU to issue preliminary rulings) had such effect; and if no, whether Article 18(1) TFEU (the prohibition of discrimination based on nationality) had such effect.[30] The German FCJ saw no reason to set aside the award on the grounds of violation of public policy and it focused on the questions to be referred to the CJEU.[31] However, it clearly preferred the view on the arbitration clause's compatibility with EU law taken by the Frankfurt HRC, and it referred the questions to the CJEU only due to the lack of definite clarity on the matter.[32]

All in all, the arguments made by national courts in Germany in the *Achmea* case mirror those that have been made by arbitral tribunals dismissing intra-EU objections.[33] Furthermore, the Frankfurt HRC avoided raising the issue to the level of EU institutions, by rejecting to make a reference for a preliminary ruling to the CJEU. And while the German FCJ did make a referral, it was acting as a national court of final instance, where no further appeal was possible, which means it was not *able*, but *required* to make a referral.[34]

6.2.1.2. *Aftermath*

Following the judgment of the Court of Justice in *Achmea*, the German FCJ had no choice but to set aside the 2012 Final Award in the *Achmea BV v Slovakia* arbitration.[35] National courts then continued applying the principle

[28] ibid paras 60–65.
[29] ibid para 48.
[30] Federal Court of Justice (Germany), Case No I ZB 2/15, ECLI:DE:BGH:2016:030316BIZB2.15.0, Decision of 3 March 2016.
[31] ibid para 20.
[32] ibid paras 21–78.
[33] cf *Eastern Sugar BV (Netherlands) v The Czech Republic*, SCC Case No 088/2004, Partial Award (27 March 2007), para 170 (it is up to discriminated persons to seek extension of rights); *Eureko BV v Slovakia* (Jurisdiction, Arbitrability, and Suspension) (n 11) paras 276 (Article 344 inapplicable to private-public arbitration) and 266–267 (remedy for discrimination is extension of rights); and, after the Frankfurt HRC's 2012 ruling, *European American Investment Bank Ag (Austria) v Slovakia* (n 14) paras 257 (Article 344 TFEU inapplicable to private-public arbitration), 259 (award reviewable by domestic courts which can make preliminary reference) and 272 (reviewing arbitral conclusions that it is up to discriminated persons to seek extension of rights).
[34] TFEU (n 16) Article 267(3).
[35] Federal Court of Justice (Germany), Case No I ZB 2/15, ECLI:DE:BGH:2018:311018BIZB2.15.0, Decision of 31 October 2018.

established by the Court of Justice in other cases too. On 11 February 2021, the Frankfurt HRC declared arbitration inadmissible in the case of *Raiffeisen Bank International AG and Raiffeisen Bank Austria DD v Croatia*, on the ground that the arbitration clause in the Austria-Croatia BIT was invalid under EU law, and no arbitration agreement could have been concluded.[36] The Frankfurt HRC explicitly held that the effect of the judgment of the Court of Justice in *Achmea* extends to all intra-EU BITs.[37] The entire reasoning was upheld by the German FCJ, finding the appeal inadmissible.[38] Then, on 19 April 2022, the Paris Court of Appeal (Paris CA) set aside the awards in two Polish arbitrations – *Strabag SE and others v Poland* and *Slot Group AS v Poland* – finding the arbitration clauses in the Austria-Poland and Czechia-Poland BITs invalid and also acknowledging *Achmea*'s general effect.[39]

The general and direct application of the *Achmea* principle to all intra-EU BITs promoted by national courts of Member States differs from the practice of arbitral tribunals, which have been reluctant to attribute it direct effects.[40] However, considering that national courts of Member States are part of the EU institutional structure, such an attitude is reasonable. Still, the practice of national courts of Member States was not unanimous: in 2022, the Amsterdam District Court (Amsterdam DC) held that the effect of *Achmea* was unclear, especially where the seat of arbitration is outside the EU, finding no manifest lack of jurisdiction in an intra-EU BIT-based arbitration and declining to order the claimant to cooperate in suspension of the arbitration.[41]

At this point, the new role of national courts of Member States manifested. Addressing the arguments of investors, both the Frankfurt HRC and the Paris CA held that award set aside does not deny their legal protection or access to justice, because such protection of investors is still offered by the respondents' national courts.[42]

But the availability of remedies at the national level might present a separate issue, although so far has not received particular attention. On the one

[36] Higher Regional Court Frankfurt am Main (Germany), Case No 26 SchH 2/20, ECLI:DE:OLGHE:2021:0211.26SCHH2.20.00, Decision of 11 February 2021.

[37] ibid.

[38] Federal Court of Justice (Germany), Case No I ZB 16/21, ECLI:DE:BGH:2021:171121BIZB16.21.0, Decision of 17 November 2021.

[39] Paris Court of Appeal (France), Pôle 5 – Chambre 16, Case No RG 20/13085, Portalis 35L7-V-B7E-CCLDI, Decision No 48/2022 of 19 April 2022, paras 85, 87; Paris Court of Appeal (France), Pôle 5 – Chambre 16, Case No RG 20/14581, Portalis 35L7-V-B7E-CCPBD, Decision No 49/2022 of 19 April 2022, para 67.

[40] See eg *Fynerdale Holdings BV v The Czech Republic*, PCA Case No 2018-18, Award (29 April 2021), paras 273–283 (holding that intra-EU BITS are not 'automatically inapplicable', by distinguishing between the incompatibility with EU law and procedural consequences such as direct non-applicability, which the CJEU did not address).

[41] Amsterdam District Court (Netherlands), C/13/720363 / KG ZA 22-636, ECLI:NL:RBAMS:2022:5772, Judgment in Summary Proceedings of 1 September 2022, para 4.8.

[42] Federal Court of Justice (Germany) (31 October 2018) (n 35) para 72; Paris Court of Appeal (Decision No 48/2022 of 19 April 2022) (n 39) para 92.

hand, the conditions of local judiciary are often challenged. In *Croatia v Raiffeisen Bank International AG and Raiffeisen Bank Austria DD*, the investors argued that the *Achmea* ruling should not be followed because the lack of independence and structural issues of the local judiciary, as well as the disregard of the preliminary reference procedure, amounted to a defeat of the principles of mutual trust and sincere cooperation.[43] However, the Frankfurt HRC dismissed the argument on the ground that such considerations are irrelevant and cannot rebut the rule that arbitrating intra-EU investment disputes is contrary to EU law.[44] The German FCJ supported this point, and noted that it would be up the Commission and other Member States to take action regarding the issues of local judiciary.[45] The same argument was essentially made by the Paris CA in *Poland v Strabag and others*.[46] In contrast, the Amsterdam DC noted that the independence of local judiciary is a relevant consideration regarding the effects of *Achmea*.[47]

On the other hand, access to national courts can also be challenged from the perspective of claims and facts. In *Poland v Slot Group*, the investors argued that the award's set aside would result in a denial of justice due to the lapse of time since the adoption of the contested measures (which was spent in arbitration).[48] But the Paris CA considered that local prescription of claims was hypothetical and that it did not demonstrate denial of justice.[49] This issue is regulated in the Agreement for the Termination of Bilateral Investment Treaties between the Member States of the EU (Termination Agreement), which in Article 10 (entitled 'access to national courts') provides:

> 1. An investor shall be entitled to access the judicial remedies under national law against a measure contested in Pending Arbitration Proceedings *even if national time limits for bringing actions have expired*, within the time limits referred to in paragraph 2, on condition that:
>
>   (a) the investor withdraws the Pending Arbitration Proceedings and waives all rights and claims pursuant to the relevant Bilateral Investment Treaty or renounces execution of an award already issued, but not yet definitively enforced or executed, and commits to refrain from instituting New Arbitration Proceedings:
>
>   (i) within six months from the termination of the Bilateral Investment Treaty on the basis of which the Pending Arbitration Proceedings were initiated, where the structured dialogue pursuant to Article 9 was not used;

[43] Higher Regional Court Frankfurt am Main (11 February 2021) (n 36) s I.
[44] ibid s II.
[45] Federal Court of Justice (Germany) (17 November 2021) (n 38) paras 36–43.
[46] Paris Court of Appeal (Decision No 48/2022 of 19 April 2022) (n 39) paras 94–95.
[47] Amsterdam District Court (n 41) para 4.8.
[48] Paris Court of Appeal (Decision No 49/2022 of 19 April 2022) (n 39) para 39.
[49] ibid para 71; cf Svea Court of Appeal (Sweden), Case No T 4658-18, Decision of 13 December 2022, 43 (holding that although there was some basis for the argument of prescription, it was not proven).

(ii) within six months from the date on which the Contracting Party concerned rejects the investor's request to enter into a structured dialogue pursuant to Article 9(1) and (6); or
(iii) within six months from the date on which the last of the parties communicates its decision pursuant to Article 9(12), where the structured dialogue pursuant to Article 9 was used;

(b) *access to the national court will be used to make a claim based on national or Union law*; and
(c) where relevant, no settlement agreement was reached as a result of the structured dialogue pursuant to Article 9.

2. National time limits to access national courts pursuant to paragraph 1 shall be deemed to run from the date on which the investor, as applicable, withdraws from the relevant Pending Arbitration Proceedings or renounces execution of an award already issued, but not yet definitively enforced or executed, and commits to refrain from instituting New Arbitration Proceedings in accordance with point (a) of paragraph 1 and shall have the duration prescribed by the applicable national law.
3. For greater certainty, the provisions of Bilateral Investment Treaties terminated pursuant to this Agreement shall not be considered as part of the applicable law in proceedings brought before a national court pursuant to this Agreement.
4. For greater certainty, the provisions of this Article shall not be construed as creating any new judicial remedies which would not be available to the investor under the applicable national law.
5. The national courts shall take into account any compensation previously paid in the Pending Arbitration Proceedings with a view to avoiding double compensation.[50]

Investors are therefore given another opportunity to access national courts, but limited to claims for violation of national or EU law. How these provisions operate and whether they contain any gaps is to be seen in future practice. For example, investors whose awards were issued before 6 March 2018 but then 'set aside or annulled before the date of entry into force of this [Termination] Agreement'[51] are excluded from this possibility, and it would be interesting to see if there are any such cases. Furthermore, the explicit right to resort to national courts is granted in respect of 'Pending Arbitration Proceedings' only, which are defined as those initiated before 6 March 2018, and not in respect of 'New Arbitration Proceedings', which are initiated from that date on.[52] This is understandable, but not entirely. On the one hand, the cited article gives the impression that pending arbitrations (as defined) can continue while investors are only *encouraged* to return to domestic courts. In contrast, the Termination

[50] Agreement for the Termination of Bilateral Investment Treaties between the Member States of the European Union [2020] OJ L169/1, Article 10 (emphasis added).
[51] ibid Article 1(4)(b).
[52] ibid Article 1(5)–(6).

Agreement appears to attempt to leave new arbitrations (as defined) groundless and to force investors back to national courts.[53] On the other hand, pending and new arbitrations are treated equally when it comes to the obligation of Member States to contest arbitral jurisdiction, in either arbitrations or national courts, on the basis that arbitration clauses are contrary to EU law and inapplicable as bases of arbitrations 'as of the date on which the last of the parties to a Bilateral Investment Treaty became a Member State of the European Union'.[54]

6.2.2. ECT Arbitration Clause

On 2 September 2021, the Grand Chamber of the Court of Justice ruled that intra-EU arbitration based on the arbitration clause contained in Article 26 ECT is contrary to EU law.[55] Some would argue that this is not a proper ruling but only an *obiter dictum*, which can be disregarded.[56] The judgment was delivered in the case of *Moldova v Komstroy LLC*, concerning an extra-EU dispute (between a Ukrainian investor and Moldova). The Grand Chamber delivered a judgment in a reference for a preliminary ruling case made by the Paris CA concerning the ECT's definition of 'investment'.[57] The question of validity of intra-EU arbitration under the ECT was neither asked nor relevant at all. Nevertheless, the Court of Justice decided to opine on it and repeat its clear preference against intra-EU arbitrations.

National courts were at first rather reluctant to refer the question of compatibility of intra-EU arbitration under the ECT with EU law. Throughout 2019 and 2020, the Svea Court of Appeal (Svea CA) in Sweden rejected to make such reference on three occasions, simply noting that it was not justified.[58] It was

[53] ibid Article 5 ('Arbitration Clauses shall not serve as legal basis for New Arbitration Proceedings.').

[54] ibid Article 7 in conjunction with Article 4(1).

[55] *Republic of Moldova v Komstroy LLC* (n 5) paras 41–66.

[56] Alan Dashwood, '*Republic of Moldova v Komstroy LCC*: Arbitration under Article 26 ECT outlawed in Intra-EU Disputes by Obiter Dictum' (2022) 47 *European L Rev* 127; Séverine Ménétrey and Matthew Happold, 'L'investissement et l'arbitrage au sens du Traité sur la Charte de l'énergie vu par la Cour de justice: la dimension stratégique de l'arrêt *Komstroy* à l'aune de l'Avis 1/20' [2022] 4 *RTDEur* 693, 698–99; and for the attitude of arbitral tribunals in practice, see Damien Charlotin, 'ICSID Tribunal Hearing Claims by State-Owned German Banks Against Spain Declines to Reconsider Intra-EU Decision in Light of the CJEU's Komstroy Decision' (*Investment Arbitration Reporter*, 13 December 2021).

[57] Paris Court of Appeal (France), Pôle 1 – Chambre 1, Case No RG 18/14721, Portalis 35L7-V-B7C-B52FG, Decision of 24 September 2019, para 79.

[58] Svea Court of Appeal (Sweden), Department 02, Case No T 4658-18, Decision of 25 April 2019; Svea Court of Appeal (Sweden), Department 02, Case No T 4658-18, Decision of 27 May 2020; Svea Court of Appeal (Sweden), Department 02, Case No T 1626-19, Decision of 26 October 2020. However, in the first case, *Novenergia II – Energy & Environment (SCA) v Spain*, the Court was

only in 2021 that the Svea CA decided to make a reference for a preliminary ruling to the CJEU on the issue of intra-EU ECT arbitration,[59] but this referral was soon withdrawn due to the issuance of the CJEU's judgments in *Komstroy* and *PL Holdings* (which is discussed in the next section).[60]

The aftermath of the judgment of the Court of Justice in *Komstroy* is somewhat uncertain. On the one hand, the arbitral award in *Komstroy* was ultimately set aside by the Paris CA; however, because that was an extra-EU arbitration, the set aside did not focus on the intra-EU issue but on the definition of 'investment'.[61] On the other hand, the effects of the Court of Justice's ruling on the intra-EU issue in the ECT context are yet to be assessed. It has been reported that in April 2022 the Higher Regional Court in Berlin (Berlin HRC) did not declare arbitration inadmissible in *Mainstream Renewable Power Ltd and others v Germany*, an intra-EU ECT-based dispute, although apparently due to the applicability of the ICSID rules.[62] The Berlin HRC reportedly reasoned that ICSID arbitrations are not subject to control by national courts, and consequently, it could not check the validity of the arbitration agreement. A different view was taken by the Higher Regional Court in Cologne later that year, which ruled that two intra-EU ECT-based arbitrations were inadmissible, despite their ICSID framework.[63] The final word on this dilemma will be given by the German FCJ.[64] Lastly, although first reluctant to refer the matter to the CJEU, the Svea CA also directly applied the CJEU's *Komstroy* ruling and set aside the award in *Novenergia II v Spain*.[65]

willing to stay the enforcement of the award pending the set aside application: Svea Court of Appeal (Sweden), Department 02, Case No T 4658-18, Decision of 17 May 2018.

[59] Svea Court of Appeal (Sweden), Department 02, Case No T 3229-19, Decision of 11 February 2021.

[60] Svea Court of Appeal (Sweden), Department 02, Case No T 3229-19, Decision of 24 November 2021; Case C-155/21 *Italy v Athena Investments A/S (previously Greentech Energy Systems A/S) and others* [2021] ECLI:EU:C:2021:1032.

[61] Paris Court of Appeal (France), Pôle 5 – Chambre 16, Case No RG 18/14721 – Portalis 35L7-V-B7C-B52FG, Decision of 10 January 2023.

[62] The decision remains unpublished. See Lisa Bohmer, 'Revealed: Berlin Court Dismisses Germany's Request for Anti-Arbitration Declaration Directed at ICSID Case' (*Investment Arbitration Reporter*, 24 May 2022); Laura Halonen and Sophie Eichhorn, 'Berlin Court Finds that ICSID Arbitrations Are Immune from Achmea and Komstroy – At Least While They Are Ongoing' (*Kluwer Arbitration Blog*, 21 July 2022).

[63] Higher Regional Court Cologne (Germany), Case No 19 SchH 15/21, Decision of 1 September 2022; Higher Regional Court Cologne (Germany), Case No 19 SchH 14/21, Decision of 1 September 2022; Lisa Bohmer, '[Updated with New Document] Unpacking German Court Decision that Declared Dutch Coal Phase-Out ICSID/ECT Arbitration to be Inadmissible due to its Intra-EU Nature' (*Investment Arbitration Reporter*, 23 September 2022).

[64] Lisa Bohmer, 'RWE v. Netherlands Arbitration is Suspended, Pending Appeal Against German Anti-Arbitration Declaration' (*Investment Arbitration Reporter*, 15 November 2022).

[65] Svea Court of Appeal (13 December 2022) (n 49).

6.2.3. Individual Arbitration Clauses

On 26 October 2021, the Grand Chamber of the Court of Justice ruled in *Polish Republic v PL Holdings Sàrl* that individual (ad hoc) arbitration agreements in intra-EU investment disputes are contrary to EU law.[66] More precisely, the question concerned the permissibility of implicit arbitration agreements under national arbitration laws, entered into by virtue of the state's failure to raise jurisdictional objections within a defined period, in a BIT-based arbitration. The Court of Justice ruled that EU law precludes the validity of thus concluded individual agreements.[67] While the Court of Justice therefore reaffirmed its anti-intra-EU-arbitration attitude, it is interesting to note that the Opinion of the Advocate General in the case emphasised the function of national courts in the investment arbitration system. It advised in favour of compatibility with EU law, under the condition that 'courts of the Member States can comprehensively review the arbitration award for its compatibility with EU law, if necessary after requesting a preliminary ruling under Article 267 TFEU'.[68] However, already there, the Advocate General expressed doubt regarding the ability of national courts (in that case specifically, national courts in Sweden) to conduct such review.[69]

The theory of implicit arbitration agreements was a pragmatic and clever response to the *Achmea* ruling, and it was endorsed in 2019 by the Svea CA in *PL Holdings*.[70] The Svea CA opined that *Achmea* prohibits arbitration clauses contained in BITs concluded between states only, and not direct arbitration agreements concluded between investors and states.[71] It rejected the argument that, in line with *Achmea*, intra-EU disputes are non-arbitrable due to the need to secure the autonomy of EU law, meaning that intra-EU investment disputes are not suitable for arbitration at all.[72] It also rejected the argument that arbitrating such disputes is contrary to public policy in Sweden.[73] The central point in the decision concerned the validity of the arbitration agreement. The Svea CA agreed with PL Holdings that Poland did not raise the intra-EU objection on time, which meant that it lost its right to raise that objection.[74] The effects of this, as formulated by *PL Holdings*, are rather far-reaching: by failing to raise the intra-EU objection, the state accepts the offer to arbitrate made by the investor (not vice versa), which amounts to a new arbitration agreement. A referral

[66] *Polish Republic v PL Holdings Sàrl* (n 5) para 47.

[67] ibid para 56.

[68] Case C-109/20 *Republic of Poland v PL Holdings Sàrl* [2021] ECLI:EU:C:2021:321, Opinion of AG Kokott, paras 65, 85.

[69] ibid para 63.

[70] Svea Court of Appeal (Sweden), Department 02, Case Nos T 8538-17, T 12033-17, Decision of 22 February 2019.

[71] ibid 43.

[72] ibid 45.

[73] ibid 46–49.

[74] ibid 49–56.

to the CJEU was neither requested by the parties, nor considered necessary by the Svea CA.[75]

The decision was appealed, and in 2019, the Supreme Court of Sweden (Swedish SC) decided to refer the case to the CJEU.[76] Once again, the referral in this case was mandatory under Article 267 TFEU.[77] What is more, given that under Swedish law, appeals to the Swedish SC are subject to exceptional leave by the Svea CA, it is remarkable that the Svea CA did not consider itself to be under a duty to make a reference for a preliminary ruling to the CJEU, as a court against whose decision no further regular appeal was possible.[78] True, in 2021, after the Swedish SC referral, the Svea CA decided to refer the same question concerning ad hoc arbitration agreements, together with the question concerning the arbitration clause under the ECT, but that request was soon withdrawn due to the issuance of other decisions of the Court of Justice.[79] In the aftermath, the Swedish SC set aside the award in the *PL Holdings* arbitration in December 2022 (viewing the CJEU's ruling as part of public policy),[80] and even before that the CJEU's *PL Holdings* ruling was directly applied by the Paris CA in *Poland v Strabag and others* (as part of the law applicable to jurisdiction).[81]

6.3. NATIONAL COURTS OF MEMBER STATES IN ENFORCEMENT PROCEEDINGS

The proceedings relating to these three preliminary rulings cases are not the only occasions where the validity of arbitration agreements in intra-EU disputes was raised. The case of *Micula and others v Romania* came to prominence due to the conflict of investment treaty protections with EU state aid law,[82] which

[75] ibid 57.

[76] Supreme Court (Sweden), Case No T 1569-19, Decision of 12 December 2019.

[77] See n 34 above.

[78] See, for instances where this was argued, Joel Dahlquist, 'Analysis: Intra-EU Awards Piling up on Stockholm Court Docket, with Three ECT Awards Added in Recent Months, and New Demands by Spain and Italy for Reference to European Court of Justice' (*Investment Arbitration Reporter*, 26 May 2019). Note that referrals for preliminary rulings present a long-standing issue in Sweden: Ulf Bernitz, 'Preliminary References and Swedish Courts: What Explains the Continuing Restrictive Attitude?' in Pascal Cardonnel, Allan Rosas and Nils Wahl (eds), *Constitutionalising the EU Judicial System: Essays in Honour of Pernilla Lindh* (Hart, 2012), 177.

[79] See nn 59–60 above.

[80] Supreme Court (Sweden), Case No T 1569-19, Decision of 14 December 2022.

[81] Paris Court of Appeal (Decision No 48/2022 of 19 April 2022) (n 39) paras 64, 76–84.

[82] See generally Christian Tietje and Clemens Wackernagel, 'Enforcement of Intra-EU ICSID Awards: Multilevel Governance, Investment Tribunals and the Lost Opportunity of the *Micula* Arbitration' (2015) 16 *J World Investment & Trade* 205; Kai Struckmann, Genevra Forwood and Aqeel Kadri, 'Investor-State Arbitrations and EU State Aid Rules: Conflict or Co-existence?' (2016) 15 *European State Aid LQ* 258; Johannes Hendrik Fahner, 'Compensation or Competitive Advantage? Reconciling Investment Arbitration with EU State Aid Law' (2022) 37 *ICSID Rev – FILJ* 672.

was raised in other cases too.[83] At first sight, the issue constitutes a matter of substantive law, and does not touch upon the authority to resolve investment disputes. However, it offered another opportunity for challenging the authority of arbitral tribunals. Arbitral tribunals thus had to deal with the argument that they should decline jurisdiction because in state aid matters, their awards would be unenforceable.[84] The argument was encouraged by the European Commission's view that payments under such awards would constitute unlawful state aid, manifested in the 2015 decision to ban payment under the *Micula* award,[85] which eventually resulted in litigation before both the General Court and Court of Justice within the CJEU.[86]

Micula and others v Romania was an ICSID arbitration, and therefore the authority of the arbitral tribunal could not be re-examined by national courts in set aside or recognition proceedings, but attempts towards that end have been made in a series of enforcement proceedings in both Member States and third states. While the United Kingdom (UK) was still part of the EU, the award was registered there for the sake of enforcement, which the state attempted to set aside. The main issue concerned the effect of the Commission's decision prohibiting payments under the arbitral award, which overlapped with the questions before the the CJEU (the decision was challenged before the General Court), and consequently the High Court of Justice in England (EWHC) decided in 2017 to stay the UK enforcement proceedings.[87] The Commission used this occasion to argue that the underlying Sweden-Romania BIT was invalid due to the conflict with EU law, which meant that the award was invalid too.[88] But the EWHC made a bold statement regarding its abilities:

> The English court cannot rule on the validity of a treaty between Sweden and Romania, though it perhaps could refer the question to the CJEU (see below). However, the court agrees with the claimants that, reference aside, validity of the Romania-Sweden BIT is not relevant to the issues to be decided in this case.[89]

This is an odd statement when compared to the practice discussed above, where national courts did rule on the validity of treaty dispute settlement provisions

[83] eg *RWE Innogy GmbH and RWE Innogy Aersa SAU v Kingdom of Spain*, ICSID Case No ARB/14/34, Award (18 December 2020), para 293. See ch 8.

[84] eg *CEF Energia BV v The Italian Republic*, SCC Arbitration V (2015/158), Award (16 January 2019), paras 69–72; *BayWa re Renewable Energy GmbH and BayWa re Asset Holding GmbH v Kingdom of Spain*, ICSID Case No ARB/15/16, Decision on Jurisdiction, Liability, and Directions on Quantum (2 December 2019), para 568.

[85] Commission Decision (EU) 2015/1470 of 30 March 2015 on State Aid SA.38517 (2014/C) (ex 2014/NN) Implemented by Romania – Arbitral award Micula v Romania of 11 December 2013 (notified under document C(2015) 2112) [2015] OJ L232.

[86] Cases T-624/15, T-694/15 and T-704/15 *European Food SA and others v Commission* [2019] ECLI:EU:T:2019:423; Case C-638/19 P *Commission v European Food SA and others* [2022] ECLI:EU:C:2022:50.

[87] *Viorel Micula and others v Romania* [2017] EWHC 31 (Comm), paras 90–112.

[88] ibid para 178.

[89] ibid para 180.

between two other states,[90] as well as to the practice of the EWHC itself in other, mainly non-EU cases.[91] Furthermore, the EWHC omitted to notice the possibility of examining the validity of a treaty as an incidental question.[92] Nevertheless, the premise that the EWHC cannot rule on the validity of a treaty between two other states undoubtedly supported the correct outcome, which seems to be decided on the account of irrelevance, considering that in ICSID cases, national courts cannot examine arbitral jurisdiction, which includes the validity of arbitration agreements, and therefore BITs. Finally, the EWHC refused to make a referral to the CJEU, because the questions were vague and the challenge of the Commission's decision was already pending before the General Court, noting that it 'd[id] not consider a reference to be appropriate, bearing in mind that a reference by a first instance court is discretionary'.[93] The decision staying the enforcement was appealed, reaching first, the Court of Appeal in England, and then the Supreme Court of the UK (UKSC), but the arguments about the validity of the BIT, or the authority of the arbitral tribunal, did not reach those instances.[94]

Besides the foundational issue of arbitral authority to adjudicate, which is tied to the validity of intra-EU BITs, the real question in these proceedings was whether EU law obliged Member States not to enforce the award, which was enforceable under the ICSID Convention.[95] The UKSC ultimately lifted the stay on enforcement of the award in 2020.[96] For context, the UKSC decided on the issue of enforcement after the 2019 decision of the General Court to annul the Commission's ban on payment, but before the judgment of the Court of Justice that the General Court was wrong, which was rendered in 2022.[97] The UKSC considered that the General Court's decision affected the 2015 ban only, but not preparatory acts (mainly the decision to open investigation), implying

[90] See specifically section 6.2.1.2 above.

[91] cf *Gold Pool JV Limited v The Republic of Kazakhstan* [2021] EWHC 3422 (Comm) (finding that Canada and Kazakhstan had implicitly agreed to the latter's succession to a BIT).

[92] cf *Viorel Micula and others v Romania* [2020] UKSC 5, para 110 ('Neither the EU courts nor domestic courts have competence to give an authoritative decision, binding as between States, as to the existence and extent of obligations under a prior multilateral convention. The convention itself will usually make provision for the resolution of disputes. In the case of the ICSID Convention that function is reserved to the International Court of Justice by article 64. However, both the EU courts (for example, in infringement proceedings or direct actions) and domestic courts (in national proceedings) have competence to consider and rule upon the effect of a multilateral treaty, insofar as it may bear upon the outcome of the proceedings before them.').

[93] *Viorel Micula and others v Romania* (EWHC) (n 87) para 181.

[94] *Viorel Micula and others v Romania* [2018] EWCA Civ 1801; *Viorel Micula and others v Romania* (UKSC) (n 92).

[95] Convention on the Settlement of Investment Disputes Between States and Nationals of Other States (signed 18 March 1965, entered into force 14 October 1966) 575 UNTS 159 (ICSID Convention), Article 54(1) ('Each Contracting State shall recognize an award rendered pursuant to this Convention as binding and enforce the pecuniary obligations imposed by that award within its territories as if it were a final judgment of a court in that State.').

[96] *Viorel Micula and others v Romania* (UKSC) (n 92) para 118.

[97] See n 86 above.

a continued duty of sincere cooperation on the part of the UK and its national courts.[98] Also, the pending appeal before the Court of Justice required a stay of enforcement in accordance with the duty of sincere cooperation.[99] However, the UKSC then turned to the UK's obligations under the ICSID Convention. That Convention obliged the UK to recognise and enforce ICSID awards, and, therefore, an indefinite stay on enforcement for the reasons not contemplated under the ICSID Convention was inappropriate.[100] Finally, the UKSC concluded that the UK's obligations under the ICSID Convention, which pre-dated the UK's accession to the EU, are owed to all ICSID contracting states, and, therefore, were unaffected by EU law by virtue of Article 351 TFEU.[101]

National courts of other Member States have been more obedient to EU law. The Nacka District Court (Nacka DC) in Sweden decided in early 2019 that enforcement could not proceed, holding that the principle of sincere cooperation under EU law required respect for the Commission's decision prohibiting payments under the award, despite the fact that the decision was under appeal at the time.[102] In Belgium, a first instance court stopped the enforcement process in 2016 due to the Commission's ban on payment, and then, in 2019, an appeals court decided to refer questions concerning the effect of the ban on the enforcement proceedings in other Member States to the CJEU.[103] The response came in September 2022, and the CJEU repeated its reasoning from earlier that year in the main *Micula* litigation regarding the invalidity of the arbitration agreement.[104]

Finally, after an appeals court in Luxembourg held in 2021 that Romania was not immune from that state's jurisdiction due to the arbitration clause in the Sweden-Romania BIT, the Court of Cassation in Luxemburg (Luxembourg CC) ruled in 2022 that the arbitration clause ceased to be valid as of Romania's accession to the EU.[105] The Luxembourg CC concluded that Romania was immune from the jurisdiction of national courts in Luxembourg, and that, consequently, the award could not be declared enforceable in that state.[106] The Luxembourg CC cited *Achmea*, but was also encouraged by the latest ruling of the Court of Justice in *Micula*,[107] which held that the former ruling was relevant in the

[98] *Viorel Micula and others v Romania* (UKSC) (n 92) para 51.

[99] ibid para 56.

[100] ibid paras 84–87.

[101] ibid para 104; cf *Viorel Micula and others v Romania* (EWHC) (n 87) paras 136–152 (avoiding addressing the issue).

[102] Nacka District Court (Sweden), Case No Ä 2550-17, Decision of 23 January 2019.

[103] Tribunal of First Instance (Francophone) of Brussels (Belgium), Case Nos 15/7241/A and 15/7242/A, Judgment of 27 January 2016; Brussels Court of Appeal (Belgium), Case Nos 2016/AR/393 and 2016/AR/394, Decision of 12 March 2019.

[104] Case C-333/19 *DA and others v Romanian Air Traffic Services Administration (Romatsa) and others* [2022] ECLI:EU:C:2022:749.

[105] Court of Cassation (Luxembourg), Case No CAS-2021-00061, Decision No 116 /2022 of 14 July 2022, 29–30.

[106] ibid 30.

[107] *Commission v European Food SA and others* (n 86).

latter case, in the sense that the arbitration clause in the Sweden-Romania BIT was invalid.[108] The Court of Justice in the *Micula* case held so, even though the dispute concerned events prior to Romania's accession to the EU, because the award was delivered after that date and it involved damages relating to the post-accession period.[109] Both the Court of Justice and the Luxembourg CC were wrong in this respect. It is a well-established rule of international adjudication that the critical date for the establishment of jurisdiction of an international court or tribunal is the date of the institution of proceedings before that court or tribunal (limited exceptions are possible only if the conditions of jurisdiction are met subsequently).[110] Once established, jurisdiction cannot be revoked, or cease to exist.[111] The same date, which in investment arbitration constitutes the date of the conclusion of arbitration agreement, is relevant in domestic judicial proceedings for confirmation of an award and governs the question whether a state is entitled to immunity.[112] The critical date in the *Micula* arbitration was 2 August 2005, when the claimants filed the request for arbitration, which was before Romania's accession to the EU in 2007.[113] The Court of Justice in *Micula* wrongly assumed that the expression of state consent found in a BIT must remain valid throughout the arbitration process,[114] while the Luxembourg CC wrongly assumed that such expression of consent must remain valid even at the time of recognition/declaration of enforceability.[115]

[108] Court of Cassation (Luxembourg) (14 July 2022) (n 105) 29–30.

[109] *Commission v European Food SA and others* (n 86) para 140; *DA and others v Romanian Air Traffic Services Administration (Romatsa) and others* (n 104) para 35.

[110] *Application of the Convention on the Prevention and Punishment of the Crime of Genocide (Croatia v Serbia)* (Preliminary Objections) (2008) ICJ Rep 412, paras 79–81.

[111] ibid para 80 ('That is why the removal, after an application has been filed, of an element on which the Court's jurisdiction is dependent does not and cannot have any retroactive effect. What is at stake is legal certainty, respect for the principle of equality and the right of a State which has properly seised the Court to see its claims decided, when it has taken all the necessary precautions to submit the act instituting proceedings in time.'); ICSID Convention (n 95) Article 25(1) ('When the parties have given their consent, no party may withdraw its consent unilaterally.').

[112] United Nations Convention on Jurisdictional Immunities of States and Their Property (adopted 2 December 2004, not in force), Article 17. See, also, for the application of this principle in practice, *Ioan Micula and others v Government of Romania*, No 17-cv-02332 (APM) (US District Court for the District of Columbia, 22 December 2022), 14.

[113] *Ioan Micula and others v Romania*, ICSID Case No ARB/05/20, Decision on Jurisdiction and Admissibility (24 September 2008), para 7.

[114] *Commission v European Food SA and others* (n 86) paras 137–145, and particularly para 145 ('since, with effect from Romania's accession to the European Union, the system of judicial remedies provided for by the EU and FEU Treaties replaced that arbitration procedure, the consent given to that effect by Romania, from that time onwards, lacked any force').

[115] Court of Cassation (Luxembourg) (n 105) 29–30, and particularly 30 ('Dès lors cependant qu'à partir du 1er janvier 2007, date de l'adhésion de la Roumanie à l'Union européenne, le système des voies de recours juridictionnel propre à l'Union européenne s'est substitué à la procédure d'arbitrage du TBI liant le Royaume de Suède à l'Etat de Roumanie et que le consentement du demandeur en cassation à voir toiser le différend en application de la clause d'arbitrage y contenue est dépourvu de tout objet, les juges d'appel, en statuant comme ils l'ont fait [concluding that Romania waived its immunity from jurisdiction by concluding the arbitration agreement], ont violé tant les articles 267

6.4. NATIONAL COURTS OF THIRD STATES IN INTRA-EU CASES

The *Micula* controversy also reached national courts outside the EU. The investors managed to convert the award into a judgment in *ex parte* proceedings in a district court, in the Southern District of New York (NY) in the United States of America (US), which Romania attempted to vacate and/or stay, with the support of the Commission. The US District Court for the Southern District of NY swiftly dismissed the argument that Romania was forbidden by the Commission to pay out the due amount, which, according to Romania, could be addressed only in plenary proceedings for recognition, holding that awards cannot be denied recognition on that basis.[116] The Commission further unsuccessfully argued that the judgment should be vacated on account of its sovereignty and the doctrines of international comity, act of state, and foreign compulsion, presenting the dispute as its internal affair.[117] The argument of international comity was creative and received most attention, as it held that national courts in the US should defer the matter concerning the *Micula* award to the CJEU, or national courts in Member States, but it failed because the US proceedings were limited to the recognition of the award, which the US was obliged to recognise under the ICSID Convention.[118] As regards the foreign compulsion doctrine, although its applicability was doubtful, the US District Court for the Southern District of NY made a notable remark that 'any "compulsion" [of Romania] by the E.U. is offset by Romania's voluntary submission to the ICSID process through its treaty with Sweden'.[119] The judgment was ultimately vacated by the Court of Appeals for the Second Circuit, but for procedural reasons, following its holding in *Mobil Cerro Negro Ltd v Venezuela* that the Foreign Sovereign Immunities Act (FSIA) applied to the enforcement of ICSID awards, and that the investors had to file a plenary action, as opposed to *ex parte* proceedings, for recognition.[120]

In November 2017, the case was brought in a plenary action to another US district court, this time the US District Court for the District of Columbia, and soon after the *Achmea* ruling was rendered in March 2018. At this point, it was argued that national courts in the US did not have jurisdiction to enforce the award under the FSIA because the Sweden-Romania BIT arbitration clause was invalidated as a consequence of *Achmea*.[121] But the argument failed before the

et 344 TFUE que le principe de droit international public de l'immunité de juridiction de l'ETAT DE ROUMANIE.').

[116] *Ioan Micula and others v The Government of Romania*, 15 Misc 107 (Part I) (US District Court for the Southern District of New York, 5 August 2015), 7–8.

[117] ibid 11–14.

[118] ibid 12–13.

[119] ibid 14.

[120] *Ioan Micula and others v Government of Romania*, No 15-3109-cv (US Court of Appeals for the Second Circuit, 23 October 2017).

[121] *Ioan Micula and others v Government of Romania*, No 17-cv-02332 (APM) (US District Court for the District of Columbia, 11 September 2019), 16–17.

US District Court for the District of Columbia for three reasons: the events in dispute occurred prior to Romania's accession to the EU; only the BIT, not EU law, supplied the applicable substantive law; the General Court confirmed these points and even distinguished *Micula* from *Achmea* on that basis[122] (note that this was before the CJEU's ruling that *Achmea* was relevant in *Micula*). Romania also advanced arguments based on the act of state and foreign sovereign compulsion doctrines, invoking the Commission's ban on payment under the award as an obstacle to the award's recognition. But the US District Court for the District of Columbia found the arguments unpersuasive in light of the General Court's annulment of the Commission's prohibition of payment (clarifying that the judgment of the General Court affected not only the ban itself, but also the opening of an investigation and the issuance of a suspension injunction, in contrast to the UKSC above).[123] The latter attempts by Romania to rely on these doctrines did not receive significant attention.[124] After the delivery of the Court of Justice's judgment in *Micula*, Romania attempted to reopen the case, however unsuccessfully. Among others, the US District Court for the District of Columbia affirmed that the Court of Justice did not invalidate Romania's agreement to arbitrate with the claimants.[125]

That is not to say that national courts in the US have never shown any deference to the EU judiciary. In *Novenergia II – Energy & Environment (SCA) v Spain*, a non-ICSID arbitration, the claimants moved to enforce the award in the US, and Spain objected that national courts in the US lacked jurisdiction under the FSIA, due to the lack of an arbitration agreement.[126] However, in 2020, the US District Court for the District of Columbia decided to first stay the proceedings until the Svea CA in Sweden decides on the application for set aside,[127] in light of the latter court's decision to stay the enforcement of the award.[128] Among the reasons for granting a stay, the US District Court for the District of Columbia reviewed international comity, and concluded that 'the more prudent course of action is to allow courts within the EU to first decide the issues [of jurisdiction, ie, the existence of an arbitration agreement in light of EU law]'.[129]

In contrast, the Federal Tribunal of Switzerland (Swiss Federal Tribunal) was mostly able to avoid dealing with the merits of EU law arguments, citing procedural grounds. In *EDF International SA v Hungary*, the state attempted to set

[122] ibid 19–22. See also *Ioan Micula and others v Government of Romania*, No 19-7127 (US Court of Appeals for the District of Columbia Circuit, 19 May 2020), para 3 (upholding the reasoning of the District Court).

[123] *Ioan Micula and others v Romania* (Columbia District Court 2019) (n 121) 22–26.

[124] *Ioan Micula and others v Government of Romania*, No 17-cv-02332 (APM) (US District Court for the District of Columbia, 20 November 2020), para 13.

[125] *Ioan Micula and others v Romania* (Columbia District Court 2022) (n 112) 14.

[126] *Novenergia II – Energy & Environment (SCA) v The Kingdom of Spain*, No 18-cv-01148 (TSC) (US District Court for the District of Columbia, 27 January 2020), para 6.

[127] ibid paras 8–25.

[128] See n 58 above.

[129] *Novenergia II – Energy & Environment (SCA) v Spain* (US District Court) (n 126) para 24.

aside the award, arguing, among others, that it was contrary to public policy because the order for payment would force the state to violate the EU law on state aid.[130] The Swiss Federal Tribunal held that the arbitral tribunal reasoned that there was no conflict between the imposed obligation and EU law.[131] The argument that the arbitral tribunal omitted to take into account certain criteria and procedures under EU law was seen by the Swiss Federal Tribunal as going more to the right to be heard than public policy.[132] Because it was not pleaded as such, the argument could not be addressed, and in any event it was not conclusive as regards the violation of public policy.[133] In another case, the Swiss Federal Tribunal dismissed the request to set aside an award for failure to re-examine the intra-EU objection in the ECT context, which the arbitral tribunal initially dismissed in 2014. However, it appears that a key component in that outcome was that the state did not challenge the award on jurisdictional grounds as such (at least not on time), but rather on the procedural limb of public policy, which standard the alleged illegality failed to satisfy.[134]

6.5. CONCLUSION

National courts in Member States obviously have a new role to play, now being the main carriers of the direct protection of individual investor rights in intra-EU disputes. However, they appear to have been reluctant to actively engage in pushes within the EU towards that change and have demonstrated commitment to the traditional system, offering the protection of individual rights in international arbitration and only a limited review of arbitral decisions in domestic adjudication. National courts in third states acting in intra-EU cases have shown a somewhat similar attitude, which means that there has been some general adherence of national courts to their marginal profile. Now when that marginal profile is about to forcefully disappear when it comes to national courts in Member States and intra-EU disputes, the next task is to continuously monitor how the new role of national courts is being carried out.

[130] Federal Tribunal (Switzerland), Case No 4A_34/2015, Decision of 6 October 2015, para 5.2.
[131] ibid para 5.3.2.
[132] ibid paras 5.3.2.1–2.
[133] ibid paras 5.3.2.2.
[134] Federal Tribunal (Switzerland), Case No 4A_187/2020, Decision of 23 February 2021, s 6.

7

The Incompatibility of the ISDS Mechanism in the Energy Charter Treaty with EU Law: Nothing New Under the Sun

NICOLAS DE SADELEER

7.1. INTRODUCTION[1]

ALONG WITH INTERNATIONAL trade, investment policy is an essential part of the world economy, given that economic development is dependent on foreign capital inflows. However, investors are wary of state courts, which they criticise for their lack of independence and impartiality. To assuage their fears, many states have concluded bilateral investment treaties (BITs), which confer on investors particularly extensive substantive and procedural rights against state authorities: most favoured nation clause, fair and equitable treatment, free transfer of capital, prohibition on direct and indirect expropriations, and so forth. Regarding litigation, the investors who are nationals of the state that concluded the investment treaty may either initiate proceedings before the courts of the host state, or bring the dispute directly before an independent arbitral tribunal without having to exhaust judicial remedies in that state. As a result, investors can thus have recourse to arbitration, without the host state being able to object. Constituting a way of circumventing the jurisdiction of state courts, ISDS was developed on the initiative of developed capital-exporting states in order to protect their investors in other, third states. It thus differs from international commercial arbitration, in that the host state of the investment gives its consent to the arbitration in advance, with such consent being detached from any contractual relationship.

[1] This contribution is partly the result of discussions between the author and his colleague Ivana Damjanovic in Brussels in June 2022. Any errors or omissions remain the author's own.

This absence of a contractual basis thus characterises ISDS in relation to international commercial arbitration, and ISDS has become remarkably successful over the past few decades, given that such a mechanism removes investment disputes from the jurisdiction of state courts, which are more inclined to strike a balance between economic rights and the general interest. Since state courts often impose relatively strict conditions for the invocability of international treaties, arbitral tribunals appear to investors to be the most appropriate forum for settling their disputes with host states.[2] Moreover, the relative speed of the procedures and their confidentiality, and the amount of compensation awarded by these tribunals seem to meet investors' expectations better than traditional court procedures before state courts. ISDS also allows for the de-politicisation of investment disputes, without generating tensions between the investor's home state and the host state.[3]

In recent times, ISDS has given rise to heated debate. In 2014, *The Economist* published a critical analysis of ISDS:[4] the implementation of laudable ideas to protect investors from discrimination or expropriation was branded as 'disastrous'. For the esteemed, right-of-centre publication, it stated that, '[m]ultinationals have exploited woolly definitions of expropriation to claim compensation for changes in government policy that happen to have harmed their business'. At the same time, academics have started to question whether ISDS delivers the benefits it is supposed to. Due to broadly defined investment protection standards, investors can use ISDS to bring a wide variety of claims, also challenging host states' actions that seek to achieve legitimate public policy goals, such as the protection of health, the environment, or public safety.

The broad interpretation by the investment tribunals of the protection afforded to investors in the BITs has called into question state regulatory powers in sensitive areas such as public health and safety, financial regulation, or environmental protection. It follows that states' ability to regulate in policy matters of public concern is constrained by the existence of these treaties, which ultimately impinge on state sovereignty. There is a widespread belief that arbitral awards made by arbitral tribunals are generally favourable to foreign investors, and that international arbitrators ignore considerations of public health, the environment, or fundamental rights.[5] Furthermore, ISDS has come under fire during the course of negotiations for the Comprehensive Economic and Trade Agreement (CETA) with Canada, and the proposed Transatlantic Trade and

[2] Opinion of Advocate General Wathelet, Case C-284/16 *Achmea* ECLI:EU:C:2017:699, para 206.

[3] See generally I Damjanovic, *The EU and International Investment Law Reform: Between Aspirations and Reality* (CUP, 2023).

[4] 'The arbitration game' (*The Economist*, 10 October 2014), p 74.

[5] Empirical studies show, however, that investors are often unsuccessful in environmental litigation. See D Behn and M Langford, 'Trumping the Environment? An Empirical Perspective on the Legitimacy of Investment Treaty Arbitration' (2017) 18 *Journal of World Investment & Trade* 14–61.

Investment Partnership (TTIP) with the United States of America. Against this background, the EU has been pushing for the replacement of the current arbitration system with a mechanism for adjudicating investment disputes that enjoys greater legitimacy, specifically, a permanent Investment Court System (ICS), comprised of a permanent tribunal and an appeal tribunal.[6]

In the aftermath of the fall of the Berlin wall, individual Member States concluded around 190 BITs with Central and Eastern European (CEE) states before they joined the EU in 2004, 2007 and 2013. These treaties quickly gave rise to a number of questions. Could international arbitrators be allowed to interpret EU law, whereas the EU Treaties give the CJEU a monopoly on interpretation? Why resort to arbitration when state courts – national courts in Member States – are already required to uphold the fundamental freedoms of the internal market over national measures purporting to restrict them? Is effective judicial protection, enshrined in Article 47 of the EU Charter of Fundamental Rights, not an integral part of the rule of law, a founding value of the EU within the meaning of Article 2 TEU? Would it be conceivable, moreover, for an investor incorporated in, say, Massachusetts in the United States to claim compensation before an international investment tribunal for damage caused by regulations adopted in Utah? To ask the question is, in fact, to answer it.

In March 2018, the Court of Justice ruled in *Achmea* that the ISDS regime under an intra-EU investment treaty was incompatible with EU law.[7] While the *Achmea* ruling has already taken its place in the pantheon of the major decisions handed down by the Court of Justice,[8] its consequences met with strong opposition amongst the arbitral tribunals created by the intra-EU BITs, which are not willing to relinquish their jurisdiction.

In order to comply with the lessons of the *Achmea* judgment, on 5 May 2022, 23 Member States concluded an international agreement terminating 181 BITs that they had concluded between themselves.[9] However, divided on the compatibility of the ECT with EU law, these Member States had not denounced the later treaty.[10] In a dispute which, at first sight, seemed to be unconnected with

[6] CETA Ch 8, F, Resolution of investment disputes between States and investors.

[7] Case C-284/16 *Achmea* ECLI:EU:C:2018:158. See especially N de Sadeleer, 'The End of the Game. The Autonomy of the EU Legal Order Opposes Arbitral Tribunals under Bilateral Investment Treaties Concluded between Two Member States' (2018) 1 *European Journal of Risk Regulation* 355–70.

[8] Xavier Groussot and Marja-Liisa Öberg. 'The Web of Autonomy of the EU Legal Order: Achmea' in Graham Butler and Ramses A Wessel (eds), *EU External Relations Law: The Cases in Context* (Oxford, Hart Publishing, 2022), 927–38.

[9] Agreement for the termination of Bilateral Investment Treaties between the Member States of the European Union [2020] OJ L169/1. The agreement was concluded by all Member States except Ireland, the Republic of Austria, the Republic of Finland and the Kingdom of Sweden.

[10] Recital 10 of the preamble.

EU law,[11] insofar as it opposed the Republic of Moldova and a Ukrainian company, the compatibility of the ISDS mechanism established by the ECT with EU law was raised before the CJEU in the *Komstroy* case.[12] In this case, the CJEU was asked by the Paris Court of Appeal (Paris CA) to give a preliminary ruling on an action for annulment against an award issued by an ad hoc tribunal constituted under the Arbitration Rules of the United Nations Commission on International Trade Law (UNCITRAL) sitting in Paris which had been brought by a third state, Moldova. It concluded, in light of the Court of Justice's judgment in *Achmea*, that the ISDS provided for by the ECT violated EU law. The aim of this chapter is to explain the salience of the reasoning of the Court of Justice concerning the subjection of an ISDS mechanism provided for under a mixed agreement – concluded by both the EU and its Member States – to the key EU constitutional obligations.

7.2. THE ENERGY CHARTER TREATY, AND APPLICATION OUTSIDE THE EU LEGAL ORDER

The ECT, to which the EU and all its Member States except Italy are contracting parties, was concluded in the aftermath of the Cold War in 1994 to ensure the political and economic transition of the energy markets in the countries of CEE and the former USSR. As a strong supporter of this multilateral treaty, the EU sought at the time to protect investments in CEE made by companies incorporated in Member States. Currently, there are 53 Contracting Parties to the ECT.

The ECT has the same status in the EU legal order as an EU-only agreement, to the extent to which its provisions fall within the scope of EU competence.[13] However, since the ECT is a mixed agreement concluded by the EU and its Member States, it follows that it is implemented and managed jointly by the EU and the Member States. In addition, the compliance by EU secondary law with obligations under the ECT may be subject to review by the CJEU. In particular, insofar as this treaty is a mixed agreement, 'the EU is legally bound by the obligations of the fair and equitable treatment and non-expropriation contained in it and resembling the substantive provisions of the Investment Protection Agreement'.[14] As a result, the 27 Member States are bound by the obligations falling within the exclusive competences of the EU (investment,[15] energy and environment when the subject matter has been harmonised,[16]

[11] Opinion of Advocate General Szpunar, Case C-741/19 *Komstroy* ECLI:EU:C:2021:164, para 1.
[12] Case C-741/19 *Komstroy* ECLI:EU:C:2021:655.
[13] Case C-213/03 *Pêcheurs de l'étang de Berre* ECLI:EU:C:2004:464, para 25.
[14] Opinion of Advocate General Jääskinen, Case C-264/09 *Commission v Slovakia* ECLI:EU:C:2011:150, para 60.
[15] Article 3(1) TEU and Article 207 TFEU.
[16] Article 3(2) TEU.

etc).[17] Furthermore, EU secondary law must be interpreted in accordance with the obligations arising from the ECT.[18]

In particular, the ECT provides for the fair and equitable treatment of investors (Article 10 ECT), freedom from expropriation of investors' assets (Article 13 ECT), compensation (except where Article 13 ECT applies) (Article 12 ECT).[19] In addition, Article 26(6) ECT allows an investor from one contracting state, in the event of a dispute concerning its energy investments in the territory of the other contracting state, to bring an action against that state before an ad hoc arbitral tribunal. Unlike commercial arbitration, arbitral tribunals arise from the ECT itself, and not from the autonomy of the parties to the dispute.[20]

In *Komstroy*, the arbitral tribunal ordered Moldova to pay a sum of money to the Ukrainian company on the basis of its ECT obligations. Moldova challenged the tribunal's jurisdiction in an action brought before national courts in France under Article 1520 of the French Code of Civil Procedure. The Paris CA found in favour of Moldova, holding that the dispute concerned the settlement of a claim for the supply of electricity, which could not be classified as an 'investment', which was an essential criterion for the jurisdiction of the ad hoc tribunal under Article 26 ECT. The Court of Cassation of France (CCF), however, quashed the judgment of the Paris CA, holding that the latter had supplemented the definition of an investment by a condition not provided for by the ECT. The case was therefore referred back to the Paris CA for a decision on the merits. The Paris CA then referred questions through the reference for a preliminary ruling procedure to the CJEU, first, to determine whether the claim arising from an electricity sales contract that did not involve a contribution by the investor in the host state fell within the definition of investment (thereby justifying the application of the ECT), and, secondly, to verify the jurisdiction of the arbitral tribunal.

According to the Court of Justice, as from its entry into force, the provisions of the ECT form an integral part of the EU legal system. It follows that the CJEU has jurisdiction to give decisions through the reference for a preliminary ruling procedure concerning the interpretation of such an international agreement. That being said, the CJEU stated that it does not, in principle, have jurisdiction to interpret such an international agreement with regard to its application in a dispute outside the EU.[21]

[17] The ECT is not a case of 'facultative mixity' on the grounds that the ISDS mechanism does not fall within an exclusive competence. See *Opinion 1/17* ECLI:EU:C:2019:341 (*EU-Canada CETA*). See further Kieran Bradley, 'Investor-State Dispute Tribunals Established under EU International Agreements: Opinion 1/17 (EU–Canada CETA)' in Graham Butler and Ramses A Wessel (eds), *EU External Relations Law: The Cases in Context* (Oxford, Hart Publishing, 2022).

[18] Case C-61/94 *Commission v Germany* ECLI:EU:C:1996:313, para 52.

[19] See Damjanovic, *The EU and International Investment Law Reform* (n 3).

[20] Case C-741/19 *Komstroy* (n 12) para 59.

[21] Case 181/73 *Haegeman* ECLI:EU:C:1974:41, paras 2 and 4; Case C-321/97 *Andersson and Wåkerås-Andersson* ECLI:EU:C:1999:307, para 26.

However, both Advocate General Szpunar and the judgment of the Court of Justice held that this was not the case when the referring court might be called upon, in a case directly falling under EU law, to rule on the interpretation of the provisions of a mixed agreement,[22] which the ECT was. In effect, where a provision can apply both to situations falling within the scope of EU law, and to situations not falling within that scope, it is clearly in the EU interest that, in order to forestall future differences of interpretation, that provision should be interpreted uniformly.[23] Accordingly, the Court of Justice acknowledged its jurisdiction to interpret provisions of a treaty that binds the EU in a dispute which falls outside the EU legal order.

In addition, the Court of Justice underscored that the parties to the dispute decided to establish the seat of arbitration in Paris, France – in the EU.[24] It follows that the national courts in France have jurisdiction to hear actions to set aside an arbitral award made in France for lack of jurisdiction of the arbitral tribunal given that EU law forms part of the law in force in every Member State.[25]

7.3. INTRA-EU ISDS AND THE DISPUTE SETTLEMENT MECHANISM ESTABLISHED BY ARTICLE 26 ECT

The Court of Justice declared itself competent to rule on the provisions of the ECT, since the international agreement, being concluded by the EU, constitutes a legal act of its own legal order.[26] The question then arose whether the *Achmea* judgment of the Court of Justice and subsequent case law could be transposed to this dispute, given that these cases involved bilateral investment treaties to which two Member States were parties, and not a mixed treaty.[27]

7.3.1. The Judgment in *Achmea* and Subsequent Judgments

In its landmark *Achmea* judgment, the Court of Justice ruled that recourse to an arbitral tribunal established on the basis of an investment agreement between the Netherlands and Slovakia was not permitted within the EU legal order. The Court of Justice's reasoning in *Achmea* rests on two pillars: on the one hand, the autonomy of the EU legal order deriving from a combined reading of Article 2

[22] Case C-741/19 *Komstroy* (n 12) paras 29–31; Opinion of Advocate General Szpunar, Case C-741/19 *Komstroy* ECLI:EU:C:2021:164, para 45.

[23] Case C-53/96 *Hermès* ECLI:EU:C:1998:292, para 32; Case C-741/19 *Komstroy* (n 12) para 29.

[24] Case C-741/19 *Komstroy* (n 12) paras 32–33.

[25] Alternatively, investors could choose the seat of the arbitration outside the EU in an attempt to escape the incompatibility of their jurisdiction with EU law.

[26] Opinion of Advocate General Szpunar, Case C-741/19 *Komstroy* (n 22) para 29; Case C-741/19 *Komstroy* (n 12) para 49.

[27] Opinion of Advocate General Szpunar, Case C-741/19 *Komstroy* (n 22) para 49.

TEU and Article 19 TEU and, on the other hand, the principle of mutual trust deriving from Article 2 TEU,[28] which goes hand in hand with the principle of loyal cooperation enshrined in Article 4(3) TEU. The reasoning was that, since the EU is based on shared values with the Member States, the national courts of Member States must cooperate with the CJEU, which guarantees the unity of interpretation of EU law.[29] In particular, the preliminary ruling procedure provided for in Article 267 TFEU is the 'keystone' of the EU judicial system.[30] The object of that procedure is to secure the 'uniform interpretation of EU law, thereby serving to ensure its consistency, its full effect and its autonomy as well as, ultimately, the particular nature of the law established by the [EU] Treaties'.[31]

Starting from these premises, the CJEU reasoned in three stages. First, the arbitral tribunal instituted by the Netherlands-Slovakia BIT 'may be called on to interpret or indeed to apply EU law, particularly the provisions concerning the fundamental freedoms, including freedom of establishment and free movement of capital'.[32] Second, as the tribunal at issue cannot be classified as a court or tribunal 'of a Member State' within the meaning of Article 267 TFEU,[33] and therefore is not part of the EU judicial system, ie, subject to no appellate jurisdiction nor oversight from the CJEU,[34] the tribunal is unable to make a reference for a preliminary ruling to the CJEU. Third, the judicial review can only be exercised by national courts of Member States 'to the extent that national law permits',[35] and the German Code of Civil Procedure provides only for limited review.

The CJEU therefore concluded that the dispute settlement mechanism in question was calling into question not only the principle of mutual trust between the Member States, but also the preservation of the particular nature of the law established by the EU Treaties, ensured by the preliminary ruling procedure provided for in Article 267 TFEU, and was not therefore compatible with the principle of sincere cooperation.[36]

Following on from this, the Court of Justice ruled in *PL Holdings* that an ad hoc arbitration agreement allowing the continuation of arbitration proceedings which had been initiated on the basis of an arbitration clause identical in content to that contained in the BIT concluded between Belgium and Luxembourg, on the one hand, and Poland, on the other, was incompatible with EU law. As a result, the Court of Justice ruled that, 'that clause is … incompatible with the

[28] Case C-284/16 *Achmea* ECLI:EU:C:2018:158, para 58.
[29] ibid para 35.
[30] ibid para 37.
[31] ibid para 37. See also *Opinion 2/13* ECLIEU:C:2014:2454 (*EU Accession to the ECHR II*), para 176 and the case law cited.
[32] Case C-284/16 *Achmea* (n 28) para 42.
[33] ibid para 46.
[34] ibid para 45.
[35] ibid para 53.
[36] ibid para 58.

principle of sincere cooperation set out in the first subparagraph of Article 4(3) TEU and has an adverse effect on the autonomy of EU law enshrined, inter alia, in Article 344 TFEU'.[37] The Member State is therefore obliged to challenge, before the arbitral tribunal or before the national court with jurisdiction, 'the validity of the arbitration clause or the ad hoc arbitration agreement on the basis of which the dispute was brought before that arbitration body'.[38]

Finally, *Micula*, a case at the crossroads between investment arbitration and state aid law, is also of interest, even though it was handed down by the Court of Justice four months after its judgment in *Komstroy*. Under a BIT concluded in May 2002 between Sweden and Romania, the latter at the time being a third state, investors incorporated in Sweden had initiated their proceedings before an arbitral tribunal under the ICSID Convention. These arbitration proceedings had been initiated on the basis of a BIT concluded between these two states prior to Romania's accession to the EU, and remained in force after the 2007 accession.

The Commission adopted a decision requiring Romania to immediately suspend any action that might lead to the implementation or enforcement of the arbitral award, on the grounds that such an award amounted to illegal state aid. This decision was annulled by the General Court.[39] On appeal, the Grand Chamber of the Court of Justice held that the compensation sought by the claimants who had invested in Romania did not relate exclusively to damage allegedly suffered prior to that state's accession to the EU in 2007. As a result, the dispute which those investors had initiated before the arbitral tribunal had to be regarded as being subject to 'the rules and principles' prohibiting such an arbitral tribunal from breaching Article 267 TFEU and Article 344 TFEU.[40] In this case, the Court of Justice established the principle of the immediate applicability of Union law to the future effects of a situation arising prior to accession to the Union.

7.3.2. The Scope of the Judgment in *Achmea* as Regards the ECT

However, the Court of Justice in these judgments had not settled all the questions concerning the relationship between investment arbitration and EU law. It should be recalled that the ECT – a mixed treaty concluded by the EU – is not, *a priori*, fully comparable to the bilateral investment treaty at the heart of the judgments commented on above.[41]

In *Komstroy*, the Court of Justice held that the fact that the EU is a party to the ECT and thus bound by that treaty does not obliterate the incompatibility

[37] Case C-109/20 *PL Holdings* ECLI:EU:C:2021:875, para 46.
[38] ibid para 52.
[39] Cases T-624/15, T-694/15 and T-704/15 *European Food v Commission* ECLI:EU:T:2019:423.
[40] Case C-638/19 P *Commission v European Food* ECLI:EU:C:2022:50.
[41] Opinion of Advocate General Szpunar, Case C-741/19 *Komstroy* (n 22) para 72.

of the intra-EU ISDS mechanism with EU law. On the one hand, the ECT has the effect of establishing a mechanism of judicial protection outside the national courts of state,[42] while, on the other hand, these arbitral tribunals are likely to interpret a treaty that falls within the scope of EU law without constituting a state court, and thus cooperate with the CJEU.[43]

Although Article 26(6) ECT provides that the arbitral tribunal is to decide the issues in dispute in accordance with the ECT, and 'applicable rules and principles of international law', the Court of Justice ruled that the tribunal in question may be obliged to interpret or even apply EU law.[44] The Court of Justice departed from the reasoning followed by the Stockholm Chamber of Commerce in *FREIF Eurowind Holdings v Spain*, according to which the case law in *Achmea* could not be applied to the ECT on the grounds that the latter, as a mixed agreement, was not akin to an intra-EU BIT.[45] Thus, in *Komstroy*, the Court of Jutice has solemnly affirmed the superiority of EU law over the ECT.

While in French law, the respect of public policy by the arbitral tribunal set up under the ECT is reviewed by the civil courts, the Court of Justice points out, as it did with regard to German procedural law in the *Achmea* case,[46] that the Code of Civil Procedure only provides for a limited review of the jurisdiction of the arbitral tribunal.[47] In contrast to commercial arbitration, where the review is more extensive, there is no safety valve. From there onwards, the ISDS provided for in the ECT is deemed incompatible with EU law when the disputes are between an investor from one Member State and another. In accordance with the principle of loyal cooperation,[48] all Member States must, in line with the *Achmea* and *Komstroy* judgments, denounce the ISDS clauses of intra-EU investment agreements, which is not yet the case for a minority of them,[49] challenge the jurisdiction of any court established at the request of an investor in the context of an intra-EU ISDS dispute, and ensure that their courts find such arbitral awards incompatible with public policy.

On the other hand, the Court of Justice accepts that the ECT may require Member States to comply with the arbitration mechanisms provided for by it with regard to relations with investors from third states. In practical terms, claims initiated by investors from third states (Tajikistan, Kazakhstan, etc) that are parties to the ECT will be adjudicated by arbitral tribunals, as the *Achmea* case law concerns only the intra-EU dimension of ISDS.[50] In effect, the principle

[42] Case C-741/19 *Komstroy* (n 12) paras 51–52.

[43] Opinion of Advocate General Szpunar, Case C-741/19, *Komstroy* (n 22) para 78.

[44] ibid para 75.

[45] Stockholm Chamber of Commerce final award of March 2021, case n. 2017/060 *FREIF Eurowind Holdings v Spain*, para 304.

[46] Case C-284/16 *Achmea* (n 28) para 53.

[47] Case C-741/19 *Komstroy* (n 12) para 57.

[48] Article 4(3) TEU.

[49] Therefore, both the EU and the 26 Member States should denounce Article 26 ECT, at least for intra-EU disputes, or to ratify a modifying treaty providing for a disconnection clause.

[50] Case C-741/19 *Komstroy* (n 12) para 65.

of mutual trust does not apply in relations between the EU Member States and third states, provided that the seat of arbitration is in a non-EU state.[51]

7.3.3. The Concept of 'Investment' in Article 1(6) ECT in the EU Legal Order

Finally, the Court of Justice had to verify whether the electricity supply contract constituted an investment within the meaning of the ECT. Article 1(6) ECT defines the concept of 'investment', as used in the provisions of the ECT, and determines the material scope of the ECT. This provision thus has the effect of triggering the application of the substantive protective provisions of the ECT.

The Court of Justice's reasoning can be broken down into two stages. In order to fall within the definition of investment within the meaning of the first subparagraph of Article 1(6) ECT, two cumulative conditions must be fulfilled. The first condition requires that 'it must concern an asset of a type owned or controlled directly or indirectly by an investor'. Given that a claim arising from a contract for the supply of electricity constitutes an asset held directly by an investor, this condition was satisfied in *Komstroy*.[52] The second condition is more complex. It should be noted that the assets in question should include at least one of the elements referred to in points (a) to (f) listed in the first subparagraph of Article 1(6) ECT. The Court of Justice uses as a potential criterion salient point (c) of the first subparagraph, which states that the concept of 'investment' includes 'claims to money and claims to performance pursuant to [a] contract having an economic value and associated with an investment'.

Although the claim at issue in *Komstroy* was of a fixed amount, and arose from a contract, namely the contract for the supply of electricity concluded between two undertakings,[53] it appeared that that claim did not arise from a contract connected with an investment.[54] In effect, the contractual relationship between the two undertakings concerned only the supply of electricity.

7.4. EU CLIMATE CHANGE POLICY

When the ECT was adopted, the possibility of differentiating among energy sources depending on their impact on the climate crisis was not considered during negotiations. In hindsight, the failure to address this issue seems astounding. In fact, when the ECT was signed in December 1994, the United Nations Framework Convention on Climate Change (UNFCCC) had already been in force since 21 March 1994.

[51] Opinion of Advocate General Szpunar, Case C-741/19 *Komstroy* (n 22) para 87.
[52] Case C-741/19 *Komstroy* (n 12) para 70.
[53] ibid paras 73–74.
[54] ibid para 78.

As the flagship measure of the European Green Deal (EGD) adopted in December 2019 was the adoption in 2021 of a European Climate Law,[55] that requires a drastic reduction in GHG emissions in a variety of sectors such as industry, transport, energy, agriculture and the heating and cooling of buildings. The aim is to achieve negative emissions after 2050. All in all, the EGD intended to create the largest shockwave since the creation of the single market in 1986 by turning the European Union (EU) into the first decarbonised (achieving carbon neutrality by 2050) and circular economy in the world aiming at zero pollution. In addition, the lending policy of the European Investment Bank (EIB), adopted by EU finance ministers in December 2019, is to phase out the financing of unabated fossil fuel energy. Furthermore, national courts in various Member States have increasingly adjudicated claims brought by city councils, NGOs and citizens concerning climate inaction, taking account of climate obligations under EU secondary law.[56]

While the forthcoming EU climate and energy measures will increase investment in green energy (renewables, hydrogen, etc), they will lead to a significant decline in fossil fuel investment across Europe and affect the rights of foreign investors under the ECT. Critics have been arguing that the ECT could undermine the EU's 2050 carbon neutrality target.[57] These fears were not exaggerated. Through its private arbitration mechanism, the ECT was likely to hold a sword of Damocles over national authorities that decide to move away from fossil fuels.[58]

In fact, the ECT has become the most litigated investment agreement in the world, with the majority of disputes being of an intra-EU nature. It has already given rise to more than 136 disputes, the vast majority of which involve Member States, with Spain currently the main target for private investors. It must be noted that under the ECT, the majority of the claims are brought in relation to renewable energy, and not fossil fuel production. In 2012, Vattenfall claimed EUR 4.7 billion from Germany to compensate for its alleged losses due to the phase-out of nuclear reactors. By the same token, the German company RWE claimed EUR 1.4 billion in compensation from the Netherlands for phasing out coal by 2030. Against this background, the ECT could prompt a regulatory chill. In order to avoid being taken to court, several national authorities could delay the energy transition. What is more, with the enlargement of the EU to

[55] Regulation (EU) 2021/1119 of the European Parliament and of the Council of 30 June 2021 establishing the framework for achieving climate neutrality [2021] OJ L243/1.

[56] In the Netherlands, see Case C-19/0035 *Urgenda* [2019] HR: 2019: 2006. In Germany, see BvR 2656/18, 1 BvR 96/20, 1 BvR 288/20, 1 BvR 78/20. In France, see Council of State, *Grande-Synthe*, FR:CECHR:2021:427301.2021070. In Belgium, see Brussels Court of Appeal, *Klimaatzaak*, 30 November 2021. See N de Sadeleer 'Belgian public authorities held liable for flawed climate policy: Klimaatzaak case' (2024) 24 *Elni Review* 4–11.

[57] For more on this debate, see ch 13.

[58] N de Sadeleer, 'L'avenir de la Charte de l'énergie: comment accommoder la protection des investisseurs à la transition énergétique', Blog de droit européen, Working paper 8/2022.

CEE states in 2004, and the development of a single energy market within the EU, the ECT has lost its initial relevance for the EU. The EU and several of its Member States had been expressing the view that it was necessary to align the ECT with the Paris Agreement, and to abolish the ISDS procedure provided for in Article 26 ECT.

In order to modernise the ECT, the modernisation group established by the Energy Charter Conference held 15 formal negotiation rounds between July 2020 and June 2022. After two years of intense negotiations, a tentative agreement was reached on 24 June 2022 among 53 Contracting Parties for the modernised ECT. In the absence of an EU position, the EU was unable to vote on the adoption of the modernised ECT at this conference.

The ECT Secretariat took the view that the modernised ECT will have a much stronger climate focus, will be aligned with the objectives of the Paris Agreement and will support the global energy transition while ensuring affordable energy for all.[59] By the same token, the European Commission considered in 2022 that, once approved and ratified, the modernised ECT will facilitate sustainable investments in the energy sector by creating a coherent and up-to-date framework and will fully preserve the EU's ability to develop its climate policies.[60] It must be noted that a disconnection clause for Regional Economic Integration Organisations (REIOs) has been included in the modernised treaty with a view to assuaging EU's objections. Given that the only REIO under the ECT is the EU, this provision was deemed to exclude intra-EU investment disputes from the scope of the modernised ECT. Such an exclusion appeared to be in line with the *Komstroy* judgment.

Although the modernised treaty was negotiated by the European Commission within the mandate given to it by the Council of Ministers, we took the view in 2023 that this modernised treaty would affect the competences of the Member States. Indeed, the extra-EU ISDS regime that is maintained in the new treaty was likely to cover new investments, notably in the field of biofuels, biomass and synthetic fuels. In addition, it was unlikely that the modernisation of the ECT would end the extra-EU ISDS mechanism, which as a matter of principle does not fall within the scope of exclusive EU competence.

Furthermore, the modernised ECT makes changes to the ISDS (third party financing) procedures.[61] Lastly, it revises the fair and equitable treatment clause[62] which will change the way arbitral tribunals review government measures related to portfolio investments. Straddling exclusive (direct investment, energy) and shared (indirect investment, dispute settlement) competences, the modernised ECT – if it is to see the light of day – will not only have to be concluded by the

[59] Communication of the Secretary General on the modernisation of the Energy Charter Treaty, 1 July 2022.

[60] DG Trade, Agreement in principle reached on Modernised Energy Charter Treaty.

[61] New provision, Part IV.

[62] Article 10.

Council of the EU, with the prior approval of the European Parliament,[63] but it will also have to be ratified by national parliaments.

The Energy Charter Conference of 22 November 2022 should have unanimously adopted the ECT modernisation agreement. While the Union and the 26 Member States (Italy no longer being a party since 2016) could, in accordance with the principle of loyal cooperation, have formed a united front so that the modernisation of the ECT could have been initiated, France, Germany, Spain and the Netherlands abstained during the COREPER vote on 18 November 2022. As unanimity was not possible at this stage, the Conference of the Parties decided on 22 November to postpone the approval of the amending agreement. It was therefore a case of squaring the circle. On the one hand, it was doubtful that the Council of Ministers would have been able to reach a qualified majority due to opposition from several Member States. Moreover, for the Council to conclude the modernised treaty, the European Parliament would have to approve the reform. In a resolution adopted on Wednesday 23 November 2022, the European Parliament clearly stated its opposition to the conclusion of the modernisation treaty. On the other hand, since the modernised treaty covers mainly exclusive competences, individual Member States will not be able to adopt it. Finally, it became clear that the revised ECT was not matching the EU's climate change ambition. On 30 May 2024, having obtained the European Parliament's approval, the Council of the EU agreed upon the EU and Euratom's withdrawal from the ECT.[64] This withdrawal was notified on 27 June 2024.

There was an absence of consensus between EU Member States whether to support the modernised treaty. It must be noted that amendments to the ECT must be adopted by unanimity by the Conference. On 3 December 2024, the ECT Conference adopted, at the statutory session of its 35th meeting, the decision on the modernisation of the ECT. Given the EU withdrawal, the Member States still party to the ECT had to vote themselves. The amendments are supposed to enter provisionally in force from 3 September 2025.

Lastly, the modernised ECT which is provisionally in force will not resolve every problem for the EU. While it will no longer be possible for a German investor to bring its dispute against the Belgian authorities before an arbitration tribunal, an investor with its registered office in the UK will still be able to bypass the Belgian courts by bringing a case before an arbitration tribunal. As a result, the tribunal could interpret EU law. Consequently, arbitral tribunals instituted under the ECT are likely to continue to claim that they have jurisdiction to adjudicate investment cases related to investments in a Member State,

[63] Article 218(6) TFEU.

[64] Council Decision (EU) 2024/1638 of 30 May 2024 on the withdrawal of the Union from the Energy Charter Treaty, OJ L 2024/1638; Council Decision (EU) 2024/1677 of 30 May 2024 on the approval of the withdrawal of the European Atomic Energy Community from the Energy Charter Treaty, OJ L 2024/1677.

departing from the *Achmea–Komstroy* case law.[65] The question thus arises as to whether the ISDS mechanism provided for in Article 26 ECT is compatible with the standards laid down by the Court of Justice in *Opinion 1/17*.[66]

In addition to Italy, which denounced the ECT in 2016, France and Spain have been denouncing the ECT. Furthermore, Poland, Germany, Spain, Portugal, Slovenia, the Netherlands and Luxembourg are considering denouncing the ECT.[67] The Member States that have so far denounced the ECT have been abrogating the consent that they gave to arbitration.

However, by virtue of the ECT sunset clause, these Member States could still be sued by investors, for a period of 20 years after their decision to denounce the treaty.[68] Italy is a case in point. Since its denunciation of the ECT in 2016, this Member State has been facing seven claims based on the ECT sunset clause, for an amount of USD 400 million. By way of illustration, following Italy's adoption of a law in 2015 prohibiting offshore production within a certain distance of the Italian coastline due to environmental concerns, earthquake risks, as well as strong opposition from local residents, the UK-based company Rockhopper, which was planning to develop an oil and gas field at Ombrina Mare, located less than 12 miles off the Italian coast in the Adriatic Sea, referred the matter to an ICSID arbitration tribunal. On 23 August 2022, the tribunal ordered Italy to pay EUR 190 million in compensation to the British investor.[69] In international investment law, the sunset clause is nothing exceptional given that 97% of 2,061 BITs enshrine such a clause.[70] Nonetheless, in contrast to most BITs, the 20-year period is rather long.[71]

The question therefore arises as to whether the sunset clause of the ECT could prevent denunciation. In fact, these clauses are not permanent, as states can neutralise them by concluding an amending treaty or a so-called inter se agreement, followed by the denunciation of the original investment treaty. Thus, the obstacle could be overcome. Indeed, in the past, several states have done

[65] However, there has been recently an exception to this. In *Green Power Partners K/S SCE and SCE Solar Don Benito APS v The Kingdom of Spain* (SCC Arbitration V (2016/135)) ('*Green Power*'), the arbitral tribunal held on 16 June 2022 that it had no jurisdiction to adjudicate the case on the grounds that it was bound by the primacy of EU law.

[66] I Damjanovic and N de Sadeleer, 'Values and objectives of the EU in light of Opinion 1/17: "Trade for all", above all' [2020] 4(1): 6 *Europe and the World: A law review*. On 16 June 2022, the CJEU delivered its Opinion on Belgium's request on the compatibility of intra-EU investor-state arbitration under a modernised text of the ECT with EU law. The CJEU found that it 'does not have sufficient information on the actual content of the envisaged agreement and that, therefore, the present request for an Opinion, on account of its premature nature, must be regarded as inadmissible'. *Opinion 1/20* ECLI:EU:C:2022:485 (*Modernised Energy Charter Treaty*), para 48.

[67] Article 47 ECT fleshes out Article 54 on the Law of Treaties.

[68] Article 47(3) ECT.

[69] *Rockhopper Exploration Plc, Rockhopper Italia SpA and Rockhopper Mediterranean Ltd v Italian Republic*, ICSID Case No ARB/17/1.

[70] European Parliament, *Sunset Clauses in International Law and their Consequences for EU Law*, January 2022, p 23.

[71] Indeed, 85% of IIAs containing a survival clause refer to a period of less than 20 years; most provide for a period of 10 years or less.

so by denouncing sunset clauses in bilateral investment treaties between themselves. Last but not least, in its resolution of 24 November 2022, the European Parliament calls for the conclusion of such an agreement.[72]

7.5. CONCLUSION

In *Komstroy*, the Court of Justice applied its reasoning from the *Achmea* judgment as regards the compatibility of the dispute settlement mechanism provided for in Article 26 ECT, regardless of the fact that this is a mixed agreement. Indeed, the fact that the EU is a party to the ECT, and is therefore bound by it, does not change anything. The autonomy of EU law definitively prevails over international investment law, at least as regards intra-EU investments.

A fundamental principle of mutual trust obliges the investors in intra-EU disputes to rely on the national courts of the host Member States, whether Romanian or Bulgarian. Moreover, given that EU law guarantees sufficient protection for intra-EU investments (principles of non-discrimination, proportionality, legal certainty, and protection of legitimate expectations, etc[73]), and that investors enjoy effective judicial protection before national courts, there was little point in maintaining the effects of ISDS provided for by BITs or the ECT any longer.[74]

By involving the national courts in accordance with Article 19(1) TEU, second paragraph, the reference for a preliminary ruling procedure has become the 'keystone'[75] of the EU judicial system. Accordingly, national courts are the guarantors of the correct implementation of EU law. However, the *Komstroy* judgment will not put an immediate end to the tug-of-war between the proponents of the EU orthodoxy and the number of arbitral tribunals that tend to disregard the case law of the Court of Justice.

[72] Joint Motion for a Resolution on the outcome of the modernisation of the Energy Charter Treaty (2022/2934(RSP)).

[73] See, for instance, Case C-390/12 *Pfleger and Others* ECLI:EU:C:2014:281, paras 30–37.

[74] In this connection, see, Opinion of Advocate General Szpunar, Case C-741/19, *Komstroy* (n 22) para 65.

[75] Case C-284/16 *Achmea* (n 28) para 37.

8

State Compliance with Intra-EU Investment Awards or the EU 'Elephant' in the Investment 'Porcelain Shop'

SZILÁRD GÁSPÁR-SZILÁGYI

8.1. INTRODUCTION[1]

THE EU'S ENTRY into the field of international investment law (IIL) and investment treaty arbitration (ITA) is more akin to the unwanted presence of an elephant in a porcelain shop, than the smooth entry of a new actor into a system of international law with established rules and practices, which all actors of the system ought to obey. Many will find this comparison of IIL's enforcement mechanism to a 'porcelain shop' slightly cynical, since IIL is often hailed or criticised for offering an enforcement system under international law to private investors, which is unmatched by other systems of international law.[2]

However, as those involved in research on the politics of state compliance with investment arbitration awards are in the process of realising, the compliance mechanism(s) in IIL is not as robust as often assumed. Just like a porcelain shop, it contains many hard elements, but any sudden move can easily shatter it. IIL compliance is a complex and often fragile system based on multiple, overlapping rules and variables, including the losing state's willingness to comply,

[1] The author would like to thank the editors of this volume and Maxim Usynin for their valuable comments. The research for this chapter was funded by the Norwegian Research Council, Project No 326269, 'Compliance Politics and International Investment Disputes'.

[2] Van Harten is one of the established critics of ITA. See Gus Van Harten and Martin Loughlin, 'Investment Treaty Arbitration as a Species of Global Administrative Law' (2006) 17(1) *EJIL* 121, 127–31.

protracted domestic enforcement and/or set-aside proceedings, and, more recently, conflicting legal orders.

This intricacy and fragility are evidenced by the complex questions faced by anyone who wishes to research state compliance with ITA awards: What exactly is meant by 'compliance' with an ITA award? How can such compliance be measured? What is the source of the data, and can it be confirmed by other sources? How far down the rabbit-hole of never-ending local enforcement and/or set-aside proceedings, interviews with lawyers, newspaper articles, and government decisions must one go? And, as the effects of the *Commission v Micula*[3] judgment of the Court of Justice of the European Union (CJEU) illustrate, when is a case truly over? An investor who had been fully paid by the respondent state in 2019 is now being faced with further lawsuits to have the moneys received as damages returned.[4]

Therefore, given this intricate system of compliance for which data is scarce, the EU's entry into the system, and the EU's demands that the system change in order to comply with the rules of EU law, is comparable to an elephant not only entering but barging into a porcelain shop, an action which has serious consequences.

Since the contributing authors to this volume are all experts on the relationship between the EU legal order and investment law, this chapter will not delve too much into topics that have already been well-researched in those chapters, and the literature at large. Thus, it will not go over some of the major milestones in EU investment law and policy after the post-Lisbon era,[5] such as the adoption of the Grandfathering Regulation,[6] *Opinion 2/15*,[7] or the adoption of the FDI Screening Regulation.[8] Instead, this chapter will focus on the issue of state compliance with intra-EU investment awards, concluding

[3] Case C-638/19 P *European Commission v European Food* ECLI:EU:C:2022:50, referred to in this chapter as *Commission v Micula*.

[4] Several Romanian news outlets reported in April 2022 that following the Court of Justice's judgment in the *Commission v Micula* appeal, the Romanian National Agency for Fiscal Administration (ANAF) began proceedings to recover the damages paid in 2019. A local tribunal suspended the freezing of the assets of the Micula brothers. See Adrian Artene, 'Statul român a început executarea silită a imperiului fraților Micula, dar o instanță din Beiuș s-a pus de-a curmezișul! Miza: 395 milioane de euro! ANAF încearcă să recupereze astfel despăgubirile achitate cu o grabă suspectă' (*Gândul*, 29 April 2022).

[5] For an overview of the major steps until 2018, see Szilárd Gáspár-Szilágyi, '*Quo Vadis* EU Investment Law and Policy? The Shaky Path Towards the International Promotion of EU Rules' (2018) 23(2) *EFAR* 167. See also Guillaume van der Loo and Michael Hahn, 'EU Trade and Investment Policy since the Treaty of Lisbon. Achievements and Future Priorities' (2020) CEPS Research Report.

[6] Regulation (EU) No 1219/2012 of the European Parliament and of the Council of 12 December 2012 establishing transitional arrangements for bilateral investment agreements between Member States and third countries (EU Grandfathering Regulation) [2012] OJ L351/40.

[7] *Opinion 2/15* ECLI:EU:C:2017:376 (*EU-Singapore FTA*).

[8] Regulation (EU) 2019/452 of the European Parliament and of the Council of 19 March 2019 establishing a framework for the screening of foreign direct investments into the Union [2019] OJ LI 79/1.

that the EU's insistence on another system, IIL, complying with EU law is problematic.

This chapter explains why – in the author's view – *Achmea*,[9] *PL Holdings*,[10] *Komstroy*,[11] and *Commission v Micula*, not only create unnecessary complexity for investors, states, and the Commission alike, but they also cause unforeseen consequences for judicial certainty, comity, the enforcement of Member States' existing international obligations, the issue of compliance, and they have the potential of undermining the enforcement of EU law obligations as well. It is a case of how the actions of overzealous EU institutions such as the Commission and the Court of Justice, in a field which they do not fully understand, have created several unforeseen results.

To substantiate this chapter's main arguments, the introduction is followed by a broader discussion in section 8.2 on compliance with investment arbitration awards and the difficulties posed by the *Achmea* and *Komstroy* judgments. Section 8.3 will then use the enforcement cases that have resulted from the first *Micula v Romania* ICSID award of 2013, and the judgment in *Commission v Micula* before the Court of Justice,[12] to highlight the multiple strands of complexity created by the elephant's movements in the porcelain shop. Before concluding, section 8.4 focuses in more detail on some of the unforeseen consequences of these recent 'movements' of the EU, taking the view that there is no current way of squaring the circle, since neither system is willing to give priority to the other.

8.2. THINKING ABOUT COMPLIANCE

8.2.1. The 'Porcelain Shop'

The Cambridge Dictionary defines 'compliance' as the 'act of obeying a particular law or rule, or of acting according to an agreement'.[13] Using this definition, the mechanisms of compliance and what is meant by compliance will differ depending on the perspectives taken.

From the perspective of *international law*, compliance means that states and other actors in the system, such as regional and international organisations, should obey the international 'agreements' they conclude, and/or other 'laws or rules' of international law, such as customary international law, general principles, or the rulings of an international court or tribunal which is binding on

[9] Case C-284/16 *Achmea* ECLI:EU:C:2017:699.
[10] Case C-109/20 *PL Holdings* ECLI:EU:C:2021:875.
[11] Case C-741/19 *Komstroy* ECLI:EU:C:2021:655.
[12] For a commentary see Szilárd Gáspár-Szilágyi and Maxim Usynin, 'Does the Court of Justice of the EU Misunderstand Investment Law and Investment Treaty Arbitration in *European Commission v. Micula*?' (2022) 7 *EILAR* 53.
[13] Cambridge Dictionary, 'Compliance'.

them. Thus, from the perspective of *international investment law*, a branch of international law, this implies that states and other actors that can conclude international agreements must obey their obligations under various international investment agreements (IIAs), as well as those arising from the ICSID Convention, the NY Convention, ITA awards, and so forth. By example, a party to an ICSID arbitration derives obligations from the ICSID Convention, the underlying IIA that allowed for the commencement of arbitration, and the arbitral award.

If the term 'compliance with international investment law' is narrowed down to 'compliance with ITA awards', then there is no agreed way of measuring such compliance. From a purely legalistic perspective, the payment in full of the damages by the state (whether as a direct payment or an indirect offsetting, for example, of taxes owed by the foreign investor) would amount to compliance. However, following the Court of Justice's *Commission v Micula* judgment, not even the payment of the damages owed to the investor is a certainty. From the perspective of *political science*, compliance could also mean a settlement agreement (often not public) between the foreign investor and the host state, following the ITA award, or it could mean the changing of local laws in the host state, or even the receiving of other types of concessions by the investor. From this perspective, compliance could mean any benefit accruing to the investor following the award, which is not necessarily the payment of damages. In short, once examined thoroughly, compliance with ITA awards becomes intricate, hard to define, and difficult to measure.

From the perspective of *EU law*, compliance means that institutions of the EU, its Member States, and even private parties, should obey the EU Treaties and the EU Charter of Fundamental Rights, the general principles of EU law, international agreements concluded by the EU, secondary EU legislation, and rulings of the CJEU. From the perspective of *EU Member States*, the notion of compliance is even more expansive, as it includes compliance by the state, its institutions, and private parties with various obligations under international law, EU law, and national law.

Lastly, from the perspective of a *non-EU state*, compliance means that its institutions and private parties must obey that state's international obligations, national laws, and regulations. It follows from the above that compliance entails differing degrees of complexity, depending on whether it is looked at from the perspective of international law, investment law, EU law, EU Member State law, or non-EU state law.

The dictionary definition of compliance only mentions 'obeyance' of the rules, laws, or agreements, but it does not mention the nature of this obeyance. Thus, obeyance could be *voluntary*, meaning that the actor willingly obeys the rules, or it could also be *compelled* obeyance, meaning that the actor is coerced in one form or another to obey the rules. There is often no fine line between voluntary and compelled compliance, and because of this, state compliance with international rules is an oft-debated topic in legal and political science literature.[14] For example, Stiansen's research into state compliance with judgments of the European Court of Human Rights (ECtHR) has shown that if the ECtHR's judgments contain specific remedies in them, and if strong domestic mechanisms of accountability are present in the state (civil society, media, independent courts, and such), the likelihood and speed of compliance is higher.[15] Thus, the clarity of international remedies and some form of coercion from and accountability to domestic actors can positively influence compliance.

However, these are not all the factors that can induce states to comply with their international obligations. Looking at investment law, on the surface, there are strong legal mechanisms in force to induce compliance. In the ICSID system, Articles 53 and 54 of the ICSID Convention make awards rendered pursuant to the ICSID Convention binding on the contracting parties, who must treat them as final judgments of their domestic courts, which cannot be reviewed and set aside.[16] In non-ICSID cases, Article III of the 1958 New York Convention states that arbitral awards (even though the New York Convention refers to commercial ones and not investment ones) are binding on the contracting parties, and recognition and enforcement may only be refused by the state where enforcement is sought on the limited grounds mentioned in Article V. However, not even ICSID awards are bullet proof, as some states might have sovereign immunity laws which allow for the recognition of the ICSID award but will not allow for the execution of it by freezing the assets of a foreign sovereign.[17] Furthermore, states might not have assets in the state where recognition and enforcement is sought, and domestic courts might not have experience with IIL.

There are also obvious cases of non-compliance when the losing state deliberately refuses to comply with an ITA award, and the legal mechanisms in place will not reach their intended aims. In such cases, an investor must hope that its home state and other states will apply political or financial pressure on the losing state that could induce some form of compliance. Such compliance will often entail a 'haircut' to the claims of the various creditors or some indirect, partial payment. Looking at the case of Argentina's compliance with the investment awards that it had lost, Hirsch found that some form of 'compliance' could

[14] See for example Clifford J Carrubba and Matthew J Gabel, 'International Courts and the Performance of International Agreements: A General Theory with Evidence from the European Union' (Cambridge University Press, 2015); Diana Kapiszewski and Matthew M Taylor, 'Compliance: conceptualizing, measuring, and explaining adherence to judicial rulings' (2013) 38(4) *Law & Social Inquiry* 803.

[15] Øyvind Stiansen, 'Directing Compliance? Remedial Approach and Compliance with European Court of Human Rights Judgments' (2021) 51 *British Journal of Political Science* 899.

[16] Stanimir A Alexandrov, 'Enforcement of ICSID Awards: Articles 53 and 54 of the ICSID Convention' (2009) *TDM* 1.

[17] See Andrea K Bjorklund, Lukas Vanhonnaeker and Jean-Michel Marcoux, 'State Immunity as a Defense to Resist the Enforcement of ICSID Awards' (2020) 35(3) *ICSID Review* 506; Michael Douglas and Claudia Carr, 'The Commercial Exceptions to Foreign State Immunity' (2006) 45 *Federal Law Review* 445; August Reinisch, 'European Court Practice Concerning State Immunity from Enforcement Measures' (2006) 17 *EJIL* 803.

still be induced in certain situations when the legal channels fail, and the state refuses to comply.[18] As mentioned, from a legal perspective, this type of compliance does not really meet the definition of 'compliance', since the states actively decide *not to* comply with the awards.

Looking at Argentina's compliance with ICSID awards through three theoretical lenses – a realist one, a social constructivist one, and a liberal one – Hirsch found that the period prior to 2013 'reveals that the decisions *not to comply* with a series of ICSID awards were significantly influenced by factors highlighted by the constructivist approach, mainly the "legitimacy deficit" of ICSID tribunals, as well as ideological hostility and collective memories of foreign interventions'.[19] Post-2013, however, 'realist–rational choice factors [such as Argentina's access to international financial markets, the depletion of foreign currency reserves, as well as discussions with the "Paris club",[20] and the International Monetary Fund] had considerably influenced the decision by the government of Argentina to reach the settlement agreement in mid-October 2013 and substantially comply with the ICSID awards'.[21]

Whilst these non-legal means of inducing compliance might ensure, in the end, that investors are directly or indirectly paid the damages owed to them or at least a part of them, they are a telling case that the IIL system of enforcement is less robust than one might think, and resorting to non-legal means of inducing compliance will depend on the willingness of the home state to exert such pressure, and the existence of factors in the host state that in the end might prompt some form of compliance.

Gaillard and Penushliski's empirical assessment of state compliance with 70% of the existing investment awards in 2019 has found that there can be serious cases of *non-compliance*, as exemplified by the Argentine situation pre-2013, Russia's and Venezuela's refusal to comply with investment awards, as well as the refusal of some EU Member States to comply with intra-EU awards post-*Achmea*, all of which can lead to the re-politicisation of investment disputes.[22] As they note, states may choose not to comply with the awards if the same situation leads to multiple awards (eg Argentina's financial crisis, Spain's renewable energy laws), if the awards are exorbitantly large (eg the Yukos award against Russia), or due to political reasons or questions surrounding the correctness of the awards.[23]

[18] Moshe Hirsch, 'Explaining Compliance and Non-Compliance with ICSID Awards: The Argentine Case Study and a Multiple Theoretical Approach' (2016) 19 *JIEL* 681. See also Daniel Peat, 'Perception and Process: Towards a Behavioural Theory of Compliance' (2022) 13 *JIDS* 179.

[19] ibid 698, emphasis added.

[20] See Paris Club/Club de Paris.

[21] Hirsch (n 18) 702.

[22] Emmanuel Gaillard and Ilija M Penushliski, 'State Compliance with Investment Awards' (2020) 35(3) *ICSID Review* 540. See also Nicola Strain et al, 'Compliance Politics and International Investment Disputes: A New Dataset' (2024) 27(1) *Journal of International Economic Law* 70.

[23] ibid 588–89. One of the main weaknesses of this study, as the authors recognise, is that they cannot verify the veracity of some of the information used in the study, as most of the data on compliance relies on newspaper articles or other open-source materials.

In conclusion, compliance with ITA awards is not strictly in the legal domain, and a state might have various incentives and disincentives to comply with an ITA award.

8.2.2. Methodological Difficulties

As the above examples show, testing the 'robustness' of a compliance system is not at all straightforward, and empirically testing compliance with ITA awards turns out to be very difficult. Thus, any broad comments that IIL's system of enforcement is robust, and/or one of a kind, should be made with reservations.

Firstly, there are no centralised databases in IIL in which compliance with ITA awards can be checked and assessed. Therefore, one needs to gather information (and often triangulate to confirm the veracity of that information) from various sources, including newspapers, interviews with the legal representatives of the investors, and government decisions setting aside a part of the annual budget or supplementing the budget to comply with the award. For example, when gathering data on compliance with the *Gavazzi v Romania*[24] ICSID award, there was no public information about the payment of the award. The only way to gather information was to contact the legal representatives of the investor, who confirmed that the state had paid, but only after the investors brought local enforcement proceedings before the Bucharest Tribunal, the judgment of which was appealed to the Bucharest Court of Appeals.[25]

Secondly, the amount of information and cut-off point needed to test whether compliance had occurred is often difficult to know. In non-ICSID cases, many against Russia for example, local set-aside proceedings often become so numerous that it is not possible to follow up on every single case.[26] In ICSID and non-ICSID cases alike, one is often faced with numerous and seemingly never-ending domestic enforcement and recognition proceedings, such as in the now infamous *Micula* case, which has so far involved both the General Court and the Court of Justice, US courts,[27] Belgian courts,[28] Swedish courts,[29] UK courts,[30]

[24] *Marco Gavazzi and Stefano Gavazzi v Romania*, ICSID Case No ARB/12/25, Award of the Tribunal of 18 April 2017.

[25] *Gavazzi et al v Statul Român prin Ministerul Finanţelor Public* – Tribunalul Bucureşti/Bucharest Tribunal, 20461/3/2018, Secţia a IV-a Civilă; *Gavazzi Gavazzi et al v Statul Român prin Ministerul Finanţelor Public* – Curtea de Apel Bucureşti/Bucharest Court of Appeal, 20461/2018.

[26] A great example being the never-ending enforcement and set-aside proceedings in the *Sedelmayer v Russia* (SCC) and *Yukos v Russia* (PCA case No 2005-04/AA227) cases.

[27] United States Court of Appeals for the District of Columbia Circuit, *Ioan Micula, et al v Government of Romania*, No 19-7127, Judgment.

[28] Cour d'Appel Bruxelles, *Micula v ROMATSA*, No 2016/AR/293 & 2016/AR/394, Arrêt 12 March 2019.

[29] Nacka tingsrätt, *Ioan Micula, et al v Rumänien*, Protokoll 2019-01-23.

[30] UK Supreme Court, *Micula and others v Romania*, Judgment, 19 February 2020.

and Romanian[31] courts. And, even when the state pays the money, the investor cannot be certain that the state will not later try to recover it, as shown by the effects of *Commission v Micula*.[32]

In summary, compliance with investment arbitration awards is an intricate system with numerous problematic areas that speak more about its fragility than its robustness. Its intactness depends on a variety of non-exhaustive legal and non-legal variables, such as:

- the rules under which the arbitration was brought and under which domestic set-aside, enforcement, or recognition is or can be sought,
- domestic rules on sovereign immunity, public policy, etc,
- potential conflicts with supranational or national rules,
- the clarity of the remedies in investment arbitration (mostly the payment of damages and interest),
- the presence of vocal domestic actors which are in favour of or against the investment law and arbitration system,
- the ideological leanings of the respondent government,
- the perceived correctness of the decisions,
- the amount of the compensation, or
- the respondent state's ability to raise international capital and financial help.

8.2.3. 'The Elephant Enters the Porcelain Shop'

From the aforementioned paragraphs, it can be concluded that the compliance system of IIL is understudied, intricate, and not as robust as it might have been thought, with many moving parts and some noticeable cracks in it. Following amendments to the EU Treaties by the Treaty of Lisbon, the EU was given the competence to enter the porcelain shop. First, it was the trunk (the Grandfathering Regulation), then the head (*Opinion 2/15*), followed by the body (*Achmea* and *Opinion 1/17*), and finally the tail, which started wiggling around (*Komstroy*, *PL Holdings*, and *Commission v Micula*). The main issues stem from the fact that the EU brought its own system of compliance into an existing system of compliance and insists that an already shaky system should now change its ways to accommodate this new compliance mechanism.

It is well known that Member State compliance with EU law is very robust, the CJEU often mentioning a 'complete system of legal remedies'.[33] Most of these methods of compliance represent a robust legal system in which multiple

[31] Curtea Constituţională, Decizie nr 887, 15 December 2015.
[32] Case C-638/19 P *European Commission v Micula* ECLI:EU:C:2022:50.
[33] Case 294/83 *Les Verts* ECLI:EU:C:1986:166, para 23.

actors can induce compliance, such as the EU institutions (Articles 258 and 260 TFEU, Article 7 TEU, and Regulation 2020/2092 on rule of law conditionality), other Member States (Article 259 TFEU), national courts (Article 267 TFEU), and, very importantly, private parties via the doctrines of primacy, direct and indirect effect, and state liability. All these methods are tucked into a nebulous concept[34] created by the CJEU, called the 'autonomy of the EU legal order'.

The problem is that unlike investment law – which is a creation of public international law, albeit sharing some features with private arbitration – EU law as a system is still struggling to find its place between international and national law. As Odermatt argues, the simultaneous conception of EU law as 'domestic law, international law, and "an independent source of law" potentially allows the CJEU to interpret any international agreement to which the EU is a party'.[35] The CJEU then uses the nebulous and constantly changing concept of 'autonomy' (which some authors call a structural principal[36]) as an *ex ante/post* constitutionality check for previously assumed international obligations under EU and Member State international agreements, such as those under intra-EU bilateral investment treaties (BITs), the Energy Charter Treaty, or the new generation of EU trade and investment agreements.

Moreover, the often cryptic and vague language of the CJEU's judgments does not help. As Stiansen noted, state compliance can increase if the international (supranational) tribunal indicates precise remedies. However, in *Achmea*, the remedy for incompatibility is not indicated, and from the judgment the extent of incompatibility is unclear. As several scholars have noted, the Court of Justice's repeated usage of the term 'such as', and its reference to Article 8 of the Netherlands-Slovak BIT, could easily be interpreted in the sense that only those provisions of intra-EU BITs were incompatible with EU law that were 'such as' the BIT provision in question.[37] Furthermore, from *Achmea*, it follows that only the investor-state arbitration provisions of intra-EU BITs are incompatible with EU law.[38] Other provisions for dispute resolution under intra-EU BITs, such as state-to-state arbitration, mediation, and conciliation, as well as all the remaining provisions of intra-EU BITs are *compatible* with EU law. Therefore, termination of the entirety of those BITs is not required but only an amendment/removal of their investor-state arbitration clauses.

[34] See Mads Andenas and Cristina Contartese, 'EU Autonomy and Investor-State Dispute Settlement under *Inter Se* Agreements between EU Member States: *Achmea*' (2019) 56 *CMLR* 157.

[35] Jedd Odermatt, 'Is EU Law International? Case C-741/19 Republic of Moldova v Komstroy LLC and the Autonomy of the EU Legal Order' (2021) 6(3) *European Papers* 1255, 1266.

[36] Niamh Nic Shuibhne, 'What is the Autonomy of EU Law, and Why Does that Matter?' (2019) 88(1) *Nordic Journal of International Law* 9.

[37] See Alan Dashwood, 'Article 26 ECT and Intra-EU Disputes – the Case against an Expansive Reading of *Achmea*' (2021) 4 *ELR* 415; Von Daniel Thym, 'The CJEU Ruling in Achmea: Death Sentence for Autonomous Investment Protection Tribunals' (EU Law Analysis Blog, 2018); Szilárd Gáspár-Szilágyi, 'It is Not Just About Investor-State Arbitration. A Look at Case C-284/16, *Achmea BV*' (2018) 3(1) *European Papers* 357.

[38] Case C-284/16 *Achmea* ECLI:EU:C:2017:699, operative part.

It is no wonder then that there was no consensus among all EU Member States to terminate their intra-EU BITs, and there was no consensus among the national courts of EU Member States on what to do with the recognition and enforcement of intra-EU awards.[39] Given this confusion that stems from the vague language of the *Achmea* judgment, it is also no wonder that intra-EU investor-state tribunals have criticised the judgment, and with the exception of *Green Power v Spain*, SCC tribunal,[40] all other intra-EU investment tribunals have refused to decline their jurisdiction.[41]

There was no indication whatsoever in *Achmea* that the same logic would apply to the ECT in an intra-EU setting, or to private agreements. Nevertheless, in the subsequent *Komstroy* judgment, the Court of Justice decided to go on a tangent and hold, *obiter*, that there is an incompatibility between the ECT in an intra-EU setting and EU law,[42] even though the referring national court *did not* ask the Court of Justice to discuss this issue and the case itself *did not* concern an intra-EU event. This makes it very difficult for an arbitral tribunal constituted under the ECT, a Member State involved in an intra-EU ECT arbitration, or a national court to take the *Komstroy* judgment seriously.

Komstroy points to the difficulty of the elephant being in an environment it does not fully understand, an environment which has its own system of compliance, with complex rules and variables for enforcement, in which vaguely worded judgments about incompatibility with an even vaguer concept of autonomy are not well appreciated. To this complex system, EU Member States that are respondents in intra-EU arbitrations must now add:

- the incompatibility with the autonomy of EU law of intra-EU investment awards,
- possible infringement cases brought by the European Commission,
- vaguely worded CJEU judgments, and
- possible illegal state aid investigations brought by the European Commission.

In the next section, the difficulties caused by EU law to the enforcement of the *Micula* award and all the unforeseen consequences will be examined, which, instead of increasing uniformity and certainty, have created a lot of uncertainty and have resulted in numerous protracted enforcement cases.

[39] Only 23 EU States signed the 'Agreement for the Termination of Bilateral Investment Treaties Between the Members States of the European Union', Austria, Finland and Sweden not signing it; see also section 8.3.2.2 of this chapter discussing the Svea Court of Appeal's decision in *PL Holdings*.

[40] *Green Power K/S and Obton A/S v Spain*, SCC Case No 2016/135. See Cosmo Sanderson, 'Tribunal Upholds Spain's Intra-EU Objection' (*GAR*, 22 June 2022).

[41] See Szilárd Gáspár-Szilágyi and Maxim Usynin, 'The Uneasy Relationship between Intra-EU Investment Tribunals and the Court of Justice's *Achmea* Judgment' (2019) 4 *EILAR* 29. A most recent criticism directed towards the Court of Justice's *Komstroy* judgment was made by the Tribunal in the *Renergy v Spain* award of 6 May 2022 (ICSID Case No ARB/14/18), paras 348, 356–62.

[42] See Odermatt, 'Is EU Law International? (n 35).

8.3. THE PORCELAIN HAS CRACKED: REVISITING *MICULA*

The 2013 *Micula v Romania* ICSID award[43] has over the years garnered a lot of academic and media attention. This case had initially become one of the poster-children for issues concerning the legitimacy of investor-state arbitration, and now it has become one of the focal points for the discussion on the compatibility of intra-EU investment awards with EU law. The objective in this section is not to question the correctness of the initial award, or whether legitimate expectations should be included in the fair and equitable treatment (FET) standard, or how the formerly Romanian, now Swedish investors (the Micula brothers) have conducted their investments in the 'Wild 90s' following the collapse of communism in Romania. Instead, *Micula* is utilised as an example of how an otherwise fairly simple case of compliance has ended up in years of protracted enforcement cases spanning multiple jurisdictions, pitting several legal systems against each other, throwing legal certainty out the window, and causing great frustration to the investors and the host state alike.

8.3.1. Business as Usual? A State Lost an ICSID Case, but the Trunk of the Elephant Appeared

In 2002, prior to the accession of Romania to the EU, Sweden and Romania concluded a bilateral agreement 'Concerning the Reciprocal Promotion and Protection of Investment' (Sweden-Romania BIT). The BIT provided for the standard investment treaty protections, such as FET (Article 2(3)), national treatment and most-favoured-nation treatment (Article 3(1)), the prohibition of expropriation without compensation (Article 4), and the free transfer of profits (Article 5).

Following the collapse of communism, Romania had also concluded an association agreement (Europe Agreement) with the then European Communities in 1993 and the state had enacted various measures to foster investments. In 1998, it adopted an Emergency Government Ordinance to provide certain tax incentives (exemption from customs duties and VAT) to investors investing in various 'disfavoured' regions of the country.[44] The investors in this case, Ioan and Viorel Micula, were two former Romanian citizens who fled to Sweden during the latter years of communism, and took up Swedish citizenship, renouncing their Romanian one. After the end of communism, they had returned to Romania and set up various businesses in an economically disadvantaged part of the country, making refreshments and snacks ('European Food', 'Starmill', 'Multipack'). Following the 1998 Ordinance, their businesses benefited from the tax incentives.

[43] *Ioan Micula, Viorel Micula, SC European Food SA, SC Starmill SRL and SC Multipack SRL v Romania [I]*, ICSID Case No ARB/05/20, Final Award of 11 December 2013.

[44] ibid pp 39–41.

In 2005, Romania signed the Accession Treaty with the Member States of the EU, which came into force on 1 January 2007. As a condition of accession, Romania had to bring some of its existing measures in line with the EU's competition policy concerning certain regional aids prohibited by EU law.[45] This resulted in Romania withdrawing in 2005 the previously granted tax incentives for several disfavoured regions. The same year, the Micula brothers filed a request for arbitration with ICSID,[46] alleging that – among others – Romania's withdrawal of the tax benefits breached the Sweden-Romania BIT's FET clause. The case was a complex one. It resulted in a 1,329 paragraph, 369-page long award, taking eight years until a final award was rendered, and raised several issues, among which one can mention whether the BIT had to be interpreted consistently with EU law, whether the tribunal lacked jurisdiction, and whether the arbitral award could be enforced due to EU law.

This was also a period when the Commission began submitting its position as *amicus* in several intra-EU investment arbitrations,[47] including the *Micula* case, arguing that the resulting award could not be implemented in Romania by virtue of the primacy of EU law.[48] In the end, the arbitral tribunal upheld its jurisdiction, and the majority of the constituted tribunal[49] concluded in 2013 that Romania had violated the BIT's FET clause,[50] since its measures had interfered with the investors' legitimate expectations,[51] and ordered the state to pay RON 376,433,229 (currently EUR 76 million) as damages plus interest.

Several months later, in April 2014, pursuant to Article 52 of the ICSID Convention, Romania requested the annulment of the award on three of the five grounds set forth in Article 52(1), and also requested a stay of enforcement of the award.[52] The annulment committee granted the Commission the right to intervene as a non-disputing party.[53] The annulment committee looked at several grounds for annulment, among which were the initial tribunal's failure to apply the applicable law, its failure to decide on the issues of enforceability of the award, and the failure to decide that each claimant had suffered harm. The annulment committee also analysed the Commission's intervention concerning the applicability of EU law to the dispute that would result in the lack of jurisdiction of the tribunal. However, the annulment committee did not agree with the arguments put forward, and in 2016 delivered its decision, rejecting

[45] ibid paras 246–249.

[46] ibid para 10.

[47] The first such case was in *Eastern Sugar v Czech Republic*, SCC 088/2004, Partial Award, 27 March 2007.

[48] *Micula v Romania*, Final Award (n 43) para 334.

[49] The Tribunal consisted of Dr Stanimir A Alexandrov, Prof Georges Abi-Saab, and Dr Laurent Lévy.

[50] *Micula v Romania*, Final Award (n 43), para 1329 (b).

[51] ibid paras 527–529.

[52] *Ioan Micula, Viorel Micula and Others v Romania [II]*, ICSID Case No ARB/05/20, Decision on Annulment of 26 February 2016, paras 1–2.

[53] ibid paras 62–63.

Romania's claims regarding annulment, and held that Romania should bear the costs of the annulment proceedings.[54]

The case so far is a bit unusual, but nothing out of the ordinary. A state lost both the original ICSID proceedings, and the annulment proceedings. It then proceeded to repay the damages plus interest. Nevertheless, a glimpse of the elephant's trunk could already be seen because the Commission intervened in both proceedings to argue that the tribunal should consider the BIT's European context and origin, that EU state aid law should be applicable to the international investment dispute,[55] and that the primacy of EU law will hamper the award's enforcement.[56]

8.3.2. Things Get Complicated: The Rest of the Elephant Got In

The *Micula* case could have ended then and there in 2016. Romania lost the original case and the annulment proceedings and began repaying the damages. However, this is when Romania's competing EU and international law obligations began to seriously collide and resulted in a multitude of cases in several different jurisdictions, often running side-by-side. In order to trace these developments, the cases are split into three groups.

8.3.2.1. Cases before the CJEU

In early 2014, the Commission informed Romania that any implementation or execution of the arbitral award would constitute new state aid. A month later, Romania informed the Commission that it had already paid part of the damages, by offsetting a tax debt of approximately EUR 76 million.[57] During the same time, the investors decided to enforce the award before the Romanian courts, which resulted in the freezing of the accounts of the Romanian Ministry of Finance following the actions of an executor appointed by the Bucharest Tribunal. The Commission then opened formal investigations under Article 108(2) TFEU concerning illegal state aid, and in 2015 adopted Decision 2015/1470 ordering Romania not to pay out the damages awarded, as they constituted illegal state aid. Moreover, the sums already paid needed to be recovered.[58]

This put Romania between a rock and a hard place. On the one hand, it had assumed a set of international obligations under the ICSID Convention, and

[54] ibid para 355.

[55] *Micula v Romania*, Final Award (n 43) paras 316–317.

[56] ibid paras 334–336.

[57] Cases T-624/15, T-694/15 and T-704/15 *Micula and others v Commission* ECLI:EU:T:2019:423, paras 29–38.

[58] Commission Decision (EU) 2015/1470 of 30 March 2015 on State aid SA.38517 (2014/C) (ex 2014/NN) implemented by Romania – Arbitral award Micula v Romania of 11 December 2013 [2015] OJ L232/43, Article 2(3).

after the fall of communism, it concluded numerous BITs with EU and non-EU states alike, heeding the advice of the Commission and believing that BITs promote foreign investment. On the other hand, being the new member of a regional organisation with its own set of obligations, it realised that complying with its international obligations would lead to breaching its EU law obligations. This resulted in a legally unsolvable situation as the different systems of compliance (international investment law *v* EU law *v* national law) have resulted in conflicting outcomes, making compliance dependent on a political decision in the end, which now has been turned upside down after the Court of Justice's judgment in the *Commission v Micula* appeal.

Following the Commission's Decision 2015/1470, the investors brought annulment proceedings under Article 263 TFEU against the Decision. In 2019, the General Court ended up annulling the Commission's Decision, arguing that the Commission lacked competence in this case, EU law was inapplicable to a situation predating Romania's accession to the EU, and that the amount of money awarded as damages could not constitute illegal state aid under EU law.[59] The Commission appealed the judgment, and in January 2022 the Court of Justice set aside the judgment of the General Court. The Court of Justice argued that the General Court erred in its judgment when it concluded that the Commission had no competence under Article 108 TFEU to adopt the Decision on state aid.[60] Furthermore, for the Court of Justice, its prior judgment in *Achmea* also precluded the investor-state arbitration provisions under intra-EU BITs, and Romania's consent to the arbitration system laid down in the BIT became inapplicable following its accession to the EU.[61]

The Court of Justice referred the case back to the General Court to adjudicate on several pleas raised before it. Among these was 'the question whether the compensation granted by the [ICSID] award may constitute "[s]tate aid"', over which the Court of Justice had no power to decide, as it was not the subject matter of the appeal.[62] If the General Court is to decide that the repayment of the ICSID award constitutes illegal state aid, then the investors would face the possibility of repaying the compensation, which they had already received in late 2019.[63] This in turn could lead to another appeal before the Court of Justice, creating even more legal uncertainty, and Romania would breach its obligations under the ICSID Convention. According to the most recent news in the Romanian media, Romania began proceedings to recover the damages paid to the Micula brothers, following *Commission v Micula*.[64]

[59] Cases T-624/15, T-694/15 and T-704/15 *Micula* (n 57) para 90.

[60] Case C-638/19 P *European Commission v Micula* ECLI:EU:C:2022:50, para 126.

[61] For a more detailed critique of the Court's arguments see Gáspár-Szilágyi and Usynin (n 12).

[62] Case C-638/19 P *European Commission v Micula* (n 60) para 131.

[63] In January 2022 a representative of the Micula brothers confirmed to me that they had received the compensation from the Romanian State. This is also mentioned in the Romanian Govt Decision/Hotărârea nr 917/2019, Art 2 of which mentions explicitly the payment of compensation in the ICSID case ARB/05/20 in the value of RON 912 million.

[64] Case C-638/19 P *European Commission v Micula* (n 60).

In conclusion, from the perspective of EU compliance, Romania had not only infringed its EU law obligations concerning illegal state aid, but, from the perspective of EU law, Romania's consent to arbitrate became inapplicable following its accession to the EU. This, however, does create plentiful problems when it comes to compliance with investment law. Firstly, under international law, Romania concluded a valid international agreement in 2002, and it only terminated it in March 2020.[65] Thus, that agreement – based on which the ICSID tribunal had jurisdiction – was in force throughout the life of the original ICSID arbitration. Secondly, Romania has obligations not only under the BIT, but also under the ICSID Convention. Under the ICSID regime, consent to arbitrate needs to be given in writing (Article 25(1) ICSID), which has been interpreted by arbitral tribunals as including a state's standing offer to arbitrate in a BIT, which is then accepted by the investor upon commencing arbitration against the state.[66] Moreover, once consent has been given, parties cannot withdraw it unilaterally. In other words, the EU system of compliance will not affect compliance under investment law, and the Court of Justice's holding that Romania's accession to the EU makes its consent to arbitrate inapplicable after 2007 will not affect the existence of Romania's obligations under the BIT and the ICSID Convention. It will simply make compliance with investment law obligations within the EU legal order extremely difficult, if not impossible.

8.3.2.2. *Cases Involving EU Member State Courts*

Following the Court of Justice's judgment in *Achmea*, followed by *Komstroy, PL Holdings*, and now *Commission v Micula*, the enforcement of intra-EU investment awards in the EU has become pretty much impossible. As mentioned in section 8.2.1, compliance with an international court's judgments can be increased if the remedy provided therein is well defined. However, in *Achmea*, there is no remedy provided. As discussed, the judgment is not clear whether it applies only to investor-state arbitration clauses that were 'such as' the ones under the Netherlands-Slovakia BIT. Furthermore, it does not define whether the consequences of incompatibility are the non-application of the incompatible provision or the termination of all intra-EU BITs or just the amendment of their ISDS clauses.

It is no wonder then that ITA tribunals are very critical of *Achmea*, and do not decline their jurisdiction based on a vaguely worded judgment of the CJEU.[67] Member State courts have also accepted the *Achmea* judgment differently. Some have accepted the primacy of their states' obligations under EU law without question, while others did not accept the effects of these recent CJEU judgments without raising their own concerns and questions.

[65] Investment Policy Hub, 'Romania-Sweden BIT'.
[66] See Jan Paulsson, 'Arbitration Without Privity' (1995) 10 *ICSID Review* 232.
[67] See Gáspár-Szilágyi and Usynin (n 41) and the Tribunal in the *Renergy v Spain* (n 40).

In the first group, one can mention the Romanian Constitutional Court (RCC). The investors sought enforcement of the ICSID award before the Romanian courts in 2014. Back then, the Bucharest Tribunal declined to make a reference for a preliminary ruling to the CJEU and ordered the freezing of the accounts of the Romanian Ministry of Finance. This judgment was then suspended from execution until the Bucharest Court of Appeals decided the appeal.[68] However, in separate proceedings launched before lower courts in the county of Bihor, Romania, the investors raised a request for constitutional review before the RCC, concerning the alleged unconstitutional nature of several Romanian laws and ordinances concerning state aid. The RCC rejected the requests. It acknowledged Romania's competing international and EU law obligations but argued that in areas of exclusive EU competence, Romania is bound to implement its EU obligations, regardless of what international obligations assumed by the country might require it to do.[69]

The Nacka District Court (*Nacka tingsrätt*) was also faced with two competing obligations. On the one hand, the obligations of Sweden under Article 54 ICSID Convention not to review an ICSID award; and, on the other hand, Sweden's obligations under EU law.[70] Among other grounds, the Nacka District Court decided that the ICSID tribunal was not competent to decide on matters relating to EU law, and, in the end, rejected the appeal by the investors.

However, there are also instances when courts and tribunals of EU Member States have not come to such a clear conclusion following the imprecise wording of *Achmea*. For example, in *PL Holdings*, the Svea Court of Appeal (*Svea hovrätt*) was not willing to apply *Achmea* to *ad hoc* arbitration agreements.[71] Furthermore, in the enforcement cases for the *Micula* award launched before the courts in Belgium, which resulted in the freezing of the accounts of ROMATSA (the Romanian Air Traffic Administration Authority), the Brussels Court of Appeals had partially accepted Micula's appeal, and made a reference for a preliminary ruling to the CJEU under Article 267 TFEU.[72] The final judgment awaits the Court of Justice's judgment on several questions concerning the compatibility of the award with EU law, and at the time of writing was also awaiting the results of the annulment action against the Commission's Decision on state aid and the subsequent appeal.[73]

[68] Cases T-624/15, T-694/15 and T-704/15 *Micula* (n 57) paras 26–27.

[69] Curtea Constituțională, Decizie nr. 887, 15 December 2015, para. 75.

[70] Nacka District Court (*Nacka tingsrätt*), *Ioan Micula, et al v Rumänien* (n 29) pp 4–5. See also the Supreme Court of Latvia in Lietuvos Aukščiausiojo Teismo Civilinių bylų skyriaus 2022 m sausio 18 d nutartis civilinėje byloje Nr e3K-3-121-916/2022 [Order of the Civil Cases Division of the Supreme Court of Lithuania dated January 18, 2022, in civil case no e3K-3-121-916 / 2022].

[71] Case C-109/20 *Republiken Polen v. PL Holdings Sàrl* EU:C:2021:875, paras 29–30.

[72] Cour d'Appel Bruxelles, *Micula v ROMATSA* (n 28).

[73] Joined Cases T-624/15, T-694/15 and T-704/15 RENV, *European Food and Others v Commission* [case in progress] and Case C-333/19 *Romatsa and Others* ECLI:EU:C:2022:749 in which the Court of Justice ordered on 21 September 2022 that the execution of the *Micula* award in Belgium be set aside.

The Court of Justice also seems to neglect the very important point that, whilst the ISDS provisions of intra-EU BITs might be incompatible with EU law, 26 Member States (except for Poland) are parties to the ICSID Convention, which has yet to be rendered incompatible with EU law. Many EU States, especially the more recent Central and Eastern European (CEE) States that are often at the receiving end of ITA awards, have concluded this agreement prior to their accession to the EU. Therefore, if the Court of Justice has yet to decide that the ICSID Convention is incompatible with EU law, then under the very rules of EU law (Article 351 TFEU) the latter may not affect Member States' obligations under international agreements prior to their accession to the EU. However, the Court of Justice is forcing Member States to break their ICSID obligations, obligations which, as shall be seen in the next section, will be enforced by non-EU courts and tribunals.

8.3.2.3. Enforcement Cases before US Courts

Whilst the compliance rules of EU law require EU Member States and their courts to follow the Court of Justice's judgments in *Achmea* and *Commission v Micula* (regardless of whether they consider either of these cases to be based on sound legal reasoning), the same rules do not apply to the courts of non-EU states tasked with the enforcement of a binding international arbitral award.

From the perspective of a non-EU state, compliance means that its institutions and even private parties must obey that state's international obligations, and its national laws and regulations. For 154 ICSID members, their international obligation is to recognise an ICSID award and to enforce the pecuniary obligations under it as if that award were a final decision of their own courts (Article 54(1) ICSID Convention). They cannot question the correctness of the award or set it aside. When the Commission joins such local enforcement cases as *amicus*, or when it submits observations, it fails to realise that EU law with its system of compliance is irrelevant for non-EU states, since their obligations flow from the ICSID Convention.[74]

A case in point is the ongoing enforcement of the *Micula* award in the United States. According to the District of Columbia Court of Appeals in the *Micula v Romania*[75] enforcement case, the arbitration agreement was not nullified by Romania's accession to the EU,[76] since Romania joined the EU after the events that formed the basis of the *Micula* award, a point which was raised in a recent critique of the Court of Justice's judgment in the *Micula* appeal.[77] This decision

[74] It also seems disingenuous to ask a non-EU State not to enforce an ICSID award due to issues internal to the EU, when the EU itself includes ICSID enforcement in its new trade and investment agreements.

[75] United States Court of Appeals for the District of Columbia Circuit, *Ioan Micula, et al v Government of Romania* (n 27).

[76] ibid.

[77] Gáspár-Szilágyi and Usynin (n 12) at 65.

also highlights some key points that often make the enforcement of ITA awards difficult, or sometimes impossible. As previously mentioned, in some states, sovereign immunity rules can apply to the freezing of the assets of a foreign sovereign. Thus, whilst these national courts will recognise the enforcement of the ICSID award, its actual execution will not be possible if their local laws forbid the seizing of the assets of a foreign sovereign. The DC Court of Appeals at second instance argued that the District Court for the District of Columbia (first instance) had jurisdiction in the enforcement case against the foreign sovereign as there was an exception to the US sovereign immunity rules which covers the enforcement of arbitral awards.[78]

Two further points are warranted. Firstly, outsourcing internal EU problems to non-EU states puts those local courts in the unfortunate situation of having to assess issues internal to the EU,[79] as well as possible problems with the underlying arbitration agreement, something which the ICSID Convention does not envisage. National courts and tribunals are not supposed to conduct such a review of the underlying arbitration agreement, since there are no set-aside possibilities under the ICSID Convention on grounds similar to those included in Article V of the New York Convention. Secondly, the judgment of the DC Court of Appeals illustrates that the CJEU tends to make sweeping conclusions without considering the fine details, such as the existence of an arbitration agreement and facts prior to Romania's accession to the EU or prior to the delivery of the *Achmea* judgment. As argued elsewhere, the Court of Justice does not properly consider the temporal effects of its judgments and its effects on legal certainty for intra-EU ITA cases that have been concluded prior to the Court of Justice finding that there was any problem with the compatibility of intra-EU BITs with EU law.[80]

8.3.2.4. *Enforcement before UK Courts*

The enforcement case before UK courts is quite special, since the UK withdrew from the EU, but the case was brought prior to the UK's withdrawal. The Court of Appeal in this case decided to stay the enforcement of the *Micula* award as there was a Commission Decision forbidding its enforcement due to the damages representing illegal state aid and because the case before the EU's General Court concerning the validity of the Commission Decision was under appeal before the Court of Justice (see section 8.3.2.1). The UK Supreme Court (UKSC), however, did not agree with this conclusion and unanimously decided to enforce

[78] United States Court of Appeals for the District of Columbia Circuit, *Ioan Micula, et al v Government of Romania* (n 27).

[79] See also Damien Charlotin, 'US Court Declines to Overturn Earlier Decision to Enforce Micula v. Romania Intra-EU Award' (*IAReporter*, 17 January 2023).

[80] Gáspár-Szilágyi and Usynin (n 12) at 68–69.

the award.[81] The UKSC cited the UK's obligations under Articles 53 and 54 of the ICSID Convention and held that the EU Treaties did not have any relevant effect.[82] It argued that the UK became a signatory to the ICSID Convention prior to the UK's EU membership, and there was no conflict between the UK's ICSID obligations and EU law under Article 351 TFEU.[83] Furthermore, it held that Articles 53 and 54 of the ICSID Convention imposed on the UK obligations which it owed to all ICSID members, and not just EU Member States.

Whilst *Achmea* is not mentioned in the UKSC's decision, the UKSC points out an obvious fact. Collectively, the UK, 26 EU Member States and many non-EU states still have obligations under the ICSID Convention. These obligations do not only stand under international law but are compatible with EU law under Article 351 TFEU in the case of Romania. In other words, not complying with the *Micula* award breaches not only Romania's international obligations, but also that of the UK towards non-EU ICSID members. This is a key point that both the Commission and the CJEU seem to neglect. It must also be mentioned that following the UKSC's judgment, the Commission has launched infringement proceedings against the UK under Article 87(1) of the EU-UK Withdrawal Agreement (WA).[84] Thus, the enforcement tale goes on.

8.4. THE UNFORESEEN CONSEQUENCES

If the purpose of *Achmea* and the EU's interference with the compliance mechanisms of investment law was to create legal certainty, predictability, and the uniform application of EU law, then those aims have clearly not been met. According to Gaillard and Penushlinski:

> One may debate whether the conflict between EU law and investment law originated in truly competing legal paradigms or was actually *engineered* by structures within the EU who disliked the experience or prospect of being a respondent in investment arbitration more than they liked the protection that investment treaties offer to their own investors. But this is irrelevant for how EU States will behave in relation to adverse intra-EU awards: these are very unlikely to be complied with within the EU and *massive enforcement efforts will be required* for any State-owned assets outside the EU. [emphasis added][85]

[81] *Micula and others v Romania* [2020] UKSC 5, 19 February 2020. For a commentary see Aikaterini Florou, 'Whither Mutual Trust? Brexit, *Achmea* and the Future of Investor-State Arbitration in the EU-UK Investment Relations' (2019) 4 *EILAR* 66, 84–87 and Szilárd Gáspár-Szilágyi, 'Does Brexit Mean Brexit? The Enforcement of Intra-EU Investment Awards in the Post-Brexit Era' (2022) III *Central European Journal of Comparative Law* 75.

[82] ibid paras 86–87.

[83] ibid para 97 and beyond.

[84] European Commission, 'Sincere cooperation and primacy of EU law: Commission refers UK to EU Court of Justice over a UK Judgment allowing enforcement of an arbitral award granting illegal State aid' (9 February 2022).

[85] Gaillard and Penushliski, 'State Compliance with Investment Awards' (n 22) 589.

This unfortunate situation is the result of the elephant entering the porcelain shop, or in other words, the *evolving* rules of the EU legal system being barged into the system of compliance of IIL that follows very different rules. The unwillingness of the EU legal order to coexist with investment law in an intra-EU setting has caused, and is likely to cause, several detrimental consequences.

Firstly, from a legal perspective, the two systems of compliance cannot be squared. The EU views itself as a creation of international law and wants to act as a major participant in international law, but disregards the existing rules of international law, arguing that it is a separate legal system from it, and that international law should conform itself to the EU's unique existence. As noted by Odermatt, there is a simultaneous conception of EU law as 'domestic law, international law, and "an independent source of law"'. This, unfortunately, creates an unsolvable paradigm; depending on where the enforcement of investment awards is sought (inside or outside the EU), the results will often be different and conflicting, something which the current investment law frameworks of enforcement were meant to minimise, creating a more uniform and predicable enforcement mechanism in an otherwise highly decentralised system.

As long as there are different dispute settlement bodies (investment tribunals *v* the CJEU), interpreting the interaction between their respective legal systems according to the rules of their own systems, there cannot be one legal solution acceptable to all parties involved. The only true way out of this situation is the termination of intra-EU BITs with their sunset clauses and the renegotiation of the ECT (which is under way, but facing continued exits by several EU Member States).[86] Furthermore, this solution is not perfect since the termination agreement will not and should not affect concluded arbitrations.[87]

Secondly, instead of sowing uniformity in the application of EU law, this intrusion into investment law compliance by the EU has created differing approaches to the effects of *Achmea* by the courts of current or former EU Member States. These courts must reconcile their competing international and EU law obligations, which till very recently were compatible with each other. Furthermore, they need to apply vaguely phrased judgments of the Court of Justice to very detailed and complex legal situations, which then leads to the need of further clarifications via preliminary references, as seen in the *Micula* enforcement case before the Brussels Court of Appeals.

Thirdly, the current situation also brings undesired complexity to enforcement cases before non-EU state courts. Instead of swift recognition and enforcement, both investors and host states are stuck in lengthy enforcement

[86] See *Opinion 1/20* ECLI:EU:C:2022:485 (*Modernised Energy Charter Treaty*), in which the Court found the request of Belgium on the compatibility of the revised ECT with EU law to be inadmissible, due to the text not being available yet. See, Johannes Tropper, 'Opinion 1/20 and the Conclusion of the Modernisation Negotiations of the Energy Charter Treaty – Hitting the Home Stretch?' (Kluwer Arbitration Blog, 25 June 2022).

[87] Article 7, Agreement for the Termination of Bilateral Investment Treaties Between the Members States of the European Union.

cases in foreign jurisdictions, during which expert opinions and *amicus* briefs are submitted to judges not accustomed to the intricacies of EU law or the recent difficult coexistence between EU and investment law.

Fourthly, the elephant's presence raises further legal issues, such as the retroactive application of judgments of the Court of Justice to previous legal situations governed by international law. It also raises questions about the extra-EU application and effects of EU law, which investment tribunals have not received fondly. The Court of Justice could have offered an olive branch for the sake of judicial comity and certainty and specified that already concluded or pending arbitrations would *not* be affected by *Achmea*. Instead, in *Commission v Micula*, the Court of Justice held that Romania's consent to arbitrate under an agreement which later became an intra-EU BIT 'lacked any force' after Romania's accession to the EU, because the system of remedies provided by the EU Treaties and EU law had 'replaced' the ITA procedure.[88]

The Court of Justice's unwillingness to limit the temporal effects of *Achmea* and its subsequent judgments creates tremendous problems for cases that were concluded prior to *Achmea* (such as the *Micula* award), or for tribunals that were constituted prior to this date. This also raises the question whether investors and host states can be certain whether a case is truly over. It is almost farcical that after both the investors and the host state have gone through costly and lengthy enforcement cases in multiple jurisdictions and after the state had paid the damages, it is now put in the position to force the investor to return those moneys, causing not only serious harm to the principle of the finality of judgments and awards, but also causing uncertainty to the day-to-day operation of the investments.

Lastly, as Lavranos and Kochenov have argued, *Achmea* and the developments following this case might result in further unforeseen consequences, such as removing substantive and procedural protections offered by intra-EU BITs from investors who invest in EU Member States where there is democratic or rule of law backsliding.[89]

Besides the legal consequences, however, there are quite serious non-legal consequences as well. The first one is a reputational one. Whilst we know that there is no conclusive data on whether BITs promote investment, non-compliance with investment awards (see Argentina or Venezuela) is a clear sign that the host state is not willing to abide by its international commitments and it is potentially not a safe place to invest. This, in turn, could lead to foreign investors restructuring their investments to benefit from extra-EU BITs, or to leave the EU market.

Then, there is the wider signal these recent developments send to various international financial and lending institutions. The post-2013 Argentine

[88] Case C-638/19 P *European Commission v Micula* ECLI:EU:C:2022:50, para 145.

[89] Dimitry Kochenov and Nikos Lavranos, '*Achmea* versus the Rule of law: CJEU's Dogmatic Dismissal of Investors' Rights in Backsliding Member States of the European Union' (2021) *Hague Journal on the Rule of Law*.

example very clearly illustrates that receiving international aid or loans from institutions such as the IMF or the World Bank can be conditioned by the country's compliance with adverse investment awards (especially since ICSID is a branch of the World Bank).[90] The last financial crisis has resulted in several EU Member States requesting IMF assistance.[91] Therefore, even if EU Member States will not comply with an intra-EU investment award due to their legal obligations pursuant to EU law, in case they will get into financial difficulty, they might have to comply in order to receive international financial assistance.

Compliance with IIL is not a purely legal decision. As Hirsch's discussion of Argentina's pre- and post-2013 compliance with investment awards has shown, there might be multiple rationales behind compliance or non-compliance, some of which are social constructivist in nature, while others are rational choice based. The latter approach is also illustrated by the decision of the Prime Minister of Romania in 2019 to supplement the national budget to comply with the *Micula* award,[92] even if the payment of the damages was contrary to EU law.

Romania's choice can be explained from a rational choice, cost-and-benefit perspective. The cost of non-compliance with the ICSID award was larger, and the consequences of non-compliance were more immediate and pressing than breaching EU law. Romania had spent considerable sums defending itself in a multitude of different jurisdictions, meanwhile the original amount of damages had significantly increased thanks to the penalising interest rates imposed in the ICSID award.[93] However, financial matters aside, the final straw that broke the camel's back was the freezing of ROMATSA's accounts in Belgium, which would have halted air traffic over the Romanian skies. In other words, when push came to shove, the Government of Romania chose to pay up, even though both the Commission and the Constitutional Court of Romania indicated not to. This points to the unforeseen practical difficulties caused by the EU's interference with the compliance mechanisms of investment law, which can lead a state's executive to disregard the decisions of EU institutions and national court rulings to remedy a pressing situation with real-life implications.

The EU's challenge to the system of compliance of investment law has really rattled the porcelain shop and ended up causing a lack of legal certainty, protracted and very expensive enforcement cases, the accrual of penalising interest, the blocking of state accounts in different jurisdictions, and a loss of faith in the value of an international arbitral award.

[90] See section 8.2.1.

[91] See Krisztina Than, 'Hungary Requests Financial Help from IMF, EU' (*Reuters*, 21 November 2011); Luiza Ilie, 'IMF gives Romania more time to meet aid targets' (*Reuters*, 29 January 2013).

[92] Romanian Govt Decision/Hotărârea nr 917/2019, Art 2.

[93] In the end Romania ended up paying RON 912 million, or EUR 184 million instead of the initial amount of EUR 76 million.

8.5. CONCLUSIONS

Understanding the EU's more recent and increasing presence in IIL and trying to make sense of the Court of Justice's case law concerning the autonomy of EU law and its relationship to other international dispute settlement mechanisms is not a straightforward task. There are probably both legal and non-legal rationales behind the hostility that the Commission and the Court of Justice have shown to investment law and intra-EU BITs in particular. This might be due to the long-held desire of the Commission to gain competences over investment law,[94] or its desire to reform investment treaty arbitration. It might also be the Court of Justice 'jealously' guarding its interpretative powers in a complex international legal landscape it might not fully comprehend, which leads it to issue judgments of constitutional significance based on certain fictions and hypotheticals.[95] This hostility might also be part of a wider ideological scepticism and legitimacy challenge of international law and international tribunals.

Be that as it may, this chapter was meant to show that the EU's – more specifically the Commission and the Court of Justice's – recent barging into a complex and fragile system of international compliance is causing unforeseen consequences, and more harm than good. Twenty years ago, no one knew that there was an incompatibility between EU and investment law. As Advocate General Wathelet noted in his Opinion on *Achmea*:

> For a very long time, the argument of the EU institutions, including the Commission, was that, far from being incompatible with EU law, BITs were instruments necessary to prepare for the accession to the Union of the countries of Central and Eastern Europe. The Association Agreements between the Union and candidate countries also contained provisions for the conclusion of BITs between Member States and candidate countries.[96]

Those same Member States now find themselves being dragged through multiple foreign jurisdictions, trying to make sense of the legal rules they should comply with; either way, they will be the ones picking up the tab.

[94] See Sophie Meunier, 'Integration by Stealth: How the European Union Gained Competence over Foreign Direct Investment' (2017) 55(3) *JCMS* 593.

[95] See Szilárd Gáspár-Szilágyi, 'Between Fiction and Reality: The External Autonomy of EU Law as a "Shapeshifter" after Opinion 1/17' (2021) 6(1) *European Papers* 675.

[96] Opinion of Advocate General Wathelet, Case C-284/16 *Achmea*, ECLI:EU:C:2017:699, para 40.

9

State-to-State Arbitration in EU Investment Protection Agreements

GESA KÜBEK

9.1. INTRODUCTION

INVESTOR-STATE ARBITRATION IS a salient feature of bilateral investment agreements (BITs) and the most well-known way to resolve disputes in international investment law. It allows private foreign investors to challenge state measures before an arbitral tribunal. Yet, investor-state arbitration is not the only dispute settlement mechanism contained in BITs. Almost all BITs also include state-to-state arbitration[1] to resolve disputes between the contracting parties of BITs. In fact, early BITs, such as the very first one between Germany and Pakistan, exclusively provided for state-to-state arbitration.[2] The recently negotiated, but not ratified, EU-China Comprehensive Agreement on Investment (CAI) revives this model by relying on a modernised state-to-state dispute resolution system, without simultaneously providing for investor-state arbitration.[3]

In practice, state-to-state arbitration has, so far, had limited relevance, with only four cases emerging over the years.[4] Conversely, the use of investor-state

[1] For the sake of simplicity, this chapter uses the term 'state-to-state arbitration' also in the context of EU international agreements, although the EU is not a state. *Opinion 2/13* ECLI:EU:C:2014:2454 (*EU Accession to the ECHR II*), para 156: 'the EU is, under international law, precluded by its very nature from being considered a [s]tate.'

[2] Article 11 of the Germany-Pakistan BIT (1959), BGBl 1962, Part II, p 793.

[3] Section V of the EU-China Agreement in principle, reached in December 2022.

[4] The first dispute is *Ecuador v USA*, where Ecuador sought an interpretation of specific terms of the BIT. See PCA Case No 2012-5, *Republic of Ecuador v United States of America*, Award, 29 September 2012. The second case is *Peru v Chile*, where Italy unsuccessfully attempted to stop ongoing investor-state proceedings. In fact, the case is only known through its mentioning in ICSID Case No ARB/03/4, *Empresas Lucchetti SA and Lucchetti Peru SA v Peru*, Award on Jurisdiction, 7 February 2005, paras 7, 9. The third case is *Italy v Cuba*, where Italy aimed to espouse its national's claim though the state-to-state arbitration procedure. See *Italian Republic v Republic of Cuba*, ad hoc state-to-state arbitration, Interim Award, 15 March 2005, and Final Award, 15 January 2008. Lastly, in *USA v Mexico*, Mexico used state-to-state arbitration to settle a dispute about a breach of the terms of NAFTA with the US. See NAFTA Arbitration Panel, Secretariat File No USA-MEX-98-2008-01, *USA v Mexico*, Cross-Border Trucking Services, 6 February 2001.

arbitration has increased steeply, especially in the past decade. The heavy reliance on investor-state arbitration has brought to the fore grave systemic shortcomings, resulting in fierce political and public controversy.[5] Against that background, several states have exited and/or pushed for ways to recalibrate the system. The EU has exited the Energy Charter Treaty after failed modernisation attempts. It has also developed an investment court system (ICS), which addresses several shortcomings of traditional investor-state arbitration, but '[a]t its core ... stays loyal to established arbitration rules'.[6] The EU's 'hybrid' reform model has not gained support from all of its trading partners, for very different reasons, as the cases of Japan, New Zealand and Australia highlight.[7] As a result, the EU, amongst others, has pushed for the multilateralisation of international investment law[8] and, specifically, for the establishment of a Multilateral Investment Court (MIC).[9] But in the current geopolitical climate, the future of the MIC project is more uncertain than ever before. In the face of declining compliance with basic principles of international law (eg Russia's war of aggression against Ukraine), a growing number of exits from multilateral organisations (eg Brexit, The Philippines' and Burundi's exit from the Rome Statute, Russia's exit from the European Convention on Human Rights (ECHR), or the United States' withdrawal from the Paris Agreement and the World Health Organization) and a simultaneous destruction of other international organisations from within (eg WTO Appellate Body crisis, EU rule of law crisis), it is not clear whether the idea to establish a new multilateral institution will fall on fertile ground.

In light of this, it may be relevant to consider the one existing alternative to investor-state arbitration, namely state-to-state arbitration. While some scholars have done so for national BITs,[10] hardly any attention has been paid to state-to-state

[5] To name but a few: inconsistent decision-making, insufficient regard to the host states' right to regulate by some tribunals, foreign investor bias etc. See further eg Stefan W Schill, 'Reforming Investor-State Dispute Settlement (ISDS): Conceptual Framework and Options for the Way Forward' (2015) E15Initiative, *International Centre for Trade and Sustainable Development/World Economic Forum Working Paper*; and M Sornarajah, *Resistance and Change in the International Law on Foreign Investments* (CUP, 2009).

[6] Hannes Lenk, 'The EU Investment Court System: A Viable Reform Initiative?', Juridiska institutionens skriftserie 32 (School of Business, Economics and Law at University of Gothenburg, 2019) 288. See further also ch 14.

[7] The EU and Japan carved out investment from the scope of their trade agreement, as Japan did not agree on the ICS while the EU insisted that 'there can be no return to old style [investor-state dispute settlement]'. See EU-Japan, The Agreement in Principle, 6 July 2017. The EU's envisaged trade agreements with Australia and New Zealand do not include investment protection and investor-state dispute settlement. Both countries are well-known opposers of investor-state dispute settlement.

[8] Stefan Schill, *The Multilateralization of International Investment Law* (CUP, 2009).

[9] On the MIC see eg Rob Howse, 'Designing a Multilateral Investment Court: Issues and Options' (2017) 36 *Yearbook of European Law* 209, and ch 15.

[10] See esp Michele Potestà, 'State-to-State Dispute Settlement Pursuant to Bilateral Investment Treaties: Is There Potential?' in Nerina Boschiero et al (eds), *International Courts and the*

arbitration in the EU's latest investment protection agreements (IPAs).[11] These agreements establish modernised state-to-state arbitration systems that, as this chapter explores, include several design features that could make state-to-state arbitration a more functional alternative to investor-state arbitration. So far, the EU has negotiated and/or signed four IPAs, with Canada, Vietnam, Singapore and China respectively. These agreements are still pending ratification in all the Member States, and therefore also face an uncertain future. As the main controversial feature of the EU's external investment policy remains investor-state arbitration, the state-to-state arbitration systems of these agreements are nevertheless worth exploring. It is arguably unlikely that investment agreements with like-minded states that only include state-to-state arbitration will face similar political problems within the Member States.

The present chapter questions to what extent the state-to-state arbitration mechanism, as foreseen in EU IPAs, could be used as an alternative or, at least, in parallel to investor-state arbitration. It is structured as follows. As a background for discussion, it explains the emergence of the EU's first (stand-alone) IPAs, and the design of their state-to-state arbitration mechanisms. The chapter then proceeds to outline the potential use of state-to-state arbitration in the context of EU IPAs – both on its own, and, as it is currently foreseen, in parallel to other investment arbitration mechanisms established by EU trade and investment agreements. Lastly, it discusses the future potential of state-to-state arbitration as an alternative dispute settlement technique in EU investment practice.

9.2. STATE-TO-STATE ARBITRATION IN EU IPAS: A BRIEF OVERVIEW

For a long time, only the Member States themselves negotiated and concluded BITs in their sovereign capacity. The Treaty of Lisbon brought about a power shift in the field of investment, which in practice led to the emergence of four IPAs negotiated by the EU in its own right (section 9.2.1). Their state-to-state arbitration mechanism replicates the one contained in the EU's new generation free trade agreements (FTAs), which is more comprehensive than the mechanism traditionally foreseen in BITs that Member States have in place (section 9.2.2).

Development of International Law: Essays in Honour of Tullio Treves (Springer, 2013) 753; and, most recently, Angshuman Hazarika, *State-to-state Arbitration based on International Investment Agreements* (Springer, 2021).

[11] Hazarika's (n 10) comparative analysis expands to EU IPAs but does not specifically focus on them. The agreements are also considered, albeit not as specific case studies, in Rodrigo Polanco, *The Return of the Home State to Investor-State Disputes: Bringing Back Diplomatic Protection?* (CUP, 2019). Most recently, Driessen considered reform options for EU IPAs. Yet, he did not further examine state-to-state dispute settlement as one of these options, deeming it not sufficiently attractive for investors. See further Bart Driessen, 'A New Route to European Investment Agreements? Some Reflections on a Possible Alternative' (2025) 50 *European Law Review* 156, 170.

9.2.1. Emergence

With the entry into force of the Treaty of Lisbon in 2009, the EU was equipped with exclusive competence over foreign direct investment.[12] In a 2012 regulation, the EU institutions decided to gradually 'grandfather' Member State BITs with EU IPAs.[13] The Comprehensive Trade and Investment Agreement (CETA) with Canada was signed as the first-ever EU IPA.[14] At the time, the EU had also finalised negotiations of comprehensive trade and investment agreements with both Singapore and Vietnam respectively. As the scope of the EU's exclusive competence was confined, as per its text, to foreign *direct* investment, the breath of the EU's new external investment agenda (including both direct and non-direct investments, as well as investor-state arbitration) soon raised legal concerns. In *Opinion 2/15*, the Court of Justice of the European Union (the Court) held that the Member States partially retain competence over foreign non-direct investments and investor-state arbitration.[15] As a result, the EU institutions decided to split comprehensive trade and investment agreements into separate FTAs and IPAs. FTAs can be concluded by the EU alone, whereas IPAs are to be concluded by the EU and the Member States jointly as mixed agreements.[16] Soon after, the EU announced the 'split' of the negotiated agreements with Singapore and Vietnam, resulting in the EU's first-ever stand-alone investment protection agreements (EUSIPA and EUVIPA, respectively). CETA was not split, as it was already provisionally applied at the time that *Opinion 2/15* was delivered.[17] At present, CETA, the EUVIPA and the EUSIPA are pending ratification by all Member States.

Most recently, the EU negotiated a Comprehensive Agreement on Investment (CAI) with China. In the face of recent geopolitical developments, it is unlikely

[12] On the evolution of EU investment law post-Lisbon see eg Angelos Dimopoulos, *EU Foreign Investment Law* (OUP, 2011); Federico Ortino and Piet Eeckhout, 'Towards an EU Policy on Foreign Direct Investment' in Andrea Biondi et al (eds), *EU Law after Lisbon* (OUP, 2012) 312; and Marise Cremona, 'Distinguished Essay: A Quiet Revolution – The Changing Nature of the EU's Common Commercial Policy' (2017) 8 *European Yearbook of International Economic Law* 3.

[13] Regulation (EU) No 1219/2012 of 12 December 2012 [2012] OJ L351/40. On the EU's new generation IPAs see esp Catharine Titi, 'International Investment Law and the European Union: Towards a New Generation of International Investment Agreements' (2015) 26 *European Journal of International Law* 639.

[14] Council Decision (EU) 2017/37 of 28 October 2016 [2017] OJ L11/1. The first-ever envisioned IPA was the Transatlantic Trade and Investment Partnership (TTIP) with the USA, which however failed.

[15] *Opinion 2/15 (FTA with Singapore)* ECLI:EU:C:2017:376. See esp Marise Cremona, 'Shaping EU Trade Policy post-Lisbon: Opinion 2/15 of 16 May 2017' (2018) 14 *European Constitutional Law Review* 231.

[16] On the new architecture of EU FTAs and IPAs see further Gesa Kübek and Isabelle Van Damme, 'Facultative Mixity and the European Union's Trade and Investment Agreements' in Merijn Chamon and Inge Govaere (eds), *EU External Relations Law Post-Lisbon: The Law and Practice of Facultative Mixity* (Brill, 2020) 137, 159 et seq; and Gesa Kübek, *EU Trade and Investment Treaty-Making Post-Lisbon: Moving Beyond Mixity* (Hart Publishing, 2024) 177.

[17] Notably, the investment part of CETA is largely carved out from its provisional application. See Council Decision (EU) 2017/38 of 28 October 2016 [2017] OJ L11/1081.

that the CAI will ever be ratified. In terms of its design, the CAI is nevertheless an interesting case study, because it is the first new generation EU investment agreement that provides only for state-to-state, and not for investor-state, arbitration. According to the Commission, the '[s]tate-to-[s]tate dispute resolution mechanism underpinning the [CAI] meets the highest standards found in existing EU trade agreements'.[18] Irrespective of its viability, the CAI will thus be used as a fourth case study for this chapter, alongside CETA, the EUSIPA and the EUVIPA.

9.2.2. Architecture

Architecturally, state-to-state arbitration in EU IPAs follows the 'EU trade model'. The EU's new generation FTAs, including CETA, devote an entire chapter to state-to-state arbitration.[19] That chapter has been 'copied and pasted' into the EU's stand-alone investment agreements with Singapore, Vietnam and China.[20] When it comes to state-to-state arbitration, the EU's IPAs therefore differ significantly from the Member States' model of BITs, which typically includes only a single article on state-to-state arbitration.[21] That article typically contains one paragraph on the scope of the settlement of inter-party disputes ('compromissory clause'), one paragraph on consultations, one or two paragraphs on the composition of the tribunal, and one paragraph on the bindingness of its decisions.

State-to-state arbitration in EU IPAs is a much more complex system, both procedurally and institutionally. For the purpose of this chapter, a brief overview of the process of state-to-state arbitration foreseen in EU IPAs suffices.[22] EU IPAs prescribe that the parties to the agreement must first attempt to solve conflicts amicably. As a result, the parties are required to enter into consultations with a view to finding a mutually agreed solution.[23] In addition, any party may request to enter into a mediation procedure.[24] If the matter is not resolved through consultation within a certain time frame, the requesting party may refer it to an arbitration panel. The agreements set out complex rules for the composition of

[18] Press release, 'EU and China reach agreement in principle on investment', 30 December 2020.

[19] Chapter 29 CETA. Cf also Chapter 14 EUSFTA, Chapter 15 EUVFTA and Chapter 21 EU-Japan FTA.

[20] Chapter 3, Section B EUSIPA; Chapter 3, Section A EUVIPA; Section V CAI.

[21] See eg Article 9 of the Germany Model BIT (2008); Article 27 of the Slovakia Model BIT (2019); Article 25 of the Netherlands Model BIT (2019); or Article 30 of the Italy Model BIT (2021). For analysis of state-to-state dispute settlement clauses contained in BITs, see eg Giorgio Sacerdoti, 'Bilateral Treaties and Multilateral Instruments on Investment Protection' (1997) 269 *Collected Courses of the Hague Academy of International Law* 428; Paul Peters, 'Dispute Settlement Arrangements in Investment Treaties' (2009) *Netherlands Yearbook of International Law* 91, 102 et seq; or Hazarika (n 10) 26 et seq.

[22] For a more detailed analysis of the architecture of state-to-state arbitration in the context of EU FTAs (which is essentially the same for IPAs) see eg Cornelia Furculiţă, *The WTO and the New Generation EU FTA Dispute Settlement Mechanisms* (Springer, 2021).

[23] Article 29.4 CETA; Article 3.26 EUSIPA; Article 3.3 EUVIPA; Article 3 Section V CAI.

[24] Article 29.5 CETA; Article 3.27 EUSIPA; Article 3.4 EUVIPA; Article 4 Section V CAI.

arbitration panels that seek to prevent the possibility of a party paralysing the arbitration process at the stage of panel selection.[25] The arbitration panel shall issue an interim report, and subsequently a final report within a certain time frame.[26] EU IPAs generally require the report to be made publicly available.[27] The responding party must comply with the arbitration panel's report within a reasonable time frame,[28] and there is a compliance review mechanism.[29] If the responding party does not comply with the findings of the report, it must enter into negotiations with the requesting party, with a view to finding a mutually acceptable agreement on compensation. If an agreement on compensation cannot be reached within a certain time, the requesting party is entitled to take countermeasures at a level equivalent to the nullification or impairment caused by the violation.[30]

9.3. POTENTIAL USE: SCOPE OF STATE-TO-STATE ARBITRATION IN EU IPAS

Any type of investment dispute can theoretically be settled through state-to-state arbitration. This includes disputes that purely concern the interpretation of a BIT provision (so-called abstract interpretation claims, section 9.3.1); disputes about a measure by one party to a BIT that allegedly caused damage to the other party of that BIT (so-called concrete interpretation claims, section 9.3.2); and disputes about a measure by one party to a BIT that allegedly caused damage to a national of the other party to that BIT (so-called diplomatic protection claims, section 9.3.3). Yet, past case law in the context of state BITs has brought to the fore legal and practical hurdles for triggering state-to-state arbitration in certain situations. This section explores whether the modernised state-to-state arbitration system in EU IPAs addresses these hurdles.

9.3.1. Abstract Interpretation Claims

State-to-state arbitration may be launched with a view to obtaining an 'abstract interpretation' of a specific investment treaty clause. According to Rosenfeld,

[25] Article 29.7 and 29.8 CETA; Article 3.29 EUSIPA; Article 3.7 and 3.8 EUVIPA: Article 7 and 8 Section V CAI. Unfortunately, the EU's IPAs simply copy and paste the relevant provisions of the FTAs, without fixing certain pre-identified design issues. On the design problems and the remaining potential for paralysis see further Furculiță (n 22) 71 et seq; 83 et seq.

[26] Article 29.9 and 29.10 CETA, Article 3.31 and 3.32 EUSIPA; Article 3.10 and 3.11 EUVIPA; Article 12 Section V CAI.

[27] Article 29.10(3) CETA; Article 3.43(2) EUSIPA; Article 3.22(2) EUVIPA, Article 12.7 Section V CAI.

[28] Article 29.12 and 19.13 CETA; Article 3.33 and 3.34 EUSIPA; Article 3.12 and 3.13 EUSIPA; Article 13 and 14 Section V CAI.

[29] Article 29.13(2) CETA; Article 3.35 EUSIPA; Article 3.14 EUVIPA; Article 15 Section V CAI.

[30] Article 29.14 CETA; Article 3.36 EUSIPA; Article 3.15 EUVIPA; Article 16 Section V CAI.

the notion of abstract interpretation may be defined as 'the determination of a norm's legal content that is made (i) without reference to concrete facts, and (ii) with binding force for all those subjects to which the norm applies'.[31] In the context of state-to-state investment arbitration, one could think of a situation where one contracting party brings a claim against an (in)action of the other contracting party that allegedly violates the terms of the BIT but has not yet caused damage to either the first party and/or one of its investors.[32] Under the 'abstract interpretation' procedure, state-to-state arbitration tribunals thus take up the role of 'conflict preventors', as they are asked to provide an authoritative reading of a BIT provision before the underlying legal uncertainty causes material damage.

Notably, it would not be possible to launch investor-state arbitration for abstract interpretation claims, as the occurrence of loss or damage by a foreign investor is typically a precondition for the exercise of jurisdiction by an investor-state arbitration tribunal.[33] Conversely, the occurrence of material loss or damage is generally not a prerequisite for launching state-to-state arbitration proceedings.

Past case law, however, highlighted that it is difficult to launch state-to-state investment arbitration proceedings for abstract interpretation claims in the absence of a 'dispute' between the parties. The compromissory clause of most BITs, including CETA and the CAI, requires the existence of a dispute to trigger state-to-state arbitration. The compromissory clause of the 2019 Dutch Model BIT, for example, reads as follows: '[a]ny *dispute* between the Contracting Parties concerning the *interpretation* or *application* of this Agreement, which cannot be settled within a reasonable amount of time by means of diplomatic negotiations, shall … be submitted, at the request of either Contracting Party, to an arbitral tribunal …'.[34] The definition of a dispute is contested.[35] The Permanent Court of International Justice (PCIJ) provided a rather broad definition, qualifying a dispute as a 'disagreement on a point of law or fact, a conflict of legal views or of interests between two persons'.[36] Although the International Court of Justice (ICJ) continues to recall this definition, it practically narrowed it down

[31] Friedrich Rosenfeld, 'Abstract Interpretations in International Investment Law' in Photini Pazartzis et al (eds), *Reconceptualising the Rule of Law in Global Governance, Resources, Investment and Trade* (Hart Publishing, 2016) 331, 332.

[32] See also Potestà (n 10) 755.

[33] Article 8.18(2) CETA; Article 3.1(1) EU-Singapore IPA; Article 3.27(1) EUVIPA.

[34] Article 25 of the Netherlands Model BIT (2019), emphasis added.

[35] On the definition of legal disputes see Paolo Palchetti, Max Planck Encyclopedias of International Law [MPIL], article last updated in December 2018; Christoph Schreuer, 'What is a legal dispute?' in Isabelle Buffard et al (eds), *International Law between Universalism and Fragmentation: Festschrift in Honour of Gerhard Hafner* (Martinus Nijhoff, 2008) 959–80; or Robert Jennings, 'Reflections on the Term "Dispute"' in Ronald St J Macdonald (ed), *Essays in Honour of Wang Tieya* (Martinus Nijhoff, 1994) 401.

[36] PCIJ, *Mavrommatis Palestine Concessions (Greece v Great Britain)* [1924] PCIJ (Ser A) No 2, Judgment of 30 August 1924, at 11.

in a series of case law. It considered a dispute as 'a situation in which the two sides hold clearly opposite views concerning the question of the performance or non-performance of certain treaty obligations'.[37] In a 2016 judgment, the ICJ further held that a dispute only exists 'when it is demonstrated, on the basis of the evidence, that the respondent was aware, or could not have been unaware, that its views were "positively opposed" by the applicant'.[38]

For a party that merely seeks an interpretation of a certain treaty norm, it may be difficult to demonstrate that the other party is opposed to its legal views. As a result, it may be difficult to establish the existence of a dispute in abstract interpretation claims under BITs, and with it the jurisdiction of state-to-state arbitration tribunals. This was illustrated in *Ecuador v USA*.[39] In this case, Ecuador sent a request to the US about the interpretation of BIT clauses which had, in Ecuador's legal view, been misread by an investor-state arbitration tribunal, and asked the USA to confirm its legal views. The USA did not respond to Ecuador's request. Ecuador subsequently brought the matter before the BIT's state-to-state arbitration tribunal, arguing that the USA's silence amounted to a dispute. Conversely, the USA maintained that there had not been a dispute because the parties had not 'put themselves into a positive opposition to one another over a concrete case involving a breach under the treaty'.[40] The tribunal sided with the USA. It dismissed the case on grounds of lack of jurisdiction due to the absence of the dispute.[41]

The *Ecuador v USA* case illustrated the difficulty of demonstrating the existence of a dispute for purely interpretative claims, which may be one reason why state-to-state arbitration has so far hardly been used to qualify the terms of BITs. One way to solve this problem is redesigning the compromissory clause of BITs. Notably, this has been done for the EUSIPA and the EUVIPA. The clauses on the 'scope' of state-to-state arbitration in these two agreements do not, as

[37] ICJ, *Interpretation of the Peace Treaties with Bulgaria, Hungary and Romania* [1950] ICJ Reports 65, Advisory Opinion of 30 March 1950 (first phase), para 74.

[38] ICJ, *Obligations concerning Negotiations relating to Cessation of the Nuclear Arms Race and to Nuclear Disarmament (Marshall Islands v United Kingdom)* [2016] ICJ Reports 833, Judgment of 5 October 2016, para 37. See also earlier ICJ, *South West Africa (Ethiopia v South Africa; Liberia v South Africa)* [1962] ICJ Reports 319, Judgment of 21 December 1962, p 328. In prior decisions, the ICJ had, however, held that the lack of refutation and/or response by the responding party does not negate the existence of a dispute (ICJ, *Applicability of the Obligation to Arbitrate under Section 21 of the United Nations Headquarters Agreement of 26 June 1947* [1988] ICJ Report 12, paras 37–38). Whether the criterion of 'positive opposition' will remain a hard one therefore remains to be seen. For a more lenient definition of 'dispute' see esp Schreuer (n 35) 965: 'The decisive criterion for the existence of a dispute is not an explicit denial of the other party's position but a failure to accede to its demands.'

[39] *Ecuador v USA* (n 4).

[40] ibid para 56. The USA here relied on the expert opinion by Prof Christian Tomuschat, *The Construction of Article VII of the Bilateral Investment Treaty between the United States and Ecuador*, 24 April 2012.

[41] ibid para 228. Prof Raúl Emilio Vinuesa contested the narrow definition of dispute given by the tribunal in his Dissenting Opinion of 29 September 2012, United Nations Reports of International Arbitral Awards, Vol XXXIV, 81–123, para 217.

per their text, require the existence of a dispute between the parties as a precondition for the exercise of jurisdiction by the arbitration tribunals. Pursuant to Article 3.2 of the EUVIPA, the chapter on state-to-state arbitration applies 'with respect to the *avoidance* and settlement'[42] of disputes about the interpretation and application of the treaty. The clause thus explicitly suggests using state-to-state arbitration to avoid disputes from arising in the first place, irrespective of whether the parties hold opposing views. Article 3.25 EUSIPA does away with the word 'dispute' altogether, and replaces it with the word 'difference'.[43] That change of wording suggests that claims about the interpretation of treaty clauses can be brought before an arbitral tribunal in situations where the parties do not share the same legal views, without such views being in opposition to each other. The design of state-to-state arbitration under the EUSIPA and the EUVIPA thus facilitates abstract interpretation claims as conflict resolution tool. As was mentioned above, the compromissory clause of CETA and the CAI, by contrast, refer to the notion of 'dispute'.[44] For these two agreements, the requesting party will have to jump through the procedural hoop of demonstrating the existence of a dispute.

9.3.2. Concrete Interpretation Claims

State-to-state arbitration could also be triggered to obtain a 'concrete interpretation' of treaty clauses with a view to resolving an ongoing dispute about the interpretation or application of a BIT between the contracting parties.[45] In contrast to abstract interpretations, these types of claims are made with the intention of being immediately applied to a set of concrete facts.[46] In the context of state-to-state arbitration, one could imagine a situation where one party seeks to obtain compensation for a harm that it has allegedly incurred from a breach of the terms of the BIT by the other party. Notably, in this scenario, the requesting party brings a claim on its own behalf, and not on behalf of one of its investors. It is true that a breach of a BIT by the host state usually causes damages to foreign investors and not the home state. The *Italy v Cuba* case, however, demonstrated that contracting parties may bring compensatory claims on their own behalf.[47] In this case, Italy requested 'the symbolic amount

[42] Emphasis added.

[43] See similarly Article 10 of the Switzerland-Sudan BIT (1974).

[44] Article 29.2 CETA; Article 2 Section V CAI. Notably, the clause on the 'objectives' of the state-to-state arbitration mechanism of the CAI refers to the 'avoidance' of disputes (Article 1, Section V). That objective is, however, more difficult to fulfil if the scope of the chapter on state-to-state arbitration – and thus the jurisdiction of the tribunal – is confined to situations where a dispute already exists (Article 2, Section V).

[45] Hazarika (n 10) 67.

[46] Rosenfeld (n 31) 333.

[47] *Italy v Cuba* (n 4). See further esp Michele Potestà, 'Republic of Italy v. Republic of Cuba' (2012) 106 *American Journal of International Law* 341.

of 1 euro for the continued and reiterated violation of the terms, the spirit and the purposes of the BIT, and for the refusal, the indifference and the silence by the Cuban authorities vis-à-vis the several diplomatic initiatives directed at the amicable settlement of the disputes concerning the Italian investors'.[48] Although the tribunal did not ultimately find state injury, the case highlights that the parties to a BIT can use state-to-state arbitration to protect their own prerogatives.

The text of the EU's IPAs makes clear that state-to-state arbitration can be used by a party to invoke concrete interpretation claims. First, their respective chapter on state-to-state arbitration expressly applies to the interpretation *and* application of the treaty, and, thus, also to its concrete implementation by the parties. This is, secondly, underpinned by a clause contained in three out of the four EU IPAs, which stipulates that state-to-state arbitration may be used when a 'measure is alleged to have breached the Agreement as regards a *specific* investment …'.[49] As host state measures breaching a BIT regarding specific investments usually (also) affect foreign investors, the home state might, however, consider bringing a diplomatic protection claim.

9.3.3. Diplomatic Protection Claims

Lastly, state-to-state arbitration could be used by a contracting party with a view to espousing its national's claim and, in doing so, exercising diplomatic protection. Diplomatic protection is an elementary principle of international law,[50] and has been defined by the Draft Articles on Diplomatic Protection as 'the invocation by a [s]tate, through diplomatic action or other means of peaceful settlement, of the responsibility of another State for an injury caused by an internationally wrongful act of that State to a natural or legal person that is a national of the former State with a view to the implementation of such responsibility'.[51] The wording of standard compromissory clauses (which, as explained above, concern the interpretation *and* application of BITs) suggests that state-to-state arbitration can be seized of claims relating to the concrete implementation of substantive treaty norms by a host state in a situation involving foreign investors.[52]

[48] *Italy v Cuba*, Final Award (n 4) para 96.

[49] Article 8.42(2) CETA; Article 3.23(2) EUSIPA; Article 3.58(2) EUVIPA, emphasis added. A similar clause cannot be found in the CAI because that agreement does not include investor-state dispute settlement.

[50] Richard B Lillich, 'The Diplomatic Protection of Nationals Abroad: An Elementary Principle of International Law Under Attack' (1975) 69 *AJIL* 359. For a historical and critical analysis of the role of the principle in international investment law see Polanco (n 11) 11 et seq, 212 et seq.

[51] Article 1 Draft Articles on Diplomatic Protection (2006).

[52] See also Potestà (n 10) 756.

Yet, in the absence of an express exception, local remedies in the home state have to be exhausted before the host state may give diplomatic protection to its investor.[53] The exhaustion of local remedies rule principally applies to international claims arising from injury to individuals. It ensures that the '[s]tate where the violation occurred should have an opportunity to redress it by its own means, within the framework of its own domestic legal system'.[54] The Draft Articles on Diplomatic Protection stipulate a limited number of exceptions to the rule, including waivers, which will be further discussed below in the context of the EU's IPAs.[55] Most BITs, however, remain silent in this regard. In such situations, investors must exhaust local remedies in the host state before their home state can bring a diplomatic protection claim on their behalf before a state-to-state arbitration tribunal. This was shown in the *Italy v Cuba* case. Italy had not only sought to protect its own rights (see above[56]), but further espoused a claim on behalf of its investors.[57] While recognising that Italy may espouse its national's claim under the state-to-state arbitration procedure, the tribunal underlined the requirement for Italian investors to first exhaust local remedies in Cuba.[58]

The *Italy v Cuba* case brought to the fore a key imbalance between investor-state and state-to-state arbitration. While the exhaustion of local remedies is waived for the former, it is strictly applied to the latter.[59] That imbalance makes diplomatic protection claims a procedurally more extensive and thus a more time-consuming and costly alternative to investor-state arbitration, which might partially explain why state-to-state arbitration is rarely used in practice. Notably, the EU's IPAs – apart from the EUVIPA (see further below) – have addressed this imbalance in their design by precluding investors from invoking the IPA before domestic courts ('no direct effect').

The EU's IPAs with Canada, Singapore and China include a 'no direct effect' clause.[60] Accordingly, 'nothing in [these agreements] shall be construed as conferring rights or imposing obligations on persons, other than those created by the parties under public international law'. Arguably, the 'no direct effect' clause constitutes a waiver of the exhaustion of local remedies rules within the meaning of Article 15(e) of the Draft Articles on Diplomatic Protection. Although the exclusion of direct effect does not exclude a foreign investor from bringing a claim before the domestic courts of the host state, it excludes the

[53] See also Potestà (n 10) 756 et seq; Hazarika (n 10) 42; Polanco (n 11) 293.

[54] ICJ, *Interhandel Case* [1959] ICJ Reports 6, Judgment of 21 March 1959, p 25.

[55] Article 15 Draft Articles on Diplomatic Protection (2006).

[56] Section 3.2 (Concrete Interpretation Claims).

[57] *Italy v Cuba*, Final Award (n 4) paras 24–25.

[58] ibid paras 89–91. See further Potestà (n 47) 343.

[59] Italy indeed claimed that there was no room for the exhaustion of local remedies rule in state-to-state arbitration in case the relevant investment treaty also provided for investor-state arbitration where that rule is waived. The tribunal, however, dismissed Italy's claim. See *Italy v Cuba*, Interim Award (n 4) paras 41 et seq. See further Potestà (n 47) 343.

[60] Article 30.6 CETA; Article 4.11 EUSIPA; Article 14 Section VI CAI.

investor from invoking the IPA before these domestic courts. The investor can only pursue national (constitutional) rights before domestic courts. In essence, the 'no direct effect' clause thus has the effect of separating the jurisdictions of domestic courts, and international courts and tribunals. As a result, domestic (or: local) remedies are no longer an alternative to international remedies, but a means to invoke a different legal right in a different legal order. In contrast to most BITs, the EU's IPAs with Canada, Singapore and China therefore waive the exhaustion of local remedies rule for diplomatic protection claims under the state-to-state arbitration mechanism. While that does not solve all the problems associated with diplomatic protection,[61] it arguably addresses one of the key ones.

Although the EUVIPA also includes a 'no direct effect' clause, it remains a more difficult case.[62] That is because the second sentence of the 'no direct effect' clause stipulates that 'Viet Nam may provide otherwise under its domestic law'. That sentence goes against the very purpose of the clause, as reiterated in its title: no direct effect. It will be for domestic courts, and international courts and tribunals, to make sense of this apparent contradiction, and for state-to-state arbitration tribunals to decide whether that provision implies that European investors must exhaust local remedies in Vietnam before the EU and/or their Member State can bring a diplomatic protection claim.

9.4. POTENTIAL PARALLELISM: STATE-TO-STATE ARBITRATION AND OTHER ARBITRATION SYSTEMS

Most BITs include state-to-state *and* investor-state arbitration. At present – and with one notable recent exception (the CAI) – state-to-state arbitration is thus not viewed as an alternative but a parallel option to investor-state arbitration. In light of this reality, this section discusses the potential issues that arise from the parallel existence of different investment dispute settlement systems in EU IPAs and FTAs. The CAI will not be further discussed in this section, as it does not provide for any parallel arbitration systems alongside the IPA's main state-to-state arbitration. This section thus focuses on CETA, and the EU IPAs and FTAs with Singapore and Vietnam.

CETA, the EUVIPA and the EUSIPA contain both state-to-state and investor-state arbitration (section 9.4.1). In addition, the separate FTAs with Singapore and Vietnam include their own state-to-state arbitration mechanism (section 9.4.2). The different types of arbitration systems in EU FTAs and IPAs are technically not competing because they involve different parties and are established on different legal bases. Their coexistence nevertheless raises

[61] See esp Polanco (n 11) 274 et seq.
[62] Article 4.18 EUVIPA.

questions with regard to coordinating multiple proceedings on substantively equivalent or related matters under EU IPAs and FTAs.

9.4.1. State-to-State and Investor-State Arbitration in EU IPAs

The EU's IPAs with Canada, Singapore and Vietnam expressly design investor-state and state-to-state arbitration as alternative procedural avenues for settling investment disputes, with broadly overlapping scopes of application. Indeed, any dispute arising under EU IPAs that could trigger investor-state arbitration would also fall within the scope of the state-to-state arbitration mechanism provided in these agreements. Despite the resulting risk for conflicting and/or parallel proceedings, the EU's IPAs with Canada, Singapore and Vietnam do not contain a clause managing the coexistence of investor-state and state-to-state proceedings. Quite the contrary: parallel proceedings on the same or related matters are acknowledged and expressly allowed.

Pursuant to Article 8.18(1) CETA, the submission of a claim by an investor against a host state is '*without prejudice* to the rights of the Parties under Chapter Twenty-Nine [on state-to-state arbitration]'.[63] That wording implies that the initiation of investor-state proceedings does not affect the parties' rights to settle disputes inter se, possibly on the same subject matter. This logic is further outlined by the so-called 'Role of the Parties' clause contained in CETA, the EUVIPA and the EUSIPA.[64] At first sight, the 'Role of the Parties' clause appears to replicate Article 27 ICSID.[65] Article 27 ICSID prevents home states from providing diplomatic protection in respect of a dispute between the host state and one of their nationals. The first paragraph of the 'Role of the Parties' clause contained in the EU's IPAs with Canada, Singapore and Vietnam indeed precludes the contracting parties from giving diplomatic protection or bringing an international claim in respect of a dispute between one of their investors and the other party. The second paragraph of the 'Role of the Parties' clause, however, differs from Article 27 ICSID, in that it includes a carve-out for state-to-state arbitration under the same agreement. Accordingly, 'paragraph 1 *shall not exclude the possibility of a Party having recourse to [state-to-state arbitration]* in respect of a measure of *general application* even if that measure is alleged to have breached the Agreement *as regards a specific investment in respect of which a claim has been submitted* [under the investor-state arbitration system]'.[66] The broad wording of that exception, relating to both measures of general application and specific disputes, authorises the contracting parties to bring both

[63] Emphasis added.

[64] Article 8.42 CETA; Article 3.23 EUSIPA; Article 3.58 EUVIPA.

[65] On Article 27 ICSID see eg Christoph Scheuer, 'Article 27' (1997) 12 *ICSID Review – Foreign Investment Law Journal* 205.

[66] See eg Article 3.23(2) EUSIPA, emphasis added.

abstract and concrete interpretation claims *in parallel* to ongoing investor-state proceedings, either on their own behalf or on behalf of their investors.

There are three main moments in time where the EU and its treaty partners could launch state-to-state arbitration to (purposefully) interact with investor-state arbitration.[67] First, an abstract interpretation claim could be launched *before* investor-state proceedings are initiated. The state-to-state arbitration tribunal would thus interpret the same treaty provisions before the investor-state tribunal renders its award in the concrete dispute. By inference, state-to-state arbitration could be seized *after* an investor-state tribunal has delivered an award with a view to clarifying the investor-state tribunal's reading of the BIT. This was attempted in the above-mentioned *Ecuador v USA* case discussed above. Thirdly, a state-to-state arbitration tribunal may be launched *while* investor-state proceedings are underway, and the state-to-state tribunal renders its award on the same or closely related subject matter before the investor-state tribunal rendered its award. This was attempted in *Peru v Chile*. In that case, Peru had initiated state-to-state investment proceedings in response to the claim brought against it by the Chilean investor Lucchetti. After initiating the state-to-state arbitration, Peru requested a suspension of the proceedings in *Luchetti v Peru*. The investor-state tribunal, however, denied Peru's request, which ultimately led Peru to withdraw the state-to-state arbitration claim.[68]

The *Peru v Chile* case illustrates the uncertain legal parameters of the relationship between state-to-state and investor-state arbitration mechanisms contained in the same BIT. That uncertainty has not been addressed by the EU's IPAs with Canada, Singapore and Vietnam. Although these agreements explicitly acknowledge the possibility of parallel proceedings, they do not stipulate any rules on the legal relationship between the two arbitration procedures and tribunals. Do investor-state arbitration tribunals have to await pending state-to-state arbitration proceedings on a substantively equivalent or closely related matter before rendering their award? Do investor-state arbitration tribunals have to give utmost consideration to the interpretation of a treaty provision by a state-to-state arbitration tribunal? And what happens if cases on substantively equivalent or closely related matters brought before state-to-state and investor-state tribunals yield into different normative interpretations and/or applied outcomes?[69] Evidently, these uncertainties could cause serious practical difficulties if the parties to EU IPAs consider making more frequent use of state-to-state arbitration in parallel to investor-state arbitration.

[67] See also Michele Potestà, 'Towards a Greater Role for State-to-State Arbitration in the Architecture of Investment Treaties?' in Shaheeza Lalani and Rodrigo Polanco Lazo (eds), *The Role of the State in Investor-State Arbitration* (Brill, 2015) 241, 264.

[68] *Empresas Lucchetti SA and Lucchetti Peru SA v Peru* (n 4), paras 7–9.

[69] On these questions see esp Gabrielle Kaufmann-Kohler et al, 'Consolidation of Proceedings in Investment Arbitration: How Can Multiple Proceedings Arising from the Same or Related Situations Be Handled Efficiently?', Final Report on the Geneva Colloquium held on 22 April 2006.

9.4.2. State-to-State Arbitration in EU IPAs and FTAs

Because EU FTAs and IPAs cover different substantive areas, the state-to-state arbitration mechanisms established by these agreements should theoretically function independently of each other – each mechanism within the scope of the agreement it is based upon. Indeed, the EU's FTAs and IPAs with Singapore and Vietnam were neatly split along substantive lines: While the FTAs cover trade and investment liberalisation, the IPAs cover investment protection and investor-state dispute settlement. Yet, the boundary between investment liberalisation and protection is sometimes difficult to draw, and certain material overlaps between the scope of self-standing EU FTAs and IPAs remain. The EUSFTA, EUSIPA, EUVFTA and EUVIPA, for example, all include rules on market access, national treatment, and most favoured nation treatment for establishments. As a result, Singapore, for example, might be able to challenge an allegedly discriminatory EU internal measure concerning foreign establishments under the FTA or the IPA – or, possibly, both simultaneously. Indeed, the EUSFTA and EUSIPA do not preclude parallel proceedings on substantively equivalent matters. Conversely, parallel FTA and IPA proceedings are expressly prohibited under the EUVIPA and the EUVFTA. These agreements contain a so-called 'Choice of Forum' clause, which precludes the parties from bringing a dispute on a substantially equivalent matter before a court or tribunal established by any other international agreement to which they are both parties.[70] As a result, the risk of conflicting parallel decisions is greatly reduced. The risk of inconsistent awards on substantively related (but not equivalent) claims however remains. Neither one of the agreements with Singapore or Vietnam includes rules on coordinating decision-making by IPA and FTA arbitration tribunals on closely related matters.

The relationship between state-to-state and other arbitration mechanisms found in EU IPAs and FTAs arguably requires further clarification and specification, including in the design of such treaties. If state-to-state arbitration is envisioned to become a practical option alongside investor-state arbitration, then the coordination of multiple proceedings on substantively equivalent or closely related matters requires closer attention.

9.5. POTENTIAL ALTERNATIVE AND OUTLOOK: THE FUTURE OF STATE-TO-STATE ARBITRATION IN EU IPAS

The analysis arguably showed that a carefully crafted state-to-state arbitration system can fulfil the same functions as investor-state dispute settlement. The CAI demonstrates that EU policymakers indeed consider state-to-state

[70] Article 3.24 EUVIPA; Article 15.24 EUVFTA.

arbitration on a par with investor-state arbitration, at least in certain political circumstances. In the face of the current geopolitical climate, which puts a strain on multilateralism and impedes global system-building, the design and function of state-to-state arbitration in EU IPAs arguably deserves further exploration. There are at least a couple of arguments that underpin the potential usefulness of state-to-state arbitration as an alternative to investor-state arbitration.

First, disputes on certain subject matters could only be resolved using state-to-state arbitration; investor-state arbitration would not be an option. EU IPAs, for instance, exclude some matters from the scope of investor-state arbitration but not (fully) from state-to-state arbitration. For example, pursuant to Annex 8 C CETA, decisions by Canada following a review under the Investment Canada Act, a piece of national legislation, can in principle not be subjected to either form of dispute settlement. However, the EU and/or the Member States may seize state-to-state arbitration to challenge the consistency of such decisions with Canada's schedules of concessions. Another example are abstract interpretation claims. Because triggering investor-state arbitration in EU IPAs presupposes that an investor has occurred loss or damage, these tribunals cannot be seized for purely interpretative claims. Conversely, the occurrence of (individual) loss or damage is not a precondition for the exercise of jurisdiction by state-to-state arbitration tribunals. Most BITs – including CETA and the CAI – however, require the existence of a dispute as a precondition to the exercise of jurisdiction by the tribunal. The EU IPAs with Singapore and Vietnam show that a carefully worded compromissory clause, which explicitly waives the criterion of the existence of a dispute, allows state-to-state tribunals to assume jurisdiction over abstract interpretation claims. By providing an authoritative reading of the terms of the BIT before the underlying legal uncertainty has caused damage, state-to-state arbitration tribunals could take up an important 'conflict prevention function'.

Secondly, any dispute that could trigger investor-state arbitration would principally also fall within the scope of state-to-state arbitration. EU IPAs leave broad room for the parties to espouse their investors' claims – even in parallel to ongoing investor-state arbitration proceedings. In contrast to many BITs, the EU's IPAs with Canada, Singapore and China waive the requirement for foreign investors to exhaust local remedies in the host state before their home state can bring a diplomatic protection claim before the state-to-state arbitration tribunal on their behalf. In doing so, these agreements solve a key procedural inefficiency associated with diplomatic protection claims in the realm of international investment law. The EUVIPA includes a 'no direct effect' clause, whose content is opposed to its own title and purpose, as it appears to allow Vietnam to grant direct effect to the IPA after all. It will be for state-to-state arbitration tribunals to decide whether this clause implies that European investors must exhaust local remedies in Vietnam before the EU and/or their Member State can bring a diplomatic protection claim.

The examples of the 'no direct effect' clause in the EUVIPA, and the 'compromissory clauses' in CETA and the CAI, demonstrate that even marginal differences in the design of state-to-state arbitration mechanisms can have broad repercussions for their functionality. As state-to-state arbitration mechanisms included in EU IPAs have different strengths and weaknesses,[71] they must be read together to create a blueprint for future agreements.

Irrespective of potential future treaty design adaptations, investors will likely prefer bringing a direct claim before an investment arbitration tribunal over requesting an espousal by their home state. They do not have to align their interests with the ones of their home state, they retain control over the proceedings, they avoid the more politicised atmosphere of diplomatic protection and, in case they win, they receive direct compensation.[72] Whether state-to-state investment arbitration will experience a revival will thus likely depend on the desire of the treaty parties – and not their investors – to make more practical use of it. An increased use of state-to-state arbitration could help the parties 'to regain control as "masters" of the investment treaties, aiming to minimize risks in the interpretation of those agreements in potential future disputes with foreign investors'.[73] In doing so, the parties could decrease their exposure to investor-state arbitration. Yet, the use of state-to-state arbitration in EU IPAs would likely come with new problems. In particular, the relationship between different arbitration mechanisms in EU IPAs and FTAs remains unclear, which raises questions about the effective coordination of multiple proceedings on substantially equivalent or related matters. Recent practice in the realm of EU FTAs nevertheless indicates that state-to-state arbitration can be a viable alternative for failing multilateral dispute resolution systems.[74] In the field of investment, not all hope in multilateralism is lost, and there are various roads to changing the existing system. It remains to be seen if state-to-state arbitration, in a modernised design, will be considered as one of these alternative roads.

[71] On improving the design of state-to-state arbitration in EU FTAs (and hence also IPAs) see further also Furculiță (n 22).

[72] See also Potestà (n 10) 766.

[73] Polanco (n 11) 6.

[74] See esp *Restrictions applied by Ukraine on exports of certain wood products to the European Union*, Final Report of the Arbitration Panel, 11 December 2020. For a discussion see Iryna Polovets, 'Report of Arbitration Panel in Restrictions applied by Ukraine on exports of certain wood products to the European Union' (2021) 48 *LIEI* 1; and Gesa Kübek, 'Sustainable Development Chapters in EU FTAs and Dispute Settlement: Lessons Learned from *Ukraine – Wood Products* and *Korea – Labour Rights*' in Elaine Fahey and Isabella Mancini (eds), *Understanding the EU as a Good Global Actor* (Edward Elgar Publishing, 2022).

10

Investor-State Dispute Settlement from the Perspective of EU Law

CLAES GRANMAR

10.1. INTRODUCTION

According to economic theory, foreign direct investment (FDI) promotes economic growth.[1] In most instances, a prerequisite for a private party in one country to start a business, develop infrastructure, provide funding, make acquisitions, or gain control through similar economic transactions over resources in another country is that there are legal remedies for protection of the investments. Without an agreement between the countries concerned that ensures rights and remedies in the host state, the investor can only hope to be treated fairly by the authorities and courts of that state. Hence, the right for a private party to take legal action against the state where the investments have been made in a tribunal that is set up *ad hoc*, instead of having the case tried in the domestic courts of that state, is an important step towards a rule-based as opposed to power-based international order. Indeed, at an early stage of economic integration, an investor-state dispute settlement (ISDS) mechanism established by a bilateral investment treaty (BIT), a multilateral agreement on investment (MIA) or a comparable agreement promote the rule of law. Having said that, at least in a liberal democracy that embraces a social market economy model, the protection of FDI must not undermine other objectives of general interest or rights and freedoms conferred on legal entities. As the world is brought together the frictions increase, making even the basic assumption that interdependencies create peace and prosperity seem idealistic, and the states need to approximate their external commitments and internal policies beyond investment protection to ensure a sustainable development.

[1] See an attempt to qualify the assumptions on which economic theories rely: SD Cohen, *Multinational Cooperations and Foreign Direct Investments: Avoiding Simplicity, Embracing Complexity* (Oxford University Press, 2007).

Contrary to the horrific events that are currently taking place in eastern Europe and the weaponising of energy supply, the development of the European Union (EU) is a good example of how economic integration can promote human wellbeing in the broader sense *if combined with shared fundamental values*. From being a free trade area that could only be accepted with great difficulty within the framework of the General Agreement on Tariffs and Trade (GATT), the European Economic Community (EEC) matured into a European Community (EC) towards the end of the Cold War and became the central 'pillar' of the EU structure introduced by the Treaty of Maastricht in 1993.[2] In addition, the EU Treaty consolidated the work on developing a Common Foreign and Security Policy (CFSP) and cooperation in the field of justice and home affairs (JHA) in two more 'pillars'.[3] In a way, the European integration process has always promoted the *rule of law* in its purest form by limiting the political room for manoeuvre in accordance with a basic regulatory framework. However, the Member States have been reluctant to relinquish their constitutional powers. Apart from the *democratic deficit* resulting from the difficulties of making the European Parliament work, *fundamental rights* beyond equal treatment became binding primary law only in 2009, when the Treaty on European Union (TEU) and the Treaty on the Functioning of the European Union (TFEU) were adopted as a result of the Lisbon revision. In accordance with Article 6(1) TEU the Charter of Fundamental Rights of the European Union (EU Charter) gained the same legal value as the Treaties.[4] Nonetheless, fundamental rights were early recognised as general principles, and there has always been a common ambition to protect shared values in relation to non-Member States (third states). Ever since the unification project started to attract more attention in the wake of the oil crises in the early 1970s, only countries adhering to the idea of a social market economy based on the rule of law, democracy and fundamental rights can become members. Indeed, the value-based Union emerged from the interplay between internal and external actions.

[2] F McKenzie, 'The GATT-EEC Collision: The Challenge of Regional Trade Blocs to the General Agreement on Tariffs and Trade, 1950–67 (June 2010) 32(2) *The International History Review* 229–52.

[3] See, with respect to the CFSP and the incorporation of this second pillar in the EU legal order, G Butler, *Constitutional Law of the EU's Common Foreign and Security Policy* (Hart Publishing, 2019) 17–71.

[4] Consolidated version of the Treaty on European Union; Consolidated version of the Treaty on the Functioning of European Union [2012] OJ C326/1; and the Charter of the Fundamental Rights of the European Union [2012] OJ C326/391. See as to the concept of fundamental rights as general principles in Article 6(3) TEU. The first general election to the European Parliament took place 1979. For further reading see R Rose, *Election and Parties in New European Democracies* (CQ Press, 2003). As to equal treatment beyond discrimination on basis of nationality, see eg Case 43/75 *Defrenne v Sabena* ECLI:EU:C:1976:56 (*Defrenne II*).

Many current EU Member States had prior to their accession concluded BITs with existing Member States. Indeed, the Member States were encouraged to strengthen the economic ties with neighbouring states to pave the way for an enlargement of the Union within the auspices of the World Trade Organization (WTO) which superseded GATT in 1994. However, along with the consolidation of the EU legal order and the emphasis on system-coherency as a core element of the rule of law, it became increasingly clear that intra-EU ISDS regimes could undermine the functioning of the internal market and the overall consistency of EU law. Accordingly, the European Commission began discouraging the Member States from using the ISDS system.[5] After the Lisbon revision, it became untenable to consider fundamental rights and substantive EU law regarding, eg, commerce, establishment, public procurement and state aid as a mere matter of fact in disputes where a private investor in one Member State invoked a BIT against another Member State.[6] Investors established in the Union cannot circumvent the scope of internal EU law in relation to a Member State just as little as investors established in a Member State cannot circumvent domestic public law in relation to the same state by invoking public international law. After much debate, the tension between internal EU law and intra-EU BITs was partly resolved in 2021 as most of the Member States signed the Agreement for the termination of intra-EU BITs.[7] Eventually, intra-EU ISDS systems under MIAs have also been deemed incompatible with the *sui generis* Union legal order.[8]

As a result of the Treaty of Lisbon revision, the Union was also afforded exclusive competences to negotiate and conclude BITs and MIAs with third countries within the scope of the Common Commercial Policy (CCP).[9] Hence, the EU speaks with one voice, for instance in the process of modernising the Energy Charter Treaty (ECT). As nothing would be more 'inefficient' for unification than to be left at the mercy of hostile powers, a high degree of self-sufficiency may in many instances seem more appealing than globalisation. In these troubled times, European security has become the top priority of EU policy makers. In that connection, the Union has adopted an investment 'screening mechanism' for information sharing and cooperation between the Commission and the Member States regarding FDIs.[10] Although the screening mechanism is

[5] An early measure was to require better statistics on FDI; see Regulation (EC) No 184/2005 on Community statistics concerning balance of payment, international trade in services and foreign direct investment [2005] OJ L35/23.

[6] See Case C-638/19 P *Commission v Micula* ECLI:EU:C:2022:50.

[7] Agreement for the termination of Bilateral Investment Treaties between the Member States of the European Union, SN/4656/2019/INIT [2020] OJ L169/1. For instance, Sweden has not signed the agreement.

[8] Case C-741/19 *Komstroy* ECLI:EU:C:2021:655.

[9] For further reading see eg P Strik, *Shaping the Single European Market in the Field of Foreign Direct Investments* (Hart Publishing, 2016).

[10] Regulation (EU) 2019/452 establishing a framework for the screening of foreign direct investments in the Union, PE/72/2018 Rev 1 [2019] OJ L791/1; and Commission delegated Regulation (EU)

without prejudice to the Member States' responsibility for national security, it identifies areas where a dialogue is appropriate, and the Commission can issue opinions. It is old news that the sustainable development of Europe envisaged in Article 3(3) TEU implies that short-term allocative efficiency must be reconciled with broader public interests and fundamental rights and, hence, the Union legal order knows of no such thing as 'European economic law'.[11]

In order to ensure consistency between external actions and internal policies, the Union has since 2015 been seeking to establish permanent tribunals or 'investment courts' through its trade and investment agreements.[12] Furthermore, the Union is promoting the creation of a multilateral investment court, in for instance Working Group III of the United Nations Commission on International Trade Law (UNCITRAL). By contrast, the United States (US) remains in favour of the WTO *ad hoc* ISDS system. Perhaps the categorical division into federal powers and state powers makes the reliance on casuistic decisions by arbitrators in investment disputes easier to accept in US law than in the context of the integrated legal framework for cohesive socio-economic development in Europe.[13] Arguably, the European experience of amalgamation of old societies into a Union by law may be of interest on the international scene, and in this piece ISDS is discussed from that point of view.

10.2. THE ARDUOUS UNIFICATION OF EUROPEAN WELFARE STATES

Soon after the end of World War II, the US took several initiatives to restore international trade and collaboration. Following the Bretton-Woods conference in 1944, the International Monetary Fund (IMF) was established within the framework of the United Nations (UN) in December 1945 with a view to (based on the ideas of Harry Dexter White and John Maynard Keynes) securing financial stability, facilitating international trade and promoting high employment and sustainable economic growth. Despite the support from more than 50 countries in the UN to also set up an international trade organisation, the US

2021/2126 amending the Annex to the aforementioned Regulation, C/2021/6924 [2021] OJ L432/1. For the time being the Union is also developing the 'emergency instrument', see eg COM(2022) 459 Proposal for a Regulation establishing a single market emergency instrument and repealing Council Regulation No (EC) 2679/98.

[11] See, on the relationship between competition law and data protection, Opinion by Advocate General Rantos, Case C-252/21 *Meta Platforms v Bundeskartellamt* ECLI:EU:C.2022:704.

[12] In 2015 the Commission issued a reformed investment dispute settlement approach. See eg COM(2017)0493 final. Recommendation for a Council Decision authorising the opening of negotiations for a Convention establishing a multilateral court for the settlement of investment disputes. See also Regulation (EU) No 912/2014 establishing a framework for managing financial responsibility linked to investor-state dispute settlement tribunals established by international agreements to which the European Union is party [2014] OJ L257/121.

[13] See, originally, Joined Cases C-6/90 and C-9/90 *Francovich and Bonafaci and others* ECLI:EU:C:1991:428, regarding the possibility for private parties to bring cases for compensation against a Member State.

withdrew from the negotiations and promoted a less ambitious framework.[14] On 30 October 1947, GATT was signed by 23 countries in Geneva, Switzerland.[15] In addition, to jump-start the world economy, the US unilaterally launched the European Recovery Plan, better known as the Marshall plan, to help Western Europe rise from the ashes. Considering the history from the Enlightenment to the end of World War II, there can be no surprise that the idea of universal human rights also gained a more general acceptance in the late 1940s. In 1948 the Universal Declaration of Human Rights, drafted by the Human Rights Commission chaired by Eleonor Roosevelt, was adopted at the third session of the UN General Assembly in Paris. Moreover, the North Atlantic Treaty Organisation (NATO) was set up shortly thereafter, in 1949.

In this context of international efforts to stabilise and promote socio-economic development, the new political leaders in Western Europe started the process of reconciliation through ever-closer cooperation. In 1949 the Council of Europe was founded by 10 countries to secure the *rule of law*, *democracy* and *human rights* by transposing and operationalising the UN Declaration of Human Rights.[16] Less than a year later, in 1950, the European Convention on Human Rights (ECHR) was adopted and it could enter into force on 3 September 1953. In the same period, the Treaty establishing the European Coal and Steel Community (ECSC) was adopted by Belgium, France, Italy, the Netherlands, Luxembourg and West Germany in Paris 1951. Evidently, the ultimate objective of the ECSC was to prevent an arms race and war by controlling the use of strategic resources. As the collaboration deepened, the same countries adopted the Treaty establishing the European Atomic Energy Community (Euratom) and the EEC Treaty in 1957.[17] Much inspiration for the EEC Treaty was originally drawn from the ordoliberal school of thought.[18] Besides the creation of a customs union by the abolition of customs duties and trading quotas between the Member States, and a common system for external customs control, the Community was based on the principles of 'deregulation' in terms of reduced direct state control, non-discrimination on the basis of geographical origin of products and legal entities, and approximation of behind the border measures.

In contrast to many international agreements, the EEC Treaty was silent on its effect in the Member States. True, unlike the overarching multilateral legal

[14] See McKenzie, 'The GATT-EEC Collision' (n 2).

[15] See, for an overview, F McKenzie, *GATT and Global Order in the Postwar Era* (Cambridge University Press, 2020).

[16] The Council of Europe was founded by Belgium, Denmark, France, Ireland, Italy, Luxembourg, the Netherlands, Norway, Sweden and the United Kingdom (UK), and within a year Greece, Iceland, Turkey and West Germany also became members. Originally 'the Convention for the Protection of Human Rights and Fundamental Freedoms'.

[17] Treaty Establishing the European Economic Community signed in Rome on 25 March 1957 and applicable from 1 January 1958 (EEC Treaty); Belgium, France, the Netherlands and the United Kingdom also established the Western Union Defence Organisation, but it had been disbanded in 1951.

[18] See, T Biebricher, W Bonefeld and P Nedergaard (eds), *The Oxford Handbook of Ordoliberalism* (Oxford University Press, 2022).

framework established by GATT, there was nothing in the structure of the Treaty that prevented it from conferring legal rights upon private parties. But since the EEC Treaty was, like all other international agreements, concluded by governments, it could appear to be left to each signatory party to decide how to transpose it into domestic law. Whereas for instance the ECHR formed part of a *monist legal system* as soon as the agreement was approved by the national parliament, it needed to be transformed or incorporated into a *dualist legal system*. Having said that, all countries have at closer inspection a rather *pluralistic approach* to international commitments.[19] In any event, the EEC established an institutional framework with potentially far reaching normative powers. This, in combination with the shared vision of a high level of economic integration, made the US and other countries hesitant to accept the EEC as a free trade area under GATT. In addition to the legislative powers, the Court of Justice which later on became the Court of Justice of the European Union (CJEU) soon took the opportunity to confirm, in two seminal rulings handed down in the 1960s, that Treaty provisions could apply directly as law in the Member States and confer rights on private parties, ie have direct effect, against the 'state' broadly defined.[20] Economic transactions known as FDI under public international law were central to the realisation of the internal market but needed to be reconciled with social objectives.[21] Hence, the EU approach to BITs with direct effect and *ad hoc* ISDS must be seen in the light of a long history of reconciling conflicting interests in order to establish and maintain the internal market.

10.2.1. Primacy of an Underdeveloped International Legal System

Following the realisation of the customs union in 1968, the European Commission could intensify efforts to legislate away measures behind the borders having an effect equivalent to quantitative restrictions (MEQRs) on exchanges between the Member States, and to deepen economic integration. As the domestic markets were brought together by the agreements between the Member States (primary law) and legislative acts adopted on the basis of primary law (secondary legislation), the corresponding limitations on the right to regulate on national level became more and more palpable. Inevitably, the competences conferred on the supranational institutions to promote market integration had repercussions for the basic structures of domestic law as well as for national policy making.

[19] See, C Granmar, 'Economic Globalisation and the Rule of Law', *Europarättslig tidskrift* 2017 nr 3, p 489. See also D Bederman and C Keitner, *International Law Frameworks*, 4th ed. (Foundation Press).

[20] Case 26/62 *Van Gen en Loos* ECLI:EU:C1963:1; and Case 6/64 *Costa v ENEL* ECLI:EU:C:64:34.

[21] See, for instance, International Labour Organization Charter; Opinion of Advocate General Dutheillet de Lamothe, Case 80/70 *Defrenne v Belgium* ECLIEU:C:1971:43 (*Defrenne I*); and Opinion of Advocate General Trabucchi, Case 43/75 *Defrenne v Sabena* ECLI:EU:C:1976:39, regarding the 'social objectives' of the Community and referred to by the Court in the same case.

In the system of cooperation between the domestic courts and the CJEU now enshrined in Article 267 TFEU, the implications of the sources of EU law could be clarified through *preliminary rulings*.

One of the many regulations adopted by the Council of Ministers on the proposal of the Commission in the 1960s with implication for the external trade relations, concerned the common organisation of the market in cereals and more particularly a deposit guarantee scheme requiring the producers of cereals to lodge a security to obtain an export licence. As this duty was considered to impose an undue burden on small and medium sized producers (SMEs) contrary to the right to conduct a business under the Basic Law of the Federal Republic of Germany, an administrative court of first instance referred questions to the CJEU on the validity of secondary legislation deemed incompatible with fundamental rights under constitutional law. In response, the CJEU explained unambiguously in *Internationale Handelsgesellschaft* that directly applicable secondary legislation prevails over all domestic law including constitutional rights.[22] If instead domestic law could override supranational measures to promote the functioning of the internal market, it would no longer be possible to ensure a 'level playing field' for the market participants.[23] Nonetheless, upon appeal, the German Constitutional Court upheld its competence to assess whether or not supranational rules were compatible with basic rights under domestic law 'as long as' the integration process had not come so far as to embrace 'a catalogue of fundamental rights'.[24] Evidently, neither the Commission, nor the Council or the CJEU advocated that human rights or the broader category of fundamental rights, encompassing also collective rights, should be set aside. However, the combination of limited competences and the primacy of the supranational sources of law resulted in an economisation of law on account of broader social interests that was uncalled for.[25]

In order not to ride roughshod over national welfare systems and particularly fundamental rights, the CJEU started to recognise the rights guaranteed by the ECHR and, as they result from the constitutional traditions common to the Member States, as general principles that could justify necessary and, hence, proportionate limitations on free movement and the protection of economic interests.[26] In 1986, the German Constitutional Court found it opportune to clarify that it would no longer need to assess whether primary law and secondary legislation tallied with the Basic Law 'as long as' effective protection for fundamental rights was ensured by the supranational institutions.[27] However, several

[22] Case 11/70 *Internationale Handelsgesellschaft* ECLU:EU:C:1970:114.
[23] See also Case C-213/89 *Factortame* ECLI:EU:C:1990:257.
[24] BverfGE 37, 291, 29 May 1974 (*Solange I*).
[25] Compare with the Single European Act [1987] OJ L169/3.
[26] See, as one of many examples, Case 36/75 *Rutili* ECLI:EU:C:1975:137.
[27] BverfGE 73, 339, 22 October 1986 (*Solange II*).

Supreme Courts remain sceptical of the primacy of EU law to this day.[28] This approach is difficult to reconcile though with the fact that the Member States, pursuant to Declaration 17 concerning the Treaty of Lisbon, recognise the case law on primacy and 'that the law stemming from the treaty, an independent source of law, could not, because of its special and original nature, be overridden by domestic legal provisions, however framed, without being deprived of its character as Community law and without the legal basis of the Community itself being called into question'.[29] Since the case law of the CJEU leaves no room for doubts about the primacy of EU law, the German Constitutional Court has in recent times developed the more credible line of reasoning that the EU institutions are sometimes acting *ultra vires*, ie, beyond their conferred powers under the Treaties.

Contrary to the internal paradox where the Member States were on the one hand reluctant to confer constitutional competences on the supranational institutions, and on the other hand the supranational institutions had a duty to take a variety of social interests into account when approximating the domestic legal systems, the Member States could ensure that only countries sharing their values acceded to the Community. Hence, the countries on the Iberian and Attic Peninsulas could join the project only in the 1980s as their authoritarian regimes had been replaced by proper democracies and *trias politicas* systems. Towards the end of the Cold War, the importance of a common identity moved into the limelight and more clarity in the negotiation with aspirant states was called for. At a meeting just some months after the entry into force of the Treaty of Maastricht in Copenhagen, the Council adopted a set of criteria for the assessment of whether a country is eligible to accede to the Union.[30]

On the international scene, the multilateral negotiations within the auspices of the GATT were also expanded. Whereas the competences of the European Commission to negotiate tariffs and trade in goods had been fairly uncontroversial, trade in services and the interfaces with intellectual property rights were addressed in the course of the Uruguay rounds which ran between 1986 and 1994. Consequently, both the Commission and the Member States participated in the negotiations, and the uncertainties surrounding the delegations' competences translated into a tug of war. As the WTO agreement was about to be signed, questions were referred to the CJEU for clarification. In its seminal *Opinion 1/94*, the Court provided a detailed account in many respects on how to draw the line between the CCP and Member State competences under public

[28] See as to Germany BverfGE 89, 155, 12 October 1993 (*Solange III*); and BverfGE 102, 147, 7 June 2000 (*Solange IV*); and at to French approaches, eg Conseil d'Etat, 30 October 2009, 298348 Mme Perreu. See also Conseil d'Etat, 1 October 2014, 365054, Mme BA et Mme A; Conseil d'Etat, 30 December 2013, 350191, Association CIMADE.

[29] A declaration concerning provisions of the Treaties – 17, Declaration concerning primacy, 12008E/AFI/DCL/17, [2008] OJ 115/344.

[30] Presidency Conclusion, Copenhagen European Council 21–22 June 1993, Accession Criteria (Copenhagen criteria), now, Article 47 TEU.

international law.[31] At the end of the day, the WTO agreement and the appendices thereto needed to be signed by both the Member States and the Union. Consequently, both the Union and its Member States needed to realise their international commitments within the scope of their respective powers.

Although the answers from the CJEU were agreeable in the external dimension, they soon created uncertainties regarding the internal distribution of competences between the Union and its Member States. In a series of preliminary rulings regarding the right to interpret Appendix 1C to the WTO Agreement regarding Trade-Related Aspects of Intellectual Property Rights (TRIPS), the Court explained that it must have the last word in order to ensure a consistent legal development within the Union.[32] Whereas internal Union measures translated into external competences along the lines of parallelism and implied powers, external Union measures must not upset the internal system-coherency.

10.2.2. Consistency, Teleology, and the Rule of Law

Even as the European Parliament has gained more and more powers along with the development of the Union and is now placed on equal footing with the Council as a legislator in most instances, the complexity of the legislative procedures often makes it difficult to discern a clear will of the EU legislator. At first blush, there still seems to be a 'democratic deficit' that undermines the unification. Indisputably, the central role of the Commission, the intergovernmental features of the legislative processes and the fact that the unification ultimately hinges on the principle of *pacta sunt servanda*, distinguish the Union from a federation and make it appear as a *sui generis* polity. However, as Plato recognised, democracy has its weaknesses, and the Union legal order may prove to be a bulwark against populism and polarisation, not least in the wake of digital globalisation.[33] Instead of understanding 'law' as mainly a tool in the hands of the legislator to realise policy decisions as the ordoliberalists did, the integration project is anchored in values and objectives which the Union and its Member States must abide by pursuant to the principle of sincere cooperation. Legal obligations in turn make the Member States less susceptible to shifting political winds which is beneficial also for the industry. Teleology anchored in legal

[31] Case C-660/13 *Council v Commission* EU:C:2016:616 (*Swiss MoU*). See A Neergaard, 'Institutional Balance in the Conclusion of Non-binding International Agreements Revisited: Council v Commission (Swiss MoU)' in G Butler and RA Wessel (eds), *EU External Relations Law: The Cases in Context* (Hart Publishing, 2022).

See also, as to the effects of this 'turf-war', M Gatti and P Manzini, '*External Representation of the European Union in the Conclusion of International Agreements*' (2010) 49 *CML Rev* 1703–34.

[32] See, eg, Case C-130/95 *Giloy* ECLI:EU:C:1997:372; Case C-53/96 *Hermès* ECLI:EU:C1998:292; and Joined Cases C-300/98 and C-392/98 *Dior and Others* ECLI:EU:C:2000:688.

[33] Plato, *Republic* (Penguin Classic, 2007).

obligations often speaks in favour of *a consistent legal development* which is an essential element of the rule of EU law.

Given the efforts to define common core values, it may have seemed logical for the EU to join the ECHR system. In fact, the European Commission had suggested in 1993 that the Community should do so.[34] However, in *Opinion 2/94 (EU Accession to the ECHR I)*, the CJEU explained that it was not possible since the Member States had at the time not conferred competences on the EU institutions in the field of human rights and, hence, the Union could not enter into such an agreement.[35] Arguably, this position became untenable in the late 20th century as 'EU-phoria' turned into a war in the Balkans and the Member States realised the need to manifest the protection of fundamental rights on Union level. On 18 December 2000, the Council, Commission and Parliament solemnly proclaimed the adoption of the EU Charter but without a clear legal basis in the Treaty despite a recent Treaty reform.[36]

Because of the uncertainties surrounding the legal effect of the Charter, the CJEU took the opportunity to reconstruct some provisions in such an extensive way that they were virtually set aside.[37] Contrary to the letter of Article 53 of the Charter, the Court was prepared to restrict and even disregard human rights and fundamental freedoms as recognised by the Member States constitutions, in order to ensure consistency of the Union legal order. Famously, in *Melloni*, the CJEU explained that the principle of mutual trust as particularised in the European Arrest Warrant could not be overridden for the purpose of avoiding an adverse effect on the right to a fair trial guaranteed by the Constitution of Spain.[38] A person who had been sentenced by an Italian court *in absentia* to 10 years' imprisonment for bankruptcy and fraud, and who had been arrested in Spain, opposed the decision by a Spanish court to surrender him to Italian authorities in order to serve the sentence imposed on him. Although the arrest warrant states unambiguously that the Member States shall respect the criminal law systems of one another, the Spanish court considered the absence of a right of appeal in Italy incompatible with the Constitution of Spain and referred questions to the CJEU for a preliminary ruling. In its response, the Court stated that Article 53 of the EU Charter does not allow a Member State to make a surrender conditional upon the conviction being open for review in the issuing Member States and, hence, that the national constitution had to yield to the principle of mutual respect enshrined in secondary legislation. In the absence

[34] As a legal basis, the Commission suggested Article 235 ECT affording a broad right to regulate, eg if it is necessary to attain an objective of the Community. For further reading, see B Brandtner and A Rosas, 'Human Rights and the External Relations of the European Community: An Analysis of Doctrine and Practice' (1998) 9 *European Journal of International Law* 468–90.

[35] *Opinion 2/94* EU:C:1996:140 (*EU Accession to the ECHR I*).

[36] Treaty of Amsterdam [1997] OJ C340/1 that entered into force on 1 May 1999 see also Treaty of Nice [2001] OJ C80/1 that entered into force on 1 February 2003.

[37] Case C-399/11 *Melloni* ECLI:EU:C:2013:107.

[38] Case C-399/11 *Melloni*, paras 55–65.

of harmonised rights, mutual respect between the Member States prevailed over domestic fundamental rights in the Spanish legal system contrary to the letter of Article 53 of the EU Charter.

In the case of international agreements, it often follows from their very purpose and structure that they are only binding on the contracting parties, as opposed to applying as law to legal entities in the states. For instance, most trade agreements turn on the principle of reciprocity between the contracting parties. Even if the agreements prevent discrimination of legal entities, the rights are not considered to be unconditional or clear and precise enough to confer rights on the private parties.[39] These sources of EU law have neither direct applicability nor direct effect in the Member States. Consequently, the CJEU has a certain leeway to adapt international commitments to internal systematics, and to confine the scope of fundamental rights if necessary to ensure internal system-coherency.

Conversely, the CJEU may condition the Union's external commitments on internal fundamental rights. For instance, in *Kadi*, the Court explained that a UN resolution to freeze the assets of persons who were believed to be affiliated with the network behind the terrorist attack against the US on September 11, 2001 could only be enforced in the Union insofar as they were entitled to an effective remedy and to a fair trial pursuant to Article 47 of the EU Charter.[40] Having said that, beyond the essence of the fundamental rights recognised in the EU Charter, the CJEU has been susceptible to the fact that they can still have a different meaning in domestic law. For instance, human dignity may justify a prohibition against an installation for live war games known as 'laserdome' in Germany, whereas that may seem far fetched in a Member State such as Sweden.[41]

Article 52 of the Charter confirms the consistent line of reasoning of the CJEU regarding the need to limit the scope of opposing general interests and fundamental rights if necessary to reconcile them. As the Union has its roots in a free trade area, the right to conduct a business under Article 16 of the EU Charter is often the starting point for the analysis, and other general interests and fundamental rights appear as justification grounds or mandatory requirements when regulating a market.[42] Furthermore, secondary legislation largely details the proportionality tests in various fields. Then again, when zooming out from the particularities of the many different fields of EU law, it becomes clear that the Union legal order is held together by a multidimensional concept of consistency. In addition to the vertical consistency between primary law and secondary legislation, the CJEU as well as the EU legislator seeks to ensure a

[39] For further reading, see J Wouters et al, *The Law of EU External Relations: Cases, Materials and Commentary on the EU as an International Legal Actor*, 3rd edn (OUP, 2021), p 6 et seq.

[40] Joined Cases C-402/05 P and C-415/05 *Kadi and Al Barakaat* ECLI:EU:C:2008:416. See further C Eckes, 'The Autonomy of EU Law vis-à-vis International Law: Kadi I and Kadi II' in G Butler and RA Wessel (eds), *EU External Relations Law* (n 31).

[41] Case C-36/02 *Omega Spielhallen* ECLI:EU:C:2004:614.

[42] Case C-112/00 *Schmidberger* ECLI:EU:C:2003:333.

consistent legal development over the time, and this in turn requires consistency between internal market law and external actions as well as consistency between various fields of substantive law.

In the beginning of the new millennium, the creation of a proper EU Constitution was on the agenda, but the project came to an end primarily as a result of the referendums in France and the Netherlands. Nevertheless, the EU institutions immediately continued the work to revise the EU Treaties. As the three 'pillars' of the Union were merged into one basic legal framework consisting of the TEU and TFEU in 2009, the EU Charter was pursuant to Article 6 TEU elevated to primary law. At the same time, the Union was granted exclusive competences with regard to direct investments from third countries, as FDI was included in the CCP under Article 207 of the TFEU.

10.2.3. The Post-Lisbon Revision Source Code of the Unification Program

According to Article 19 TEU, the CJEU and the General Court shall 'ensure that in the interpretation and application of the Treaties the law is observed'. Considering the fact that the Treaties are the primary sources of law in the EU legal order potentially prevailing over external commitments, the reference to the 'law' as a yardstick when applying the Treaties may seem puzzling. However, the notion of 'law' must in this connection be understood as referring to a set of meta norms in the Treaties constituting a 'source code of the unification program', as this author has reiterated.[43]

According to Article 5(2) TEU, the EU institutions shall act only within the limits of the powers conferred by the Member States on the Union in the Treaties to *attain the objectives* set out therein. At the highest level of abstraction, the Member States have written into Article 3(1) TEU that the overarching objective of the Union is to promote peace, its values and the well-being of its peoples. According to Article 2 TEU, the Union 'is founded on the values of respect for human dignity, freedom, democracy, equality, the rule of law and respect for human rights, including the rights of persons belonging to minorities', and as mentioned the EU Charter specifics the fundamental rights.

Notably, the EU Charter is no smorgasbord of rights and freedoms that can be invoked upon convenience. It is the starting point for all normative measures taken by the EU institutions and the Member States within the scope of the powers conferred upon the Union and a yardstick for assessing the validity of Union measures. Furthermore, the impact of the fundamental rights within the scope of the domestic legal systems of the Member States was made utterly clear by the CJEU in *Åkerberg Fransson* regarding the meaning of *ne bis in idem*:

[43] C Granmar, 'Global Applicability of the GDPR in Context' (2021) 11(33) *International Data Privacy Law* 225.

> Since the fundamental rights guaranteed by the Charter must therefore be complied with where national legislation falls within the scope of European Union law, situations cannot exist which are covered in that way by European Union law without those fundamental rights being applicable. The applicability of European Union law entails applicability of the fundamental rights guaranteed by the Charter.[44]

Indeed, the teleology of the Union legal order has been manifested in Article 13 TEU requiring the Union to have 'an institutional framework which shall aim to promote its values, advance its objectives and serve its interests, those of its citizens and those of the Member States'. When it comes to the external dimension, the Union shall according to Article 3(5) TEU in its relation with the wider world 'promote its values and interests, and contribute to the protection of its citizens'. More to the point, the Member States require pursuant to Article 21(1) TEU that the 'Union's actions on the international scene shall be guided by the principles which have inspired its own creation, development and enlargement, and which it seeks to advance in the wider world: democracy, the rule of law, the universality and indivisibility of human rights and fundamental freedoms'.

Then again, competing interests and rights need to be reconciled by proportionate limitations, and ultimately the CJEU needs to ensure internal/external, vertical and horizontal as well as evolutionary consistency. Consequently, the Member States stipulate in Article 13 TEU that the EU institutional framework shall 'ensure the consistency, effectiveness, and continuity of its policies and actions'. Article 7 TFEU confirms the need to apply the teleological and systematic interpretative methods by stating that 'the Union shall ensure consistency between its policies and activities, taking all of its objectives into account and in accordance with the principle of conferral of powers'.

As the Union had obtained unambiguous powers with regard to fundamental rights, the Commission started negotiation with a view to acceding to the ECHR in accordance with Article 6(2) TEU. Also many Member States promoted an accession of the Union to the ECHR system in order to avoid norm conflicts on a national level. However, pursuant to the CJEU in *Opinion 2/13 (EU Accession to the ECHR II)*, it would be incompatible with the primacy, consistency and nature of the legal order to subject the EU institutions to review by the Council of Europe and the ECtHR.[45] Ultimately, the autonomy of the *sui generis* EU legal order can according to the CJEU be justified only as long as the essential characteristics of the system can be safeguarded by the Court. After all, there is a vast amount of secondary legislation that particularises the fundamental rights, and according to Article 19 of the TEU, the EU Court shall ensure a consistent legal development.

[44] Case C-617/10 *Åkerberg Fransson* ECLI:EU:C:2013:105, para 21.

[45] *Opinion 2/13* ECLI:EU:C:2014:2454 (*EU Accession to the ECHR II*). See K Ziegler, 'The Second Attempt at EU Accession to the ECHR: Opinion 2/13' in G Butler and RA Wessel (eds), *EU External Relations Law* (n 31).

10.3. SYSTEM-COHERENCY, INVESTMENT PROTECTION AND THE MEMBER STATE

In the light of the aforementioned, it would be an infringement of the EU Treaties, and hence *contra legem*, not to align the protection of FDIs in the Union with the teleology and consistency of EU law. Since BITs and MIAs with ISDS mechanisms confer rights on private parties against contracting polities or states, they have contrary to international trade agreements *per definition* vertical direct effect. Even if an *ad hoc* ISDS tribunal may take broad social interests into account and the arbitrators may be well versed in 'constitutional' EU law, the mere fact that the tribunal is not a 'court or tribunal of a Member State' in accordance with Article 267 TFEU makes the ISDS award anomalous in EU law.[46]

Without the possibility for the arbitrators to request a preliminary ruling from the CJEU, there is no way that the CJEU can fulfil its duty under Article 19 TEU to ensure that the law is observed in the case. True, the *raison d'être* of ISDS is to afford private investors access to justice and to have their cases decided by arbitrators which may be less inclined than a court to side with the polity or state concerned. And as long as the investor can chose to bring the case before a national court instead, there is no infringement of the right to an effective remedy and a fair trial under Article 47 of the EU Charter. But to have cases regarding, for instance, trade in goods such as energy decided without a possibility for the CJEU to ensure system-coherency could create a parallel legal regime within the Union. That brings questions about non-discrimination based on nationality under primarily Article 18 of the TFEU to the fore. Furthermore, the Union must ensure a high and consistent level of data protection, solidarity, consumer protection and environmental protection, just to mention a few other fields of substantive EU law.

Contrary to the view that a parallel system for investment protection sits uncomfortably with the Union legal order and may undermine the unification project, the recognition of ISDS mechanisms may seem to be a matter of *pacta sunt servanda* from an international law perspective. If two or more countries have agreed to set up an extra-judicial system for enforcement of the contractual clauses, they need to abide by the agreement also if they happen to be EU Member States. Indeed, the relation between a BIT or MIA and the EU Treaties should be governed by the Vienna Convention on the Law of Treaties (VCLT) just as any other conflict between international agreements.[47] Even though the EU is not a signatory to the VCLT, its provisions inevitably apply as *jus cogens*, and it should be reminded that neither the CJEU not the General Court has categorically disregarded the possibility of applying the VCLT on formalistic

[46] Case C-638/19 P *Commission v Micula* (n 6) para 142.

[47] The Vienna Convention on the Law of Treaties, concluded in Vienna (Austria) on 23 May 1969 (*United Nations Treaty Series*, Vol 1155, p 331).

or procedural grounds.[48] However, when choosing between *pacta sunt servanda* under public international law and *sincere cooperation* under Article 4(3) TEU, the EU Courts are compelled to opt for the latter alternative. At the end of the day, EU law as opposed to international law has primacy within the jurisdiction.

10.3.1. Categorical Approaches to Investment Protection in the EU

With a view to facilitate enlargement by levelling economic conditions, the EU seemed to be in favour of, or at least not against, BITs between Member States and neighbouring countries in the 1990s. Many countries concluding these BITs, as well as the ECT framework for energy cooperation originally adopted in 1994 (although it did not enter into force until 1998), later became EU Member States. On that note, the Treaties shall pursuant to Article 351 TFEU not affect rights and obligations arising from an agreement between one or more Member States on the one hand, and one or more third countries on the other hand, in a country that becomes a Member State after concluding the agreement.[49] Nonetheless, such a Member State is pursuant to paragraph two thereof required to take all appropriate steps to eliminate incompatibilities between the international agreement and the EU Treaties. That may create a friction with the international commitments.

As foreign investors according to BITs and MIAs shall abide by rules and regulations in the host state the foreign investor enjoy is equal treatment in most instances. However, investment protection also includes protection of legitimate expectations, which implies that a legal change in the host state can constitute an infringement of the BIT or MIA. Hence, it can be costly for a country to adapt the legal system when becoming an EU Member State. However, BITs and MIAs can of course be renegotiated and amended by the contracting parties.

According to Article 59(1) VCLT an agreement shall be terminated or partly suspended insofar as all the signatories later conclude an agreement relating to the *same subject-matter* and it appears from that agreement that the parties have intended to govern the matter by the later agreement, or the provisions of the two agreements are not capable of being applied at the same time. As for instance the ECT has been updated, the original version has been superseded by the later versions. Along those lines it could be argued that the TFEU superseded all pre-existing intra-EU BITs and MIAs between Member States within the scope of EU law in 2009, albeit it could also be argued that most of the

[48] See eg Case C-104/16 P *Council v Front Polisario* ECLI:EU:C:2016:973, regarding the territorial scope of the Association and Liberalisation Agreement concluded between the EU and Morocco.

[49] Notably the time of entering into an agreement may be irrelevant for the competence of the Union to take measures with regard to decisions based on the agreement; see Case C-638/19 P *Commission v Micula* (n 6) para 135; and Cases T-624/15, T-694/15 and T-704/15, *European Food and Others v Commission* ECLI:EU:T:2019:423.

relevant provisions enshrined in the revised EU Treaties existed already before the Lisbon revision.

Even more controversially, the CJEU has on occasion taken the liberty of interpreting international agreements often concluded by Member States before they acceded to the Union, in order to promote internal system-coherency, despite the fact that the Union *per se* has not signed the agreement.[50] In *SGAE*, the CJEU re-interpreted the concept of 'communication to the public' enshrined in Article 11 of the Berne Convention for the Protection of Literary and Artistic Work with a view to avoid a norm conflict in the domestic legal systems which transposed an EU directive approximating copyrights, even though the Member States but not the Union were parties to the Convention.[51]

Conversely, if two or more Member States would enter into intra-EU BITs or MIAs after becoming EU Member States, they would be considered infriging the EU Treaties by not recognising the duty to cooperate sincerely under Article 4(3) TEU.[52] By contrast for a long time the European Commission steered clear from intervening against new agreements between Member States and third countries. Because, even if a BIT or MIA with ISDS could undermine the right to regulate with regard to the internal market, the Member States retained exclusive external powers to enter into BITs and MIAs with ISDS clauses until 2009 when FDI was included in the CCP. This distribution of competences induced ISDS tribunals in the 2000s to conclude that a BIT between a Member State and a third country is compatible with EU law even if the third country later on becomes a Member State, since the Agreement and the Treaties are *not relating to the same subject-matter*.

That was the approach in *Eastern Sugar BV (Netherlands) v Czech Republic* concerning measures in connection with the Czech Republic's accession to the EU to protect European sugar production.[53] By categorically excluding the FDI from the scope of EU law, it was possible to avoid a debate on whether a BIT could override EU law pursuant to Article 30 VCLT, and the Member State could rest assured that there was no risk of infringement proceedings under Articles 258–260 TFEU. In the case, the Commission intervened by its own motion and submitted observations. Although the Commission did not object to the line of reasoning and had in any event no formal power to affect the outcome, it required the Member States to commence a termination procedure.

However, to categorically consider EU measures regarding FDI *ultra vires* seemed strained, considering the potential effects on the right to regulate the internal market. As the enlarged Union was consolidated, the Commission

[50] J Rosén and C Granmar, 'Länkning på internet – EU domstolen i konflikt med internationell rätt', *Svensk Juristtidning* 4/15, 2015, p 347.

[51] Case C-306/05 *SGAE* ECLI:EU:C:2007:764.

[52] Case T-69/89 *RTÉ v Commission* ECLI:EU:T:2091:89, para 103.

[53] *Eastern Sugar BV (Netherlands) v Czech Republic*, SCC Case No 088/2004.

started to oppose intra-EU ISDS in 2006.[54] In fact, the Union had adopted an abundance of secondary legislation regarding, eg, financial markets, transportation services, the energy sector and the environment with direct implications for FDI. Then again, investors must always comply with the rules and regulations in the host state, and a BIT or MIA can be invoked only insofar as domestic law is considered discriminatory or unfair, eg, in the sense of legal changes that are incompatible with legitimate expectations.

In *Electrabel SA v Hungary* concerning a power purchase agreement between a Belgian company and Hungary that was terminated by the Commission under EU rules regarding state aid, the ISDS tribunal elaborated on the concept of EU law as *a matter of fact* that was not subject to interpretation.[55] Indisputably, the tribunal constructed only the provisions of the ECT in the case. However, the decision reveals that it is little more than a play on words to call a legal regime that creates a situation where a state needs to compensate an investor pursuant to a BIT 'a matter of fact'. Although the arbitrators did not consider themselves authorised to interpret EU law regarding state aid, they took the reasoning of the European Commission into account when deciding on the award.[56] In other words, the tribunal assessed to what extent the Commission had made a convincing case without the possibility for an EU court to assess the effects of the tribunal's decision on the internal market.[57]

As the Member States finally transferred exclusive competences to the Union regarding FDI pursuant to the Lisbon revision in 2009 and, hence, waived the right to conclude new BITs and MIAs, the Union intensified its endeavours to promote normative consistency, primarily within the Union. In 2012 the Union adopted a regulation or 'transitional instrument' that established a system for information sharing and coordination of measures by the Member States and the Union in the field.[58] In relation to third countries, the Member States may according to the 'grandfathering clause' in Article 3 thereof maintain their BITs in force until the Union has entered into a BIT or MIA with the same country.

Conversely, it follows from the letter of that provision that it does not apply to intra-EU BITs. Instead, the Commission issued a 'reformed investment approach' in 2015 to ensure internal consistency.[59] Soon thereafter, in 2016, the Commission issued a formal request to Austria, the Netherlands, Romania,

[54] 2 BvR 73, 859/15, 5 May 2020.

[55] *Electrabel SA v Hungary*, ICSID Case No ARB/07/19, para 4.195.

[56] *Electrabel SA v Hungary* (n 55) para 4.198.

[57] Case C-638/19 P *Commission v Micula* (n 6).

[58] Regulation (EU) No 1219/2012 establishing transitional arrangements for bilateral investment agreements between Member States and third countries [2012] OJ L351/40. Additional measures have been taken with regards to capital markets, see eg Directive (EU) 2014/65/EU [2014] OJ L173/349; Directive (EU) 2019/878 [2019] OJ L150/253; and Directive (EU) 2019/2034 [2019] OJ L314/64.

[59] Reformed investment dispute settlement approach 2015 (n 12).

Slovakia and Sweden to terminate all their intra-EU BITs as soon as possible.[60] From an EU law point of view, a parallel system of intra-EU BITs does more harm than good. Investments are already protected under primary and secondary law, and investors from one Member State can easily bring actions for compensation before the courts of another Member State. In a Union based on mutual trust, the argument that national courts may side with the receiving state in an investment dispute carries little weight, and if a Member State considers that investors established in the state are being discriminated against or treated unfairly in another Member State, the dispute between the two Member States should be submitted to the CJEU pursuant to Article 259 TFEU.[61] In addition, any court or tribunal in a Member State may, and the courts of last instance must, refer questions in law for preliminary rulings to the CJEU in cases regarding investment protection.

10.3.2. System-coherency and the View on Intra-EU Arbitration

As long as no disputes regarding BITs were brought before national courts or tribunals in the Member States, and infringement proceedings were brought to an end by satisfactory responses to the arguments raised by the Commission, no cases regarding the validity of BITs reached the EU Courts. However, there is often the possibility to appeal an award in the courts of a designated country. That is how the decision by an ISDS tribunal under the BIT concluded in 1991 between the Netherlands and the Czech Republic and Slovakia regarding investments made by a Dutch company in order to provide sickness insurance services in Slovakia found its way to the CJEU in *Achmea*.[62] Due to measures by the Slovak state to nationlise the market, the ISDS in the BIT was triggered.

As the parties agreed to locate the arbitration to Frankfurt am Main, German law became applicable. During the proceedings, Slovakia had raised questions about jurisdiction and argued that the arbitration clause in the BIT was incompatible with Articles 18, 267 and 344 TFEU. As the tribunal dismissed the objection, Slovakia turned to the German regional courts. It follows from the preliminary ruling that an award can pursuant to German law be set aside if it is, for instance, incompatible with the laws to which the parties are subject

[60] COM(2018)547 final, Communication from the Commission on protection of intra-EU investment. In more recent times the Commission has opened infringement proceedings, eg against the Czech Republic for not protecting investments in the railway sector in accordance with Directive 2012/34/EU, see December infringement package INF/21/6201, 2021.

[61] See, as to mutual trust, Case C-399/11 *Melloni* ECLI:EU:C:2013:107. On Article 259 TFEU procedures, see Graham Butler, 'The Court of Justice as an inter-state court' (2017) 36 *Yearbook of European Law* 179.

[62] Case C-284/16 *Achmea* ECLI:EU:C:2018:158. See Xavier Groussot and Marja-Liisa Öberg, 'The Web of Autonomy of the EU Legal Order: Achmea' in G Butler and RA Wessel (eds), *EU External Relations Law* (n 31).

or contrary to 'public order'. Whereas both the court of first instance and the appeal court dismissed the action, the German Federal Court of Justice (*Bundesgerichtshof*) granted leave of appeal and referred questions to the CJEU.

Contrary to the reasoning of the ISDS tribunal in *Electrabel SA v Hungary* mentioned above, the CJEU clarified that since the intra-EU BIT in question explicitly stated that the arbitral tribunal should take 'the law in force of the contracting party concerned and other relevant agreements between the contracting parties' into consideration, it could be required to interpret EU law.[63] On the one hand, sources of EU law have direct applicability and direct effect in the Member States, and on the other hand the unification project is based on agreements between the Member States.[64] In particular, the provisions concerning fundamental economic freedoms safeguarded under Article 16 of the EU Charter such as the freedom of establishment and the free movement of capital may be applicable.[65] In view of this, the CJEU established that even if an award can in some respects be appealed to a national court, the fact that an arbitral tribunal can interpret EU law without the possibility to ask the CJEU for clarification is incompatible with the procedural system set up under Article 267 TFEU. Indeed, the contracting Member States have then removed disputes which may concern the application or interpretation of EU law from the jurisdiction of their own courts contrary to the duty to provide sufficient remedies to ensure efficient legal protection in the fields covered by EU law under Article 19(1) TEU.[66]

Furthermore, the CJEU clarified, with reference to *Opinion 2/13* regarding the Union's accession to the ECHR, that an international agreement cannot 'affect the allocation of powers fixed in the Treaties or, consequently, the autonomy of the EU legal system, observance of which is ensured by the Court'.[67] Since the Member States must pursuant to Article 344 TFEU not submit disputes concerning the interpretation and application of the Treaties to a method that is not provided in the Treaties, the Member State infringes the Treaties when concluding a BIT with an ISDS mechanism according to the CJEU. Article 344 TFEU must namely be read in the light of the overall nature and scheme of EU law, including the principles of conferral, primacy and sincere cooperation.

Consequently, the CJEU concluded that Article 267 TFEU and Article 344 TFEU preclude a provision in an intra-EU BIT that makes it possible to circumvent the Court's *interpretative prerogative* under Article 19(1) TEU, which in

[63] Case C-284/16 *Achmea* (n 62) para 40.

[64] Case C-284/16 *Achmea* (n 62) para 41.

[65] Case C-284/16 *Achmea* (n 62) para 42. In fact, the domestic legal systems form to a great extent integral parts of the EU legal order. See Article 51 of the EU Charter, establishing that both the Union institutions and the Member States shall respect the rights, observe the principles and promote the application of the Charter in accordance with their respective competences. See as to the interrelation between services monopolies and the internal market, eg, Case C-347/09 *Dickinger and Ömer* ECLI:EU:C:2011:582, paras 56–57, 61–63, 71 and 100.

[66] Case C-638/19 P *Commission v Micula* (n 6) para 139.

[67] Case C-284/16 *Achmea* (n 62) para 32.

turn ensures that the Treaties are interpreted and applied in accordance with the 'law'. As mentioned, the 'law' referred to is in turn a set of meta norms enshrined in primary law provisions constituting a normative source code of EU law. Since the ISDS mechanism in the BIT was considered incompatible with the primacy, teleology and consistency of EU law, there was no need to make inquiries into whether such a parallel legal system could also give rise to discrimination on grounds of nationality contrary to Article 18 TFEU.

Implicitly, the preliminary ruling in *Achmea* repudiates the very *raison d'être* of intra-EU BITs. There is no need for a separate legal regime for protection of investments made in a Member State by a private party established in another Member State, beyond the scope of the Union legal order. In the wake of the explanations provided by the CJEU and the targeted actions of the Commission, the perceived problem with intra-EU BITs within the *sui generis* EU legal order was partly solved in 2021 as the agreement for the termination of BITs between 21 EU Member States was concluded.[68]

However, for various reasons there may remain questions regarding BITs to be resolved. In 2022, the CJEU handed down its ruling in *Commission v Micula* where the Court partly set aside the judgment of the General Court on the validity of a Commission decision regarding state aid by payment of an arbitral award pursuant to a BIT between Sweden and Romania.[69] Although the BIT concluded in 2002 was inapplicable, the Commission is decision that Romania's payment of the award in 2014 and 2015 constituted state aid was contested in 2015 by the beneficiaries. In accordance with Article 263 TFEU, the private investors brought direct revocation proceedings before the General Court, and on appeal from the Commission the CJEU decided the legal issues. If there were previously doubts about the relationship between ISDS mechanisms and EU law, at least the interrelations between the payment of an award and EU state aid law have now been clarified.

In contrast to the transitional instrument providing a legal framework for the Member States' withdrawal from BITs concluded with third countries, no such measure has been taken regarding MIAs. In 2019 an *ad hoc* arbitration procedure initiated by a Ukrainian energy distributing company against Moldova under the ECT reached the CJEU on winding procedural roads. Since the arbitral award was made in Paris, and the *ad hoc* tribunal decided against Moldova, the state appealed in accordance with the BIT the decision to the appeal court of Paris. That court in turn should decide the case in accordance with French law. After granting leave of appeal, the court stayed the proceedings and referred questions to the CJEU regarding the meaning of an investment pursuant to Articles 1(6) and 26(1) of the ECT.

[68] Agreement for the termination of Bilateral Investment Treaties between the Member States of the European Union [2020] OJ L169/1, see above (n 7).

[69] Case C-638/19 P *Commission v Micula* (n 6).

Although the Union had acceded to the revised ECT in 2015, several Member States which remained signatories alongside the Union intervened in the case and argued that the CJEU must not have jurisdiction to interpret and apply the MIA *a fortiori* in a case not concerning a Member State. However, in the preliminary ruling in *Komstroy*, delivered in September 2021, the Court explained that since exclusive competences regarding FDI had been bestowed on the Union in 2009 and it had gained shared competence with regard to indirect portfolio investment, it was entitled to clarify the intra-EU validity of an ISDS award under a MIA to which also third countries are signatories.[70] In other words, the CJEU took the opportunity to explain the interrelation between ISDS in MIAs and EU law in intra-EU cases almost as an *obiter*, in a dispute with no immediate connection to the Union. In light of this, the rather obvious answer to the questions actually referred from the French Court, that the claim arising from a contract for the supply of energy which is not connected with an actual investment is not an 'investment', has passed virtually unnoticed in the debate that has followed.

Along the lines of *Achmea*, the Court started by emphasising the 'constitutional structure of the Union', the importance of the judicial system established by the Treaties to ensure the 'autonomy' of the EU legal order, and 'the consistency and uniformity in the interpretation of EU law'.[71] It continued by establishing that it cannot be permitted under EU law that an international agreement removes disputes between a Member State and an investor in another Member State concerning EU law from the judicial system of the Union so that the effectiveness of that law is not guaranteed.[72] The Court further provided that although the ECT is a MIA, it is in intra-EU Cases 'intended, in reality, to govern bilateral relations between two of the Contracting Parties, in an analogous way to the provision of the [BIT] at issue' in *Achmea*. According to the CJEU, this implies that the provisions in the ECT establishing an ISDS mechanism 'must be interpreted as not being applicable to disputes between a Member State and an investor of another Member State concerning an investment made by the latter in the first Member State'.[73]

Considering the fact that an ISDS award *per definition* concerns a dispute between a private party and a contracting state as opposed to a dispute between two contracting states, it is far from convincing that the CJEU emphasises that a MIA would in fact govern bilateral relations between two signatories. Although it is conceivable that the relationship between an intra-EU award under a MIA and EU law, on the one hand, and an intra-EU award under a BIT and EU law on the other hand is the same, the reason for this is not that the agreements govern

[70] Case C-741/19 *Komstroy* (n 8).
[71] Case C-741/19 *Komstroy* (n 8) paras 43–45.
[72] Case C-741/19 *Komstroy* (n 8) para 62.
[73] Case C-741/19 *Komstroy* (n 8) para 66.

bilateral relations between two Member States. Instead, the reason is that EU law applies to both the Member State concerned and the private investor.

In any event, ISDS mechanisms established by MIAs no longer apply in intra-EU investment disputes. By contrast, a private investor established in a third country may still bring an arbitration procedure in an *ad hoc* tribunal against a Member State pursuant to provisions in a MIA such as the ECT. Since, on the one hand, third country investors can still have resort to arbitral tribunals in cases against EU Member States and, on the other hand, investors in the Union can have resort to arbitral tribunals in cases against third countries, the absence of such a possibility may arguably create a situation of reverse discrimination against legal entities in the Union that seek to resolve intra-EU investment disputes. However, it would be a contradiction in terms to argue on the one hand that the CJEU has exaggerated the risk of awards undermining the internal market, and on the other hand to argue that a third country investor would be put in an advantageous position if EU law is substituted by an award.

Notably, the CJEU has so far steered clear from ruling on the risk of discrimination, and even if a case on reverse discrimination could be made, the line of reasoning regarding agreements concluded by EU Member States could be elevated to the external relations *of the Union*. Whereas third state-based investors enjoy the right to non-discrimination and the principle of most favoured nation in the Union, that does not prevent EU law from applying instead in intra-EU disputes. Conversely, if the possibility to seek an arbitral award in a third country induces legal entities in the Union to make investments in that third country instead of in the Union, that may be a price worth paying for the Union in order to ensure cohesive socio-economic development. Anyhow, as the Union gained exclusive competence regarding FDI in 2009, it is concluding new international agreements regarding investment protection with third countries that replace the residual Member State BITs. In many instances, investment protection with direct effect in the Union is forming part of more comprehensive EU agreements.

10.3.3. EU External Actions to Promote Internal Consistency

In 2018 the Union signed the trade and investment protection agreement with Singapore, and as the European Parliament and all the Member State endorsed the agreement, it entered into force in 2019. At the outset, the Commission negotiated the agreement without participation of the Member State. After all, the scope of Article 207 TFEU that defines the competences conferred on the Union regarding the CCP was significantly extended pursuant to the Lisbon revision. In addition, the Commission could rely on the parallelism laid down in Article 3(2) TFEU, which establishes an exclusive competence whenever necessary not to undermine internal Union measures.

However, some Member States raised concerns regarding the powers of the Union to enter into such a far-reaching agreement, and the Commission requested an Opinion from the CJEU on the matter in 2015. Although the CJEU clarified in *Opinion 2/15 (EU-Singapore FTA)* that the Member States no longer have exclusive competences in the fields of external trade and investment protection, they share competences with the Union regarding indirect investment, ie, portfolio investments and to set up dispute settlement mechanisms.[74] However, with regard to dispute settlement mechanisms, the Court explained that a distinction must be made between the resolution of disputes between the Union and Singapore on the one hand, and an ISDS between one of the contracting parties and a private investor on the other hand. Since arbitration between the signatories cannot remove cases from the jurisdiction of national courts, the Union has, according to the CJEU, exclusive competences to establish horizontal arbitral regimes between the contracting parties. By contrast, the Member States must agree to the right for private investors in a third country to seek vertical redress against the State before an arbitral tribunal instead of trying the case in national courts. Nonetheless, the Union had shared implied powers, pursuant to Article 216(1) TFEU in these regards, since an ISDS mechanism would help the EU to achieve its objectives pursuant to Article 21 TEU.[75]

Although the distinction between horizontal and vertical dispute settlement makes perfect sense, the readiness of the Union to accept ISDS mechanisms in its external relations may appear to sit uncomfortably with *Achmea*, where they were deemed inapplicable in intra-EU investment disputes. However, on closer inspection, this distinction promotes system-coherency because without an ISDS mechanism, EU law applies to the parties in an intra-EU dispute, but in a dispute between a private investor in the EU and Singapore the courts in Singapore would apply domestic law in that country. Conversely, investors in Singapore would have to accept the jurisdiction of Member State courts. Whereas intra-EU disputes are expected to take upon the features of disputes in one and the same country because of the principle of mutual trust and checks and balances under the Treaties, the investor located in Singapore could face the risk of unfair treatment in national EU courts. An ISDS mechanism that facilitates FDI is a step forward when integrating economies within different jurisdictions, but a step backward when developing a cohesive society within the same jurisdiction. In addition, the EU habitually accepts a trade and investment protection agreement only insofar as fundamental rights are explicitly recognised in the agreement. Because, the Union shall as mentioned promote its values on the international

[74] *Opinion 2/15* ECLI:EU:C:2017:376 (*EU-Singapore FTA*). See C Kaddous, 'The EU Competence to Conclude the New Generation of Free Trade Agreements: Opinion 2/15 (EU–Singapore FTA)' in G Butler and RA Wessel (eds), *EU External Relations Law* (n 31).

[75] *Opinion 2/15* (n 74) paras 285–293.

scene pursuant to Articles 3(5) and 21 TEU, and it advocates stable conditions for a consistent legal evolution whenever possible.

In the mixed Comprehensive Economic and Trade Agreement (CETA) between Canada, of the one part, and the EU and its Member States, of the other part, a permanent investment court was established. A decision by the court in a case between either Canada and a private investor in the EU, or a private investor in Canada and the EU or one of its Member States, can be appealed to an appellate body. Since such a two-tier court can develop a consistent body of case law, normative powers are transferred from the contracting parties. Consequently, several Member States and, indeed, political groupings and organisations across Europe considered the creation of a supra-supra-investment protection regime to be a step too far. Hence, the Commission turned once more to the CJEU for clarifications regarding the Union's external competences. In *Opinion 1/17*, the CJEU explained that the EU has implied powers to set up such a court.[76] Interestingly enough, the CJEU caught on to the reasoning of the arbitral tribunal in the *Electrabel SA v Hungary* case mentioned above, and waived aside the argument that precedents from the CETA courts may reduce the right to regulate within the Union, by explaining that EU law and the domestic legal systems in the Member States will just be a 'matter of fact' when the CETA is interpreted.[77] Naturally, the Commission supports this view in its explanatory notice regarding the CETA.[78] However, in parity with the conclusion reached by the Commission and the CJEU that an arbitral tribunal may apply EU law, a CETA court may interpret EU law as well as the Member State's laws and entail a risk of regulatory chill. Because of the remaining concerns, the CETA entered into force only provisionally in 2017.

With a view to promote economic exchanges and at the same time avoid potentially disruptive *ad hoc* tribunals, the Union has since 2015 also worked for the creation of a two-tier international investment court. For the time being, it seems difficult to find common ground on the issue with, for instance, the US. Perhaps the zeal for globalisation that followed the establishment of the WTO in 1994 has subsided. Perhaps we are facing a brave new world where the borders between the material world and metaverse collapse, and it becomes necessary to entirely disconnect jurisdiction from geographical borders. In any event, there are pros and cons with the transfer of powers to judges beyond the *trias politicas*. Whereas the absence of democratic anchoring may be troubling, an *ad hoc* tribunal may be worse. From an EU perspective, primary law requires that system-coherency is promoted and it would simply be *contra legem* for

[76] *Opinion 1/17* ECLI:EU:C:2019:341 (*EU-Canada CETA*). See K Bradley, 'Investor–State Dispute Tribunals Established under EU International Agreements: Opinion 1/17 (EU–Canada CETA)' in G Butler and RA Wessel (eds), *EU External Relations Law* (n 31). See also, Case C-284/16 *Achmea* (n 62) para 57; and Case C-741/19 *Komstroy* (n 8) para 61.

[77] *Opinion 1/17* (n 76) paras 130–131.

[78] Joint interpretative Instrument on the Comprehensive Economic and Trade Agreement (CETA) between Canada and the European Union and its Member States [2017] OJ L11/3.

the Union not to promote its objectives and values internationally and, hence, internally. Indeed, the international agreements on which the Union is based limit the freedom of the EU institutions to accept international agreements that may undermine the Treaty obligations, and this is what distinguishes the *sui generis* polity from a fully fledged federation that relies more clearly on political mandates to regulate.

10.4. CONCLUSION

Along with the development from a Community structured around a free trade area into a value-based Union, the Member States have conferred increased competences regarding FDI on the supranational institutions. Normative consistency is the guiding star in the process of amalgamating the socio-economic systems of the Member States, and it has given the impetus for the accumulation of Union powers. As a *sui generis* polity based on international agreements, the Union cannot justify its internal and external measures by the will of a legislator to the same extent as the domestic norm giving powers. Although the democratic anchoring can no longer be called into question considering the institutional balance between the Council of Ministers and the European Parliament manifested in the Treaties, the EU institutions must pursuant to Article 5(2) TEU act only within the limits of the competences conferred upon them by the Member States to attain the objectives set out in the Treaties, as well as to ensure consistency between the Union's policies and activities. Ultimately, the Member States require the CJEU to ensure that, in the interpretation and application of the Treaties, the 'law' so defined is observed under Article 19(1) TEU. Even if the meta-instructions on how to develop the Union legal order are directed to the EU institutions, the Member States also have a duty to cooperate sincerely pursuant to Article 4(3) TEU and, hence, to give primary EU law and secondary legislation the intended legal effects in domestic law. There is no longer room for any uncertainty about the primacy of these sources of EU law, and even international agreements must be fitted into the normative system to ensure its multidimensional consistency.

Furthermore, primary law and secondary legislation often apply directly as law in the Member States, and as many provisions confer rights on private parties, they have direct effect in the Union. For instance, the fundamental rights enshrined in the EU Charter must always be complied with on EU level and on national, regional and local level within the territorial and substantive scope of EU law. By contrast, only the signatories are normally bound by international agreements, and the polities and states also retain the right to decide how to transpose provisions on the rights of private parties. Then again, BITs and MIAs with ISDS mechanisms cut through this distribution of competences. Consequently, arbitral awards may challenge the system-coherency required by the EU Treaties.

External BITs and MIAs, such as the ECT, entered into by the Member States were for a long time considered to escape the scope of EU law, albeit the normative overlaps were well understood in some quarters. Indeed, the Union's hands-off approach around the turn of the millennium is better explained by the intention to pave the way for the enlargement than by a categorical absence of conferred competences. By facilitating investments in the third countries concerned, the economic differences could be reduced prior to their accession. However, as the number of Member States increased from 15 to 28 in the 2000s, the objectives changed to primarily stabilise the project by uniting around core values and a consistent integration. Whereas democracy has sometimes been seen as the foundation of the rule of law, the rule of law in the strict sense of limiting political leeway became the foundation of a deepened unification process.

Although the Member States retain their autonomy in many ways, and the Union respects their national identities, the directly applicable and effective sources of EU law inevitably transform the domestic legal systems, and the Union's legal personality is promoted. An important aspect of this process is the judicial system established by the Treaties, and particularly the dialogue between national courts and tribunals and the CJEU pursuant to Article 267 TFEU. Since an *ad hoc* tribunal established under a BIT or MIA can finally settle a dispute involving a Member State and one or more legal entities in another Member State without the possibility to participate in this dialogue, the arbitral tribunal is anomalous in EU law. Indeed, to contract away disputes which may concern the application or interpretation of EU law from the jurisdictions of the Member States' courts and the CJEU is incompatible with the duty to cooperate sincerely under Article 4(3) TEU. Furthermore, by entering into a BIT or MIA that establishes an ISDS mechanism, the Member State submits future disputes that potentially concern the interpretation and application of the Treaties to another method for settlement than those provided for therein, contrary to the letter of Article 344 TFEU. Indisputably, an *ad hoc* arbitral tribunal established pursuant to a BIT or MIA constitutes another method for dispute settlement between a state and a private party than those recognised in the Treaties.

Whereas most Member States shall terminate all intra-EU BITs in accordance with the international agreement concluded in 2021, the CJEU has deemed provisions regarding ISDS mechanisms in MIAs inapplicable in disputes between a Member State and one or more private investors in other Member States. By contrast, third country investors may still rely on ISDS mechanisms in disputes with EU Member States under BITs that remain in force pursuant to the transitional instrument adopted in 2012. Obviously, the same applies with regard to dispute settlement between such parties under a MIA. Although this may seem to discriminate against an investor in the Union that seeks redress against an EU Member State, it is at closer inspection a logical approach to promote economic integration with third countries while ensuring that the EU legal order is not circumvented within the Union. Based on the CCP in conjunction with the broad, vague and sometimes shared 'implied powers' enshrined in Article 216(1) TFEU, the Union is also promoting a more system-coherent development of its internal and external legal spheres by the establishment of permanent investment courts. For instance the CETA is designed to set up a two-tier investment court with jurisdiction to interpret the Agreement. Ultimately, the Union is opting for an international investment court that can over time develop a consistent body of case law regarding agreements concluded between countries and polities which, as a minimum denominator, recognise at least the provisions of the UN Declaration of Human Rights. It is, indeed, difficult to imagine another path for the EU when trying to reconcile investment protection with a consistent development of the Union legal order.

Part III

Investment and Sustainability

11

Sustainable Development in EU Trade and Investment Agreements

HANNES LENK

11.1. INTRODUCTION

TRADE LIBERALISATION, IN spite of the macroeconomic benefits, is bound to produce negative externalities, as the scale, composition and technique of international trade can have discernible effects on climate change, social inclusion and poverty.[1] This linkage of trade and sustainable development was made explicit both in the Rio Declaration of 1992[2] and in the preamble to the Marrakesh agreement.[3] At least nine out of the 17 Sustainable Development Goals (SDGs) adopted by the United Nations (UN) General Assembly in 2015 have a clear trade dimension.[4] Indeed, trade and investment policy are increasingly seen as part of a broader governance regime that aims to achieve sustainable development with preferential trade agreements (PTAs)[5] and, to a lesser degree, international investment agreements, which are being instrumentalised to pursue social and environmental objectives.

[1] United Nations Conference on Trade and Development, 'Better Trade for Sustainable Development: The role of voluntary sustainability standards' (2021); WTO, 'Mainstreaming trade to attain the Sustainable Development Goals' (2018). For a comprehensive discussion of the case against free trade, see eg Douglas A Irwin, *Free Trade under Fire,* 5th edn (Princeton University Press, 2020).

[2] United Nations, Report of the United Nations Conference on Environment and Development, Rio de Janeiro, 3–14 June 1992, A/CONF.151/26/Rev.l (Vol l), Annex 1, principle 12.

[3] Marrakesh Agreement Establishing the World Trade Organization, 15 April 1994, 1867 UNTS 154 (1994).

[4] Joachim Monkelbaan, 'Using Trade for Achieving the SDGs: The Example of the Environmental Goods Agreement' (2017) 51(4) *Journal of World Trade* 575, 578–80.

[5] For a recent survey, see Lorand Bartels, 'Social issues: Labour, environment and human rights' in Simon Lester, Bryan Mercurio and Lorand Bartels (eds), *Bilateral and Regional Trade Agreements: Commentary and Analysis* (CUP, 2016) 364, 368 et seq.

This is also reflected in the design and structure of the European Union's (EU) Common Commercial Policy (CCP). In EU primary law, Article 3(5) TEU requires that, 'in its relations with the wider world, the Union … shall contribute to peace, security, [and] the sustainable development of the Earth.' Article 207(1) TFEU further stipulates that 'the common commercial policy shall be conducted in the context of the principles and objectives of the Union's external action', which in Article 21 TEU include a plethora of social and environmental objectives. The EU, thus, frequently uses trade policy instruments as a platform to promote sustainable development and other non-trade policy objectives.[6] Instrumentalising its significant economic clout as a trading bloc, the EU projects itself in this way as a powerful global actor that attempts to shape the fabric of global governance through its trade and investment policy.[7] This chapter analyses how sustainable development objectives have been integrated into the EU's treaty-making practice post-Lisbon, comparing the EU's trade with its nascent investment policy.

Three methodological considerations ought to be made. First, the EU concludes international agreements concerning trade under the umbrella of its CCP,[8] as well as in the form of association agreements (AAs).[9] For the purpose of this analysis, both types of agreements are considered PTAs, unless differentiated explicitly.

Second, some of these agreements include comprehensive chapters on investment; others include investment liberalisation commitments that are complemented with separate investment protection agreements (IPAs). It is, therefore, not always possible to separate the EU's trade from its investment policy with surgical precision.

Third, this analysis focuses on post-Lisbon developments. It has been observed in scholarship that the 'Global Europe'[10] and the Lisbon Strategy have triggered the legalisation of labour and environmental provisions – resulting in

[6] Joris Larik, 'Good Global Governance through trade: constitutional moorings' in Jan Wourters, Axel Marx and Dylan Garaets (eds), *Global Governance Through Trade: EU Policies and Approaches* (Edward Elgar, 2015) 43.

[7] Be that as a normative power (see eg Ian Manners, 'Normative power Europe: a contradiction in terms?' (2002) 40 *Journal of Common Market Studies* 235), market power (see eg Chad Damro, 'Market power Europe' (2012) 19 *Journal of European Public Policy* 682) or a power through trade (see Sophie Meunier and Kalypso Nicolaïdis, 'The European Union as a Trade Power' in Christopher Hill and Michael Smith (eds), *International Relations and the European Union*, 2nd edn (Oxford University Press, 2011) 275–98, 294).

[8] Consolidated versions of the Treaty on European Union and the Treaty on the Functioning of the European Union [2012] OJ C326/1 [hereinafter 'TEU' and 'TFEU' respectively], Article 207 TFEU.

[9] Article 217 TFEU.

[10] European Commission, 'Global Europe: Competing in the World: A Contribution to the EU's Growth and Jobs Strategy', COM(2006) 567 final, Brussels, 4 October 2006.

the systematic inclusion of trade and sustainable development (TSD) chapters.[11] Additionally, the EU's post-Lisbon trade policy has witnessed the strengthening of the European Parliament, as well as the emergence of new actors with a particular interest in sustainable development, such as NGOs and civil society, that now exert significant influence over the formation of the EU's policy preferences.[12] Most importantly, the Treaty of Lisbon introduced exclusive competence of the EU over foreign direct investment (FDI), establishing the EU as a foreign investment policy actor.

The following section traces the origin of sustainable development as a concept in EU external relations law. Having become a fashionable term in the late-1980s, this section concludes that the Treaties now provide a robust framework for the pursuit of non-trade objectives, including sustainable development. Section 11.3 illustrates these general conclusions through the example of TSD chapters, alluding to the variations in the content, scope and enforcement of these provisions; this section concludes that the concept is strategically used to further the EU's economic interests, and garner public support for the EU's neoliberal trade policy in the wake of the 2006 'Global Europe' strategy. This section also provides some brief remarks on the Commission's recent TSD review. Section 11.4 examines whether the established practice of TSD chapters is consistently extended to the EU's investment policy. The chapter concludes that inconsistencies between PTAs with comprehensive investment chapters and IPAs, and the decentralisation of the EU's investment policy, undermine the EU's constitutional responsibility to consistently integrate sustainable development in its external policy.

11.2. SUSTAINABLE DEVELOPMENT: THE CONCEPT AND ITS APPLICATION IN EU TRADE POLICY

The notion of sustainable development has deep roots in economic scholarship.[13] In *The Economics of Welfare*, Pigou warned as early as 1920 of the 'over-hasty exploitation of stored gifts of nature, which must make it harder for future generations to obtain supplies of important commodities'.[14] And yet, the dominant economic development theories in the post-war era focused primarily on industrial productivity and free trade as a prerequisite for unbridled export-led

[11] With respect to labour provisions, see eg James Harrison et al, 'Governing labour standards through free trade agreements: limits of the European Union's trade and sustainable development chapters' (2019) 57(2) *Journal of Common Market Studies* 260, 266.

[12] Alasdair R Young and John Peterson, 'The EU and the new trade politics' (2006) 13(6) *Journal of European Public Policy* 795, 800–02.

[13] Although in his brief etymological account, Sand finds the historical roots of the term 'not so much in mercantile economics, but in subtle national geopolitics'; see Peter H Sand, 'Sustainable Development – of Forests, Ships, and Law' (2007) 37 *Environmental Policy and Law* 201, 203.

[14] Arthur Cecil Pigou, *The Economics of Welfare* (Macmillan, 1920) 28.

economic growth.[15] Embracing the boundaries that the limited carrying capacity of the Earth sets for economic globalisation, *sustainable* development addresses the utilisation of scarce resources that are non-regenerative or regenerate at a slower rate than current consumption. As an economic concept, sustainable development realises the need for environmental protection to guarantee sustained (ie, long-term or continuous) *economic* development. The Brundtland report later broadened the term, and firmly established sustainable development as a concept in economic development policy. Accordingly, sustainable development 'meets the needs of the present without compromising the ability of future generations to meet their own needs'.[16]

The Johannesburg Plan[17] later defined what has now become the dominant conception of sustainable development, embracing 'economic development, social development and environmental protection – as interdependent and mutually reinforcing pillars'.[18] The economic dimension is well reflected in the intergenerational aspect of sustainable development, ie, economic growth must take the needs of future generations into account. The environmental dimension is equally straightforward, in that it focuses on the ecosystem, and imposes limits for the use of natural resources as economic inputs. The social dimension is more difficult to grasp, however, because it refers to a system of social organisation that alleviates poverty by way of facilitating the basic conditions needed for everyone to realise their needs. This rather extensive concept entails, *inter alia*, human rights, equality, and the rule of law.[19]

A link between EU trade policy and environmental protection can be traced back to the 1970s. The First Environmental Action Programme of the EU in 1973 proclaimed that '[e]ffects on the environment should be taken into account at the earliest possible stage in all … decision-making processes',[20] and explicitly recognised that international measures concerning the environment could ultimately fall within EU exclusive competence, such as trade.[21] The Court of Justice of the European Union acknowledged in the mid-1970s that trade policy can

[15] Although the relationship between exports and growth in the two decades following 1950 in Western Europe remains contested; see eg Andrea Boltho, 'Export-led growth or growth-led exports? Western Europe in the "golden age"' (2020) 17(2) *European Journal of Comparative Economics* 185.

[16] United Nations, 'Report of the World Commission on Environment and Development' (1987), UN Doc A/42/427, Annex.

[17] United Nations, 'Report of the World Summit on Sustainable Development' (2002), A/CONF.199/20, 6.

[18] ibid 8; Justice Mensah, 'Sustainable Development: Meaning, History, Principles, Pillars, and Implications for Human Action: Literature Review' (2019) 5(1) *Cogent Social Sciences* 1, 8.

[19] Mensah (n 18) 10.

[20] [1973] OJ C112/1, Declaration of the Council of the European Communities and of the representatives of the Governments of the Member States meeting in the Council of 22 November 1973 on the programme of action of the European Communities on the environment, 6.

[21] ibid 11 and 47; for a recognition of the trade/labour nexus by the EU institutions, see eg European Commission, Communication from the Commission to the Council, the European Parliament and the Economic and Social Committee on Promoting core labour standards and improving social governance in the context of globalization COM(2001) 416 final, especially 10 and Annex 1.

be put to use for the pursuit of social[22] and environmental objectives,[23] demonstrating that long before today's strong basis in the EU Treaties, the pursuit of non-trade objectives through trade policy was deeply embedded in the history of the European integration project.[24]

In EU primary law, an obligation to integrate environmental objectives in all EU policies – the so-called environmental integration clause – was introduced in 1987 with the Single European Act.[25] It was not until the Treaty of Maastricht, however, that sustainable development was introduced into the legal terminology of EU primary law. The Treaty of Maastricht did not provide a definition of the concept,[26] and although later Treaty revisions embedded sustainable development ever more firmly in the EU's institutional architecture,[27] a definition remained conspicuously absent. In addition, sustainable development and environmental protection were by design treated as separate Treaty objectives. With respect to EU external action, sustainable development, as a Treaty objective, was explicitly mentioned only as a part of development cooperation,[28] whereas a separate Treaty chapter dealt explicitly with environmental protection. This structure reinforced the ideational belonging of sustainable development to the domain of economic development policy and did not reflect the conceptual understanding of sustainable development as a concept that balances three interdependent and mutually reinforcing dimensions. It is therefore that references in the EU Treaties to sustainable development were understood to express a political commitment towards long-term economic growth aimed to improve social cohesion,[29] with environmental protection setting external boundaries, within which sustainable *economic* development could be realised. To fully implement the three dimensions of sustainable development consistently across

[22] Joined Cases 37 and 38/73 *Sociaal Fonds voor de Diamantarbeiders v NV Indiamex and Association de Fait de Belder and its partners JWL and R De Belder* EU:C:1973:165.

[23] *Opinion 1/78 (Natural Rubber)* EU:C:1979:224. See also Per Cramér, 'Defining the Scope of the Treaty-Making Competence for the Formulation of the Common Commercial Policy: Opinion 1/78 (Natural Rubber)' in Graham Butler and Ramses A Wessel (eds), *EU External Relations Law: The Cases in Context* (Oxford, Hart Publishing, 2022) 123–32.

[24] See eg Marise Cremona, 'The External Dimension of the Single Market: Building (on) the Foundations' in Catherine Barnard and Joanne Scott (eds), *The Law of the Single European Market: Unpacking the Premises* (Bloomsbury, 2002) 351, 386–87; Angelos Dimopoulos, 'The Effects of the Lisbon Treaty on the Principles and Objectives of the Common Commercial Policy' (2010) 15(2) *European Foreign Affairs Review* 153, 157–58; for a history of the development of the common commercial policy with respect to its link with non-trade policy objectives, see Larik (n 6) 43, 46 et seq.

[25] [1987] OJ L169/1, Single European Act, Article 130r(2): 'Environmental protection requirements shall be a component of the Community's other policies'.

[26] TEU, Article B, and Declaration No 20 on assessment of the environmental impact of Community measures.

[27] Treaty of Amsterdam amending the Treaty on European Union, the Treaties establishing the European Communities and certain related acts [1997] OJ C340/1, Articles 1(2), 1(5), and 2(2).

[28] Treaty establishing the European Communities [2002] OJ C325/33, Article 177.

[29] Ludwig Krämer, 'Sustainable Development in EC Law' in Hans Christian Bugge and Christina Voigt (eds), *Sustainable Development in International and National Law* (Europa Law Publishing, 2008) 375, 379.

all policy fields proved, thus, unsurprisingly difficult in practice.[30] In spite of its substantive vagueness, however, the concept was clearly *en vogue* throughout the 1990s, as references to sustainable development proliferated in EU policy and legal instruments.

Having failed to lobby successfully for the inclusion of labour standards in multilateral negotiations in the late 1990s, the EU started to unilaterally propose labour rights and environmental protection in the special incentive arrangement under its Generalised System of Preferences (GSP)[31] and through PTAs.[32] Notably, the first explicit reference to sustainable development in an EU PTA dates back to the EU-Hungary AA of 1993, one of the Europe Agreements, that defined the concept in relation to the full incorporation of environmental considerations into policies 'designed to bring about economic and social development'.[33] Most EU PTAs during this early period, however, incorporated sustainable development through the permissive treaty language of the general exception clauses only. These general exception clauses, which are either modelled on Article 36 TFEU or Article XX GATT (Article XIV GATS for services),[34] remain an important element even for post-Lisbon PTAs.[35] Indeed, both the WTO Appellate Body and the Court of Justice have clarified that these exceptions provide ample space to regulate in the interest of environmental protection, or for the protection of human rights, including core labour standards.[36]

[30] Wybe T Douma, 'The Promotion of Sustainable Development through EU Trade Instruments' (2017) 28(2) *European Business Law Review* 197, 202–03.

[31] Regulation (EU) No 978/2012 of the European Parliament and of the Council of 25 October 2012 applying a scheme of generalised tariff preferences and repealing Council Regulation (EC) No 732/2008 [2012] OJ L303/1, Article 9.

[32] On the relationship of the WTO with environmental and labour standards, see eg Bartels (n 5) 365–67.

[33] Europe Agreement establishing an association between the European Communities and their Member States, of the one part, and the Republic of Hungary, of the other part [1993] OJ L347/2, Article 70(2).

[34] On this point, see eg Gracia Marín Durán and Elisa Morgera, *Environmental Integration in the EU's External Relations beyond Multilateral Dimensions* (Hart Publishing, 2012) 114 and 115.

[35] eg Comprehensive Economic and Trade Agreement (CETA) between Canada, of the one part, and the European Union and its Member States, of the other part [hereinafter 'CETA'] [2017] OJ L11/23, Article 28.3; Free Trade Agreement between the European Union and the Republic of Singapore [hereinafter 'EU-Singapore FTA'], Articles 2.14 and 8.62; Trade Agreement between the European Union and its Member States, of the one part, and Colombia and Peru, of the other part, as amended by [2016] OJ L356/1, Council Decision of 11 November 2016 on the signing, on behalf of the Union, and provisional application of the Protocol of Accession to the Trade Agreement between the European Union and its Member States, of the one part, and Colombia and Peru, of the other part, to take account of the accession of Ecuador [hereinafter 'EU-Colombia/Peru/Ecuador FTA'], Articles 106 and 167; Trade and Cooperation Agreement between the European Union and the European Atomic Energy Community, of the one part, and the United Kingdom of Great Britain and Northern Ireland, of the other part [hereinafter 'EU-UK TCA'], Article 412.

[36] Lorand Bartels, 'Human Rights, Labour Standards, and Environmental Standards in CETA' in Stefan Griller, Walter Obwexer and Erich Vranes (eds), *Mega-Regional Trade Agreements: CETA, TTIP, and TiSA: New Orientations for EU External Economic Relations* (Oxford University Press, 2017) 202, 212–14; on the interpretation of Article XX GATT, see eg Markus W Gehring, 'Sustainable Development in World Trade Law: A Short History' in Hans Christian Bugge and

From the mid-2000s onwards, an external dimension of sustainability really started to emerge. The 'Global Europe' strategy was particularly significant in this respect, as it laid the foundation for a stronger focus on sustainable development in the EU's trade policy through, on the one hand, institutionalising sustainable impact assessments that now precede negotiations, and, on the other hand, the integration of non-trade objectives (ie, sustainable development) in bilateral international agreements concerning trade. Although the sustainable development nexus clearly included environmental protection, the social pillar was limited to labour standards,[37] a conceptualisation that has carried over into the current design and structure of TSD chapters.

The Treaty of Lisbon finally brought about a process of constitutionalisation. The horizontal environmental integration clause was sharpened, and now reads: '[e]nvironmental protection requirements *must* be integrated into the definition and implementation of the Union's policies and activities, in particular with a view to promoting sustainable development'.[38] Systematic horizontal integration was furthermore broadened by introducing a new provision that focuses on the social dimension of sustainable development.[39] Most importantly, the Treaty of Lisbon embedded the pursuit of sustainable development through trade policy in a constitutional mandate.[40] A common set of principles and objectives for EU external action was introduced in Article 21 TEU, and anchored in the CCP – the framework for the EU's trade and investment policy.[41] Article 21(3) TEU requires that the EU shall 'pursue the objectives set out in paragraphs 1 and 2 in the development and implementation of the different areas of the Union's external action'. Article 205 TFEU further stipulates that '[t]he Union's action on the international scene … shall be guided by the principles, pursue the objectives and be conducted in accordance with the general provisions laid down in [Article 21 TEU]'. Accordingly, the EU shall 'foster the sustainable economic, social and environmental development of developing countries, with the primary aim of eradicating poverty',[42] and 'help develop international measures to preserve and improve the quality of the environment and the sustainable management of global natural resources, in order to ensure sustainable development'.[43] The Treaty of Lisbon, in other words, decoupled sustainable development from development cooperation, and recognised its significance across the boundaries of any specific policy field.

C Voigt (eds), *Sustainable Development in International and National Law* (Europa Law Publishing, 2008) 269, 282 et seq.

[37] ibid 9: 'strengthen sustainable development [by] incorporating new co-operative provisions in areas relating to labour standards and environmental protection'.

[38] Article 11 TFEU (emphasis added); the mandatory character of Article 11 TFEU was previously confirmed by the Court of Justice in Case C-62/88 *Greece v Council* ECLI:EU:C:1990:153, para 20.

[39] Article 9 TFEU.

[40] Article 3(5) TEU.

[41] For a discussion, see eg Douma (n 30) 198.

[42] Article 21(2)(d) TEU.

[43] Article 21(2)(f) TEU.

Against this backdrop, the Court of Justice recently observed that 'the objective of sustainable development henceforth forms an integral part of the common commercial policy'.[44] The Treaty of Lisbon constructed, in other words, a common framework that provided the 'necessary legal foundation … for pursuing non-trade objectives through the adoption of [common commercial policy] measures'.[45] The Commission's latest trade policy review clearly illustrates that this is understood to include all three dimensions of sustainable development.[46]

The EU's post-Lisbon approach to sustainable development in trade policy, thus, rests on both impact assessments and the inclusion of TSD chapters. Impact assessments are important *ex ante* process-based tools for the integration of sustainable development into EU trade policy that highlight trade-offs between the three dimensions of sustainable development.[47] Although they do not provide normative assessments regarding the weight that ought to be given to any dimension, impact assessments can establish important guiding principles for the process of decision-making that ultimately requires political judgment.[48] The Commission has committed to conduct independent impact assessments in a timely and transparent manner for all trade negotiations.[49] In practice, however, the final report is seldom published in time to assist negotiators in any meaningful way, reducing the legitimacy and practical relevance of sustainability impact assessments.[50] Sustainability impact assessments are also vulnerable to be used as a rhetoric that pays lip-service to the social and environmental dimension of trade and investment agreements, without substantively pursuing the necessary trade-offs.[51] The perhaps most glaring example of this is the EU-Mercosur Association Agreement (AA). Negotiations were concluded in June 2019 without a final sustainability impact assessment.[52] The final report

[44] *Opinion 2/15*, ECLI:EU:C:2017:376 (*EU-Singapore FTA*), para 147.

[45] Dimopoulos (n 24) 161; see also Larik (n 6) 53.

[46] European Commission, 'Trade Policy Review – An Open, Sustainable and Assertive Trade Policy' (Communication) COM(2021) 66 final, pt 2.2.

[47] Bernard Hoekman and Hugo Rojas-Romagosa, 'EU Trade Sustainability Impact Assessments: Revisiting the Consultation Process' (2022) 25(1) *Journal of International Economic Law* 45, 47.

[48] Sander RW van Hees, 'Sustainable Development in the EU: Redefining and Operationalizing the Concept' (2014) 10(2) *Utrecht Law Review* 60, 68.

[49] European Commission, 'Impact Assessment' (Communication) COM(2002) 276 final, 5 June 2002; European Commission, 'Trade for All – Towards a more responsible trade and investment policy' (Communication) COM(2015)0497 final, 12; European Commission, 'Handbook for trade sustainability impact assessment', April 2016, 26.

[50] Douma (n 30) 209.

[51] In case of the EU-Colombia/Peru/Ecuador negotiations, the Commission position paper on the final report justified negotiating options *ex post* instead of guiding formulation of policy choices *ex ante*, see Douma (n 30), 212.

[52] The European Ombudsman later found this to amount to maladministration, see European Ombudsman, Decision in case 1026/2020/MAS concerning the failure by the European Commission to finalise an updated 'sustainability impact assessment' before concluding the EU-Mercosur trade negotiations, 19 March 2021.

was ultimately published in December 2020.[53] The Commission continues to support the agreement, in spite of serious concerns over its effects on *inter alia* deforestation.

The combined effect of the 'Global Europe' strategy of 2006 and the Treaty of Lisbon of 2009 has furthermore led to 'widened and deepened'[54] TSD commitments in the form of labour and environmental standards,[55] that has given rise to the comprehensive TSD chapters that are now an integral part of EU trade policy.[56]

11.3. TRADE AND SUSTAINABLE DEVELOPMENT CHAPTERS

The first comprehensive TSD chapter appeared in the EU-Korea FTA of 2011,[57] and similar chapters have since been introduced in the four subsequent trade agreements.[58] Additionally, TSD chapters form part of the EU's AA with Central America,[59] as well as the deep and comprehensive free trade areas developed under the EU's AAs with Ukraine,[60] Georgia[61] and Moldova.[62] The EU-UK Trade and Cooperation Agreement (TCA)[63] and the EU-Japan Economic Partnership Agreement (EPA)[64] also include TSD chapters. Consequently, a total of 11 EU

[53] Max Mendez-Parra et al, 'Sustainability Impact Assessment in Support of the Association Agreement Negotiations between the European Union and Mercosur', Final Report, December 2020.

[54] Lore van den Putte and Jan Orbie, 'EU bilateral trade agreements and the surprising rise of labour provisions' (2015) 31(3) *International Journal of Comparative Labour Law and Industrial Relations* 263, 265.

[55] See eg European Commission, 'Trade, Growth and World Affairs, Trade Policy as a Core Component of the EU's 2020 Strategy' (Communication) COM(2010) 612, 4–5.

[56] Douma (n 30) 204.

[57] Free Trade Agreement between the European Union and its Member States, of the one part, and the Republic of Korea of the other part [2011] OJ L127/6 [hereinafter 'EU-Korea FTA']; note that the EU-CARIFORUM Economic Partnership Agreement ([2008] OJ L289/4) includes strong commitments towards sustainable development but falls short of a TSD chapter in the form that has transpired in the EU's recent treaty-making practice.

[58] EU-Colombia/Peru/Ecuador FTA; CETA; EU-Singapore FTA; Free Trade Agreement between the European Union and the Socialist Republic of Viet Nam [2019] OJ L186/3 [hereinafter 'EU-Vietnam FTA'].

[59] Agreement establishing an Association between the European Union and its Member States, on the one hand, and Central America on the other [2012] OJ L346/3 [hereinafter 'EU-Central America AA'].

[60] Association Agreement between the European Union and its Member States, of the one part, and Ukraine, of the other part [2014] OJ L161/3 [hereinafter 'EU-Ukraine AA'].

[61] Association Agreement between the European Union and the European Atomic Energy Community and their Member States, of the one part, and Georgia, of the other part [2014] OJ L261/4 [hereinafter 'EU-Georgia AA'].

[62] Association Agreement between the European Union and the European Atomic Energy Community and their Member States, of the one part, and the Republic of Moldova, of the other part [2014] OJ L260/4 [hereinafter 'EU-Moldova AA'].

[63] EU-UK TCA.

[64] Agreement between the European Union and Japan for an Economic Partnership [2022] OJ L330/3 [hereinafter 'EU-Japan EPA'].

international agreements featuring TSD chapters are fully or provisionally applied (as a group these agreements are hereafter referred to as PTAs). Nine additional international agreements concerning trade or AAs with TSD chapters are, at the time of writing, still under negotiation, or await ratification.[65]

Although TSD chapters have thus been an integral part of the EU's negotiation template for PTAs for over a decade,[66] their scope and content, but even their bindingness, enforceability and transparency, varies significantly.[67] Some level of variation ought to be expected as third states would be less likely to adopt regulatory policies imposed by the EU 'unreflexively, with a single model promoted to all its partners regardless of their context'.[68] Moreover, the normative rhetoric of the EU's value-based trade policy would suggest that the EU takes full account of the trading partners' level of development.[69] Another possible explanation is based in the distribution of market power between the EU and its trading partners.[70] But these accounts only partly explain the variations in TSD chapters actually negotiated. There is, indeed, convincing evidence that the Commission, in negotiating PTAs, manages the interests of organised societal groups within the EU where export-oriented industries wish to gain access to new markets and cheaper components, whereas import-competing industries fear the competitive pressure from foreign producers.[71] The costs compliance with environmental and labour regulation is in this regard an important factor to maintain a 'level playing field' in trade relations.

Lastly, the emergence of new actors in EU trade policy is another relevant factor for understanding TSD chapters in EU PTAs. Since the adoption of the 'Global Europe' strategy in 2006, EU trade policy has experienced increasing politicisation, with NGOs and civil society becoming more involved in what has historically been the playing field of a few trade policy wonks in the Commission and Member States' foreign ministries, and academics. With the Treaty of Lisbon, the European Parliament assumed a stronger position in trade

[65] EU-Mercosur Trade Agreement; EU-Mexico Trade Agreement; EU-Australia Free Trade Agreement; modernization of the EU-Chile Association Agreement; deepening of the EU-Easter and Southern Africa Economic Partnership Agreement; EU-New Zealand Free Trade Agreement; EU-Philippines Free Trade Agreement; EU-China Comprehensive Agreement on Investment; for a comprehensive overview of the state-of-play, see https://policy.trade.ec.europa.eu/eu-trade-relationships-country-and-region/negotiations-and-agreements_en.

[66] eg Harrison (n 11) 261.

[67] For a recent review of the TSD chapters, see Jean-Baptiste Velut, 'Comparative Analysis of Trade and Sustainable Development Provisions in Free Trade Agreements' (LSE, 2022).

[68] Federica Bicchi, '"Our size fits all": normative power Europe and the Mediterranean' (2006) 13(2) *Journal of European Public Policy* 286, 293.

[69] Arlo Poletti, Daniela Sicurelli and Aydin B Yildrim, 'Promoting sustainable development through trade? EU trade agreements and global value chains' (2020) 51 *Italian Political Science Review* 339; Arlo Poletti and Daniela Sicurelli, *The Political Economy of Normative Trade Power Europe* (Palgrave Macmillan, 2018) 124; Putte and Orbie (n 54).

[70] eg Alasdair A Young, 'Liberalizing trade, not exporting rules: the limits to regulatory co-ordination in the EU's "new generation" preferential trade agreements' (2015) 22 *Journal of European Public Policy* 1253.

[71] Poletti, Sicurelli and Yildrim (n 69) 341–43.

policy, elevating pressure for the inclusion of TSD commitments, and making the Commission accountable for the interests of civil society.[72] Non-trade provisions such as labour standards and environmental protection, thus, became important strategic instruments for, on the one hand, imposing regulatory costs on foreign competitors and, on the other hand, rallying public support for the EU's trade liberalisation agenda.[73]

11.3.1. Scope, Content, and Nature of Commitments

With the exception of EU-Canada CETA, and the EU-UK TCA, all the above-mentioned EU agreements include a single comprehensive TSD chapter.[74] AAs usually complement TSD chapters with additional commitments on, for instance, social standards[75] and environmental protection.[76] The EU-Canada CETA features a horizontal chapter on TSD,[77] and a separate chapter on labour,[78] as well as the environment.[79] The EU-UK TCA departs entirely from the comprehensive approach. Some provisions on labour and social standards,[80] as well as on the environment and climate,[81] are followed up with a horizontal chapter on 'other instruments for trade and sustainable development'.[82]

Although the structure and content of TSD chapters is broadly similar, the individual provisions vary significantly.[83] TSD commitments can, thus, be categorised as tackling, on the one hand, environmental aspects, and, on the other hand, social standards – reflecting the two non-trade pillars of the sustainable development concept. With respect to the environmental dimension, most of the agreements require the contracting parties to effectively implement national laws and multilateral environmental agreements (MEAs) to which they are party.[84] Often, the PTAs will specify the relevant MEAs.[85] TSD chapters include

[72] With respect to labour provisions, see eg Harrison (n 11) 266.

[73] Ida Bastiaens and Evgeny Postnikov, 'Social standars in trade agreements and free trade preferences: an empirical investigation' (2020) 15 *Review of International Organizations* 793.

[74] eg Chapter 13 EU-Singapore FTA; Chapter 16 EU-Japan EPA; Chapter 13 EU-Ukraine AA.

[75] eg Articles 41–48 EU-Central America AA; Articles 419–425 EU-Ukraine AA; Articles 348–354 EU-Georgia AA.

[76] eg Articles 50–51 EU-Central America AA; Articles 360–366 EU-Ukraine AA; Articles 301–312 EU-Georgia AA.

[77] Chapter 21 CETA.

[78] Chapter 22 CETA.

[79] Chapter 23 CETA.

[80] Articles 386–389 EU-UK TCA.

[81] Articles 390–396 EU-UK TCA.

[82] Articles 398–407 EU-UK TCA.

[83] Marco Bronckers and Giovanni Gruni, 'Taking the enforcement of labour standards in the EU's free trade agreements seriously' (2019) 56 *Common Market Law Review* 1591, 1595.

[84] Article 13.5(2) EU-Korea FTA; Article 292 EU-Ukraine AA; Article 230 EU-Georgia AA; Article 400(4) EU-UK TCA; Article 24.4(2) CETA.

[85] eg Convention on International Trade in Endangered Species of Wild Fauna and Flora, 1 July 1974, 993 UNTS 243 [hereinafter 'CITES']; Protocol on Substances that Deplete the Ozone

different types of commitment from 'reaching the objectives',[86] to 'cooperate on the implementation',[87] and 'effectively implement' the MEAs.[88] The level of legal commitment also varies across the agreements, from aspirational language (ie, 'confirm their commitment to effectively implement' or 'shall endeavour'), to strict legal commitment (ie, 'undertake to ensure that they have ratified by the date of entry into force of this Agreement'[89]). All of the above PTAs include specific provisions on 'trade in forest products',[90] or 'trade in fish products', but these provisions vary greatly in scope and the level of legal commitment.[91]

Provisions made with respect to labour standards are in principle linked to existing ILO instruments. All the TSD chapters require ratification of the core ILO conventions. Beyond that, the scope of TSD chapters is fairly inconsistent. Whereas the EU-Canada CETA includes rather far-reaching binding commitments with respect to a set of ILO Conventions regarding, *inter alia*, health and safety of workers and migrants,[92] the EU-Vietnam FTA is rather limited in scope,[93] and in many cases, TSD chapters take a decidedly weaker approach 'reaffirming their commitment to' respect, promote and realise, or effectively implement ILO conventions.[94] Generally speaking, the coverage of MEAs and the level of legal commitment reflects both the power of the EU's respective trading partner and their prior level of participation in global environmental governance.

All the TSD chapters include a right or the contracting parties to set their own levels of environmental protection.[95] This is, however, qualified in all cases by binding non-regression clauses that lock in the existing level of environmental

Layer, 16 September 1987, 1522 UNTS 3; Basel Convention on the Control of Transboundary Movements of Hazardous Wastes and their Disposal, 22 March 1989, 1673 UNTS 57; Convention on Biological Diversity, 29 December 1993, 1760 UNTS 79; United Nations General Assembly, United Nations Framework Convention on Climate Change, 20 January 1994, UN Doc A/RES/48/189; Kyoto Protocol to the United Nations Framework Convention on Climate Change, 11 December 1997, UN Doc FCCC/CP/1997/L.7/Add. 2; Nagoya Protocol on Access to Genetic Resources and the Fair and Equitable Sharing of Benefits Arising from their Utilization to the Convention on Biological Diversity, 29 October 2010, UN Doc UNEP/CBD/COP/DEC/X/1; United Nations Framework Convention on Climate Change, Paris Agreement, 12 December 2015, UN Doc FCCC/CP/2015/10/Add.1;.

[86] eg Article 13.5(3) EU-Korea FTA; Article 287(2) EU-Central America AA; Article 230(4) EU-Georgia AA.

[87] eg Article 13.6(1) EU-Vietnam FTA.

[88] eg Article 400(4) EU-UK TCA; Article 24.4(3) CETA; Article 12.6 EU-Singapore FTA.

[89] eg with respect to CITES Article 287(3) EU-Central America AA.

[90] Alternatively 'trade and forest', see eg Article 403 EU-UK TCA; or 'Trade in Timber and Timber Products', see eg Article 12.7 EU-Singapore FTA.

[91] compare eg Article 294 EU-Ukraine AA and Article 233 EU-Georgia AA.

[92] Article 23.3(2) CETA; similar language whereby the parties 'commit' to the promotion and implementation of ILO conventions, eg Article 229(2) EU-Georgia AA and Article 269 EU-Colombia/Peru/Ecuador FTA; EU-Singapore FTA.

[93] Article 13.4 EU-Vietnam FTA.

[94] eg Article 286 EU-Central America AA; Article 16.3 EU-Japan EPA.

[95] Article 13.3(1) EU-Korea FTA; Article 268(1) EU-Colombia/Pero/Ecuador FTA; Article 285(1) EU-Central America AA; Article 290(1) EU-Ukraine AA; Article 228(1) EU-Georgia AA; Article 364(1) EU-Moldova AA; Article 391 EU-UK TCA; Article 24.3 CETA; Article 12.2(1) EU-Singapore FTA; Article 13.2(1) EU-Vietnam FTA.

and labour protection, preventing parties from lowering their environmental standards, even if this were compatible with their MEA and ILO commitments. In theory, this guarantees a continuous upwards trajectory in the level of environmental and social protection. It is noteworthy, however, that the majority of post-Lisbon PTAs qualify non-regression clauses to actions 'affecting trade or investment between the parties'.[96] Conditioning the lowering of labour and environmental standards to effects on trade alone can cause problems.[97] Even more contentious are formulations that further limit non-regression clauses to administrative or regulatory actions aimed at 'encouraging trade and investment'.[98]

All of the PTAs include best endeavour provisions, whereby the parties 'seek to ensure that … laws and policies provide for and encourage high levels of … protection',[99] with respect to labour and environmental standards. Though not drafted in a legally binding fashion, these provisions are crucial, as they could still be invoked against laws and policies that fall short of the environmental and labour standards pronounced in the PTA, and should not, therefore, be dismissed as purely aspirational.[100]

TSD chapters clearly instrumentalise trade policy to further environmental and social objectives. Many of the agreements incorporate explicitly a three-pillar concept of sustainable development that pivots economic development, against social and environmental protection as interdependent and mutually reinforcing elements, in that 'trade should promote sustainable development in all its dimensions'.[101] The economic growth brought about by an upwards trajectory of trade and continuous global economic integration is, nonetheless, at the heart of PTAs. In all the agreements, and EU trade policy more generally, the trade/labour or trade/environment nexus is depicted in terms of economic growth. Accordingly, PTAs can facilitate trade and investment in green technologies, and goods and services with a distinct environmental dimension. The reduction of barriers to trade is more generally projected to yield upsides for social and environmental protection, and sustainable development policies such as labour standards are believed to improve economic efficiency and productivity. Many of the agreements refer therefore to 'trade-related aspects' of labour and environmental policies, or, indeed, allow regulatory flexibility in domestic sustainable development-related policies, as long as these do not affect trade or investment. Nothing in the agreements, however, encourages the EU or its

[96] eg Article 13.7 EU-Korea FTA; Article 12.12 EU-Singapore FTA; Article 13.3(2) EU-Vietnam FTA; Article 277(2) EU-Colombia/Peru/Ecuador FTA; Article 291(2) EU-Central America AA; Article 296 EU-Ukraine AA; Article 387 EU-UK TCA.

[97] Bronckers and Gruni (n 83) 1605 and 1606.

[98] eg Article 16.2(2) EU-Japan EPA; Article 13.3(3) EU-Vietnam FTA; CETA provides a similar wording but does not combine this with an effect-on-trade requirement, Article 23.4 CETA.

[99] eg Article 23.3 CETA (on labour); Article 13.3 EU-Korea FTA; Article 12.2(2) EU-Singapore FTA;.

[100] Bartels (n 36), 206.

[101] Article 13.6 EU-Korea FTA.

trading partners to adopt positive actions that restrict trade and investment as a trade-off for longer-term high levels of environmental and social protection. On the contrary, these types of measures are presumed to be protectionist in character unless covered by the general exception clause.[102]

11.3.2. Implementation and Enforcement Mechanism

All PTAs establish an institutional structure that oversees the implementation of the TSD chapter, usually comprising a bilateral committee,[103] or board,[104] on trade and sustainable development, in combination with national contact points. These bilateral structures are charged with promoting cooperation towards achieving the labour and environmental objectives, carry out impact assessments, and making recommendations for the proper implementation of the TSD chapter. As part of the broader civil society dialogue, most agreements require the parties to establish domestic advisory groups (DAG), comprising affected stakeholders, and a civil society forum that brings together representatives of civil society organisations for regular dialogues on sustainable development aspects of the PTA.[105] All of the PTAs include provisions on regulatory cooperation.[106] The EU-Vietnam FTA,[107] the EU-Colombia/Peru/Ecuador FTA,[108] as well as the EU-Central America AA,[109] include provisions on technical assistance and capacity building with respect to both labour and environmental provisions. Notably, the three AAs with Moldova, Georgia and Ukraine provide for capacity building outside of the framework of the TSD chapter, and only with respect to social policies, including labour standards.[110] All but the EU-Central America AA allow for civil society participation as part of the impact assessment, and all PTAs allow for public submissions to the parties directly or through the DAG.[111]

The enforcement mechanism of non-regression obligations in most agreements is of a cooperative nature, including commitments to put in place a system of labour inspections,[112] access to effective administrative and judicial

[102] eg Article 13.2(2) EU-Korea FTA; Article 12.1 EU-Singapore FTA; Articles 16.3(6) and 16.4(5) EU-Japan EPA; Articles 286(4) and 287(5) EU-Central America AA.

[103] eg Article 22.4 CETA; Article 13.12 EU-Korea FTA; Article 13.15 EU-Vietnam FTA; Article 280 EU-Colombia/Pero/Ecuador FTA; Article 376 EU-Moldova AA.

[104] eg Article 294 EU-Central America AA; Article 12.15 EU-Singapore FTA.

[105] Bartels (n 36) 207.

[106] eg Article 23.8(5) CETA (on labour) and Articles 24.7(3) and 24.13(5) CETA (on environment).

[107] Article 13.14(3)(c) EU-Vietnam FTA.

[108] Article 286 EU-Colombia/Peru/Ecuador FTA.

[109] Article 302 EU-Central America AA.

[110] Article 420 EU-Ukraine AA; Article 349 EU-Georgia AA; Article 32 EU-Moldova AA.

[111] Article 13.13(3) EU-Korea FTA; The EU-Colombia/Peru/Ecuador FTA allows for public submissions to be made directly to the sub-committee on trade and sustainable development, see Article 280(7).

[112] Article 23.5(1) and 24.6(1) CETA.

proceedings,[113] and other means of cooperation.[114] With respect to the ratification and implementation of environmental and labour conventions, the enforcement mechanisms are equally cooperative and, thus, match the aspirational language of the substantive commitment. The EU-CARIFORUM EPA is the only PTA with a robust dispute settlement mechanism (DSM) for disputes arising out of the implementation of, or non-compliance with, the TSD provisions. All post-Lisbon PTAs incorporate a specific DSM with respect to their TSD chapters. If a disagreement cannot be resolved through state-state consultation, a panel of experts is charged to provide recommendations on how to remedy violations. The committee on trade and sustainable development oversees the implementation of the panel of experts' recommendations, but nothing in the agreements requires the parties to comply with the recommendations.

With the exception of the EU-UK TCA,[115] which provides for the temporary suspension of trade concessions, TSD chapters in EU PTAs generally lack the possibility to impose sanctions. Many scholars have criticised this soft approach as the core weakness of EU TSD chapters.[116] Van den Putte and Orbie, on the other hand, view the soft approach as a strength, which allows the EU to reinforce its image as a normative power seeking to instil long-term change through learning, best practices, and socialisation.[117] Be that as it may, the EU still has the possibility, at least in theory, to react more assertively to violations of the TSD chapters, including through the imposition of sanctions where such violation concerns core labour standards that fall, in principle, under the EU's human rights conditionality clause.[118]

The effectiveness of TSD chapters does not, however, merely depend on the choice between a cooperation or sanction-based approach. On the contrary, the promotion of sustainability objectives through trade and investment policy instruments requires a deeply held conviction to prioritise environmental and labour objectives over the EU's economic interests. Poletti and Sicurelli, however, found a correlation between the strength of TSD chapters in EU PTAs and the level of economic integration between the EU and its trading partner in global value chains.[119] This seems to suggest that export-oriented industries are effective in mobilising against the inclusion of far reaching TSD chapters, and the resulting higher

[113] Article 23.5(2) and 24.6(2) CETA.

[114] eg Article 395 EU-UK TCA.

[115] Articles 410(2) and (3) in combination with Article 749 EU-UK TCA.

[116] eg Bronckers and Gruni (n 83) 1610; Giovanni Gruni, 'Law or Aspiration? The European Union Proposal for a Labour Standards Clause in the Transatlantic Trade and Investment Partnership' (2016) 43(4) *Legal Issues of Economic Integration* 399, 404; Bartels (n 36) 208; Emilie M Hafner-Burton, 'Trading human rights: how preferential trade agreements influence government repression' (2005) 59 *International Organizations* 593, 599.

[117] Putte and Orbie (n 54) 270–71.

[118] Bronckers and Gruni (n 83) 1614; note that recent treaty practice may restrict the possibility, see eg Strategic Partnership Agreement between the European Union and its Member States, of the one part, and Canada, of the other part [2016] OJ L329/45, Article 28(7).

[119] Poletti, Sicurelli and Yildrim (n 69) 350.

regulatory cost for trading partners. As a consequence, the balance of the three dimensions of sustainable development in these TSD chapters clearly prioritises economic objective over the promotion of environmental or social protection.[120]

To date, the DSM has only been tested once in respect of labour standards in the TSD chapter of the EU-Korea FTA. In late 2017, the EU requested consultations with Korea for failing to respect a labour obligation and having repeatedly fallen short of its commitments to ratify core ILO conventions.[121] Korea has, for some time, been painted as a poster-child for the ineffectiveness of TSD chapters to deliver social change. Unable to resolve the matter in consultations, the EU requested in mid-2019 the establishment of a panel of experts.[122] In its final report, published in January of 2021,[123] the panel found certain provisions of Koreas national legislation to be in breach of the binding obligation to implement relevant ILO conventions.[124] Although Korea shortly after publication of the final report ratified ILO Conventions Nos 29, 97 and 98, it remains unclear to what extent this can be credited to the effectiveness of the EU's cooperation-based approach to TSD chapters. The panel of experts proceeding was nonetheless significant for a better understanding of the explicit restriction of TSD chapters to 'trade-related aspects of labour and environment'.[125] The panel of experts, adopting a contextual interpretation of the TSD chapter, concluded that individual obligations to comply with core ILO conventions (eg, the abolition of slavery or child labour) cannot be understood as having been limited to trade-related aspects only.[126] If replicated, this reading would debunk 'trade-relatedness' as a general limitation to the material scope of the TSD chapters.

11.3.3. TSD review

Under increasing pressure from the Parliament to 'include comprehensive, enforceable and ambitious [TSD] chapters',[127] the Commission in 2017

[120] Gerda Van Roozendaal, 'Where symbolism prospers: an analysis of the impact on enabling rights of labour standards provisions in trade agreements with South Korea' (2017) 5(4) *Politics and Governance* 19, 26.

[121] Request for consultations by the European Union on compliance with obligations under Chapter 13 of the EU – Korea Free Trade Agreement, 17 December 2019.

[122] Request for the establishment of a Panel of Experts by the European Union on compliance with obligations under Chapter 13 of the EU – Korea Free Trade Agreement, 4 July 2019.

[123] Panel of Experts proceeding constituted under Article 13.15 of the EU-Korea Free Trade Agreement, Report of the Panel of Experts, 20 January 2021; for a discussion of the panel's findings see eg Aleydis Nissen, 'And so it begins: trade and sustainable development recommendations by panel of experts under a European Union free trade agreement' (2021) 7 *International Labor Rights Case Law* 257.

[124] Panel of Experts Report, paras 107, 175 and 227.

[125] Article 13.2 EU-Korea FTA; similar language is included in Article 13.1(1) EU-Vietnam FTA.

[126] Panel of Experts Report, para 66.

[127] eg European Parliament resolution of 5 July 2016 on implementation of the 2010 recommendations of Parliament on social and environmental standards, human rights and corporate responsibility (2015/2038(INI)), para. 21.

announced a 'thorough stocktaking of the EU TSD provisions'.[128] Either the EU would address concerns more assertively through existing structures, or shift to a sanctions-based model of TSD enforcement. Other options were suggested in scholarship, including public participation in complaints procedures, a pre-ratification requirement to ratify relevant ILO conventions, and a stricter enforcement mechanism.[129] Although the 15-point action plan on how to 'revamp the TSD chapters'[130] did not consider a sanctions-based model as desirable, the Commission in its review of the TSD policy in 2022 introduced temporary and proportionate trade sanctions in limited circumstances.[131]

At present, the Commission further proposes a 'tailored approach' that is sensible to target the specific needs of developing countries in identifying and prioritising sustainable development objectives. Though generally welcome, it carries the risk of further eroding the coherence and consistency of TSD chapters. Considering that the existing variances across agreements cannot satisfactorily be explained by the development needs of third states, this may instead reflect the interests of well-organised interest groups, with a tailored approach potentially leading to a weakening of TSD chapters in PTAs with economies that are well integrated with the EU in global value chains. Additionally, the Commission's plans to mainstream TSD commitments by reinforcing environmental and labour standards outside of TSD chapters, thereby increasing the role of private stakeholders in lodging complaints with the Chief Enforcement Officer.[132] The Commission also, more generally, envisages strengthening the role of the civil society dialogue within the framework of the TSD implementation. All of these suggestions are welcome, and are likely to increase transparency in the implementation of the EU's TSD policy.

11.4. SUSTAINABLE DEVELOPMENT AND EU INVESTMENT AGREEMENTS

The Treaty of Lisbon of 2009 substantively broadened the EU's competence under the CCP to include FDI,[133] reflecting the intricate relationship of trade and

[128] European Commission, 'Trade and sustainable development (TSD) chapters in EU Free Trade Agreements (FTAs)', 11 July 2017, p 5.

[129] Louise Curran and Jappe Eckhardt, 'EU Trade Policy in a Trade-Skeptic Context' in Wolfgang Weiß and Cornelia Furculita (eds), *Global Politics and EU Trade Policy* (Springer, 2020) 140, 145 et seq; Harrison (n 11); Bronckers and Gruni (n 83); Gregory Shaffer, 'Retooling trade agreements for social inclusion' (2019) *University of Illinois Law Review* 1.

[130] European Commission, 'Feedback and way forward on improving the implementation and enforcement of Trade and Sustainable Development chapters in EU Free Trade Agreements', 26 February 2018.

[131] European Commission, 'The power of trade partnerships: together for green and just economic growth' (Communication) COM(2022) 409 final.

[132] In her mission letter to the trade commissioner, Ursula von der Leyen outlined the role of the Chief Enforcement Officer with respect to TSD provisions in EU PTAs, Ursula von der Leyen, Mission letter to Phil Hogan – Commissioner for Trade, 1 December 2019, p 5.

[133] See ch 4.

investment in international economic governance. The EU has since established itself as a serious actor, pushing its own rules on foreign investment in multiple fora.[134] Negotiations on the multilateral[135] and bilateral[136] level are accompanied by unilateral policies, such as an investment screening framework.[137] These efforts focus in varying degree on both the pre-establishment phase of FDI, such as investment liberalisation, and the post-establishment phase, such as investment protection and dispute settlement. Out of the post-Lisbon constitutional mandate to integrate environmental and social objectives in all EU policies arises a need for coherence and consistency across all aspects of the CCP. Trade and investment policy instruments should therefore clearly integrate sustainable development objectives.

11.4.1. Five Types of Investment Agreements

The structure and design that the EU uses to regulate foreign investment through bilateral and regional agreements varies significantly. Five different approaches stand out. First, deep and comprehensive trade agreements such as the EU-Canada CETA, or the now dormant (if not dead) EU-US Transatlantic Trade and Investment Partnership Agreement (TTIP), comfortably couch a comprehensive chapter on investment liberalisation, protection, and dispute settlement amongst its trade provisions.[138] Second, the EU-Japan Economic Partnership Agreement (EPA) includes general investment liberalisation commitments,[139] but only a distant promise to revisit investment protection and dispute settlement in separate negotiations.[140] This approach is not very different from earlier agreements such as the EU-Korea FTA, or the EU-Colombia/Peru/Ecuador FTA, although investment liberalisation commitments beyond trade in services (ie, GATS disciplines) are in these agreements covered under the heading of 'establishment'.[141]

Third, the EU FTAs with Singapore and Vietnam have as their objective to facilitate both trade *and* investment,[142] and contain general trade in services, as well as specific liberalisation commitments, such as, for example, regarding

[134] Julien Chaisse and Matthieu Burnay, 'Introduction – CAI's Contribution to International Investment Law: European, Chinese, and Global Perspectives' (2022) 23(4) *Journal of World Investment & Trade* 497, 498.

[135] eg WTO, UNCITRAL, and ECT.

[136] eg PTAs and IPAs.

[137] Regulation (EU) 2019/452 of the European Parliament and of the Council of 19 March 2019 establishing a framework for the screening of foreign direct investments into the Union [2019] OJ L79I/1. See ch 3.

[138] CETA, Chapter 8.

[139] Articles 8.14 to 8.19, EU-Japan EPA.

[140] Commission Press Release, 'EU-Japan trade agreement enters into force' (31 January 2019).

[141] EU-Korea FTA, Chapter 7, section C; EU-Colombia/Peru/Ecuador FTA, Title IV, Chapter 2.

[142] Article 1.2 EU-Vietnam FTA; Article 1.2 EU-Singapore FTA.

investments in renewable energies.[143] Unlike the EU-Japan EPA, however, these agreements were negotiated in parallel to specific Investment Protection Agreements (IPAs).[144] Notably, the EU-Vietnam FTA explicitly includes investment liberalisation,[145] including market access commitments,[146] national treatment and most favoured nation treatment (MFN),[147] and performance requirements.[148] The structure and design of the agreement is, thus, closer to the EU-Japan EPA, whereas the EU-Singapore FTA follows the EU-Korea FTA model, in that it subsumes investment liberalisation under its establishment provisions. The EU-Singapore FTA furthermore limits non-discriminatory market access to national treatment.[149] Ultimately, however, the scope of investment liberalisation included under these two agreements appears to be broadly similar.[150] What stands out is that the approach draws a clearer line between pre- and post-establishment disciplines. Arguably, this primarily responds to concern over the division of competences between the EU and its Member States for the negotiation of investment agreements covering portfolio investment and ISDS, which was caused by *Opinion 2/15* of the Court of Justice on an earlier draft of the EU-Singapore FTA.[151]

Fourth, as the only pure investment liberalisation agreement, the envisaged EU-China Comprehensive Agreement on Investment (CAI)[152] has a unique structure that resembles neither trade, nor fully-fledged investment agreements.[153] Without investment protection, the envisaged EU-China CAI encompasses market access, technology transfers, state-owned enterprises, and subsidies.[154]

[143] Article 7.3 EU-Vietnam FTA; Article 7.3 EU-Singapore FTA.

[144] Council Decision (EU) 2018/1599 of 15 October 2018 on the signing, on behalf of the European Union, of the Free Trade Agreement between the European Union and the Republic of Singapore [2018] OJ L267/1; Council Decision (EU) 2019/753 of 30 March 2020 on the conclusion of the Free Trade Agreement between the European Union and the Socialist Republic of Viet Nam [2018] OJ L186/1.

[145] EU-Vietnam FTA, Chapter 8, section B.

[146] Article 8.4 EU-Vietnam FTA.

[147] Articles 8.5 and 8.6 EU-Vietnam FTA.

[148] Article 8.8 EU-Vietnam FTA.

[149] Unlike the EU-Korea FTA, see Article 7.14.

[150] Petros C Mavroidis and André Sapir, 'What Is so Special about CAI?' (2022) 30(2) *Asia Pacific Law Review* 348, 351–52.

[151] *Opinion 2/15* ECLI:EU:C:2017:376 (*EU-Singapore FTA*); for a discussion of the case, see eg Hannes Lenk, 'Prior Judicial Involvement in Investor-State Dispute Settlement: Lessons from the Court's Rhetoric in Opinion 2/15' (2018) 13(1) *Global Trade And Customs Journal* 19; Marise Cremona, 'Shaping EU Trade Policy Post-Lisbon: Opinion 2/15 of 16 May 2017' (2018) 14(1) *European Constitutional Law Review* 23; Merijn Chamon, 'Implied exclusive powers in the ECJ'S post-Lisbon jurisprudence: The continued development of the ERTA doctrine' (2018) 55(5) *Common Market Law Review* 1101.

[152] European Commission, 'EU and China reach agreement in principle on investment', 30 December 2020.

[153] Markus Krajewski, 'Dancing with the Dragon: The new EU-China Investment Agreement' (*Verfassungsblog*, 5 January 2021).

[154] For a brief overview of the CAI, its meaning for EU investment policy, and the criticism against it, see eg Hannes Lenk, 'Developments in International Investment Law and Policy in the European Union' in Lisa Sachs, Lise Johnson and Jesse Coleman (eds), *Yearbook on International Investment*

This structure has been presented as 'a glimpse of what investment treaties could look like if they responded to the problems businesses actually face, rather than assumptions about how legal protections would promote investment',[155] and may well be replicated in future negotiations. Overall, the agreement appears to lock in commitments that broadly reflect the mutualisation of openings already made by China with other trading partners and adds, therefore, little in terms of market access.[156] Like other PTAs, however, the envisaged EU-China CAI includes a comprehensive chapter on 'investment and sustainable development'.

Lastly, a significant portion of bilateral investment agreements are currently negotiated by the Member States themselves with third states. These agreements are sanctioned under the 'Grandfathering Regulation',[157] subject to monitoring by the Commission.[158] These agreements are, at least, partly covered by the CCP, and Member States should therefore be considered to exercise EU exclusive competence.[159] Although the EU is now under a constitutional mandate to promote sustainable development through all of these agreements – including investment agreements concluded by Member States with third states – the level of integration varies in practice significantly between pre- and post-establishment of FDI.

11.4.2. Pre-establishment

Sustainable development and investment liberalisation commitments are generally well integrated in PTAs. Being part of the same agreement, investment liberalisation provisions are generally subject to horizontal TSD chapters in both the EU-Canada CETA model and also in the EU international agreements

Law & Policy 2020 (Oxford University Press, 2021) 293, 302–08; see also Axel Berger, 'The China–EU Investment Agreement Negotiations: Rationale, Motivations, and Contentious Issues' in Yuwen Li, Tong Qi and Cheng Bian (eds), *China, the EU and International Investment Law: Reforming Investor-State Dispute Settlement* (Routledge, 2019) 11; and Bryan Mercurio, 'Putting the Comprehensive Agreement on Investment (CAI) into Perspective: Five Key Points' (*University of Adelaide Institute for International Trade*, 2 February 2021), https://iit.adelaide.edu.au/news/list/2021/02/02/putting-the-comprehensive-agreement-on-investment-cai-into-perspective-five.

[155] Lorenzo Cotula, 'EU–China Comprehensive Agreement on Investment: An Appraisal of its Sustainable Development Section' (2021) 6 *Business and Human Rights Journal* 360, 361.

[156] François Godement, 'Wins and Losses in the EU-China Investment Agreement (CAI)' (January 2021) Institut Montaigne Policy Paper; Mercurio (n 154).

[157] Regulation (EU) No 1219/2012 of 12 December 2012 establishing transitional arrangements for bilateral investment agreements between Member States and third countries [2012] OJ L 351/40. See ch 12.

[158] For a statistical overview over the number of post-Lisbon investment agreements negotiated and concluded by Member States with third countries, see European Commission, 'Report from the Commission to the European Parliament and the Council on the Application of Regulation (EU) No 1219/2012 Establishing Transitional Arrangements for Bilateral Investment Agreements between Member States and Third Countries' COM(2020)134 final.

[159] Philip Strik, *Shaping the Single European Market in the Field of Foreign Direct Investment* (Hart Publishing, 2014) 184.

with Korea, Japan, Singapore and Vietnam. The parties recognise, for instance, that it is 'inappropriate to encourage trade *or investment* by weakening or reducing the protections afforded by their domestic labour and environment law'.[160] TSD chapters, thus, cover investment as an economic activity insofar as it is covered by EU PTAs, which in all cases includes investment liberalisation. The investment and sustainable development chapter in the envisaged EU-China CAI broadly adopts the same approach as TSD chapters in EU PTAs. Although the envisaged EU-China CAI does not, in principle, go beyond China's already existing international obligations with respect to ILO conventions, the inclusion of an explicit commitment to make 'continued and sustained efforts' to sign and ratify ILO Conventions 29 of 1930 and 105 of 1957 is significant.[161] Indeed, China has included references to labour rights in its investment agreements previously, but these were markedly geared towards preserving China's regulatory policy space.[162] Whether the envisaged EU-China CAI, if it is ever ratified, is capable of instigating a lasting policy change vis-à-vis labour rights in China remains to be seen.[163]

With respect to international agreements of Member States, however, the picture is rather bleak. Although the Commission asks for an 'affirmation of the right to regulate; …; the prohibition of investment enhancement by lowering or relaxing domestic environmental or labour legislation or standards, or by failing to effectively enforce such legislation and standards; a reference to human rights and sustainable development',[164] references to human rights and sustainable development may in practice be limited to preambular language.[165] None of the agreements, however, appears to include a comprehensive TSD chapter or equivalent. The idea that Member States through their own investment agreements can 'act as advocates of the modernised EU standards in regions where there is no Union agreement'[166] is, therefore, unsubstantiated. Overall, how efficiently investment liberalisation and sustainable development are integrated in EU investment policy depends, first and foremost, on the strengths of the TSD chapter.

[160] eg Article 23.4 CETA; Article 12.1(3) EU-Singapore FTA; Article 13.3(1) EU-Vietnam FTA (emphasis added).

[161] Comprehensive Agreement on Investment, Section IV (22 January 2021), subsection 3, article 4 (hereafter 'CAI Section IV').

[162] Manjiao Chi, 'Addressing Sustainable Development Concerns through IIAs: A Preliminary Assessment of Chinese IIAs' in Julien Chaisse (ed), *China's International Investment Strategy: Bilateral, Regional, and Global Law and Policy* (Oxford University Press, 2019) 105, 110–11; Godement also points out that 'China in the past has been extremely generous with non-binding, or non-sanctioned, or non-precisely defined commitments', see Godement (n 156).

[163] Krajewski (n 153).

[164] Commission (n 158) 6.

[165] See Agreement between the Government of Hungary and the Government of the Republic of Cabo Verde for the promotion and reciprocal protection of investments (signed 28 March 2019) (Hungary–Cabo Verde BIT).

[166] Commission (n 158) 9.

11.4.3. Post-establishment

Much more problematic is the situation with respect to investment protection. Only the EU-Canada CETA integrates sustainable development objectives and investment protection. This is vividly illustrated in the Joint Interpretative Instrument that accompanied the signing of that agreement.[167] Accordingly, that agreement 'preserves the ability of the European Union and its Member States and Canada to adopt and apply their own laws and regulations that regulate economic activity in the public interest, to achieve legitimate public policy objectives such as … the environment, public morals, social or consumer protection …'.[168] The instrument is clearly intended to provide the EU and Canada with greater flexibility in adopting domestic regulations that relate to sustainable development, without triggering a breach of the agreement. This not only provides context to the non-regression clauses of the TSD chapters, and the right to set levels of environmental and social protection, but effectively circumscribes the scope of investment protection standards such as fair and equitable treatment, or the prohibition on indirect expropriation.[169] The investment court with the EU-Canada CETA, adopting a contextual approach, would naturally take account not only of the interpretative statement but also the TSD chapters in the agreement.

The EU's IPAs with Singapore and Vietnam, on the other hand, are not explicitly linked to the TSD chapters of the accompanying FTAs. This context is, thus, effectively removed from the interpretative matrix. Although joint interpretative instruments could be adopted to provide interpretations of the right to regulate in these IPAs, little else in the agreements hints at the importance of environmental and labour standards. The adoption of measures that are well in line with the TSD chapters of the FTAs, or perhaps justified under the general exception clause, may nonetheless violate the investment protection standards of the IPA.

Although the separation of pre- from post-establishment provisions may appear reasonable from the point of view of the division of competences and, thus, the efficiency in the ratification of PTAs, it severely undermines the coherence and consistency in the integration of sustainable development in the EU's investment policy. This is only exacerbated by the fact that the enforcement of TSD chapters under the PTAs remains relatively weak, compared to the right of private investors to initiate proceedings before the investment court system under the IPAs. Conscious or not, this reflects a policy choice that elevates the concrete economic interests of private investors over the systemic concerns of long-term sustainable development objectives.

[167] Joint Interpretative Instrument on the Comprehensive Economic and Trade Agreement (CETA) between Canada and the European Union and its Member States, 27 October 2016, EU Council Doc 13541/16.

[168] ibid Article 2.

[169] Bartels (n 36) 212.

Member State agreements with third states fare even worse. These agreements lack strong sustainable development objectives with respect to both the pre- and post-establishment dimension, and lack the institutional safeguards that the investment court system (ICS) is projected to provide. Instead, traditional investor-state arbitral tribunals will be the arbiters of whether or not environmental or social policies in the host state violate the investment agreement.

11.5. CONCLUSION

The EU started to integrate sustainable development in its laws and policies as a response to developments in the multilateral fora. Both the Brundtland report and the three-pillar model that requires a balancing of economic, social, and environmental objectives continue to influence the implementation of sustainable development. It was not until the mid-2000s, however, that sustainable development was clearly rooted in the EU's external action, including its trade and investment policy. Today, comprehensive TSD chapters are standard elements of all EU PTAs. Comparing TSD chapters and their implementation in EU trade and investment agreements, this chapter made four observations.

First, rather than becoming a workable legal principle, sustainable development has become 'a fashionable and rhetoric phrase – to which everyone pays homage but nobody seems to define with precision and exactitude'.[170] The term 'non-trade' objectives is itself telling that social and environmental objectives are not part and parcel of an integrated conception of sustainable development. Rather, trade policy conceives of these two pillars as incidental to the achievement of the EU's economic objectives. As such, sustainable development has been used by the EU strategically to legitimise its free trade and investment agenda by appealing to the broader concerns of civil society, which has become influential in an increasingly politicised arena, while simultaneously pushing its economic interests through the negotiation of bilateral trade and investment agreements.

Second, while the environmental dimension is strongly represented in the EU's conception of sustainable development, the social dimension is restricted to labour standards. Other social gains with respect to, for instance, poverty or development, are assumed to result from the overall macroeconomic benefits of free and fair markets. But even environmental and labour aspects are in EU PTAs often limited to 'trade-related' aspects – underlining the primary objective of EU trade and investment agreement that is opening markets and fostering economic growth.

Third, although the soft model of enforcement has long been advocated by the EU as a long-term perspective to instigate lasting policy changes in third

[170] Mensah (n 18) 2.

states with respect to labour, empirical studies suggest that the effect is much more limited than expected. As the geoeconomic[171] landscape is shifting, the EU's market power will increasingly come under pressure to deliver the changes inherent in the EU's value-based trade and investment policy. The recent TSD review appears to open the doors to a more assertive enforcement of TSD commitments. With that said, the effects of TSD chapters must be seen in context. They may lack the level of enforceability that may be desirable from an environmental or labour law perspective, yet at the time of conclusion, Chapter 13 of the EU-Korea FTA represented the most far-reaching labour commitment in any of Korea's FTAs,[172] and the same would be true for the envisaged EU-China CAI.

Lastly, only EU PTAs with comprehensive chapters on investment, ie, those including investment liberalisation, protection, and dispute settlement under a single institutional roof, are comprehensively linked to the EU's TSD commitments. But these agreements are few and far between. Overall, therefore, EU investment policy appears to have taken a deliberate choice to exclude investment protection standards, and its ICS, from the comprehensive cover of its TSD commitments. In the case of parallel IPAs, sustainable development is reduced to the scope of the right to regulate, which protects the possibility of adopting environmental or social policies where the political will for doing so is present in third countries. Most significantly, however, by shifting responsibility for the negotiation of IIAs with third states to the Member States, even the broader context of the agreements is removed from the value-driven trade and investment policy that the EU openly advocates.

[171] '[T]oday's battles for supremacy and hegemony will not have a mainly geopolitical, but much more a *geoeconomic* character. This means that beyond military, state-centered forms of 'hard' power contentions, today's global landscape is being governed by more economic, network-centered, and complex forms of confrontation, competition, and cooperation.' Milan Babić, Adam D Dixon and Imogen T Liu, 'Geoeconomics in a Changing Global Order' in Milan Babić, Adam D Dixon and Imogen T Liu (eds), *The Political Economy of Geoeconomics: Europe in a Changing World* (Palgrave Macmillan, 2022) p 1.

[172] Nissen (n 123) 7–8.

12

The EU's Powers to Green International Investment Law

LAURENS ANKERSMIT

12.1. INTRODUCTION[1]

ACCORDING TO THE International Energy Agency (IEA), no new investments can be made in fossil fuel projects as of December 2021 if the world is to achieve net-zero emissions by 2050 (the net-zero emissions (NZE) scenario).[2] The NZE scenario gives the world a chance to stay within 1.5 degrees of global warming. The European Union (EU) and its Member States have committed to net-zero emissions by 2050. The Commission's European Green Deal strategy aims for NZE, and the recently adopted EU secondary legislation puts this objective into law: 'Union-wide greenhouse gas emissions and removals regulated in Union law shall be balanced within the Union at the latest by 2050, thus reducing emissions to net zero by that date, and the Union shall aim to achieve negative emissions thereafter'.[3]

Nevertheless, neither the EU nor its Member States are planning on banning investments in fossil fuel projects in the EU, or by EU investors in third states. To the contrary, Member State governments are still planning new fossil fuel projects in their territories after December 2021. The governments of Germany and the Netherlands, for instance, recently handed out permits for gas extraction in the North Sea above the Waddenzee, a UNESCO world heritage site. In third states, governments are seeking to take advantage of high energy prices in the wake of Russia's invasion of Ukraine. The government of the Democratic Republic of Congo, for instance, is auctioning large amounts of old-growth

[1] The author wishes to thank Jessica Lawrence and Christina Eckes for their comments.

[2] Stéphanie Bouckaert et al, *Net Zero by 2050: A Roadmap for the Global Energy Sector* (IEA, 2021).

[3] Article 2 of Regulation (EU) 2021/1119 of the European Parliament and of the Council of 30 June 2021 establishing the framework for achieving climate neutrality and amending Regulations (EC) No 401/2009 and (EU) 2018/1999 ('European Climate Law') [2021] OJ L243/1.

rainforests that extend into Virunga National Park for oil exploration and drilling because it wants to become 'the new destination for oil investments'.[4] The peatlands and rainforests in the Congo Basin are hugely important for storing carbon. French energy company TotalEnergies is reportedly involved in this new fossil fuel project.

What is more, the EU and its Member States have in the past decades ensured that investments in such projects are also *protected*. Investments of fossil fuel companies in third states, like TotalEnergies, or by companies in third states investing in the EU often benefit from favourable standards of protection under international investment agreements concluded by the EU and its Member States.[5] Such international agreements have been concluded either as a means of protecting exported capital abroad, or as a means of making their states more attractive for foreign investors. They typically protect foreign investments through standards of protection, and allow investors to make use of investor-state dispute settlement (ISDS) to claim damages for any measure in breach of these international agreements that affects their investments. Investment agreements typically offer fossil fuel investors generous and open-ended worded rights, higher sums in compensation, and several procedural advantages that make them attractive.[6] Revoking exploration permits or tracking back on earlier commitments in order to get back on track for NZE and the goals of the Paris Agreement, therefore, presents significant financial risks for governments. A recent study in *Science* found that if governments want to achieve NZE by 2050, 'global action on climate change could generate upward of $340 billion in legal claims from oil and gas investors' from *known* upstream projects in oil and gas alone (the study did not cover investments in coal).[7] This makes climate action more costly, as investors in fossil fuel projects need to be compensated.[8] What is more, the threat of litigation, or even the mere existence of such agreements, can compel governments to delay or abandon government climate action.[9]

[4] Ruth Maclean and Dionne Searcey, 'Congo to Auction Land to Oil Companies: "Our Priority Is Not to Save the Planet"' (*New York Times*, 24 July 2022).

[5] Investments by French companies such as TotalEnergies in Congo are protected under the DRC-France Bilateral Investment Treaty of 1975. See Convention entre le Gouvernement de la République Française et le Gouvernement de la République du Zaire sur la Protection des Investissements (the Democratic Republic of Congo – France) (signed 5 October 1972, entered into force 1 March 1975).

[6] Kyla Tienhaara et al, 'Investor-state disputes threaten the global green energy transition: Global action on climate change could generate upward of $340 billion in legal claims from oil and gas investors' (2022) 376(6594) *Science* 701–03; Kyla Tienhaara, 'Regulatory Chill in a Warming World: The Threat to Climate Policy Posed by Investor-State Dispute Settlement' (2018) 7 *Transnational Environmental Law* 229.

[7] Tienhaara et al, 'Investor-state disputes threaten the global green energy transition' (n 6) 701–03.

[8] See ch 13.

[9] Tienhaara, 'Regulatory Chill in a Warming World' (n 6).

Governments are already facing claims and significant financial liability from awards under investment agreements for climate action from fossil fuel companies. Italy has been required to pay over €250 million in compensation as a result of a claim from UK-based Rockhopper for the denial of an oil drilling concession in the Adriatic Sea under the Energy Charter Treaty (ECT).[10] The Netherlands is facing two claims from German energy companies Uniper and RWE for its plans to phase out the use of coal by 2030 under the ECT.[11] In 2022, UK-based oil and gas company Ascent Resources started arbitration proceedings under the ECT and the UK-Slovenia Bilateral Investment Treaty (BIT) with a claim of over €500 million because the Slovenian environment authority determined that Ascent needed an environmental impact assessment for the exploration of an oil and gas field in Slovenia.[12] In fact, the fossil fuel industry is responsible for 20% of all known ISDS cases.[13]

Alarmed by these developments, the European Parliament has called for significant reform of international investment agreements. In June 2022, the Parliament passed a resolution on the future of EU international investment policy, in which it noted that 'an increasing number of legal proceedings before investment tribunals target environmental measures', and 'deplore[d] the fact that various countries, including the Member States, are being sued in relation to policies on climate, the phasing out of fossil fuels, or the just transition'.[14] It subsequently called for a number of significant reforms to green international investment law. These reforms can be placed in three broad categories. First, in terms of the *scope* of such agreements, the Parliament called for a limitation of the type of investments protected: a carve-out for the protection of investments in fossil fuels.[15] Second, in terms of *standards* contained in such agreements, the Parliament called for better circumscribed standards of investment protection to ensure public policies such as climate change policies cannot be affected and for investor obligations.[16] Third, in terms of *dispute settlement*, it called for introducing third-party rights and requiring foreign investors to exhaust domestic remedies first.[17]

[10] Rockhopper Exploration plc, 'Succesful arbitration outcome' (*Investis Digital*, 24 August 2022).

[11] Due to the balance of payments difficulties experienced by Uniper as a result of Russia's invasion of Ukraine and the subsequent takeover by the German government, Uniper and the Netherlands agreed to suspend the proceedings as part of the German government's demand to withdraw the case. See *Uniper SE, Uniper Benelux Holding BV and Uniper Benelux NV v Kingdom of the Netherlands*, ICSID Case No ARB/21/22, 26 August 2022.

[12] Ascent resources plc, 'Arbitration Initiation and Revised Damages Estimate' (*Polaris*, 15 August 2022).

[13] Lea Di Salvatore, 'Investor–State Disputes in the Fossil Fuel Industry' (*IISD publications*, 31 December 2021).

[14] European Parliament resolution of 23 June 2022 on the future of EU international investment policy (2021/2176(INI)), point 20.

[15] ibid point 21.

[16] ibid points 27, 30.

[17] ibid points 25, 32.

The Parliament's call for reforms hinges on the EU's powers under EU law to green international investment law. This chapter will evaluate the EU's powers to make the three types of reforms the Parliament has called for. It will argue that the ability for the EU to green international investment law is made more difficult because of the current division of powers between the EU and its Member States.

This contribution will set out three arguments why EU law on the division of powers between the EU and the Member States makes such reform limited and more difficult. First, it will argue that the EU is not currently in a position to compel the Member States to introduce such reforms to their existing bilateral investment agreements, or to new international agreements that its Member States are negotiating. Second, the EU's ability to replace old Member State investment agreements is cumbersome because the scope of the EU's exclusive powers is not wide enough to cover both reforms that relate to the *scope* of international investment agreements, and reforms that relate to the *standards* contained in such agreements. As a result, the legal basis for EU action is not only legally murky, but also the EU may not be politically willing to exercise any competences it shares with its Member States. Third, in terms of *dispute settlement*, while some reforms may facilitate the exercise of EU exclusive competence, the lack of clarity in the case law of the Court of Justice in *Opinion 2/15 (EU-Singapore FTA)* does not provide a solid enough basis to assume exclusive competences over such reforms. Other reforms (such as third-party rights) may make the exercise of EU competences more difficult.

12.2. COMPELLING MEMBER STATES TO GREEN INTERNATIONAL INVESTMENT LAW: THE GRANDFATHERING REGULATION

This section will discuss the ability of the EU to compel Member States to green their investment agreements with third states in light of the reforms called for by the Parliament. It will argue that the EU is in no realistic position to do so, despite the fact that 'foreign direct investment' is an exclusive EU competence under the Common Commercial Policy (CCP) since the entry into force of the Treaty of Lisbon. The EU's Grandfathering Regulation offers almost no possibilities for the EU to compel Member States to reform their existing international agreements, and very little possibilities to green their approach in line with the Parliament's desired reforms for any *new* international investment agreements the Member States conclude.[18] This is an important first point as a very extensive network of such agreements already exists, and Member States

[18] Commission, 'Report from the Commission to the European Parliament and the Council on the application of Regulation (EU) No 1219/2012 establishing transitional arrangements for bilateral investment agreements between Member States and third countries' COM(2020) 134 final, 3–4.

remain active in negotiating new agreements. The maintenance of such agreements as they stand, or even their expansion, would significantly impede the actual reform of the international investment law regime as it currently stands.

The EU is a relatively new player in negotiating international investment agreements.[19] Member States, on the other hand, have been prominent players in this field since the very beginning, and have a long history and established practice in negotiating them. Member States concluded them with newly independent developing states as a means of securing economic assets in (among others) former colonies in return for investments in those states in the wake of nationalisation campaigns in those states.[20] Member States had 1,360 international investment agreements in force before the EU obtained exclusive competence under the CCP over 'foreign direct investment' in 2009.[21] The transfer of the competence over 'foreign direct investment' from the Member States to an exclusive competence of the EU was the result of entrepreneurship on the part of Commission negotiators that eventually was reformed into the Treaty of Lisbon.[22] In areas of exclusive competence, 'only the Union may legislate and adopt legally binding acts, the Member States being able to do so themselves only if so empowered by the Union'.[23] The loss of competence over this area by Member States resulted in a push from the Member States to limit the effects of this blow to their powers and their existing networks and practices. The Grandfathering Regulation, adopted in 2012, was introduced to ensure a smooth transition of powers from the Member States to the EU in this area.[24] The Grandfathering Regulation ensures that Member States can maintain their existing bilateral investment agreements (they are thus 'grandfathered' into a new area of exclusive competence of the EU). It also authorises the Member States to negotiate and conclude new international investment agreements, but subject to an assessment made by the Commission that these new international investment agreements do not conflict with EU law, or conflict with the EU's own negotiations for an international agreement on investment.

[19] The EU is currently only party to one international agreement containing investment provisions such as ISDS: the Energy Charter Treaty. It has negotiated several more since the entry into force of the Treaty of Lisbon, but these agreements have not yet entered into force.

[20] Kenneth J Vandevelde, 'A Brief History of International Investment Agreements' (2005) 12 UC Davis Journal of International Law & Policy 157–94; Muthucumaraswamy Sornarajah, *The International Law on Foreign Investment*, 5th edn (Cambridge University Press, 2021) 19–28; Bart-Jaap Verbeek, *The Making of the EU Investment Policy. A Critical Political Economy Perspective* (PhD thesis, Radboud University Nijmegen, 2021) 89–144.

[21] Article 207 TFEU.

[22] Robert Basedow, 'International Investment Policy ten years on: the Policy-Making Implications of Unintended Competence Transfers' (2021) 59 *Journal of Common Market Studies* 643.

[23] Article 2(1) TFEU.

[24] Regulation (EU) No 1219/2012 of the European Parliament and of the Council of 12 December 2012 establishing transitional arrangements for bilateral investment agreements between Member States and third countries [2012] OJ L351/40.

Article 3 of the Grandfathering Regulation stipulates that the existing agreements of the Member States with third states notified to the Commission can be maintained in force, until the EU has concluded its own international agreement with that same third state that replaces the Member State international agreement. The Grandfathering Regulation does not require Member States to modify their existing agreements, for instance, by greening them to facilitate compliance with emerging EU climate legislation.

There are only two rather remote possibilities under current EU law that would allow the EU to compel the Member States to make (modest) changes to their existing agreements. First, the Grandfathering Regulation specifies that this authorisation is done 'without prejudice to other obligations of the Member States under Union law'. This provision refers to the fact that some of these investment agreements have been found to be incompatible with EU law, for instance where they prevent the EU institutions from regulating capital flows to and from third states under Article 64 TFEU.[25] In *Opinion 1/17 (EU-Canada CETA)*, the Court of Justice found that international agreements of the EU that would allow investment tribunals 'to call into question the choices democratically made within a Party relating to', inter alia, the protection of the environment are incompatible with the EU's autonomous legal order.[26] Such international agreements, according to the Court of Justice, violate the EU's own legal order because they negatively affect the independence of EU institutions involved in the regulatory process. As such, international agreements containing ISDS must also contain a number of substantive safeguards that limit the jurisdiction of such tribunals and accordingly preserve the ability of EU institutions to regulate in the public interest.

Opinion 1/17 (EU-Canada CETA) was about the compatibility of international agreements negotiated by the EU with EU law. However, the Opinion does seem to have some application to Member State activity as well. The Court of Justice was referring to the possibility of awards of investment tribunals resulting in Member States amending or withdrawing legislation when they implement EU law.[27] If this is correct, investment agreements concluded by the Member States would also need to include the safeguards the Court of Justice referred to in *Opinion 1/17 (EU-Canada CETA)* in order to ensure that they are compatible with EU law. In essence, this would require Member States to circumscribe the standards of investment protection in a more precise manner. This issue of the extent of reform of investment protection standards is returned to below in section 12.3. Given the ambiguity of *Opinion 1/17 (EU-Canada CETA)* on this matter, it is unlikely that Member States would feel compelled to change their

[25] See, for instance, Case C-249/06 *Commission v Sweden* ECLI:EU:C:2009:119.

[26] *Opinion 1/17* ECLI:EU:C:2019:341 (*EU-Canada CETA*), para 148; Laurens Ankersmit, 'Regulatory autonomy and regulatory chill in Opinion 1/17' (2020) 4(1) *Europe and the World*.

[27] *Opinion 1/17* ECLI:EU:C:2019:341 (*EU-Canada CETA*), para 150. This section of the Opinion also at various parts refers to 'Parties', and Member States are parties to the CETA.

standards in existing agreements because of *Opinion 1/17 (EU-Canada CETA)*, and there is no indication that the Commission is considering the pro-active step of beginning infringement proceedings on this point against Member States.

Second, the Commission may, under Article 5 of the Grandfathering Regulation, consider that existing agreements 'constitute a serious obstacle to the negotiation or conclusion by the Union of bilateral investment agreements with third countries, with a view to the progressive replacement of' those bilateral investment agreements. The Commission could encounter a situation, for instance, where a third state is not willing to negotiate an investment agreement with the EU that would replace the investment agreement with the Member State because it does not want to introduce green reforms in a proposed agreement. If this is the case, the Commission may 'assess' these international agreements of Member States, and it is not clear what the consequences of this assessment might be.

While such existing agreements might be incompatible with EU law, the Court of Justice has made clear in *Opinion 2/15* that the EU does not have the power under EU law to terminate such international agreements of Member States with third states. This has to do with the fact that the scope of those Member State investment agreements with third states goes beyond EU exclusive competence.[28] In a nutshell, these international agreements of Member States protect portfolio investments, whereas the EU only has exclusive competence for direct investments. Moreover, ISDS is a competence that is 'shared' with the Member States.

In relation to *new* agreements or *renegotiated* agreements by the Member States, the EU is in a slightly better position to scrutinise such agreements on the basis of green reforms. This is because, for such agreements, the Member States need to obtain explicit authorisation from the Commission to negotiate and conclude such agreements. Article 9(1) of the Grandfathering Regulation lists the limited grounds for refusal. The Commission can refuse such authorisation if such an agreement is 'in conflict with Union law'. The Commission can also make such a refusal where the agreement would 'be inconsistent with the Union's principles and objectives for external action as elaborated in accordance with the general provisions laid down in Chapter 1 of Title V of the Treaty on European Union'. In relation to the former, the Commission could base refusal on *Opinion 1/17*, as discussed above. In relation to the latter, the Commission could refer to its external climate change policy and argue that insufficient green reforms hamper the EU's goal to 'help develop international measures to preserve and improve the quality of the environment and the sustainable management of global natural resources, in order to ensure sustainable development'.[29]

[28] *Opinion 2/15* ECLI:EU:C:2017:376 (*EU-Singapore FTA*), paras 245–256.
[29] Article 21(2)(f) TEU.

The Parliament in its resolution has called on the Commission 'to ensure that all of the Member States' BITs are fully compatible with EU law, and are consistent with the EU's objectives and values', and has expressed support for the Commission 'in applying in a strict manner the conditions for authorising the negotiation, signature and conclusion by Member States of new agreements'.[30] However, so far, the Commission has simply authorised most requests by Member States, and not refused a single new agreement on grounds that insufficient reforms have been introduced. It has granted 241 authorisations, and only rejected six requests.[31] All six requests were rejected on grounds that the EU was already negotiating an investment agreement.

12.3. COVERAGE: THE TYPES OF INVESTMENT PROTECTED

A key feature of international investment agreements is the wide coverage of foreign investments that fall within the scope of these agreements (*coverage*). This section will argue that the wide scope of these agreements has consequences for the division of powers between the EU and the Member States and, as a result, complicates the ability of the EU to green international investment law. The EU only has exclusive competence under the CCP over direct investment ('foreign direct investment'), whereas investment agreements typically also cover portfolio investments, a competence that is shared between the EU and its Member States.

Typically, international investment agreements use a so-called 'asset-based' definition of 'investment'. Covered investment is defined through a non-exhaustive list of investments, such as shares, bonds, moveable or immovable property, loans, securities, intellectual property rights, and claims to money. This approach is, as the Court of Justice notes in *Opinion 1/17 (EU-Canada CETA)*, 'particularly broad' permitting tribunals 'to hear a wide range of disputes'.[32] Under this 'asset-based' definition, both direct investment (where investment is intended to create lasting links between the investor and the host state) and portfolio investment (where the investor simply seeks to make an investment, for instance through shares, without any intention to exercise control over a company in the host state) fall under the coverage of an agreement. A small number of investment agreements use a less broad 'enterprise-based' definition, where capital is committed with the view of creating an enterprise in the host state.

International investment agreements do not distinguish in terms of coverage between the type of investment made. All foreign investments are protected. The neoliberal rationale for this is that all foreign investments are seen as beneficial

[30] European Parliament resolution on the future of EU international investment policy (n 14) at 37.
[31] Commission (n 18) 3–4.
[32] *Opinion 1/17* ECLI:EU:C:2019:341 (*EU-Canada CETA*), para 139.

to the host state, in that they can help with economic growth of a state. Thus, an international investment agreement will normally not distinguish between 'good' and 'bad' investments. Thus, foreign investments in renewables, nuclear energy, fossil fuels, arms, tobacco, infrastructure, telecommunications, pharmaceuticals, agriculture, or manufacturing are all treated the same and are covered by these agreements. In other words, international investment agreements do not make an attempt to distinguish between investments on the basis of economic sectors, or on the basis of public policy.

The notable exception to this approach is the ECT. That agreement has a focus on the energy sector as western European states sought to safeguard their energy supply by seeking access to fossil rich countries to the East, in particular access to Russia.[33] The ECT uses an 'asset-based' definition of investment, but limits the scope of the agreement to 'any investment associated with an economic activity in the energy sector'. 'Economic activity in the energy sector', in turn, concerns economic activities that are listed in an annex to the agreement. The parties to the ECT have recently renegotiated the text of the agreement under an effort to 'modernise' the ECT. Under pressure from a number of EU Member States and the Parliament, an attempt has been made to remove fossil fuel investments from the annex.

Under a 'flexibility mechanism', new investments in fossil fuels from 15 August 2023 would no longer be protected in a number of parties to the ECT, including the EU, its Member States, and the UK. In addition, existing investments in fossil fuels in the territories of those parties would be protected for an additional 10 years once the proposed renegotiated ECT enters into force. Investments made by investors in fossil fuels from the EU and the UK in the territories of other parties would continue to be protected under the modernised ECT. However, the Parliament and several Member States consider that these negotiated reforms do not go far enough to ensure compatibility with the EU's climate objectives. The Parliament has called for a coordinated withdrawal by the EU and the Member States from the ECT, while seven Member States (including France, Germany, Spain, Poland and the Netherlands) have announced their intention to withdraw from the ECT.[34]

In *Opinion 2/15 (EU-Singapore FTA)*, the Court of Justice employed its test developed in *Daiichi Sankyo* to find that investment agreements that protect foreign investments fall within the exclusive competence of the EU under the CCP, insofar as these agreements protect direct investments. According to the Court of Justice, the CCP is a policy that 'relates to trade with third [s]tates'. However, international agreements that merely have 'implications for trade' between the EU and third states do not fall within the scope of the CCP. An

[33] Christina Eckes and Laurens Ankersmit, 'The compatibility of the Energy Charter Treaty with EU law' (ClientEarth, 27 April 2022).

[34] European Parliament resolution of 22 November 2022 on the outcome of the modernisation of the Energy Charter Treaty (2022/2934(RSP)), points 18–20.

EU act only falls within the CCP 'if it relates specifically to such trade in that it is essentially intended to promote, facilitate or govern such trade and has direct and immediate effects on it'.[35] This effects-based test, as Cremona has put it,'favours flexibility over predictability'.[36] An effects-based test is, moreover, a test that allows for a wide interpretation on the scope of the CCP. Measures more easily have a direct impact on trade than, for instance, the environment, where impacts of measures, both negative and positive, can take much longer to materialise.

In *Opinion 2/15 (EU-Singapore FTA)*, the Court of Justice found that by including 'foreign direct investment' within the scope of Article 207 TFEU, the EU had exclusive competence 'to approve any commitment vis-à-vis a third [s]tate relating to investments made by natural or legal persons of that third State in the European Union and vice versa which enable effective participation in the management or control of a company carrying out an economic activity'.[37] The definition of 'foreign direct investment' reflects, according to the Court of Justice, the rationale of the scope of the CCP which is that the CCP covers acts that have direct and immediate effects on trade by promoting, facilitating, or governing such trade.[38] In other words, if investors are only making a capital commitment with the view of making a profit without actually influencing the conduct of a business, measures that govern such activity fall outside the scope of the CCP, as there are no direct effects on trade in goods or services. However, where investors are able to influence the decision-making in a company in a third state, the Court of Justice assumes that there are direct effects on trade in goods and services between the EU and the third state, and therefore any measure that relates to such investments falls within the scope of the CCP.

Commitments on portfolio investments, however, fall outside the scope of the CCP. Such investments fall within the scope of the free movement of capital (a shared competence) because their intention is to make an investment, without intending to influence the management and control of a company. The Court of Justice found that in relation to those foreign investments, the EU can negotiate agreements that regulate such capital flows on the basis of an implied competence derived from Article 63 TFEU that the EU shares with its Member States.[39]

The Court of Justice's case law on the of division of powers in the area of foreign investment makes clear that it is not dependent on the economic sector, such as mining or energy, to which the foreign investment relates. Nor is it dependent on the impact of foreign investment for policy areas such as climate change mitigation or environmental protection. The key criterion for the Court

[35] Case C-414/11 *Daiichi Sankyo and Sanofi-Aventis Deutschland* ECLI:EU:C:2013:520, para 51; *Opinion 2/15* ECLI:EU:C:2017:376 (*EU-Singapore FTA*), para 36.
[36] Marise Cremona, 'Shaping EU Trade Policy post-Lisbon: Opinion 2/15 of 16 May 2017' (2018) 14 *European Constitutional Law Review* 231–59 at 242.
[37] *Opinion 2/15* ECLI:EU:C:2017:376 (*EU-Singapore FTA*), para 82.
[38] ibid para 84.
[39] ibid para 240.

of Justice is whether an EU act covers foreign direct investments, or is wider and also covers portfolio investments. The fact that protecting direct or portfolio investments in fossil fuels has an impact on and undermines the EU's climate and environmental goals and rules does not affect this distribution of competences. What does matter, however, is whether a provision in an agreement is specifically targeted at regulating trade or whether the measure has direct effects on trade. Therefore, a measure that would ban foreign direct investments in fossil fuels or would protect foreign direct investments other than those made in fossil fuels would fall within the scope of Article 207 TFEU. However, a broader provision such as a more general ban on direct investments (thus a ban on both domestic and foreign direct investments) in fossil fuels or protection of all direct investments other than those made in fossil fuels does not specifically target foreign direct investments and would fall outside the scope of Article 207 TFEU.

In terms of reforms, the Parliament has urged

> the Commission and the Member States to ensure consistency between IIAs and the European Green Deal, environmental policies, …, *by excluding from treaty protection investments in fossil fuels or any other activities that pose significant harm to the environment and human rights.*[40]

As a consequence, it is not readily apparent who has the competence to decide to carve out the protection of foreign investments in fossil fuels in new or renegotiated investment agreements, such as the ECT. While doing so for direct investments in fossil fuels is clearly an EU competence, carving out protection for portfolio investments is a shared competence. This means that the EU institutions will have to decide whether or not the EU is to exercise this competence.[41] So far, as the Court of Justice has made clear in *Germany v Council (COTIF I)*, it appears that there is little political support within the Council to elect for the EU to exercise its competences in this area.[42]

What is more, the Court of Justice's reasoning in *Opinion 2/15 (EU-Singapore FTA)* does not make clear what would be the substantive legal basis on which the EU would be exercising this shared competence. The Court of Justice found implied competence for the EU in Article 63 TFEU based on Article 216(1)

[40] European Parliament resolution on the future of EU international investment policy (n 14) at 21, emphasis added.

[41] Where an international agreement falls within a competence that is shared between the EU and the Member States, the EU has the possibility to choose to exercise this competence and thus conclude the agreement on its own. However, where both the EU and the Member States partially exercise their competences, the EU and the Member States resort to a 'mixed agreement' where both the EU and the Member States conclude the agreement for the respective competences that they have exercised. See Allan Rosas, 'The European Union and mixed agreements' in Alan Dashwood and Christophe Hillion (eds), *The General Law of E.C. External Relations* (Sweet & Maxwell, 2000).

[42] Case C-600/14 *Germany v Council* ECLIEU:C:2017:935 (*COTIF I*), para 68. See further Maciej Szpunar and Roland Klages, 'The Unitary Representation of the Union in an International Forum and Clarification of Shared Competence and Facultative Mixity Post-Lisbon: Germany v Council (COTIF I) and Commission v Germany (COTIF II)' in Graham Butler and Ramses A Wessel (eds), *EU External Relations Law: The Cases in Context* (Hart Publishing, 2022) 917–26.

TFEU, but Article 63 TFEU itself is not a proper legal basis, as it does not set out a procedure for the adoption of secondary law. As a result, if the EU were to exercise this power, it is unclear *how* the EU would exercise this power. The procedure for the conclusion of international agreements in Article 218 TFEU is dependent on the procedures found in the substantive legal bases found in the EU Treaties. Without a substantive legal basis, it is unclear whether the Council needs to vote by qualified majority voting, or unanimity, and whether the Parliament needs to consent to those parts of the agreement.[43]

Given the political realities and legal complexities introduced in *Opinion 2/15 (EU-Singapore FTA)*, the consequence is that where the EU wants to negotiate (replacing) an international investment agreement that protects both direct and portfolio investments, but carves out this protection for fossil fuels, both the EU and the Member States will need to be involved in the decision-making. The sequence of events for renegotiating the ECT is illustrative. The Commission obtained a mandate and negotiating directives from the Council to negotiate, on behalf of the EU, those parts for which the EU would exercise its competence.[44] The legal basis used suggests that portfolio investment was not a matter for which the EU would exercise its competence, as no legal basis for this competence was used. The governments of the Member States meeting within the Council took a separate decision on behalf of the Member States for those areas falling within their competence.

The carve-out for fossil fuel investments, and more broadly, the definition of 'economic activity in the energy sector' under the ECT, however, transcends this division of powers. The Commission's negotiating directives do not explicitly mention negotiating such a carve-out.[45] Nonetheless, it was the Commission that proposed to the other parties of the ECT in February 2021 to carve out investments in fossil fuels from the investment protection part of the ECT (Part III). Possibly, this was the result of an amendment proposed by the Parliament in proposed secondary legislation in October 2020 that stipulated that the 'Union shall end protection of investments in fossil fuels in the context of the modernisation of the Energy Charter Treaty'. That amendment did not make it into the

[43] For instance, the text of Article 218(6) TFEU suggests the European Parliament's consent can relate to those parts of the agreement over which the EU is exercising its competence, including those parts that are not covered by Article 218(6)(a) TFEU as long as other parts are. Article 218(6)(a) TFEU makes an exception for agreements that 'exclusively' relate to the Common Foreign and Security Policy (CFSP). *A contrario* if an agreement only partially relates to the CFSP, but also to the CCP, consent would be required. The provision further does not suggest that the European Parliament can only take this decision for those parts that only relate to the CCP. The provision refers to the Council decision concluding agreements, inter alia, that are 'covering fields to which either the ordinary legislative procedure applies, or the special legislative procedure where consent by the European Parliament is required' without making any limitations.

[44] Commission, 'Recommendation for a Council Decision authorizing the entering into negotiations on the modernization of the Energy Charter Treaty' COM (2019) 231 final.

[45] The directives specify: 'the Modernised ECT should include a definition of the "economic activity in the energy sector" which allows addressing the challenges and opportunities of the transition to a safe and sustainable low-carbon, more digital and consumercentric energy system'.

adopted legislation during the ordinary legislative procedure.[46] It was nonetheless a clear incentive for the Commission to propose the carve-out during the negotiations, in order to secure the backing of the Parliament during the ratification phase.

12.4. THE POWER TO ESTABLISH THE STANDARDS OF PROTECTION AND INTRODUCE INVESTOR OBLIGATIONS IN INTERNATIONAL INVESTMENT AGREEMENTS

This section will evaluate the ability of the EU under EU law to green the standards of protection of investment agreements and introduce investor obligations. This section will first outline how investment agreements typically deal with standards of protection, and how these standards have been criticised by academics and civil society. It will subsequently assess the two key reforms (*protecting public policy space* and *investor obligations*) that the Parliament is proposing in light of the division of powers between the EU and the Member States. It will argue that the first set of reforms (*protecting public policy space*) broadly follows the same division of powers as the coverage of investment agreements discussed in section 12.2. As such, the ability of the EU to reform these standards runs into the same difficulties as discussed in section 12.2. Nonetheless, the EU itself is even compelled to introduce these reforms as a result of the Court of Justice's findings in *Opinion 1/17 (EU-Canada CETA)*. Introducing investor obligations may even fall outside the scope of the exclusive competence of the EU under the CCP in its entirety.

Investment agreements typically include a set of provisions that offer those investments made by foreign investors a substantive level of protection; they rarely introduce any corresponding obligations for foreign investors. These standards of protection are generally widely worded. An international investment agreement will offer to those foreign investors who have made investments in the host state the right to 'fair and equitable treatment' (the so-called FET standard), the right to national treatment (non-discrimination), a most favoured nation (MFN) clause, and a right against direct and indirect expropriation. The rationale for these standards is that they offer foreign investors assurances that their investments will be treated fairly by the host state as a means of encouraging foreign investors to make such investments. These standards have been interpreted in a wide manner by investment tribunals and, as a result, have come under considerable criticism in recent years.[47]

[46] Amendments adopted by the European Parliament on 8 October 2020 on the proposal for a regulation of the European Parliament and of the Council establishing the framework for achieving climate neutrality and amending Regulation (EU) 2018/1999 (European Climate Law) (COM(2020)0080 – COM(2020)0563 – C9-0077/2020 – 2020/0036(COD))(1).

[47] Gus van Harten, *Investment Treaty Arbitration and Public Law* (OUP, 2007); Sornarajah, *The International Law on Foreign Investment* (n 20).

In particular, the FET standard and its interpretation, as well as the notion of indirect expropriation, has come under considerable criticism for its vague and open-ended wording and expansive interpretation.[48] The main point of contention is whether these standards, and in particular the FET standard, are too broadly defined and interpreted so as to leave insufficient space for regulatory action in the public interest, such as climate change mitigation. Critics have argued that changing the wording of these standards themselves offers little prospect of avoiding 'regulatory chill' caused by international investment agreements. Tienhaara et al have argued, for instance, that 'reformist approaches would be time-consuming and likely ineffectual, based on the experience of previous efforts'.[49] Aischner and Sarmiento have argued that:

> Over the past two decades, scholars, states, and international organizations have focused much of their reform energy on a new generation of IIAs. Among other things, these new treaties have phased out controversial investment protection standards, inserted additional clarifications, and often included novel general exceptions. This combination, it was thought, would ensure a better balance between protecting investments and safeguarding host states' policy space in investment arbitration.
>
> Yet, surprisingly, this expectation has not materialized in practice. When we look at the first wave of investment arbitration awards rendered under these new-generation treaties, we instead see that tribunals tend to interpret these new treaties just like old ones: exceptions are ignored or watered down, clarifications are disregarded, and controversial investment protections that had been phased out in treaty practice are brought back in through the back door. In short, rather than address the concern that investment treaties unduly restrict policy space, new treaties have produced old interpretive outcomes.[50]

The Commission, however, is a major proponent of expanding the network of international investment agreements that include reformed standards of protection. It now follows a similar approach for all agreements negotiated by the EU. Firstly, the Commission seeks to introduce 'right to regulate' clauses. These provisions seek to 'reaffirm the right to regulate' to achieve legitimate policy objectives by stating that 'the mere fact' that a party has adopted a public interest measure cannot amount to a breach of one of the FET, or expropriation, standards. The national treatment and MFN standards are usually excluded from these clauses. Second, the Commission seeks to more elaborately define the FET standard. It does so by introducing a list of situations when the standard has been breached in order to avoid overly broad interpretations. Third, the Commission has introduced a definition of indirect expropriation in an attempt

[48] See van Harten (n 47); Sornarajah (n 20); Wolfgang Alschner, *Investment Arbitration and State-Driven Reform* (Oxford University Press, 2022); Tienhaara, 'Regulatory Chill in a Warming World' (n 6).

[49] ibid.

[50] Wolfgang Alschner and Florencia Sarmiento, 'An interview with Wolfgang Alschner on Investment Arbitration and State-Driven Reform: New Treaties, Old Outcomes' (ITN, 4 July 2022).

to limit the scope of that concept and exclude certain instances where regulatory measures in the public interest could be seen as amounting to indirect expropriation. The approach by the Commission has been criticised as merely codifying existing arbitration practice, and not doing enough to limit the scope of these standards. For instance, the current approach of the Commission even codifies arbitration practice that considers violating 'legitimate expectations' of a foreign investor by a host government to be a breach of the FET standard. This is relevant for climate change mitigation efforts, as governments will have to go back on earlier commitments towards oil and gas companies in order to achieve the NZE scenario, and thereby affect currently known investments generating up to EUR 313 billion in claims.[51]

The Parliament appears to be more sceptical about the effectiveness of the approach favoured by the Commission. While it has welcomed 'the fact that, since 2016, EU IIAs containing investment protection clauses include more precise wording for some protection standards, as well as the right to regulate', it has also underlined that 'EU IIAs should not allow broad protection standards to be used to challenge legitimate public policies' and has asked both the Commission and the Member States 'to avoid including ambiguous terminology in substantive clauses, and to continue reviewing protection standards on the basis of available evidence'.[52] While it has underlined 'the importance of maintaining, strengthening and implementing the clauses in all investment agreements that prohibit the lowering of standards, as they are critical to avoid a race to the bottom in countries aiming to attract foreign investment', it has called on the Commission to 'further analyse the effectiveness of such clauses, in particular in developing countries, to ensure that tax policy and development finance are aligned to support a "race to the top"'.[53]

In *Opinion 2/15 (EU-Singapore FTA)*, the Court of Justice rejected the argument put forward by the Council and several Member States that the concept of 'foreign direct investment' merely relates to the admission of such investment, and not to standards that protect foreign direct investment as soon as it has been admitted in the host state. The Court of Justice pointed out that Article 207(1) TFEU 'refers generally to EU acts concerning "foreign direct investment", without drawing a distinction according to whether the acts concern the admission or the protection of such investments'.[54] Because the standards of investment protection 'contribute to the legal certainty of investors', the Court of Justice found that these standards are intended to 'promote, facilitate and govern trade' within the meaning of the first limb of the *Daichi Sankyo* test.[55] In relation to the second limb, the Court of Justice found that insofar as these standards

[51] Tienhaara et al (n 6).
[52] European Parliament resolution on the future of EU international investment policy (n 14) at 30.
[53] ibid at 9.
[54] *Opinion 2/15* ECLI:EU:C:2017:376 (*EU-Singapore FTA*), para 87.
[55] ibid para 94.

of protection relate to direct investment they also have a direct and immediate effect on trade.

As a result, the division of powers between the EU and the Member States on establishing the standards of protection common to investment agreements simply follows the division of powers for direct and portfolio investment. This means that if an investment agreement were to only cover direct investment, the EU would have exclusive competence to negotiate and conclude the standards of protection common to international investment agreements, including the introduction of several reforms that the Commission is eager to introduce. However, if the agreement is broader in scope and includes portfolio investment, the EU is presented with a political choice to not exercise this competence and to involve the Member States in the decision-making over those standards insofar as they relate to portfolio investment.

Opinion 2/15 (EU-Singapore FTA) did not assess the so-called 'right to regulate' clauses, as they were not part of the draft text negotiated with Singapore at the time and submitted to the Court of Justice.[56] These clauses are likely to simply follow the division of powers as outlined above, because they are not only very generally worded, but also because they are merely intended to clarify the already existing scope of the standards of protection. These clauses are introduced 'for greater certainty' and 'reaffirm' an already existing 'right to regulate'.[57]

The inclusion of these 'right to regulate' clauses is, nonetheless, essential for the EU in order to be able to exercise its competences. In *Opinion 1/17 (EU-Canada CETA)*, the Court of Justice found that international agreements that would allow investment tribunals 'to call into question the choices democratically made within a Party relating to', inter alia, the protection of the environment are incompatible with the EU's autonomous legal order.[58] Such agreements violate the EU's own legal order because they negatively affect the independence of EU institutions involved in the regulatory process.[59] International investment agreements could potentially pose such risks, because under ISDS, tribunals would often be called upon to weigh 'the interest constituted by the freedom to conduct business' under the various standards of protection in such agreements against 'public interests'.[60]

Importantly, the Court of Justice's concerns with the negative effects on the regulatory autonomy of the EU institutions are much narrower than how

[56] The definitions of indirect expropriation and the FET standard are in line with current practice of the Commission that the Commission considers part of the reform of international investment law.

[57] Article 8.9 of the Comprehensive Economic and Trade Agreement (CETA) between Canada, of the one part, and the European Union and its Member States, of the other part [2017] OJ L11/23.

[58] Ankersmit (n 26).

[59] *Opinion 1/17* ECLI:EU:C:2019:341 (*EU-Canada CETA*), para 150.

[60] ibid para 137.

scholars view the concept of 'regulatory chill'. Regulatory chill is understood as the phenomenon whereby

> governments will fail to enact or enforce bona fide regulatory measures (or modify measures to such an extent that their original intent is undermined or their effectiveness is severely diminished) as a result of concerns about ISDS.[61]

This definition of regulatory chill concerns delays in regulatory action, as well as modification or abandonment of a particular course or regulatory action.[62] The Court of Justice, on the other hand, focuses on the *ex post* effects of multiple awards of tribunals on the EU and the Member States: legislation would have to be amended or withdrawn *as a result of* an assessment made by an arbitral tribunal. Regulatory chill also covers threats to use ISDS (*threat chill*) or other forms of preventive action by a government in order to avoid claims.

Nonetheless, as a result of *Opinion 1/17 (EU-Canada CETA)*, international agreements containing ISDS must contain a number of substantive *safeguards* that limit the jurisdiction of such tribunals and accordingly preserve the ability of EU institutions to regulate in the public interest. For the ISDS mechanism in CETA, the Court of Justice in *Opinion 1/17 (EU-Canada CETA)* found that the following safeguards were sufficient to protect the EU's regulatory autonomy:

- the agreement contains a general exceptions clause for public interest measures worded in a similar way to that of Article XX of GATT;[63]
- the agreement contains 'right to regulate' clauses;[64]
- there is a decision by the parties to the agreement that clarifies that the agreement cannot result in lowering levels of protection of public interests (an interpretative instrument);[65]
- the scope of the investment protection standards is circumscribed.[66]

In relation to the standards of protection, the Court of Justice took the position that the much debated and criticised reformed FET standard and indirect expropriation standards provide sufficient safeguards to protect public interests. Thus, in order for an investment agreement to be compatible with EU law, it is not necessary, for instance, to exclude 'legitimate expectations' from the FET standard. Most modern investment agreements outside of the EU do, however, do this.[67]

[61] Tienhaara, 'Regulatory Chill in a Warming World' (n 6) 233.
[62] Ankersmit (n 26) 4.
[63] *Opinion 1/17*, ECLI:EU:C:2019:341 (*EU-Canada CETA*), paras 152–153.
[64] ibid para 154.
[65] ibid para 155.
[66] ibid paras 157–159.
[67] Sarah Brewin and Lukas Schaugg, 'Modest Modernization or Massive Setback? An analysis of the Energy Charter Treaty agreement in principle' (IISD, August 2022), 15–16.

It is not clear from *Opinion 1/17 (EU-Canada CETA)* whether an agreement needs to meet all safeguards listed by the Court of Justice to conclude that an agreement is compatible with the EU Treaties. It may be that several of these safeguards, depending on their wording, will suffice. The legal value of the interpretative instrument cited by the Court of Justice, for instance (the 'Joint Interpretative Instrument') is dubious, given the imprecise language and the fact that it is not linked to any specific provision in CETA. The language of the Court of Justice suggests an overall assessment based on a reading of the provisions together. It concluded that, after 'reading provisions together', 'it is apparent from all those provisions' that the parties had 'expressly restrict[ed] the scope' of investment provisions and therefore the agreement was compatible with the EU Treaties.

Overall, these constitutional limits set by *Opinion 1/17 (EU-Canada CETA)* do not significantly constrain the EU institutions in defining the standards of protection in investment agreements. The EU is required to introduce a number of formal legal safeguards that offer a certain minimum level of guarantees that an investment agreement will not be interpreted in a way that would fundamentally undermine the EU institutions' ability to regulate in the public interest. This means that laying down the standards of protection offered to investors is still very much a political choice that has to be made by the EU institutions, rather than a significant constitutional obligation for the EU institutions.

More significant reforms, such as the introduction of obligations on the part of foreign investors, will, depending on their wording, however, change the division of powers between the EU and the Member States. The 'model BIT' investment agreement of the Southern African Development Community (SADC), for instance, introduces several obligations for foreign investors not to engage in corruption, to conduct environmental and social impact assessments, maintain environmental management systems, and respect minimum standards for human rights, the environment, and labour.[68]

The Parliament has also called for the introduction of obligations for investors. It has noted 'with concern the asymmetry of certain IIAs in which foreign investors can pursue investment cases against states, while governments, workers and affected communities are unable to pursue in arbitration transnational corporations that fail to respect human rights, public health or labour and environmental laws'.[69] To that end, the Parliament has urged the Commission to

> fully support and accelerate negotiations to expand investor obligations and their enforcement; believes that investor obligations should not only be included in EU IIAs, but should also apply via separate binding and enforceable international instruments, and via robust domestic frameworks for human rights and environmental due diligence.[70]

[68] Southern African Development Community, 'SADC Model Bilateral Investment Treaty Template with Commentary' (IISD, July 2012).

[69] European Parliament resolution on the future of EU international investment policy (n 14) 22.

[70] ibid 27.

Some of these obligations are framed in part as requirements for states to introduce such obligations in domestic law for foreign investors. They are intended to benefit mainly domestic third parties that may be negatively affected by foreign investments in a country. For instance, the SADC 'model BIT' requires parties to ensure that investors and investments are subject to civil liability under domestic law. Others are framed as obligations for investors for which a violation would result in their investments no longer being covered by the investment agreement or as specific obligations for investors or investments.[71] If introduced in international investment agreements of the EU, this wording may have an impact on the division of powers between the EU and the Member States, even if the scope of Article 207 TFEU is broad and can encompass some of these obligations.

First of all, Article 207 TFEU allows the EU to both liberalise *and* restrict trade. While the Court of Justice has maintained that the 'progressive abolition of restrictions on trade between States' is the CCP's 'main objective',[72] that objective 'cannot compel' EU institutions to liberalise trade.[73] Article 207 TFEU therefore allows the EU under Article 207 TFEU to restrict or prohibit trade, for instance when banning or restricting the trade in hazardous chemicals.[74] In *Commission v Council (Rotterdam Convention I)*, the Court of Justice made clear that Article 207 TFEU can be used if trade instruments are used such as import licences, tariffs, quantitative restrictions, and import bans as they have a 'direct and immediate effect' on trade.[75]

Furthermore, the Court of Justice has interpreted several constitutional provisions of the EU Treaties aimed at integrating the different objectives of the EU, such as environmental protection, as *enabling* the EU to do more under Article 207 TFEU rather than limiting or restricting the EU's competences.[76]

[71] For instance, engaging in corruption under the SADC model BIT results in investments made by such an investor no longer falling within the scope of the agreement. Under the same model BIT, investors have specific obligations to carry out environmental and social impact assessments and environmental management systems.

[72] Joined Cases C-446/09 and C-495/09 *Philips* ECLI:EU:C:2011:796, para 63. Marise Cremona, 'Distinguished Essay: A Quiet Revolution – The Changing Nature of the EU's Common Commercial Policy' in M Bungenberg and others (eds), *European Yearbook of International Economic Law 2017* (Springer, 2017) 3 at 8.

[73] Case C-150/94 *UK v Council* ECLI:EU:C:1998:547, para 67. See earlier Case 112/80 *Dürbeck* ECLI:EU:C:1981:94, para 44 and Case 245/81 *Edeka Zentrale* ECLI:EU:C:1982:277, para 24.

[74] Case C-94/03 *Commission v Council* EU:C:2006:2 (*Rotterdam Convention I*), para 49. See further Geert de Baere, 'The Indissociable Link between Environmental Policy and the Common Commercial Policy: Commission v Council (Rotterdam Convention I)' in Graham Butler and Ramses A Wessel (eds), *EU External Relations Law: The Cases in Context* (Hart Publishing, 2022).

[75] Case C-94/03 *Commission v Council* (n 74) para 42.

[76] 'Consistency' is required between different areas of external action (Article 21(3) TEU). Article 205 and 207 TFEU (Trade policy shall be conducted 'in the context' of other objectives and principles of external action), Article 11 TFEU states, 'Environmental protection requirements must be integrated into the definition and implementation of the Union's policies and activities, in particular with a view to promoting sustainable development.' Jan H Jans, 'Stop the Integration Principle?' (2011) 33 *Fordham International Law Journal* 1533–47 at 1540; see also Nele Dhondt, *Integration of Environmental Protection int Other EC Policies: Legal Theory and Practice* (Europa Law Publishing, 2014).

The Court of Justice's joint reading of Article 21(3) TEU and Articles 11, 205 and 207(1) TFEU lead it conclude that the 'objective of sustainable development henceforth forms an integral part of the common commercial policy'.[77]

As such, under Article 207 TFEU, the EU is empowered to make liberalisation of trade between parties conditional upon compliance with already existing international environmental commitments. According to the Court of Justice, making trade liberalisation conditional upon such compliance demonstrates 'a specific link' with trade and has 'direct and immediate effects' on trade.[78] However, Article 207 TFEU cannot be used 'to regulate the levels of social and environmental protection in the Parties' respective territory'.[79]

In light of this case law, framing investor obligations in two ways will contribute to such commitments falling within the scope of Article 207 TFEU. The first is where such obligations are specifically tied to either the direct investment made in the host state or are imposed specifically on foreign investors. Where, as in the case of corruption under the SADC 'model BIT', a breach of an obligation results in the exclusion of the direct investment from the scope of the agreement, it is more likely that the Court of Justice will find such obligations to have a 'specific link' with trade, intended to 'govern' such trade, and to have 'direct and immediate effects' on such trade. Rather than laying down environmental or social standards more generally, such obligations would be specifically tied to the direct investments made. Moreover, similar to the Trade and Sustainable Development (TSD) commitments in *Opinion 2/15 (EU-Singapore FTA)*, the obligations would contain a clear conditionality: investment protection is made conditional upon the compliance with these obligations.

The second way in which these investor obligations can be framed to make them more likely to fall within the scope of the CCP is where the obligations refer to already existing international standards, and do not create any new environmental, social, or other public interest obligations. Where an investment agreement therefore establishes any new environmental norms that would result in the agreement regulating the levels of social and environmental protection, or, put differently, if the agreement looks like an environmental agreement in that it generally lays down new environmental commitments for the parties, it falls outside the scope of the CCP. However, if the obligations are linked to both foreign investors and their investments, and do not substantively introduce new rules, such obligations can be assumed by the EU under Article 207 TFEU.

Not many existing international environmental agreements impose obligations on private parties, let alone foreign investors. International environmental agreements usually impose obligations on states to take the necessary measures, and in some instances specific measures, to achieve the levels of protection

[77] *Opinion 2/15* ECLI:EU:C:2017:376 (*EU-Singapore FTA*), paras 139–147.
[78] ibid para 166.
[79] ibid para 164.

sought in the agreement.[80] They also generally introduce monitoring and reporting obligations for states.[81] On the other hand, an increasing number of private international standards develop norms for private parties. The most well-known example is the 2011 edition of the OECD Guidelines for Multinational Enterprises, and other various, more detailed underlying sector-specific standards, such as those for the garment industry and the mining industry.[82] Environmental management systems, such as the ISO 14000 standards, can assist in ensuring that domestic environmental laws are complied with by investors. In relation to climate change, the International Accounting Standards Board (IASB) is developing reporting standards on the climate impact of businesses.[83]

On the one hand, imposing such obligations on foreign investors is – to an extent – codifying such private standards into law, and therefore can be seen as regulating the levels of protection in a state. On the other hand, the obligations (depending on how they are framed) are addressed to investors making an investment; thus it would not result in laying down standards applicable to everyone, and it would not amount to harmonisation. The key would be that those obligations are framed as addressed to foreign investors, not as an obligation on the state to implement such private standards into law.

12.5. THE POWER TO REFORM INVESTOR-STATE DISPUTE SETTLEMENT IN INTERNATIONAL AGREEMENTS

A last key area of reform of investment agreements that would reduce negative exposure of climate policies of states is reform of ISDS itself. ISDS mechanisms in international investment agreements are unusually strong compared to other forms of international dispute settlement, and are more favourable to investors than national courts of states. Investors do not have to exhaust domestic remedies first, can enforce awards in other states than the host state, are involved in the appointment of the arbitrators, can rely on greater secrecy of proceedings, and the sums of compensation are higher than in national courts. As Tienhaara et al point out:

> Increasingly, there is a tendency for tribunals to use projections of an investment's expected future income across its entire life cycle as the basis of compensation, using discounted cash flow as the method of calculation. The result has been hugely

[80] For instance, Article 3 of the Paris Agreement obliges the parties to undertake 'ambitious efforts' through 'nationally determined contributions' with a view of achieving the goal of staying well below 2 degrees of global warming. Paris Agreement [2016] OJ L282/4.

[81] Article 13 of the Paris Agreement sets up an Enhanced Transparency Framework that ensures proper reporting and monitoring of the parties' efforts to reduce greenhouse gas emissions through their nationally determined contributions.

[82] OECD, 'Guidelines for multinational enterprises' (OECD, 2011).

[83] The International Sustainability Standards Board, 'Exposure Draft: Climate Related Disclosures' (IFRS, 2022).

> inflated monetary awards in the hundreds of millions and even billions of dollars. In some cases, the amount of compensation awarded has been described as 'crippling' because it is incommensurate to the state's capacity to pay.[84]

An example is the recent arbitration award against Italy. The investor, Rockhopper, had invested EUR 40 million in a cancelled oil drilling project, but received compensation of around EUR 240 million.[85]

This section will argue that some reforms of ISDS may facilitate exercise of EU exclusive competence, but that the lack of clarity of the case law of the Court of Justice in *Opinion 2/15 (EU-Singapore FTA)* does not provide a solid enough basis to assume exclusive competences over such reforms. Other reforms (such as third-party rights) may make exercise of EU competence more difficult. This means that the EU will need to involve the Member States in reforming international agreements that contain ISDS.

The Court of Justice found in *Opinion 2/15 (EU-Singapore FTA)* that including ISDS in an international agreement is a shared competence between the EU and its Member States. Referring to previous case law, the Court of Justice held that normally institutional 'provisions are of an ancillary nature and therefore fall within the same competence as the substantive provisions which they accompany'.[86] However, this reasoning did not apply to ISDS. The Court of Justice first pointed out that not only the EU, but also the Member States could be respondents under ISDS.[87] It then pointed out the relationship between ISDS and claims before national courts. According to the Court of Justice, while it is not excluded that an investor brings a claim before a domestic court, 'the fact remains that that is merely a possibility in the discretion of the claimant investor'.[88] The Court of Justice also pointed out that a respondent state cannot oppose such a claim, as under ISDS in EU agreements, the EU and its Member States give their unconditional consent to arbitration.[89] Therefore, the Court of Justice concluded:

> Such a regime, which removes disputes from the jurisdiction of the courts of the Member States, cannot be of a purely ancillary nature within the meaning of the case-law recalled in paragraph 276 of this opinion and *cannot, therefore, be established without the Member States' consent*.[90]

As a consequence, the competence to introduce ISDS in an international agreement is 'shared between the European Union and the Member States'.[91]

[84] Tienhaara et al, 'Investor-state disputes threaten the global green energy transition' (n 6).
[85] Joe Lo, 'British company forces Italy to pay €190m for offshore oil ban' (Climate Home News, 24 August 2022).
[86] *Opinion 2/15* ECLI:EU:C:2017:376 (*EU-Singapore FTA*), para 276.
[87] ibid para 286.
[88] ibid para 290.
[89] ibid para 291.
[90] ibid para 292, emphasis added.
[91] ibid para 293.

However, as with the shared competence for portfolio investments, the Court of Justice does not make clear what the substantive legal basis is of this shared competence. There is no area of shared competence listed in Article 4(2) TFEU that would logically include the power to include ISDS in an international agreement.[92] What is more, the clarification offered in *Germany v Council (COTIF I)* that the EU can decide to exercise its shared competence without the Member States only refers to portfolio investments, and not to ISDS.[93] *Opinion 2/15 (EU-Singapore FTA)* therefore makes the conclusion of investment agreements containing ISDS as an 'EU-only' agreement a legal and practical impossibility. Any reform of Member State agreements through replacement with an EU agreement would therefore necessitate the involvement of the Member States.

The modest reforms proposed by the Commission under its proposed 'Investment Court System' (ICS) do not change this division of powers between the EU and the Member States as they do not touch upon the key aspects of the Court of Justice's ruling in *Opinion 2/15 (EU-Singapore FTA)*.[94] In essence, the Commission is seeking to replace ad hoc arbitration with a more permanent form of dispute settlement where investors are no longer involved in the appointment of arbitrators, because it sees the current form of arbitration as undermining the legitimacy of a system it would like to preserve.[95] Importantly,

[92] Article 4(2) lists non-exhaustively the following areas that are shared competence: internal market; social policy; economic, social and territorial cohesion; agriculture and fisheries; environment; consumer protection; transport; trans-European networks; energy; area of freedom, security and justice; common safety concerns in public health matters; research, technological development and space; and development cooperation and humanitarian aid. The only suitable candidate for a legal basis it is submitted is the flexibility provision of Article 352 TFEU. That article can even be used (controversially) to develop a policy area that does not yet exist. See Robert Schütze, *An Introduction to European Law*, 2nd edn (Cambridge University Press, 2015) 74–75; Marise Cremona, 'External Relations of the European Union: The Constitutional Framework for International Action' in Paul Craig,and Gráinne de Búrca (eds), *The Evolution of EU Law*, 3rd edn (Oxford University Press, 2021) 226.

[93] Oddly enough, the Commission and the Council have resorted to Article 207 TFEU as a legal basis (an exclusive competence) for the adoption of rules governing ISDS within ICSID. See Council Decision 2022/438 of 14 March 2022 on the position to be adopted on behalf of the European Union within the Administrative Council of the International Centre for Settlement of Investment Disputes (ICSID) [2022] OJ L89/9.

[94] See ch 15.

[95] Commission, 'Investment in TTIP and beyond – the path for reform' (Commission, 2015), 6–7. ICS introduces a roster of arbitrators selected by the parties to the agreement that will be allocated to cases randomly, instead of appointed by the parties to the dispute. Unlike most domestic judicial systems, however, the arbitrators are still partially paid in daily fees. This creates a financial interest in cases being brought by investors. Arbitrators are also investment law specialists. This means that they are trained in the rationale of investment law and investor rights, and do not necessarily have an understanding of the legal or political system of a responding state, nor an expertise in other areas of law such as environmental law. ICS also introduces an appellate system. The possibility of appeal goes against the rationale of ISDS, which is meant to offer a quick remedy for foreign investors; the Commission seeks to introduce more predictability and consistency in the investment law system. The appellate system would operate in a similar fashion to the WTO's Appellate Body, allowing predominantly for appeals on points of law. This is meant to ensure that tribunals will start following decisions from the Appellate Tribunal. Lastly, the ICS system incorporates the UNCITRAL Transparency Rules. This ensures that secret investment disputes that occur almost entirely in secret,

ICS maintains several key features of traditional ISDS that make it a shared competence under EU law: individual foreign investors – as opposed to states only – can bring claims, they can do so without exhausting domestic remedies first,[96] and there is automatic consent from the host state to resolve the dispute through ICS. Moreover, under ICS, only investors can bring claims for damages before ICS tribunals, to the exclusion of the host state or affected third parties. While some investment agreements (implicitly) allow host states to bring counterclaims, ICS explicitly cuts off this possibility. For instance, in *Urbaser*, an ISDS tribunal found that it had jurisdiction to hear Argentina's counterclaim on the basis of the Argentina-Spain BIT against Urbaser for failing to provide water supply services on the basis that Urbaser had violated the right to water.[97]

More significant reforms that touch upon these key features and that the Parliament has called for, however, may have an impact on the EU's powers. Two reforms will be discussed here: the introduction of an exhaustion of domestic remedies rule and reforms that would allow third parties (NGOs or affected communities) to bring claims, for instance as a result of environmental damage caused by the investor in extractive or logging activities.

In relation to exhaustion of domestic remedies, the Parliament in its 2022 resolution on EU international investment policy has emphasised that 'under both customary international law and international human rights law, individuals are required to seek redress before domestic courts before bringing international proceedings against the state for wrongful acts'. It has therefore expressed regret that international investment law 'usually does not require the exhaustion of domestic remedies', and 'believes, that IIAs should require recourse through domestic justice systems to be exhausted before foreign investors can resort to an arbitration tribunal, as is the case in international human rights law; stresses that in the event of gross denial of justice in domestic courts, foreign investors should directly be able to seek international dispute settlement'.[98]

The introduction of such a rule may ensure that reform of this aspect of existing international agreements falls within the exclusive competence of the EU. The key to the Court of Justice finding that ISDS is not merely ancillary in nature is that the regime 'removes disputes from the jurisdiction of the courts of the Member States'. This is so, according to the Court of Justice, due to the fact that the investor has the choice to bypass national courts when seeking damages. Therefore, *a contrario*, if ISDS no longer removes disputes from the jurisdiction

such as the Vattenfall claim against Germany for phasing out nuclear power, are a thing of the past under ICS.

[96] See for instance Article 8.22 CETA (n 57); however, ICS does not allow investors to have parallel proceedings before domestic courts if they are to make use of ICS.

[97] The counterclaim was nonetheless dismissed. See Markus Krajewski, 'Human Rights in International Investment Law: Recent Trends in Arbitration and Treaty-Making Practice' (SSRN, 15 April 2018).

[98] European Parliament resolution on the future of EU international investment policy (n 14) 32.

of the Member States, such provisions become ancillary to the substantive provisions they accompany.

There are two ways in which this can be achieved. The first is to remove the unilateral offer to arbitrate by host governments to foreign investors – unconditional consent – from the ISDS provisions. Governments then retain control over whether they would like to resolve a dispute through international arbitration, or through their own national courts. This option would follow the Court of Justice's reasoning closely, as the Court of Justice concludes that ISDS removes disputes from the jurisdiction of national courts precisely because Member States give unconditional consent in the international agreement containing ISDS.[99] The second option is to explicitly introduce an exhaustion of domestic remedies rule. This option would be a bit further removed from the Court of Justice's reasoning, but would offer a more solid guarantee that no disputes would be removed from the jurisdiction of the courts of the Member States. Governments would not be in the position to consent to arbitration and allow for the removal of a dispute from the jurisdiction of a national court. *Opinion 2/15 (EU-Singapore FTA)* is, however, not explicit about the potential of the exhaustion of domestic remedies rule having an impact on the nature of EU powers, and future guidance from the Court of Justice on this point is likely necessary before Member States would be willing to concede their loss of powers over ISDS if such a rule were to be introduced.

In relation to third party rights, the Parliament has called 'on the Commission and the Member States to include a right of standing for affected third parties in future IIAs'.[100] The European Parliament has also called for investor-state proceedings to be dismissed 'when determinations of fact or law might prejudice affected local or indigenous communities which are not party to the investment proceedings'.[101] The latter solution limits the jurisdiction of investment tribunals to the benefit of national courts, but it does not structurally avoid the removal of disputes from the jurisdiction of the national courts of the Member States. As such, this solution would not affect the power over the inclusion of ISDS under EU law. Who has competence to introduce the former solution (a right of standing for third parties) is a much more complicated question as it depends on how such a right is introduced. Such a right would likely be tied to investor obligations introduced by the agreement. They may simply not be provided for in the international agreement itself, as parties may agree to ensure that there are sufficient domestic remedies available to affected third parties. However, where arrangements are foreseen in the agreement, such institutional arrangements following from a right of standing would then be ancillary to the substantive obligations (discussed in section 12.3). However, to the extent that

[99] *Opinion 2/15* ECLI:EU:C:2017:376 (*EU-Singapore FTA*), paras 286–91.
[100] European Parliament resolution on the future of EU international investment policy (n 14) 25.
[101] ibid.

the ISDS provisions themselves are used, the EU's powers are shared as the Court of Justice has found these provisions to be a shared competence.

12.6. CONCLUSION

The possibilities for the EU to green international investment law are limited. This is mainly because the EU's powers under current EU law do not allow it to compel the Member States to reform the already existing investment agreements that are far from compatible with the goals of the Paris Agreement. These agreements contain provisions that protect investments in fossil fuels through widely worded standards, offer no obligations for foreign investors nor introduce third party rights, and offer significant procedural rights for such investors through ISDS.

Instead, the EU can only negotiate investment agreements of its own that can gradually replace Member State investment agreements. The EU's policy, however, is not targeted towards replacing Member State agreements, nor is this feasible as not all Member States have investment agreements with specific third states.[102] This means that instead of reforming existing agreements, the EU's own agreements are likely a combination of expanding new investment law and replacing old investment law with a new approach.

Even if such an approach were to result in a significant replacement of old international investment law, this process is cumbersome. The competence to do so does not fall entirely within the exclusive competence of the EU. These agreements cover portfolio investments and contain ISDS, both shared competences. Moreover, *Opinion 2/15 (EU-Singapore FTA)* introduces an obligation to involve the Member States in the ratification of investment agreements containing ISDS, even if it is a shared competence.

[102] For instance, Ireland has no such international agreements with third states.

13

Coal Phase-out and Investment Law: Navigating the Arbitration Barrier Through Market Forces

SARA SOINI AND ANATOLE BOUTE

13.1. INTRODUCTION[1]

COAL-FIRED POWER PLANTS are a major source of greenhouse gas (GHG) emissions within the energy sector as a whole, and to an even larger extent in the electricity sector, reaching an all-time high of 40% of the overall growth in global carbon dioxide emissions in 2021.[2] Transitioning away from coal is therefore generally considered one of the most impactful ways of mitigating climate change.[3] In order to achieve this transition, states will need 'to retire a large number of existing coal power plants early, reduce the capacity factor of those that remain, and refrain from building new coal capacity'.[4] In the EU context, the European Green Deal recognises that coal needs to be

[1] This chapter benefited from research funding by the HK Research Grants Council Project, General Research Fund project number 14609122. The analysis is up to date as of February 2023.

[2] See International Energy Agency (IEA), 'Global Energy Review: CO2 Emissions in 2021' (2022). The power sector (including the generation of electricity and heat) is itself the single largest source of CO2 emissions globally. See eg International Energy Agency (IEA), 'CO2 Emissions from Fuel Combustion' (2020) IEA Statistics Report, 6. See also IEA, 'Net Zero by 2050' (2021) at 165.

[3] See eg PA Yanguas Parra et al, 'Global and regional coal phase-out requirements of the Paris Agreement: Insights from the IPCC Special Report on 1.5°C' (2019) *Climate Analytics*. See also BM Kefford et al, 'The early retirement challenge for fossil fuel power plants in deep decarbonisation scenarios' (2018) 119 *Energy Policy* 294, 299.

[4] Yanguas Parra et al (n 3) 4 ('Unabated coal-fired power generation globally should be reduced to 80% below 2010 levels by 2030 and phased out before 2040, some 10 years earlier than previous estimates' and 'most reductions in coal in the power sector need to happen by 2030, when the share of coal in electricity generation should not exceed 13% anywhere, and be around 6% globally.').

rapidly phased out,[5] in line with international projections on the changes that are needed in the energy sector to transition to net-zero emissions.[6] For the Commission, 'by 2050[,] solids virtually disappear from the energy system'.[7]

Phasing out coal power requires ambitious environmental regulation. Before the energy crisis caused by the war in Ukraine, a number of EU Member States introduced a ban on the use of coal for electricity production.[8] Banning the use of coal is the most effective way of phasing out these polluting facilities.[9] However, as illustrated by investor claims (and threats of claims) against coal bans, energy companies can challenge phase-out decisions before international investment arbitration to protect their vested interests and obtain compensation.[10] The alternative approach, followed in the EU, is to rely on market forces to drive the decarbonisation of power generation.[11]

International investment law, and in particular foreign investors' right to directly challenge state measures before arbitral tribunals, is subject to increasing criticism concerning states' regulatory sovereignty regarding environmental protection.[12] In its Sixth Assessment Report on Climate Change, the

[5] The European Green Deal, which boosts the EU's climate ambitions for 2030 and 2050, explicitly states that in order to further decarbonise the energy system, transforming the power sector to become largely based on renewable sources must be 'complemented by the rapid phasing out of coal', and that the EU should be 'phasing out all new coal plant construction'. Commission, 'The European Green Deal' COM(2019) 640 final, 6 and 21.

[6] IEA, 'Net zero by 2050' (n 2).

[7] Commission, 'In-depth Analysis in Support of the Commission Communication COM(2018)773' (2018).

[8] For an overview of national phase-out decisions in Europe, see Europe Beyond Coal, 'Overview of national coal phase-out commitments' (January 2022).

[9] See eg B Caldecott and J Mitchell, 'Premature retirement of sub-critical coal assets: The Potential Role of Compensation and the Implications for International Climate Policy' (2014) 16 *Seton Hall Journal of Diplomacy and International Relations* 59–70; F Matthes et al, 'Assessment of the planned compensation payments for decommissioning German lignite power plants in the context of current developments' (Öko-Institut e.V, 2020), 30 www.oeko.de/fileadmin/oekodoc/Assessment-of-the-planned-compensation-payments.pdf.

[10] See eg *RWE AG and RWE Eemshaven Holding II BV v Kingdom of the Netherlands*, ICSID Case No ARB/21/4; *Uniper SE, Uniper Benelux Holding BV and Uniper Benelux NV v Kingdom of the Netherlands*, ICSID Case No ARB/21/22; *Westmoreland Coal Company v. Government of Canada*, ICSID Case No UNCT/20/3. See also ClientEarth, 'Should German coal companies get cash to close?' (2019); A Van den Berghe, 'Legal opinion on Uniper's legally misconceived ISDS threat to Dutch coal phase-out' (ClientEarth, 2019).

[11] C(2022) 481 final, 'Guidelines on state aid for climate, environmental protection and energy 2022', para 423. For a legal analysis of coal phase-out in the EU, see eg L Braaksma and R Fleming, 'Phasing out coal-fired power plants in the European Union' in M Roggenkamp and C Banet (eds), *European Energy Law Report XIII* (Intersentia, 2020), 261–87, at 263. For an in-depth analysis of the EU market-based approach to coal phase-out, see Anatole Boute, 'Phasing Out Coal Through Electricity Market Regulation' (2022) 59 *CMLR* 1007–44. Sections 13.5 and 13.6 of the present chapter to some extent build on the latter article.

[12] See eg K Tienhaara, 'Investor-state disputes threaten the global green energy transition' (2022) 376(6594) *Science* 701–03; F Marisi, *Environmental Interests in Investment Arbitration: Challenges and Directions* (Kluwer Law International, 2020); J Bonnitcha et al, *The Political Economy of the Investment Treaty Regime* (Oxford University Press, 2017); C Titi, *The Right to Regulate in*

Intergovernmental Panel on Climate Change noted that international investment agreements 'have tended to protect investor rights, constraining the latitude of host countries in adopting environmental policies'.[13] The Energy Charter Treaty (ECT) is at the centre of this criticism, with accusations that the treaty protects carbon-intensive interests, and thus constitutes an obstacle to the achievement of the decarbonisation objectives of the Paris Agreement by preventing the implementation of ambitious climate policies.[14] For the EU, a central concern is whether states can adopt ambitious decarbonisation measures, eg, 'discourage all further investments into fossil fuel', without violating their investment treaty obligations.[15] Following an attempt to 'modernise' the treaty and align it with EU and international decarbonisation ambitions, a number of EU Member States have announced their intention to withdraw from the ECT.[16] The massive damages awards issued in the energy sector (amounting in several cases to billions of USD) illustrate the risk that states face when implementing coal phase-out decisions.[17] Given the risk of massive compensation claims associated with a ban on coal, how can states phase out coal power while navigating the risk of investment arbitration?

This chapter examines coal phase-out policies from an investment law perspective, and seeks to determine the extent to which market mechanisms, by contrast to a ban on coal, can achieve the objective of moving away from coal power, while limiting the risk of investor-state arbitration claims in the low-carbon transition. The argument aims to contribute to the debate on the right to regulate under international investment law, by examining how different

International Investment Law (Hart Publishing, 2014); J Viñuales, *Foreign Investment and the Environment in International Law* (Cambridge University Press, 2012).

[13] Intergovernmental Panel on Climate Change (IPCC), 'Climate Change 2022: Mitigation of Climate Change'.

[14] See eg J Rankin, 'Why activists fear little-known treaty could slow fossil fuel phase-out' (*Guardian*, 3 November 2021); J Rankin, 'Energy treaty update fails to address climate crisis, activists say' (*Guardian*, 24 June 2022); Climate Action Network, 'Energy Charter Treaty reform: Why it has failed to deliver on the EU's own objectives' (2022) (arguing that the ECT 'include[s] the ability for fossil fuel investors to sue governments through private tribunals for multiple-billions of dollars if action on climate change and the environment damage their future profits'). See also A Belyi, 'The Energy Charter process in the face of uncertainties' (2021) 14(5) *Journal of World Energy Law & Business* 363–75.

[15] European Union, *EU text proposal for the modernisation of the Energy Charter Treaty (ECT)* (2020).

[16] European Parliament, Resolution of 24 November 2022 on the Outcome of the Modernisation of the Energy Charter Treaty (2022/2934(RSP)).

[17] K Tienhaara and L Cotula, 'Raising the cost of climate action? Investor-state dispute settlement and compensation for stranded fossil fuel assets' (2020). According to H van Asselt, 'Governing fossil fuel production in the age of climate disruption: Towards an international law of "leaving it in the ground"' (2021) 9 *Earth System Governance* 100, 118, 'the normative guidance from international investment law seems to hinder a transition away from fossil fuel production to achieve climate goals'. See, more generally, M Paparinskis, 'A Case Against Crippling Compensation in International Law of State Responsibility' (2020) 83 *Modern Law Review* (2020) 1246–86.

approaches to phase out coal interact with investment law, with varying degrees of effectiveness in achieving the transition away from fossil fuels.

The argument proceeds as follows. First, the chapter introduces the urgency of coal phase-out in the context of the EU's climate mitigation objectives. Next, the environmental effectiveness of a coal ban and its implications under international investment law is discussed, before examining market-based alternatives. The analysis introduces the benefits of the market-based approach from an investment law perspective, and examines its environmental effectiveness by looking at the interaction of the EU electricity market reform with the EU Emissions Trading Scheme (ETS) – the cornerstone of the EU climate policy. It is then concluded that market mechanisms have been more successful in navigating investors' claims than traditional regulation, and have initially achieved the closure of coal-fired power plants. However, recent market developments, in the context of geopolitical turmoil, have stalled the coal phase-out process, indicating the limits to the environmental effectiveness of this approach

13.2. THE URGENCY AND CHALLENGE OF THE COAL PHASE-OUT

From a decarbonisation perspective, it is necessary 'to focus not only on new infrastructure but also on the emissions that are "locked in" to existing systems'.[18] Even if no new coal-fired power plants are built, the emissions associated with the existing stock of coal power present a major challenge to the EU's decarbonisation goals.[19] According to the IEA, allowing the existing global energy infrastructure (including power plants currently under construction) to operate until the end of their typical lifetimes would cause a level of emissions that would by far exceed the 'remaining total CO2 budget consistent with limiting global warming to 1.5°C'.[20] Coal-fired power plants are especially critical when it comes to energy infrastructure that risks locking in emissions in the long run, due to their long-term and capital-intensive nature.[21] At the same time, the power sector is among the most cost-effective sectors in terms of reducing

[18] IEA, 'World Energy Outlook (WEO) 2019', 5.

[19] IEA, 'WEO 2020', 45. See also IEA, 'WEO 2019', 5.

[20] 'If today's energy infrastructure was to be operated until the end of the typical lifetime in a manner similar to the past, [the IEA] estimate that this would lead to cumulative energy-related and industrial process CO2 emissions between 2020 and 2050 of just under 650 Gt CO2. This is around 30% more than the remaining total CO2 budget consistent with limiting global warming to 1.5°C with a 50% probability.' IEA, 'Net zero by 2050', 39. See also IEA WEO 2020, 46. In a similar study in 2019, Climate Analytics found that 'Even if all the planned and announced coal power plants would be cancelled, shelved, or converted to other fuel, the operating coal plants would exceed the Paris Agreement benchmarks by four times in 2030 and more than twenty times by 2040'. Yanguas Parra et al, 'Global and regional coal phase-out requirements', 16.

[21] 'The electricity sector accounts for more than 50% of the total emissions that would come from existing assets; 40% of total emissions would come from coal-fired power plants alone'. IEA, 'Net zero by 2050' (n 2) 39.

emissions,[22] and closing coal-fired power plants (the most carbon-intensive form of power production) is among the most effective abatement measures. Climate and energy analysts therefore generally agree that credible decarbonisation pathways 'necessarily involve the early retirement (i.e. stranding) of coal-fired generation plants'.[23] To achieve the objectives of the Paris Agreement, 'rapidly reducing coal-based power generation down to 80% below 2010 levels by 2030, and a global phase-out by 2040 at the latest is the single most important step'.[24]

In 2021, global carbon emissions from coal power increased to the record level of 10.5 gigatons, 800 megatons higher than their 2020 level, as the exceptional surge in gas prices following the war in Ukraine incentivised a switch from gas power to coal power.[25] In the EU, emissions from coal increased by 16% in 2021, reversing the declining trend where the share of coal for electricity production had dropped by a third over the last decade.[26] In 2022, the production of electricity from coal in the EU further benefited from the energy crisis, as several Member States temporarily allowed higher production to save gas in response to the disruption of Russian supplies.[27] The EU still had around 600 coal-fired power plants with a total installed capacity of 164 gigawatts (GW), among which about 50 GW of coal capacity remained without a retirement date.[28]

The decarbonisation targets set by the 2021 European Climate Law (Regulation (EU) 2021/1119) are unlikely to be achieved without the rapid phasing out of coal.[29] However, EU law does not require the closure of existing coal-fired power plants. Banning the use of coal remains a national prerogative, in consideration of the protection of Member States' right to determine

[22] W Acworth et al, 'Emissions Trading and Electricity Sector Regulation – A conceptual framework for understanding interactions between carbon prices and electricity prices' (International Carbon Action Partnership, 2018), 2.

[23] P Simshauser and A Akimov, 'Regulated electricity networks, investment mistakes in retrospect and stranded assets under uncertainty' (2019) 81 *Energy Economics* 117, 121.

[24] Yanguas Parra et al (n 3) 22. BM Kefford et al, 'The early retirement challenge for fossil fuel power plants in deep decarbonisation scenarios' (2018) 119 *Energy Policy* 294, 299 (in a two-degree scenario, 'coal power capacity needs to be reduced by 99% capacity from 2014 to 2060').

[25] IEA, Global Energy Review, at 6.

[26] IEA, 'European Union 2020 Energy Policy Review' (2020), 288–89 (total coal consumption in the EU nearly halved from 445 Mtoe in 1990 to 228 Mtoe in 2017).

[27] IEA, World Energy Outlook 2022, at 40. See also European Commission, Communication on REPowerEU Plan COM/2022/230 final ('some of the existing coal capacities might also be used longer than initially expected'); and Anatole Boute, 'Energy Geopolitics and Climate Law: Interdisciplinary Environmental Law Scholarship in a Geopolitical World' (2023) 35(1) *Journal of Environmental Law* 157–59.

[28] IEA, 'European Union 2020 Energy Policy Review', 291. L Roberts et al, 'Global status of coal power. Pre-Covid19 baseline analysis' (2020) E3G, 16. 'The nine EU member states most reliant on lignite for power generation are Bulgaria, the Czech Republic, Germany, Greece, Hungary, Poland, the Slovak Republic, Slovenia and Romania. Germany and Poland make up about half of the EU's installed coal capacity.'

[29] COM(2019) 640 final, 'The European Green Deal', at 6.

their energy mix under EU primary law.[30] Besides this constitutional limitation to the banning of coal, the threat of investment arbitration is a potentially significant obstacle to adopting and implementing mandatory closures of coal-fired power plants in the EU, despite the environmental effectiveness of this approach.

13.3. BAN ON COAL: ENVIRONMENTAL EFFECTIVENESS VERSUS INVESTMENT ARBITRATION

Phasing out coal through direct regulation refers to legislative or regulatory measures taken by governments to end coal-fired power production. This can involve banning the use of coal for electricity generation, often by a set date, effectively forcing some plants to either switch to other fuels or to close down, by making coal-fired power generation illegal.[31] Some EU Member States have enacted coal phase-out legislation, banning the use of coal in electricity production by specific dates. For instance, the phase-out law of the Netherlands (adopted in December 2019) gave the remaining five coal-fired power plants phase-out dates based on their electrical efficiency rate.[32]

According to environmental law theory, imposing a ban on coal, or mandatory decommissioning of carbon-intensive facilities, is a radical form of technology-based command and control regulation, as it interferes with the property rights of the plant owners.[33] A coal ban is an effective way of closing

[30] Articles 191(1), 192(2) and 194(2) Consolidated version of the Treaty on the Functioning of the European Union (TFEU) [2012] OJ C 326/47. See also Case C-5/16 *Poland v Parliament and Council* ECLI:EU:C:2018:483, paras 24–35.

[31] To date, there is no international treaty specifically governing the use of coal for power generation nor the phasing out of such generation capacity. Cf A Burke and S Fishel, 'A coal elimination treaty 2030: Fast tracking climate change mitigation, global health and security' (2020) 3 *Earth System Governance*, advocating for global adoption of a treaty to prohibit and phase out the mining and burning of coal by 2030.

[32] Plants with an efficiency rate lower than 44% must be closed before 2025 while plants with an efficiency of 44% or above are banned from 2030. Act on the Prohibition on the Use of Coal in Electricity Production of 11 December 2019 (*Wet verbod op kolen bij elektriciteitsproductie*), Articles 2, 3 and 3a. Accordingly, one plant (owned by Vattenfall) had to close immediately; one plant (RWE's Amercentrale plant) will have to close before 2025; and the remaining three (including Uniper's plant) which all became operational very recently, in 2015/2016, were given until 2030 to shut down.

[33] A Boute and H Zhang, 'The Role of the Market and Traditional Regulation in Decarbonising China's Energy Supply' (2018) 30 *Journal of Environmental Law* 264, 275. See also S Kingston et al, *European Environmental Law* (Cambridge University Press, 2017) 131. In a broad sense, a regulatory phase-out can also involve more flexible types of traditional direct regulation, restricting the operations of coal-fired power plants by regulating their emissions, eg by imposing environmental performance standards (pollution control regulations). For example, the Netherlands used performance requirements to decommission five older coal-fired power plants dating from the 1970s and 1980s, by imposing an energy efficiency rate of 40%. See Advice of the Advisory Division of the Council of State, Parliamentary document 34627, 2016–2017, no 15, 24 July 2017, 1–2.

coal-fired generators,[34] and creates planning certainty for stakeholders in the coal and electricity sectors, the affected communities, and governments.[35] It is also meant to provide a more coordinated decommissioning of coal-fired power plants compared to the uncoordinated closures due to market forces.[36] For example, Germany justified its regulatory coal phase-out approach with benefits of a more targeted trajectory for the development of alternative electricity sources, and with the possibility 'to determine a gradual closure path upfront, [which would have a smaller] impact on security of supply and employees in the sector'.[37]

However, imposing a ban on coal creates possible tensions with property rights and international investment protection, as coal-fired power plants become so-called 'stranded assets' by the adoption of new laws.[38] Unrecovered investment costs and remaining economic and technical plant lifetimes in affected power plants can lay the ground for judicial action by investors before national courts, eg under the right to property, and before international arbitration, eg under the indirect expropriation and fair and equitable treatment standards.[39]

Besides its investment arbitration claim based on the ECT, the German energy company RWE challenged the legality of the Dutch coal phase-out decision based on its right to property under Article 1 of the First Additional Protocol to the European Convention on Human Rights. In its judgment of November 2022, the Hague District Court accepted that the Dutch coal law interfered with RWE's right to property but ruled that this interference was proportionate with the GHG emission reduction objective pursued and that the

[34] Caldecott and Mitchell argue that there is 'strong evidence' that the use of direct regulation, based on the rationales of reducing emissions or increasing fleet efficiency, has been effective in inducing closures of older, highly polluting coal-fired power plants in the past (eg China and the US, and older Dutch plants). B Caldecott and J Mitchell, 'Premature retirement of sub-critical coal assets' (n 9) 59–60. Effectiveness refers particularly to 'environmental effectiveness' (as opposed to economic efficiency). Kingston et al, *European Environmental Law* (n 33) 123–24.

[35] See eg F Heilmann and R Popp, 'How (not) to phase out coal: Lessons from Germany for just and timely coal exits' (2020) E3G Briefing Paper, 10–11; M Rocha et al, 'A stress test for coal in Europe under the Paris Agreement' (2017) Climate Analytics, VII.

[36] Rocha et al, 'A stress test' (n 35) VII; Heilmann and Popp, 'How (not) to phase out coal' (n 35) 10.

[37] Alternative policy options Germany had considered to achieve the envisaged CO2 emission reductions included (i) relying on the EU ETS and existing targets for renewable energy, (ii) a national minimum price for CO2 for sectors covered by the EU ETS, and (iii) regulatory closure of hard coal without a tender procedure. See Commission Decision, *Tender mechanism for the phase-out of hard coal in Germany*, SA.58181 (2020/N), 25 November 2020, para 9.

[38] International Renewable Energy Agency (IRENA), 'Stranded assets and renewables: how the energy transition affects the value of energy reserves, buildings and capital stock' (2017), at 21, defining stranded assets in the power generation sector 'as fossil fuel power plants that call for closure before the end of their anticipated technical lifetimes'.

[39] For example, it was foreseen that the Dutch coal utility-owners would resist closing their plants without compensation, 'given that they are still generating positive cash flows'. G Wynn, 'The Dutch Coal Mistake' (2016) IEEFA, 3.

claimant's interests had been sufficiently considered.[40] RWE could have expected that such measure could be imposed on its investment, if it would not manage to significantly reduce its carbon emissions, eg by using biomass instead of coal or by retrofitting its facilities with carbon capture and storage. The transition period foreseen in the Dutch coal law also enabled the company to continue to receive revenues for a certain duration and identify alternative uses for its plants, thus limiting the financial damage to the investor. The possible risks of carbon leakage and the waterbed effect, referring to an increase in emissions elsewhere in the system because of the release of emissions trading allowances previously needed by a plant forced to close, did not undermine the efficiency of the coal ban, according to the court.

The judgment of the Hague District Court must be welcomed in the context of increasing concerns about the risk of state compensation for ambitious climate action, taken to accelerate the transition away from coal. In light of the readily available and long-standing knowledge about the adverse impacts of GHG emissions on climate change, energy companies that have invested in coal-fired power plants should bear the risk of the increasing climate and decarbonisation regulation that is affecting their investment. However, under international investment arbitration, states could be held up to a more stringent standard of investment protection compared to the level of protection of property rights under national laws and European human rights law, exposing states to potentially massive damages.

In principle, regulations implemented for public purposes in a non-discriminatory manner are not deemed expropriatory nor compensable despite the economic loss caused to foreign investments.[41] But expropriation could be established and compensation owed in cases where the economic value of assets is completely and indefinitely destroyed by otherwise legitimate regulations. According to Wälde and Kolo, 'in the extreme case of complete and indefinite destruction of the economic value of property by otherwise fully legitimate regulation, and if individuals are required by regulation to make a special sacrifice in terms of their proprietary rights for the benefit of the society at large, compensation is also owed'.[42] Although there have only been a few investment arbitration cases involving coal-fired power generation impacted by climate policy and there is little empirical evidence on the extent to which investment arbitration has actually 'chilled' state law-making,[43] an important concern is that international investment protection could dissuade states from adopting coal bans.[44] Besides

[40] *RWE Eemshaven Holding II v De Staat der Nederlanden* (Het Ministerie van Economische Zaken en Klimaat), Rechtbank den Haag, No C/09/608584, judgment of 30 November 2022.

[41] *Methanex Corporation v United States of America* (UNCITRAL, 2005).

[42] T Wälde and A Kolo, 'Environmental Regulation, Investment Protection and "Regulatory Taking" in International Law' (2001) 50 *ICLQ* 811, 846.

[43] Bonnitcha et al, *The Political Economy of the Investment Treaty Regime* (n 12).

[44] K Tienhaara, 'Regulatory chill and the threat of arbitration: A view from political science' in C Brown and K Miles (eds), *Evolution in Investment Treaty Law and Arbitration* (Cambridge

the threat of regulatory chill, compensating carbon-intensive plants for early decommissioning raises important legitimacy questions since it shifts the financial burden of decarbonisation from the coal plant operators to society.[45]

In the context of the 'modernisation' reform of the ECT, strengthening states' 'right to regulate' could reduce the protection of investors in high-carbon energy assets against regulatory measures to combat climate change.[46] In addition to a clearer 'right to regulate', proposals were made to limit the scope of protected investments under the ECT by narrowing 'economic activity in the energy sector' to climate friendly investments.[47] Negotiations on the 'modernised ECT' resulted in a 'flexibility mechanism' that 'allows Contracting Parties, based on a Conference decision, to exclude investment protection for fossil fuels in their territories, considering their individual energy security and climate goals'.[48]

Despite the option 'to carve-out fossil fuel related investments from investment protection under the ECT',[49] an increasing number of EU Member States and the European Parliament have criticised the outcome of the ECT modernisation process. According to the European Parliament Resolution of 24 November 2022 on the Outcome of the Modernisation of the Energy Charter Treaty, the final text of the modernised ECT 'is not aligned with the Paris Agreement, the EU Climate Law or the objectives of the European Green Deal'.[50] This criticism is mainly based on the fact that, in the modernised ECT, existing fossil fuel investments continue to be protected for at least 10 years.

University Press, 2011); K Tienhaara, 'Regulatory chill in a warming world: The threat to climate policy posed by investor-state dispute settlement' (2018) 7(2) *Transnational Environmental Law* 229–50.

[45] 'Arguments grounded in equity and fairness can be deployed by both sides of the stranding debate' (both the utility's and consumer's perspective), and can thus be used in favour of a partial recovery of stranded costs. See P Simshauser, 'Monopoly regulation, discontinuity & stranded assets' (2017) 66 *Energy Economics* 386.

[46] Currently, the ECT does not include any specific provision on the right to regulate in the public interest. Yet, 'more than two-thirds of the known 130 ISDS cases have related to host states' 'right to regulate'. See 'Modernisation of the Energy Charter Treaty' (2020), Table 3, at 27.

[47] eg, the Energy Minister of Luxembourg, Claude Turmes, argued that the current definition which protects fossil fuels investments 'will limit EU governments to take decisions in the direction of energy transition and reduction of CO2 emissions (and in the same time, their right to define their own energy mix) [and that] the lack of ambition in the definition of economic sectors in the ECT will give more time for investors to claims for millions/billions of indemnities for phasing out fossil energies and jeopardize the pace of our common road for climate neutrality by 2050 and to achieve at least 55% greenhouse gas emission reduction in 2030'. See 'Letter from Claude Turmes Minister of Energy Luxembourg to the European Commission – Energy Charter Treaty Modernization Process: Definition of Economic Activities to Terminate Investment Protection in Fossil Fuels – 5 February 2021'.

[48] Decision of the Energy Charter Conference, Public Communication explaining the main changes contained in the agreement in principle, 24 June 2022.

[49] The carve-out applies to 'existing investments after 10 years from the entry into force of the relevant provisions and for new investments made after 15 August 2023 as of that date with limited exceptions'.

[50] European Parliament, Resolution of 24 November 2022 (n 16).

There is great concern that the cut-off date of 2040, by which all investments in fossil fuels will no longer be protected if the parties activate the carve-out, 'is at odds with current knowledge on the speed of fossil fuel phase-out needed to limit global warming to 1.5°C above pre-industrial levels and that it will undermine the EU's climate objectives'.[51] In its Resolution of 23 June 2022 on the Future of EU International Investment Policy, the Parliament had already urged the Commission and the Member States 'to ensure consistency between [international investment agreement]s and the European Green Deal, … by excluding from treaty protection investments in fossil fuels', 'alarmed by the thousands of existing Member State [bilateral investment treatie]s which still protect fossil fuel investments' and the 'increasing number of legal proceedings before investment tribunals [that] target environmental measures'.[52]

Therefore, according to the European Parliament and an increasing number of EU Member States, the ECT should 'immediately prohibit fossil fuel investors from suing contracting parties for pursuing policies to phase out fossil fuels in line with their commitments under the Paris Agreement'.[53] In addition to individual EU Member States' reported intentions to withdraw, the Commission has presented a recommendation for a coordinated withdrawal from the ECT to the Member States as an option in response to the unsatisfying result of the modernisation negotiations.[54] In parallel to the reform of investment treaties, states can adopt less intrusive decarbonisation policies, to avoid conflicts with existing investment protection regimes. In the EU, phasing out coal through market forces is the alternative to closing coal-fired power plants through direct law-making.

13.4. PHASING OUT COAL THROUGH MARKET FORCES: LESS INTRUSIVE BUT UNPREDICTABLE

Instead of banning the use of coal for power generation, the EU relies on the Emissions Trading Scheme (ETS), as the cornerstone of its decarbonisation policy, to facilitate the transition to a green economy. A lot has been written on the regulation of the EU ETS,[55] but the role of this environmental market mechanism in achieving the closure of coal-fired power plants is less clear.[56] The

[51] ibid.

[52] European Parliament Resolution of 23 June 2022 on the Future of EU International Investment Policy (2021/2176(INI)). See also European Parliament, Resolution of 24 November 2022 (n 16) ('at least 150 investment arbitration cases have been instituted under the ECT, one third of which relate to fossil fuel investments').

[53] European Parliament, Resolution of 24 November 2022 (n 16).

[54] V Djanic, '[Updated] European Commission recommends coordinated EU withdrawal from Energy Charter Treaty' (*Investment Arbitration Reporter*, 8 February 2023).

[55] See eg S Bogojević, *Emissions Trading Schemes: Markets, States and Law* (Hart, 2013) 68.

[56] For a detailed analysis, see Anatole Boute, 'Phasing Out Coal Through Electricity Market Regulation' (2022) 59 *CMLR* 1007–44.

complexity is that, unlike a ban on coal, the phase out of coal power through market forces depends on the interaction of the EU ETS with electricity market regulation.[57] An additional issue is that EU electricity law only contains few references to the closure or decommissioning of power plants.[58] Instead, under EU law, most focus has been on adding new electricity production capacity, amidst concerns of security of supply.[59]

Coal-fired power generation was initially part of the response to energy security concerns. In 2000, the Commission estimated that coal is likely to remain a staple of the electricity mix for reasons of security and diversity of supply.[60] In the mid-2000s, the vision was to keep coal as part of the EU's energy mix even post-2020, while upgrading it with carbon capture and storage (CCS).[61] The risk of insufficient capacity was still perceived too imminent for considering phasing out coal altogether.[62] In the early 2000s, the Commission acknowledged that 'a large number of power stations are due for closure over the next few years', and that new investments would be needed to fill that capacity gap.[63] The 2005 Security of Electricity Supply Directive therefore sought to create a stable framework for long-term investment.[64] Until 2019, Member States could support

[57] See eg W Acworth et al, 'Emissions trading in pursuit of electricity decarbonisation – Market structures and regulations matter', German Environment Agency, Synthesis Report, May 2021, 32; W Acworth et al, 'Emissions trading in regulated electricity markets' (2020) 20 *Climate Policy* 60–70, 62; A Boute, 'The impossible transplant of the EU Emissions Trading Scheme' (2017) 6 *Transnational Environmental Law* 59–85.

[58] eg Regulation (EU) No 256/2014 of the European Parliament and of the Council of 26 February 2014 concerning the notification to the Commission of investment projects in energy infrastructure within the European Union [2014] OJ L84/6 (repealed by Regulation (EU) 2018/1504) defined decommissioning as 'the phase [of an investment] where an infrastructure is permanently taken out of operation'.

[59] Before the liberalisation of the electricity market, there was a capacity surplus under the monopoly markets, and investments were secured through central planning. However, this surplus started to disappear when competition was introduced, which led to increasing concerns about security of supply. See Eurelectric, 'Security of Electricity Supply – Roles, responsibilities and experiences within the EU', Eurelectric, Working Group on Security of Electricity Supply, January 2006, 13.

[60] Commission, 'Green Paper Towards a European strategy for the security of energy supply' COM(2000) 769, Annex 1, Technical background document on security of energy supply, 4. See also 3, 35, 37–39. At this time, hopes were laid on the development of cheap and efficient 'clean' coal technologies (an idea that has now been largely abandoned, at least in power production where CCS is too expensive to be viable).

[61] While the Commission recognised that it 'may be justified to discourage traditional coal-based power generation', at the same time it suggested to 'foster wide penetration and use of Sustainable Coal technologies'. Commission Communication of 10 January 2007, 'Sustainable power generation from fossil fuels: aiming for near-zero emissions from coal after 2020' COM(2006) 843 final, 7. The idea was to ensure 'that new coal fired power plants built after 2020 operate with CCS; capture-ready plants built in the previous period should be rapidly retrofitted' (ibid 10).

[62] The Commission highlighted the risk that if 'electricity operators [are] reluctant to include coal-based technologies in their considerations when replacing ageing coal-fired plants; their decisions could then impact on the security of EU energy supply' COM(2006) 843 final, 7.

[63] Commission, Proposal for a Directive concerning measures to safeguard security of electricity supply and infrastructure investment, 10 December 2003, COM(2003) 740 final, 2 and 4.

[64] Directive 2005/89/EC concerning measures to safeguard security of electricity supply and infrastructure investment [2006] OJ L33/22.

electricity production from indigenous coal through priority dispatch for security of supply reasons. In *Castelnou Energía v Commission*,[65] the General Court dealt with the legality of Spain's priority dispatch regime for coal power.[66] The Commission justified the appropriateness of the state aid measure by arguing 'that coal power plants, and in particular indigenous coal power plants, played an important role in providing support to electricity production from renewable energy and … providing balancing services to the system operator, which were essential to avoid supply disruptions'.[67] The General Court acknowledged this, and found the aid measure to be proportional in relation to its security of supply objective, noting that the scope of the priority access support was limited by law,[68] and in time.[69]

The investment gap created by the wide-scale closures of (mainly) older plants was in essence due to the ageing coal-plant fleet in Europe, and stricter emission regulations.[70] By requiring reductions in emissions of air pollutants,[71] the Large Combustion Plants Directive (LCPD) and its successor the Industrial Emissions Directive (IED) contributed to the decommissioning of the older and more inefficient coal-fired power plants.[72] However, closing more recent and

[65] Case T-57/11 *Castelnou Energía, SL v Commission* ECLI:EU:T:2014:1021. Castelnou, the owner of a combined-cycle power plant, challenged the Commission's approval of the Spanish state's aid measure supporting the production of electricity from indigenous coal. State aid case N178/2010 of 29 September 2010 C(2010) 4499.

[66] The aid measure was adopted as a means of ensuring security of electricity supply in Spain, relying on Article 11(4) of the 2003 Electricity Market Directive (EMD). Case T-57/11, *Castelnou Energía, SL v Commission* (n 65) paras 91, 92 and 95.

[67] Case T-57/11, *Castelnou Energía, SL v Commission* (n 65) para 153.

[68] The EMD permitted Member States to give power plants using indigenous fuel sources priority access, however 'only' to the extent not exceeding 15% of the overall primary energy necessary to produce the electricity consumed in that Member State (2003 EMD, Article 11(4)).

[69] The aid measure had been approved for approximately four years. Case T-57/11, *Castelnou Energía, SL v Commission* (n 65) para 166. 'The case confirmed the earlier position of the Commission that the use of indigenous primary energy sources for power generation may, under certain circumstances, be regarded as a genuine [service of economic interest], where the measure is in line with the rules applicable to State aids in the form of public service compensation.' L Hancher and M Klasse, 'Aid to Nuclear and Coal' in L Hancher et al (eds), *State aid and the energy sector* (Hart Publishing, 2018) 222. See also A de Hauteclocque et al, 'Services of General Economic Interest' in L Hancher et al (eds), *State aid and the energy sector* (Hart Publishing, 2018) 291.

[70] Commission, Green Paper 'A European Strategy for Sustainable, Competitive and Secure Energy' COM(2006) 105 final, 7. In 2007, the Commission acknowledged that over 'a third of existing coal-fired capacity in the EU is expected to reach the end of its technical lifetime in the coming 10 to 15 years'. Commission Communication of 10 January 2007, 'Sustainable power generation from fossil fuels: aiming for near-zero emissions from coal after 2020' COM(2006) 843 final, 7.

[71] Directive 2001/80/EC on the limitation of emissions of certain pollutants into the air from large combustion plants [2001] OJ L309/1, replaced by Directive 2010/75/EU on industrial emissions (integrated pollution prevention and control) [2010] OJ L334/17.

[72] 'It has been asserted that between 2008 and 2015 the LCPD was related to the closure of 35 GW of [coal-fired] capacity.' G Rentier et al, 'Varieties of coal-fired power phase-out across Europe' (2019) 132 *Energy Policy* 623. Eg, 'In France, EU legislation on air pollution regulations led to the closure of seven coal-fired units in 2015 totaling 1,758 MW of capacity': H Schindler, 'Managing the phase-out of coal – A comparison of actions in G20 countries' (Climate Transparency, 2019), 5. It was widely perceived among power generators that 'The only solution is to take the second option

more efficient installations with tighter emission performance requirements under the IED could amount to an abuse of the directive.[73]

In parallel, the EU's decarbonisation approach initially focused on adding new production capacity, in particular from renewable energy sources, with very limited attention to the decommissioning of existing, carbon-intensive production capacity. The 2001 and 2009 Renewable Energy Directives aimed to promote electricity production from renewable energy sources based on national renewable energy targets and support schemes.[74] Phase-out elements were not integrated into the EU decarbonisation and electricity market architecture until more recently. The preamble to the 2018 recast Renewable Energy Directive acknowledges that in addition to promoting 'a higher uptake of cost-efficient renewable energy projects … the Commission should … establish an adequate strategy to manage the retirement of technologies which do not contribute to the reduction of emissions or deliver sufficient flexibility'.[75] The Renewable Energy Directive also encourages the replacement of heating and cooling supply at building level (promoting renewable systems), to 'reduce the risk of fossil fuel technology lock-ins'.[76]

In comparison to the previous EU electricity acts which were largely focused on ensuring the security of electricity supply, the 2019 Electricity Directive and Regulation integrated a stronger decarbonisation dimension, including references to the exit of generators from the market.[77] In parallel, by exposing coal-fired power plants to the carbon price, the EU ETS increased the cost of carbon-intensive electricity generation, in particular coal, which in theory is supposed to gradually push coal-fired power plants out of the market. Under EU electricity and climate law, market forces thus govern the exit, ie closure and decommissioning, of coal-fired power plants.

and close such plants by the end of 2015'. S Cornot-Gandolphe, 'The European Coal Market: Will Coal Survive the EC's Energy and Climate Policies?' (Institut français des relations internationales, 2021), 35. See also B Grebot et al, 'Support to the evaluation of the Industrial Emissions Directive (Directive 2010/75/EU)' (European Commission, 2020), 21; and MM Sokołowski, 'Burning out Coal Power Plants with the Industrial Emissions Directive' (2018) 11 *Journal of World Energy Law & Business* 260, 260, considering that the effect of the IED is that 'many of the existing coal-fired power stations will be closed', in particular the older and less efficient installations.

[73] See Advice of the Advisory Division of the Council of State, Parliamentary document 34627, 2016-2017, no 15, at 1–2.

[74] Directive 2001/77/EC on the promotion of electricity produced from renewable energy sources in the internal electricity market [2001] OJ L283/33 (repealed); Directive 2009/28/EC on the promotion of the use of energy from renewable sources and amending and subsequently repealing Directive 2001/77/EC [2009] OJ L140/16 ('RED I'), repealed by Directive (EU) 2018/2001.

[75] Recital 14, Directive (EU) 2018/2001 on the promotion of the use of energy from renewable sources [2018] OJ L328/82 ('RED II').

[76] Article 15(6) RED II. The Commission defines 'technology lock-in' as 'where the approach focused on energy efficiency only triggers fossil fuel technologies being replaced by more efficient but still fossil fuel solutions'. Commission, Proposal for a Directive on the promotion of the use of energy from renewable sources (recast) COM(2016) 767 final/2, 15.

[77] See eg 2019 EMD, Article 3: Member States shall ensure that 'no undue barriers exist within the internal market for electricity as regards market entry, operation and exit'; and 2019 Electricity Market Regulation (EMR), Article 3(n).

This market-based approach proved to be effective in facilitating the market exit of coal-fired power plants until the 2021 energy crisis. Higher carbon prices following reforms of the EU ETS in 2015 impacted coal power, which contributed to 'accelerat[ing] the ongoing phase-out of coal, resulting in more market space for the use of existing natural gas power plants in the short term, ... as well as the necessary deployment of renewable electricity sources in the medium term'.[78] Energy and climate market developments allowed the Commission to state in 2020 that 'Europe is phasing out coal sooner than initially expected, which helps reduce greenhouse gas emissions and air pollution'.[79]

At the same time, the EU's market-based approach has also enabled the EU, and its Member States, to navigate the barrier of arbitration, and fend off legal challenges by investors. Most notably, in the *Arcelor* and *Romonta* cases, the General Court rejected claims that the EU ETS had negatively affected the profitability of the claimants in violation of their property rights.[80] In *Arcelor*, the General Court ruled that,

> apart from the very general claim that the contested provisions give rise to a situation in which the applicant is no longer able to exploit, in a profitable manner, its steel-production installations established within the internal market, the applicant has not made it clear to what extent its right to property in relation to certain tangible or intangible assets involved in its production process is actually affected or rendered meaningless as a result of the application [of the ETS].[81]

The General Court also rejected the argument that the obligation to cover carbon emissions with allowances under the ETS 'necessarily give[s] rise to negative financial consequences which adversely affect the applicant's right to property and its freedom to pursue an economic activity'.[82] Although the EU ETS has not yet been challenged before investment arbitration, these decisions indicate that a market-based approach to phase out coal is likely to be more difficult to oppose based on property and investment protection grounds compared to phasing out coal through direct regulation.[83]

However, exceptionally high gas prices in 2022 following the war in Ukraine have benefited coal power, threatening the effectiveness of the EU decarbonisation

[78] J Lehne et al, 'The EU ETS: From Cornerstone to Catalyst – The Role of Carbon Pricing in Driving Green Innovation', E3G, Briefing Paper, April 2021, 10.

[79] COM(2020)564 final, 'An EU-wide assessment of national energy and climate plans', 14 and 26.

[80] Case T-16/04 *Arcelor SA v Parliament and Council* ECLI:EU:T:2010:54; and Case T-614/13 *Romonta GmbH v Commission* ECLI:EU:T:2014:835. Arcelor argued that its right to property was infringed because of the impact of the ETS which would make its production loss-making, given that it was difficult to further decarbonise its production process. See further A Boute, 'Combating Climate Change and Securing Electricity Supply: The Role of Investment Protection' (2007) 16 *European Energy and Environmental Law Review* 231.

[81] Case T-16/04 *Arcelor SA v Parliament and Council* (n 80) para 154.

[82] Case T-16/04 *Arcelor SA v Parliament and Council* (n 80) para 155.

[83] See, however, K Miles, *The Origins of International Investment Law* (CUP, 2013) at 189, warning that 'the justification that satisfied the European Court of Justice [in the *Arcelor* case] is unlikely to impress an investor–state arbitral tribunal'.

approach, as Member States returned to coal as a gas saving measure in response to the disruption of Russian exports.[84]

13.5. LIMITS TO THE ENVIRONMENTAL EFFECTIVENESS OF COAL PHASE-OUT THROUGH MARKET FORCES

The EU ETS was founded upon the electricity market liberalisation paradigm, and free market pricing is key in this process.[85] The 2019 Electricity Directive and Regulation emphasise the role of free market prices in providing the right incentives for investment in electricity generation.[86] Electricity market prices should 'ensure that only those resources will exit that genuinely have no value for the system as a whole'.[87] Improving price signals thus contributes to steering the decommissioning of power plants to target the least desirable and inefficient resources (eg coal-fired power plants). To enable prices to effectively reflect scarcity, EU law disciplines government interventions that distort the price formation mechanism and can 'result in inefficient plants being artificially kept in operation through public support, or in unnecessary new generation capacity being built'.[88] Price interventions are seen as 'constituting a fundamentally distortive measure'.[89]

By increasing the operating costs of carbon-intensive sources, carbon prices push coal-fired power generation down the price- and volume-based ranking of electricity producers.[90] This so-called 'merit order' effect reduces the annual operating hours of the most carbon-intensive units, ie coal power, and can in principle threaten their economic viability.[91] Dispatching that only partially (or not at all) reflects price signals can constitute a regulatory barrier affecting the level playing field between market participants and types of resources.[92] As seen above, until 2019, electricity produced from indigenous coal was able to benefit

[84] C Moore et al, 'European electricity review 2022' (Ember, January 2022), 6. See also C Hodgson and S Bernard, 'EU wind and solar push not enough to limit global warming as coal use remains stubborn' (*Financial Times*, 1 February 2022).

[85] European Commission, 'Proposal for a Directive Establishing a Scheme for Greenhouse Gas Emission Allowance Trading' COM(2001) 581 final, [2002] OJ C 75E/33.

[86] EMD, recitals 19 and 20; EMR, recital 22.

[87] Commission, 'Impact Assessment Accompanying the Proposal for the Fourth Energy Package' SWD(2016) 410 final, part 1/5 and 2/5 (Main text), 211.

[88] 'It is therefore critical to ensure that administrative and implicit price caps are removed in order to allow for scarcity pricing': EMR, recital 24. The Commission reaffirmed that, 'state interventions, often designed in an uncoordinated manner, have led to distortions of the wholesale electricity market', COM(2016) 861 final/2, 2 and COM(2016) 864 final, 3; and EMR, recital 6.

[89] The EMD acknowledges that public service obligations in the form of price setting 'constitute a fundamentally distortive measure': EMD, recital 22.

[90] Acworth et al, 'Emissions Trading and Electricity Sector Regulation' (n 22) 9.

[91] B Caldecott and J McDaniels, 'Stranded generation assets: Implications for European capacity mechanisms, energy markets and climate policy', January 2014, Stranded Assets Programme Working paper, 5. See also IEA, 'Implementing effective emissions trading systems' (2020), 40.

[92] Commission, 'Impact Assessment' (n 87), part 1/5 and 2/5 (Main text), 231.

from priority dispatch for reasons of security of supply, which effectively constituted a government subsidy for coal-fired power generation and a barrier to the phase-out of coal.[93] In 2019, the priority access regime for indigenous coal was removed from the Electricity Directive. Dispatching authorities must now 'take into account the economic precedence of electricity from available generating installations'.[94] Without priority access to the market, 'full utilisation of fossil fuel assets is not guaranteed'.[95] Thus, EU law indirectly weakened the economic case for coal-based generation, hence contributing to the closure of these installations through market forces.

EU law also disciplines subsidising investments in coal-fired power generation to avoid distorting the functioning of the market and supporting fossil fuel investments. In particular, the 2019 Electricity Regulation sets carbon dioxide (CO2) limits to power plants eligible for capacity mechanisms (ie 'temporary measure[s] to ensure the achievement of the necessary level of resource adequacy by remunerating resources for their availability'). For new power plants (commissioned on or after 4 July 2019), participation in a capacity mechanism is only possible if the plant emits less than 550g of CO2 per kilowatt-hour (kWh) of electricity produced. For existing power plants (in operation before 4 July 2019), the emission limit of 550g of CO2 per kWh – and a limit of 350kg of CO2 on average per year per installed kWe – will become applicable as of 1 July 2025.[96] With these CO2 emission limits, the EU restricts remuneration of the most polluting power plants, in accordance with its climate change agenda,[97] and signals the need to decommission investments in coal-fired power generation.[98] According to Frontier Economics, the CO2 limits are linked to the need to control 'supposedly fraught investments in the setup or continued operation of coal-fired power

[93] 2009 EMD, Article 15(4); 2003 EMD, Article 11(4); 1997 EMD, Article 8(4). Yoko Ito notes that this coal supporting mechanism was in contradiction with EU low-carbon policies (notably the EU ETS). Y Ito, 'EU Policy Background and Realities for "Coal Phase-out"' (The Institute of Energy Economics, Japan, November 2017), 4–5.

[94] Article 15, Directive 2009/72/EC concerning common rules for the internal market in electricity and repealing Directive 2003/54/EC [2009] OJ L211/29 ('2009 EMD').

[95] B Caldecott et al, 'The fate of European coal-fired power stations planned in the mid-2000s: Insights for policymakers, companies, and investors considering new coal' (Sustainable Finance Programme at the University of Oxford Smith School of Enterprise and the Environment, Working Paper, August 2017), 60.

[96] EMR, Article 22(4).

[97] According to Frontier Economics, the Commission is justifying the CO2 limit 'with the need to do more to protect the climate': Frontier Economics, '550g rule as an access requirement to capacity markets – How useful is such an approach?', Expert report commissioned by RWE AG, July 2017, 6. ACER describes the emission cap as 'an essential tool to limit the impact of Capacity Mechanisms on EU climate objectives' and 'a key element to enable [the energy transition]', by 'avoid[ing] financial support for generation capacity that … does not meet the environmental goals': ACER,' Capacity mechanisms: ACER publishes technical guidance for CO2 emission limits', 19 December 2019; and ACER, Opinion No 22/2019 of the European Union Agency for the Cooperation of Energy Regulators of 17 December 2019, 2.

[98] P Alves Dias et al, 'EU coal regions: opportunities and challenges ahead' (Publications Office of the European Union, Luxembourg, 2018), 37.

plants' and the premature decommissioning of coal-fired plants 'is clearly one of the [CO2 cap] regime's intended effects'.[99]

However, the energy crisis has interrupted the phase-out of coal through market forces, as high gas prices resulted in renewable energy replacing gas instead of coal in the merit order.[100] Structurally, the EU and its Member States responded to exceptionally high electricity prices in 2022 by interfering with the market to protect consumers.[101] Council Regulation (EU) 2022/1854 on an emergency intervention to address high energy prices set a cap on the market revenues of electricity produced from generators with lower marginal costs (eg wind and solar energy) at EUR 180 per MWh.[102] Although governments have a clear responsibility to protect consumers, and in particular the most vulnerable users, against exceptionally high prices in times of crisis, there is a risk that price interventions can distort the signals that are at the centre of the EU market-based approach to decarbonisation.[103]

13.6. ALIGNING REGULATED AND MARKET-BASED PHASE-OUTS

Besides regulatory intervention in the electricity market (eg through price caps), the role of the EU ETS as driver of decarbonisation can be distorted by national decisions to ban the use of coal, or phase out coal through direct regulation. Due to the 'waterbed effect', the forced closure of coal-fired power plants frees up emission allowances on the EU ETS for other polluting installations,[104]

[99] Frontier Economics, '550g rule' (n 97) 6. The European Parliament generally acknowledged that decisions by Member States 'to actively phase-out coal fired electricity generation' may be made either 'independently from or as a consequence of harmonised rules of capacity mechanisms'. The Parliament justified this by saying that a 'managed and planned retirement of coal-fired capacity would help to improve the functioning of the electricity system in addition to reaching Union climate and environmental objectives': European Parliament, Report on the proposal for a regulation on the internal market for electricity, A/2018/0042, 154–55.

[100] According to Moore et al, 'Using 2019 as the baseline, the growth in renewables output predominantly replaced coal in the first half of 2021. However, in the second half of the year, with fossil gas power more expensive than coal, new renewable output replaced fossil gas instead. Furthermore, the second half of 2021 saw some direct replacement of fossil gas with coal, equivalent to approximately 5% of total coal power generation in 2021.' Moore et al, 'European electricity review 2022' (n 84).

[101] On the political pressure to protect consumers against high energy prices, see eg European Parliament, 'Energy costs: MEPs debate measures to limit impact of price rises' (Press Release, 6 October 2021); M Khan, D Dombey and B Hall, 'France and Spain demand changes to EU energy market' (*Financial Times*, 5 October 2021).

[102] Council Regulation (EU) 2022/1854 of 6 October 2022 on an emergency intervention to address high energy prices, [2022] OJ L 261I/1.

[103] The European Union Agency for the Cooperation of Energy Regulators (ACER), 'ACER's preliminary assessment of Europe's high energy prices and the current wholesale electricity market design', November 2021, 12.

[104] In the context of the coal phase-out, 'the demand for EUAs falls significantly … yielding a market situation where EUAs are not subject to scarcity, i.e., the EUA cap lies above the level of total carbon emissions. As a consequence, the EU ETS becomes ineffective': C-P Anke et al, 'Coal

depressing carbon prices and thus improving the competitiveness of coal-fired power plants elsewhere in the system.[105] The challenge for the phase out of coal through market forces is thus 'how to ensure that ambitious national policies in one Member State do not result in other countries doing comparatively less'.[106] The scale of the waterbed effect is especially significant in the power sector, as a significant share of the demand for emission allowances comes from electricity producers.[107] Adjusting the ETS cap in accordance with the avoided emissions from a coal phase-out is commonly advocated as a way of counterbalancing the waterbed effect.[108]

In *Castelnou Energía v Commission*, the General Court used the 'reversed' waterbed effect to justify a Spanish subsidy mechanism supporting indigenous coal.[109] It was argued that on an aggregate level, the ETS will balance out the increased GHG emissions resulting from the Spanish support of coal power through the carbon price signal, driven up by the increased demand for allowances by the indigenous emitters.[110] The Court's reasoning is relevant in the coal phase-out context as it confirms that the ETS is the main instrument for controlling CO2 emissions, and acknowledges that emitting more will push up the carbon price while the cap will ensure that total system-wide emissions will not increase. Conversely, the effect of closing down coal-fired power plants through direct regulation on the carbon price can jeopardise the integrity of the market, and thus undermine the market-based phase out of coal.

With the Market Stability Reserve, established in 2015 to address the allowance surplus,[111] the EU automatically adjusts the supply of allowances to be

phase-outs and carbon prices: Interactions between EU emission trading and national carbon mitigation policies' (2020) 144 *Energy Policy* 6–7.

[105] Acworth et al, 'Emissions Trading and Electricity Sector Regulation' (n 22) 28–29.

[106] Rocha et al, 'A stress test' (n 35) 30–31.

[107] Anke et al, 'Coal phase-outs and carbon prices' (n 104) 1–2. In fact, arguably 'it is mainly the power sector with its underlying market dynamics that strongly drives equilibrium prices in the EU ETS' (ibid 2). In other words, 'the regulatory phase out of coal-fired power generators … will have a strong effect on the emissions profile of the covered sectors': Acworth et al, 'Emissions trading in pursuit of electricity decarbonisation' (n 57) 35.

[108] According to the IEA, the waterbed challenge can be overcome by adjusting the ETS cap or design: International Energy Agency (IEA), 'Implementing Effective Emissions Trading Systems: Lessons from international experiences' (2020), 37. See also Acworth et al, 'Emissions Trading in Regulated Electricity Markets' (n 57) 66; and D Keles and H Ümitcan Yilmaz, 'Decarbonisation through coal phase-out in Germany and Europe – Impact on Emissions, electricity prices and power production' (2020) 141 *Climate Policy* 11–12.

[109] Case T-57/11 *Castelnou Energía, SL v Commission*, ECLI:EU:T:2014:1021.

[110] ibid, paras 113 and 218. (The Court noted that because of the fixed cap on the total quantity of allowances, 'the alleged increase in greenhouse gas emissions from indigenous coal power plants caused by the contested measure cannot, in itself, prevent the Kingdom of Spain from complying with the emissions limits resulting from the implementation of [the ETS Directive] and, therefore, lead to an increase in harmful emissions in Spain.').

[111] Commission, Proposal for a decision concerning the establishment and operation of a market stability reserve for the Union greenhouse gas emission trading scheme and amending Directive 2003/87/EC, COM(2014) 20 final, 2. See also recitals 4 and 5 of Decision (EU) 2015/1814 concerning the establishment and operation of a market stability reserve for the Union greenhouse

auctioned.[112] This can be relevant in the context of Member States' coal phase-outs, which disrupt the demand for emission allowances and thereby the carbon price,[113] provided the mechanism can sufficiently rapidly offset the carbon price drop resulting from national coal phase-out policies.[114] The revised ETS Directive also introduced an optional mechanism for cancellation of allowances whereby Member States may reduce the total quantity of allowances they will auction when they phase out power plants.[115] The voluntary cancellation mechanism is a clear recognition of the fact that in terms of investments, decarbonisation is not just about adding low-carbon technology, but also involves phasing out generating capacity. By opting for this cancellation option, Member States can help balance the surplus of allowances that would otherwise be created in the ETS market. It is a new possibility of adapting the EU ETS cap to the effects of coal phase-outs. This should help counteract the waterbed effect and stabilise the carbon price, thus contributing to the market-based phase-out of coal. However, with calls to intervene in the ETS to bring the level of carbon prices down in the context of the energy crisis,[116] governments might find it difficult to cancel carbon allowances and thereby contribute to increasing the scarcity of allowances on the market.

13.7. CONCLUSION

The EU aims to achieve decarbonisation through market forces, and not by banning the use of coal. Electricity market reforms introduced in 2019 further

gas emission trading scheme and amending Directive 2003/87/EC [2015] OJ L264/1 (the 'MSR Decision').

[112] See recital 5 of the MSR Decision. According to Acworth et al, 'automatic cancellations of allowances above a pre-defined threshold as preordained through the MSR will reduce the emissions cap and strengthen the environmental effectiveness of the system': Acworth et al, 'Emissions trading in pursuit of electricity decarbonisation' (n 57) 32.

[113] According to IETA, 'the potential to address the problem of uncoordinated policies at the European level' is an (unstated) objective of the MSR. International Emissions Trading Association, 'Allowance Reserves Across Emission Trading Systems', Briefing note.

[114] ibid. See also Acworth et al, 'Emissions trading in pursuit of electricity decarbonisation' (n 57) at 31: 'the ability of quantity-based stabilisation instruments to adjust for structural changes such as a regulatory driven coal phase out has been debated in the EU ETS (Germany). Debate has centered on the role of the MSR *versus* direct changes to the allowance cap as well as targeted cancellation of allowances to reflect mandatory closures in fossil fuel-based generation.' See also A Marcu and D Vangenechten, 'Addressing the supply-demand imbalance in the EU ETS through the Market Stability Reserve' (European Roundtable on Climate Change and Sustainable Transition (ERCST), 8 February 2021) 5.

[115] 'In the event of closure of electricity generation capacity in their territory due to additional national measures, Member States may cancel allowances from the total quantity of allowances to be auctioned by them.' Directive 2018/410 amending Directive 2003/87/EC to enhance cost-effective emission reductions and low-carbon investments, and Decision (EU) 2015/1814 [2018] OJ L76/3, Article 12(4).

[116] M Khan, 'EU leaders battle over carbon price as energy costs soar' (*Financial Times*, 17 December 2021).

reinforced the market foundation of the EU decarbonisation policy. Until the energy crisis that started in 2021 and deteriorated in 2022 following the start of the war in Ukraine, the EU market-based approach was effective in pushing coal-fired power plants out of the market. This market-based approach has also helped the EU avoid similar arbitration challenges that Member States, having forced the closure of coal-fired power plants through direct environmental regulation, are facing. Arbitration claims against coal phase-out decisions have generated severe criticism against the legitimacy of investment arbitration and investment treaties, in particular the Energy Charter Treaty. In the context of the controversy on the constraining effect of investment law on decarbonisation, the EU experience shows that market-based decarbonisation mechanisms can play a role in moving away from coal, while limiting tensions with international investment protection.

However, the EU experience also shows the significant economic, political, and regulatory risks to which this less intrusive phase-out approach is exposed. The impact of geopolitical turmoil on energy markets can jeopardise the contribution of the market to decarbonisation, and the closure of carbon-intensive units in particular. Taking into account this important limit to the environmental effectiveness of market mechanisms, reform of international investment law is needed to ensure that states that are determined to phase out coal power, regardless of high energy prices, can do so through traditional environmental regulation.

Part IV

The Future of Investment and EU Law

14

New EU International Investment Agreements with Third States: A 'New' Paradigm and the EU Constitutional Framework Challenge

MARIA FANOU

14.1. INTRODUCTION: A NEW FRONTIER FOR THE EU COMMON COMMERCIAL POLICY[1]

AFTER THE ENTRY into force of the Treaty of Lisbon in 2009,[2] when exclusive competence in foreign direct investment (FDI) was conferred to the EU by Article 207 TFEU, investment presented itself 'as a new frontier' for the EU common commercial policy (CCP).[3] This marked the beginning of a new era in which the EU, a 'historically' not 'significant' actor in the field of investment law,[4] would gradually, albeit non-seamlessly, emerge as a 'global leader'.[5]

The transition from multiple national frameworks to a unified EU investment policy was not easy. The European Commission (hereinafter the Commission) first had to deal with the suspicion of the EU Member States, which until that point had enjoyed the competence of shaping their own investment policies.[6] Originally, European states had been pioneers in the conclusion of bilateral

[1] All views expressed are strictly personal to the author.

[2] Treaty on the Functioning of the EU (TFEU) (into force on 1 December 2009).

[3] European Commission, Communication, 'Towards a Comprehensive European International Investment Policy' COM(2010) 343 final, 7 July 2010, 2.

[4] ibid 21.

[5] European Parliament, Report on the future of EU international investment policy, Rapporteur: Anna Cavazzini (2021/2176(INI)) Committee on International Trade, A9-0166/2022, 7.

[6] Before Lisbon, Member States had only agreed to allow the EU to participate in specific investment negotiations. Such an example was the EU's participation in the negotiations of the Energy Charter Treaty (1990–1994).

investment treaties (BITs), whilst other developed states, including for instance the United States of America, hesitantly followed their lead.[7] In making use of the new competence, the EU, in light of its 'special responsibility'[8] to introduce a new paradigm in its new generation of trade and investment protection agreements, would travel in the opposite direction, moving away from traditional BITs.[9] This included, most notably, its aspiration to reform the 'old' investor-state dispute settlement (ISDS) mechanism in the form of investor-state arbitration,[10] which was subject to a generalised wave of criticisms.[11] For instance, criticisms of ISDS include allegations relating to the lack of independence and impartiality of the arbitral tribunals, the lack of systemic checks and, relatedly, a second degree of review of arbitral awards (an appellate system), as well as an alleged dearth of transparency.[12]

One of the first 'deep and comprehensive' trade deals which were bringing together trade and investment provisions was the EU-Singapore FTA (EUSFTA),[13] whilst the most 'comprehensive EU FTA' is the EU-Canada Comprehensive Economic and Trade Agreement (CETA), which was officially signed in October 2016.[14] CETA is also the first international agreement of the EU that was concluded implementing the EU's ISDS vision. Among other agreements, the following are worthy of mention: the EU-Vietnam Free Trade Agreement (EU-Vietnam FTA) and the EU-Vietnam investment protection agreement (EU-Vietnam IPA),[15] the EU and Mexico trade agreement (EU-Mexico FTA),

[7] See, eg, Rudolf Dolzer and Christoph Schreuer, *Principles of International Investment Law* (OUP, 2008), 17–18.

[8] See European Commission, 'Trade for all – Towards a more responsible trade and investment policy', October 2015, para 4.1.2.

[9] For the avoidance of any confusion, in this contribution, by traditional BITs or traditional investment agreements, we refer to agreements roughly concluded before 2010. The blueprint for these agreements that formed the European States' investment treaty practice was the 1967 OECD Draft Convention on the Protection of Foreign Property. Also, throughout this contribution we will be referring simply to EU international investment agreements or EU IIAs.

[10] The acronym ISDS stands for 'investor-state dispute settlement'. Thus, all forms of dispute settlement, including the envisaged investment court system (ICS) and other bilateral or multilateral court-solutions for investor-state disputes, are part thereof. Confusingly, ISDS is often presented as a synonym of arbitration. In this contribution, there is no attempt to attribute, implicitly or explicitly, connotations to any of these acronyms. However, only for purposes of clarity, the term 'traditional ISDS' or 'ad hoc system' is used to encapsulate pure arbitration-solutions.

[11] See for a collection of contributions on various points of critique, Michael Waibel et al (eds), *The Backlash against Investment Arbitration: Perceptions and Reality* (Kluwer 2010).

[12] See indicatively among many different summaries of critiques against ISDS, UNCTAD, 'Reform of Investor-State Dispute Settlement: In Search of a Roadmap', IIA Issues Note No 2, United Nations (2013); IBA Arbitration Subcommittee on Investment Treaty Arbitration, 'Consistency, Efficiency and Transparency in Investment Treaty Arbitration', Report (11-2018).

[13] The EU-Singapore FTA and Investment Protection Agreement (IPA) were signed on 19 October 2018. In February 2019, the European Parliament gave its consent, and the trade and investment agreements will now continue their ratification process for their entry into force.

[14] Commission, 'Trade for all …' (n 8) para 5.2.1.

[15] The agreement was signed on 30 June 2019.

on which an agreement in principle has already been reached,[16] as well as the trade deal which was too 'ambitious and strategic'[17] to materialise, but is now already obsolete, the Transatlantic Trade and Investment Partnership between the EU and the United States (TTIP).[18] Finally, negotiations for an investment agreement with several other third states have been launched, with some ongoing, and others on hold.[19]

This chapter explores the 'new' paradigm introduced by the EU in its investment agreements with third states, shedding light on its key elements in terms of content, but also on the EU constitutional law challenge it faces. First, this chapter begins with what is widely presented as the most radical novelty of the EU paradigm, that is the establishment of a permanent ICS to replace traditional ISDS (section 14.2). Thereafter, it discusses the real novelty of the EU paradigm, namely how the redefinition of substantive investment standards has helped to achieve a balance with the right to regulate (section 14.3). This novelty, the chapter argues, is intertwined with the main constitutional limitation the EU will have to face in seeing its ambitions as a global actor coming to fruition in the future (section 14.4). Section 14.5 offers a conclusion.

14.2. ISDS IN EU INTERNATIONAL INVESTMENT AGREEMENTS

ISDS provisions are one of the most common and distinctive features of investment agreements. Usually, international arbitration (whether administered or not) is the chosen form of ISDS. The debates on the reform of the ad hoc ISDS regime began at the same time as its genesis, making it a constant work-in-progress.[20] One of the most significant challenges for the EU investment policy was the EU's participation in ISDS. Soon after acquiring the new competence on FDI, the EU introduced two regulations that both had an impact on investor-state disputes. First, the Grandfathering Regulation 1219/2012 established

[16] European Commission, 'EU and Mexico reach new agreement on trade', Press Release IP/18/782 (21 April 2018).

[17] Commission, 'Trade for all …' (n 8) para 5.2.1.

[18] The negotiations started in 2013 and ended in 2016. A Concept Paper on TTIP was the first instance in which the EU introduced its proposal for an investment court. See European Commission, 'Investment in TTIP and beyond – the Path for Reform' (5 May 2015) (TTIP Concept Paper).

[19] See, eg, the EU-China negotiations on the Comprehensive Agreement on Investment (CAI). The agreement in principle only included a commitment to continue negotiations in relation to investment protection and investment dispute settlement. See in that regard, European Commission, Press Release IP/20/2541, 'EU and China reach agreement in principle on investment' (30 December 2020). The EU has also launched negotiations with India (for an investment agreement), Australia ('for a comprehensive and ambitious trade agreement'), Philippines (negotiations for an agreement 'similar' to the one with Singapore and Vietnam, currently on hold).

[20] See, indicatively, a collective account of initiatives towards reform in UNCTAD, 'Taking Stock of IIA Reform', IIA Issues Note No 1 (March 2016).

transitional arrangements for BITs between Member States and third countries (extra-EU BITs) in 2012,[21] and, two years later, the Financial Responsibility Regulation created a framework for managing financial responsibility linked to ISDS tribunals established by international agreements to which the EU is a party.[22] The Financial Responsibility Regulation aimed to address, as an internal EU law matter, the issues arising from extra-EU BITs without prejudice to the scope of the EU's competence, including the issue of who should be the respondent in each case (ie, the EU, the Member State, or both) and, therefore, who should bear the costs and be held liable to pay for the damages granted.[23] Having dealt with these two issues, the core challenge was what form of ISDS the EU would include in its agreements.

14.2.1. A Gradually Evolving EU Approach

In its extra-EU relations, the EU never questioned the need for the conclusion of investment agreements and the inclusion of ISDS.[24] Instead, the Commission has expressly linked the attractiveness of a host state as an investment destination to the availability of ISDS. As it was explicitly noted in one of the early policy documents, ISDS 'is such an established feature of investment agreements that its absence would, in fact, discourage investors and make a host economy less attractive than others. For these reasons, future EU agreements including investment protection should include [ISDS]'.[25]

[21] Regulation (EU) No 1219/2012 of the European Parliament and of the Council of 12 December 2012 establishing transitional arrangements for bilateral investment agreements between Member States and third countries [2012] OJ L351/40–46 (20 December 2012) (the Grandfathering Regulation). See also ch 12.

[22] Regulation (EU) No 912/2014 of the European Parliament and of the Council of 23 July 2014 establishing a framework for managing financial responsibility linked to investor-to-state dispute settlement tribunals established by international agreements to which the European Union is party [2014] OJ L257/121–34 (28 August 2014). See generally, Angelos Dimopoulos, 'The involvement of the EU in Investor-State dispute settlement: A question of responsibilities' (2014) 51(6) *CMLR* 1671–1720.

[23] Notably, the EU did not assume the risk for any Member States' acts in violation of their BIT obligations towards investors. See Financial Responsibility Regulation (n 22) recitals 3 and 5. So far, we have only seen one instance in which the EU was the respondent (in an extra-EU ECT case; *Nord Stream 2 AG v European Union*, PCA Case No 2020-07). Previously, in *Electrabel SA v Hungary*, ICSID Case No ARB/07/19, Decision on Jurisdiction, Applicable Law and Liability (30 November 2012), para 3.21, the Commission argued that the EU and not Hungary was the right respondent. Nevertheless, since the claimants had chosen to submit their dispute to the ICSID Centre and the EU is not (and could not since it is not a state but a REIO) a Contracting State to the ICSID Convention, it could not be a respondent to the case either.

[24] cf the approach taken by other economies. See eg the 2005 US-Australia FTA (AUSFTA). Empirical evidence available is inconclusive when it comes to the impact of investment agreements on FDI. UNCTAD, 'The Role of International Investment Agreements in Attracting Foreign Direct Investment to Developing Countries', UNCTAD Series on International Investment Policies for Development', UNCTAD/DIAE/IA/2009/5 (New York and Geneva, 2009).

[25] European Commission, 'Towards a Comprehensive …' (n 3) 10.

In light of this approach, the EU not only included ISDS in its agreements, but, in the early exploratory days of its new competence, was also willing to work out its participation in the existing *ad hoc* regime, including its accession to the ICSID Convention.[26] The investment chapter of the EUSFTA, and the ISDS mechanism originally included therein, is illustrative of this original intent.[27] Nevertheless, the EU soon realised that acceding to the ICSID Convention was not a tangible option.[28] In addition to this realisation, EU institutional actors, such as notably the European Parliament, had endorsed several of the critiques of the traditional ad hoc treaty arbitration.[29] The Commission's new policy would have to please those EU institutional actors given that, post-Lisbon, the Parliament was empowered with the final word in the conclusion of EU international agreements.[30] Against this background, opting for traditional ISDS clauses was almost a non-option. In 2015, and in the context of the then ongoing TTIP negotiations, the EU introduced its proposal for a permanent ICS.[31] In January 2016, the EU invited Canada to revisit the ISDS chapter of the CETA in order to include a permanent ICS.[32]

In a nutshell, this envisaged permanent ICS comprises a first instance tribunal as well as an appellate tribunal. Its members will not be appointed by the parties to a given dispute but by a Joint Committee of the Contracting Parties,

[26] The Convention on the Settlement of Investment Disputes between States and the Nationals of Other States, 18.03.1965, 575 UNTS 159. See on this, European Commission, 'Towards a Comprehensive …' (n 3) 21.

[27] Originally, in addition to the EUSFTA, both CETA and TTIP envisaged to include a *traditional* ISDS chapter. The issue of ISDS was left open in the Vietnam agreement even after the parties had reached an agreement on all other issues and '*in light of the new EU approach on investment dispute settlement*', as it was expressly noted in an EU Memo issued in August 2015. See European Commission, Memo, 'EU and Vietnam reach agreement on free trade deal' (4 August 2015).

[28] The ICSID Convention does not provide for the accession of Regional Economic International Organisations (Article 67 ICSID Convention). An amendment of the ICSID Convention would be the only solution for a REIO to accede to it, but such amendment would require unanimity (Articles 65–66 ICSID Convention).

[29] See also European Parliament Resolution, P7_TA(2011)0141, European international investment Policy, European Parliament resolution of 6 April 2011 on the future European international investment policy (2010/2203(INI)), para 33 (The European Parliament '[i]s aware that the EU cannot use existing … (ICSID) and … (UNCITRAL) dispute settlement mechanisms since the EU as such is a member of neither organisation; calls on the EU to include a chapter on dispute settlement in each new EU investment treaty in line with the reforms suggested in this resolution; requests that the Commission and the Member States take up their responsibility as major international players to work towards the necessary reforms of the ICSID and UNCITRAL rules'). See also European Parliament Resolution of 8 July 2015 containing the European Parliament's recommendations to the European Commission on the negotiations for the Transatlantic Trade and Investment Partnership (TTIP) (2014/2228(INI)).

[30] See, eg, Articles 207, 218(6) and 218(10) TFEU.

[31] European Commission, 'Commission Proposes New Investment Court System for TTIP and Other EU Trade and Investment Negotiations', IP/15/5651 (16 September 2015). For a more detailed discussion of the parallel and intermingling negotiations leading to this proposal and shaping the EU policy, see Maria Fanou, 'The CETA ICS and the Autonomy of the EU Legal Order in Opinion 1/17 – A Compass for the Future' (2020) 22 *CYELS* 106, 109–15.

[32] European Commission, Press Release IP/16/399, 'CETA: EU and Canada agree on new approach on investment in trade agreement (29 February 2016) (CETA Press Release).

and their appointment will be on a full-time basis.[33] As having multiple bilateral investment courts (one per EU international investment agreement) would not be sustainable in the long run, the EU plan has always been the multilateralisation of the exercise and the establishment of a multilateral investment court (MIC).[34] The EU has successfully branded this court idea as a radical departure from ISDS.[35] The question, however, is whether the proposal for a permanent ICS (multilateral or not) is in fact such a novel idea.

14.2.2. A Permanent ICS: A New Opportunity for an Old Idea?

> Plainly, the next advance to be urged along this line is to pass on from an arbitral tribunal … to a permanent court composed of judges who devote their entire time to the performance of judicial duties and proceed in accordance with a sense of judicial obligation, not to adjust or compromise differences, but to decide upon rights in accordance with the facts and the law.[36]

This quote could be an excerpt from one of the many EU policy papers issued since the 2010s advocating for a permanent ICS, and eventually a MIC,[37] but as surprising as it may be, this is not the case. These are the words of Elihu Root, the Founder of the American Society of International Law, which date back to 1912. Root's thoughts are indicative of the fact that the debate on arbitral tribunals versus permanent courts is far from new.

The need for an investment instrument and the establishment of an investment court was discussed in the 1950s at International Law Association (ILA) conferences.[38] The element of permanence is also present in the establishment of the Iran-US Claims Tribunal, which was created by a treaty to arbitrate cases

[33] For a summary of the core features of the CETA ICS, see Maria Fanou, 'The independence and impartiality of the hybrid CETA Investment Court System: Reflections in the aftermath of Opinion 1/17' (2020) 4(1) *Europe and the World* 6–8.

[34] The Council of the EU gave the Commission the mandate to negotiate the creation of a MIC in March 2018. See Council of the EU, 'Negotiating directives for a Convention establishing a multilateral court for the settlement of investment disputes', 12981/17 ADD 1 DCL 1 (20 March 2018). The establishment of a MIC is part of the discussions for the reform of ISDS under the auspices of the UNCITRAL Working Group III.

[35] ISDS has been called 'the most toxic acronym in Europe', according to one former Trade Commissioner. See Paul Ames, 'ISDS: The most toxic acronym in Europe' (*Politico*, 17 September 2015).

[36] Elihu Root, 'Towards Making Peace Permanent', Nobel Lecture 1912.

[37] Soon, it became clear that the multilateralisation (that is the MIC) is an inbuilt element to the new ICS policy (European Commission, Inception Impact Report (1 August 2016) (Inception Impact Report), 5. To this effect, a transition provision (such as the one included in Article 8.29 of CETA) is included in all EU deals. Notably, a similar transition provision is now found in the new Dutch Model BIT making clear that the MIC shall be the forum for investor-state disputes arising from extra-EU BITs.

[38] See ILA (1948), 'Draft Statutes of the Arbitral Tribunal for Foreign Investment and of the Foreign Investments Court'. Reproduced in International Investment Instruments: A Compendium', Volume III, compiled by UNCTAD, UNCTAD/DTCI/30, 259–272; ILA, 'Nationalization' (1958) 48 *Int'l L Ass'n Rep Conf* 130–239; 'Juridical Aspects of Nationalization and Foreign Property' (1960) 49 *Int'l L Ass'n Rep Conf* 175–243 and 'Juridical Aspects of Nationalization and Foreign Property'

between individuals and one of the two contracting states under UNCITRAL rules. Its members were appointed by Iran and the US.[39] The idea of a permanent court has also been part of the discussions on reforming the system in different contexts and forums, including UNCTAD,[40] the WTO[41] and the OECD.[42]

When one examines the hybrid CETA ICS, or discusses the design of a future MIC, one realises that this idea – name it old, name it new – is certainly not as radical as branded. Instead, it is coupled with some borrowed things that stem from the reliance on pre-existing tools, such as the International Bar Association Guidelines on Conflicts of Interest in International Arbitration, and organisations, such as notably the ICSID Convention and the ICSID Rules.[43] Importantly, the 'awards' that will be rendered by the envisaged permanent ICS will be enforced via existing conventions, notably, and perplexingly, the ICSID Convention and the New York Convention.[44] For instance, Article 8.41(3) CETA explicitly refers to 'final award[s] issued under the ICSID Convention'. It is beyond the scope of this contribution to discuss the question of enforcement of awards of the permanent ICS/MIC and the various questions raised by this dubious reliance. As problematic as that may be, such reliance is another indicator that radically 'new' solutions are rather scarce.

This old idea has found a new opportunity thanks to, or because of, the EU's role, assertion and persuasion as a global actor,[45] as well as timing, that being one of backlash against the system. It comes, however, with what is indeed an

(1962) 50 *Int'l L Ass'n Rep Conf* 101–55. See also Taylor St John and Yulia Chernykh, 'Déjà vu? Investment Court Proposals from 1960 and Today' (*EJIL Blog*, 15 May 2018).

[39] See generally on the Iran-US Claims Tribunal, Charles N Brower, *The Iran-United States Claims Tribunal* (1990) 224 *Collected Courses of the Hague Academy of International Law* 123–396. See also Bernd Ehle, 'Article I' in Reinmar Wolff (ed), *New York Convention on the Recognition and Enforcement of Foreign Arbitral Awards – Commentary* (Beck, Hart, Nomos 2012) 26–84, 54–55.

[40] See, eg, in 2013, UNCTAD included the alternative of a permanent investment court in its paper under the title 'Reform of Investor-State Dispute Settlement: In search of a Roadmap', Special Issue for the Multilateral Dialogue on Investment [IIA Issues Note No 2, 2013].

[41] Quite indicatively, discussions on investment were part of the Doha Round Agenda (2001) but, as it was confirmed two years later, governments were unable to reach consensus on the start of negotiations. The failure of the creation of an investment instrument within the WTO failed mainly because of the opposition of developing states. See in that regard, Muthucumaraswamy Sornarajah, *The International Law on Foreign Investment* (CUP, 2017), 2.

[42] See, eg, OECD, Negotiating Group on the Multilateral Agreement on Investment (MAI), DAFFE/MAI(98)9/FINAL (20 April 1998). The negotiations on MAI were discontinued in 1998, for several reasons including the inability to reach an agreement even between like-minded countries. See Yoshi Kodama, 'Dispute Settlement under the Draft Multilateral Agreement on Investment. The Quest for an Effective Investment Dispute Settlement Mechanism and its Failure' (1999) 16(3) *JOIA* 45–88, 47–52. See also Dolzer and Schreuer (n 7) 18–19 and 26–27.

[43] The EU has incorporated the ICSID Arbitration Rules and Additional Facility Arbitration rules in all its trade and investment agreements that include rules on investment protection – this explains the 'particular interest of the EU in ICSID'. See Commission's Proposal for a Council Decision on the position to be taken on behalf of the European Union in the International Centre for Settlement of Investment Disputes (ICSID), COM(2022) 38 final (9 February 2022), 2.1.

[44] The Convention on the Recognition and Enforcement of Foreign Arbitral Awards, 10 June 1958, 330 UNTS 3, I.

[45] The EU is also notably the largest exporter and importer of FDI in the world.

innovation of the new EU international investment agreements (IIAs), and a sign that drafters strived to learn something from the failures of the past. This is the approach taken in relation to the substantive standards of protection of foreign investments.[46]

14.3. SUBSTANTIVE STANDARDS AND THE RIGHT TO REGULATE IN EU INVESTMENT AGREEMENTS

Traditionally, IIAs include a list of substantive provisions to protect investment and investors against the conduct of the state where the investment is made (host state).[47] For example, protection against expropriation, direct or indirect, is a standard provision in most if not all investment agreements.[48] Another important standard found in investment agreements relates to fair and equitable treatment (FET).[49] Most favoured nation (MFN) treatment clauses and full protection and security (FPS)[50] are other examples of frequently included substantive standards. Historically, the language chosen for these standards was evaluative, to achieve more flexibility and adaptability to future factual scenarios, as well as circumstances that could not have been anticipated at the time of the conclusion of the agreement. Progressively, in the current era of 'recalibration',[51] and as more and more developed states found themselves on the respondent's side, there has been a significant shift towards more precise language in defining and limiting investment standards in order to preserve states' regulatory powers.[52] In this regard, the EU has been pioneering in its investment agreements.

[46] Other innovations such as market access and liberalisation go beyond the scope of this contribution.

[47] For a comprehensive account of the substantive protection of foreign investment, see Yannick Radi, *Rules and Practices of International Investment Law and Arbitration* (CUP, 2020).

[48] Protection from expropriation is found in several international texts, including the EU Charter of Fundamental Rights (Article 17) and the European Convention on Human Rights (Article 1 of the First Additional Protocol). On investment protection under the ECHR, see Maria Fanou and Vassilis Tzevelekos, 'The Shared Territory of the ECHR and International Investment Law' in Yannick Radi (ed), *Research Handbook on Human Rights and Investments* (Elgar, 2018), 93–136.

[49] On FET see generally Christoph Schreuer, 'Fair and Equitable Treatment in Arbitral Practice' (2005) 6 *Journal of World Investment and Trade* 357–86; B Choudhury, 'Evolution or Devolution? Defining Fair and Equitable Treatment in International Investment Law' (2005) 6 *Journal of World Investment and Trade* 297–320.

[50] It is sometimes referred to as protection and security, protection, full protection and legal security, most constant protection and security and adequate protection and security.

[51] See the conceptualisation of the stages of the investment regime, and the description of the current phase as one of recalibration in Jürgen Kurtz, 'The Shifting Landscape of International Investment Law and its Commentary' (2012) 106 *AJIL* 686.

[52] See indicatively the Statement of the European Union and the United States on Shared Principles for International Investment (10 April 2012), where the United States and the EU express their commitment to implementing strong investment protection 'while still preserving the authority to adopt and maintain measures necessary to regulate in the public interest to pursue certain public policies'. See also in scholarship, Federico Ortino, 'Refining the Content and Role of Investment "Rules" and "Standards": A New Approach to International Investment Treaty Making' (2013) 28(1)

Following calls from the Parliament,[53] and in line with the negotiating mandates of the Council to the Commission,[54] EU policy had to move away from the old approach, in which limitations on investment protection were rather rare. This shift has been achieved in various ways. In some instances, standard-specific limitations are included in the specific provision. In addition, a separate chapter with exceptions applicable to an entire international agreement may be included, as is the case in CETA.[55] Limitations and exceptions are inspired by pre-existing case law and debates.

Without entering into a detailed discussion of the various investment standards, this section will explore just some, focusing on how their scope has been limited in EU investment agreements (section 14.3.1) and how they have been balanced with the preservation of the states' right to regulate (section 14.3.2).

14.3.1. Limiting the Scope of Substantive Standards

Starting with expropriation, it is a right of states that is subject to conditions of legality (notably, compensation). There are distinctions to be drawn between direct and indirect expropriation. Direct expropriation is relatively straightforward as a concept involving deprivation of property, while indirect expropriation consists of measures that leave the titles of the property unaffected, but which deprive the investors of their ability to meaningfully utilise it. The vast majority of investment agreements provide no definition of indirect expropriation. Although 'it is well established that the mere exercise by government of regulatory powers that create impediments to business or entail the payment of taxes or other levies does not of itself constitute expropriation',[56] there is divergence in approaches as to which measures are tantamount to indirect expropriation.[57]

ICSID Review 152; Caroline Henckels, 'Protecting Regulatory Autonomy through Greater Precision in Investment Treaties: The TPP, CETA, and TTIP' (2016) 19 *Journal of International Economic Law* 27.

[53] See, eg, Resolution of 6 April 2011 (n 29) 23 ('future investment agreements concluded by the EU must respect the capacity for public intervention').

[54] See, eg, Council of the EU, 'Directives for the negotiation on the Transatlantic Trade and Investment Partnership between the European Union and the United States of America', ST 11103/13 DCL 1 (17 June 2013), para 23 (noting that the objective of the investment protections 'should be without prejudice to the right of the EU and the Member States to adopt and enforce, in accordance with their respective competences, measures necessary to pursue legitimate public policy objectives such as social, environmental, security, stability of the financial system, public health and safety in a non-discriminatory manner'); Council of the EU, MIC Negotiating Directives (n 34) para 6, where the Council notes that the Convention establishing the MIC should have provisions 'drafted in a way which allows their effective use by the EU'.

[55] See, eg, CETA Chapter 28 entitled 'Exceptions', and Article 28.9 therein where exceptions applicable to culture in relation inter alia to Chapter 8 (investment) are repeated.

[56] *Telenor Mobile Communications AS v The Republic of Hungary*, ICSID Case No ARB/04/15 Award (13 September 2006), para 64.

[57] See, eg, *Técnicas Medioambientales Tecmed, SA v The United Mexican States*, ICSID Case No ARB (AF)/00/2 2004, Award (29 May 2003) paras 115–116; *Telenor Mobile* (n 56) paras 64ff. See

Two main doctrines have been deployed in arbitral practice: 'sole effects'[58] and 'police powers'.[59] According to the police powers doctrine, states should not be held liable for certain measures they take when they exercise their regulatory powers, and damage is caused by non-discriminatory regulation that is adopted in good faith and protects a public welfare objective.[60] As long as these key requirements are met, state conduct will fall under the police powers doctrine, and the investor may suffer interferences with the investment. The impact of the conduct on the investment is irrelevant. As to the mitigation of the scope and effects of the doctrine, this can be achieved by examining the purpose of the national measure interfering with the investment. However, while this idea has generated – mostly academic – debate, arbitral practice has been rather reluctant to fully endorse it.[61] With respect to sole effects, only the effects of the state measure on property are examined and primarily in terms of whether they are tantamount to an expropriation.[62] The aims pursued by the national policy impacting the investment are, to a large extent, irrelevant.

The EU approach endorses a form of the customary police powers doctrine. Indicatively, CETA includes an interpretative annex on expropriation (Annex 8-A) that offers interpretative guidance about the definition of indirect expropriation. To this effect, it includes a list of factors that can be taken into account when determining whether a measure constitutes an indirect expropriation.[63] The message that stems from this Annex and the list is that the economic effect of the measure does not suffice for it to be deemed expropriatory. Other factors should carry weight, namely the duration, the degree of interference with investors' distinct and reasonable investment-backed expectations, as well as the object, context and intent of a measure.[64] The inclusion of 'intent' here presents a novelty, perhaps attributed to the EU, in comparison to the text of other IIAs which have served as a model for these

also generally Yves Fortier and Stephen Drymer, 'Indirect Expropriation in the Law of International Investment: I Know It When I See It, or Caveat Investor' (2004) 19(2) *ICSID Review* 293–327.

[58] See, eg, *Metalclad Corporation v The United Mexican States*, ICSID Case No ARB(AF)/97/1, Award (30 August 2000), para 102; *Compañiá de Aguas del Aconquija SA and Vivendi Universal SA v Argentine Republic*, ICSID Case No ARB/97/3, Award (21 November 2000), para 7.5.20.

[59] See, eg, *Saluka Investments BV v The Czech Republic*, UNCITRAL, Partial Award (17 March 2006), paras 484, 255.

[60] *MethanexCorp v USA* (UNCITRAL) Final Award on Jurisdiction and Merits (3 August 2005), para 410 ('non-discriminatory regulation for a public purpose'); *Saluka* (n 59) paras 255, 262.

[61] *Azurix Corp v Argentine Republic* (ICSID Case No ARB/01/12), Award (14 July 2006), para 310 (the tribunal found this criterion 'insufficient').

[62] *Patrick Mitchell v The Democratic Republic of Congo* (ICSID Case No ARB/99/7), Decision on the Application for Annulment (1 November 2006), para 53; *Biwater Gauff (Tanzania) LTD v United Republic of Tanzania* (ICSID Case No ARB/05/22), Award (24 July 2008), paras 463–67; *Telenor Mobile* (n 56) para 70 (where the tribunal mentions the 'divergence' of views on this matter).

[63] Article 8.12 CETA explicitly notes that Article 8.12(1) shall be interpreted in accordance with Annex 8-A. It also includes an exclusion from its scope of compulsory licenses in relation to intellectual property rights (Article 8.12(5)).

[64] CETA, Annex 8-A, Article 2(b)–(d).

provisions contained in the 'expropriation-Annex'.[65] It has thus drawn criticism.[66] When a regulatory measure aims to protect legitimate public goals (a non-exhaustive list of such goals is provided) then the threshold is higher for it to amount to indirect expropriation; it has to be manifestly excessive and discriminatory.[67]

Another controversial standard in the arbitration practice has been the FET standard,[68] which is interconnected with indirect expropriation. Different international agreements use different language to outline the definition, elements and manifestations of this standard.[69] The abstract terms in which it is formulated, 'fair' and 'equitable', explain why 'normative indeterminacy'[70] has traditionally been its key feature, leaving room for interpretative creativity. The standard has been associated with equal treatment,[71] arbitrariness,[72] transparency,[73] reasonableness, non-discrimination,[74] and good and bad faith.[75] Importantly, legitimate expectations have emerged in arbitral practice as an integral aspect of FET.[76]

[65] See, eg, Annex B of the US Model BIT (2012), which seems to have been the model for the relevant provisions in the EU agreements.

[66] See, eg, Ursula Kriebaum, 'FET and Expropriation in the (Invisible) EU Model BIT' (2014) 15 *JWIT* 454, 464–65.

[67] CETA, Annex 8-A, Article 3.

[68] The scholarship on the FET standard is vast. See among other authorities, Patrick Dumberry, 'Fair and Equitable Treatment' in Makane Moïse Mbengue and Stefanie Schacherer (eds), *Foreign Investment Under the Comprehensive Economic and Trade Agreement (CETA)* (Springer, 2019) 95–126.

[69] Dolzer and Schreuer (n 7) 121.

[70] See Radi (n 47) 81.

[71] *MTD Equity Sdn Bhd and MTD Chile SA v Republic of Chile,* ICSID Case No ARB/01/7 (25 May 2004) para 113 ('treatment in an even-handed and just manner').

[72] *SD Myers, Inc v Government of Canada*, UNCITRAL/NAFTA, Partial Award (13 November 2000) para 263. See also *Waste Management, Inc v United Mexican States*, ICSID Case No ARB(AF)/00/3, Award (30 April 2004) paras 98 and 99.

[73] *Emilio Agustín Maffezini v The Kingdom of Spain*, ICSID Case No ARB/97/7, Award (13 November 2000) para 83; *Waste Management* (n 72) para 98; *PSEG Global, Inc, The North American Coal Corporation, and Konya Ingin Electrik Üretim ve Ticaret Limited Sirketi v Republic of Turkey*, ICSID Case No ARB/02/5, Award (19 January 2007) paras 238–56; *Enron Corporation and Ponderosa Assets, LP v Argentine Republic*, ICSID Case No ARB/01/3, Award (22 May 2007) paras 251–68, and especially 260–62.

[74] *Saluka* (n 59) para 309. See also on discrimination as a basis for the breach of FET: *Loewen Group, Inc and Raymond L Loewen v United States of America*, ICSID Case No ARB(AF)/98/3, Award (26 June 2003) para 135; *Mondev International Ltd v United States of America*, ICSID Case No ARB(AF)/99/2, Award (11 October 2002) para 156.

[75] See, eg, *Alex Genin, Eastern Credit Limited, Inc and AS Baltoil v The Republic of Estonia*, ICSID Case No ARB/99/2, Award (25 June 2001) para 367.

[76] Tribunals have treated legitimate expectations differently, including finding a breach of legitimate expectations tantamount to a breach of the FET standard. Other tribunals have only taken breach of legitimate expectations as an indicator, an element to be considered. See, eg, *Tecmed* (n 57) para 154; *CMS Gas Transmission Company v Argentina*, Award (12 May 2005) paras 274–76; *Eureko BV v Poland*, Partial Award (19 August 2005) paras 231–35. For a comprehensive account of arbitral practice in relation to legitimate expectations, see Radi (n 47) 88–94.

EU IIAs, cognisant of this arbitral practice, do include an FET clause,[77] but it is limited and not linked to the international minimum standard.[78] An FET clause in EU international agreements concerning investment also comes with a specific 'menu', an exhaustive list of conducts that would breach the FET standard.[79] In this direction, Article 8.10 CETA stipulates that Contracting Parties shall accord to covered investments of the other Party and to investors with respect to their covered investments fair and equitable treatment. This obligation is breached when the measures they adopt constitute denial of justice, fundamental breach of due process, including a fundamental breach of transparency, in judicial and administrative proceedings, manifest arbitrariness, targeted discrimination on manifestly wrongful grounds, such as gender, race or religious belief, and abusive treatment of investors (eg, coercion, duress and harassment). Explicitly, legitimate expectations are only an element to be considered by the CETA tribunal when determining a breach of the FET standard.[80]

The content of the FET obligation is under review by the parties to the investment agreement. Moreover, the Committee on Services and Investment, established under Article 26.2.1(b) CETA, may develop recommendations in this regard and submit them to the CETA Joint Committee for a decision. In the context of constant review, the Commission engaged in discussions with Germany and prepared a text that 'clarified' certain provisions of CETA, with the aim of preventing 'the misuse of the ISDS mechanism by investors' (the Draft Decision).[81] For example, the Draft Decision clarifies that a measure may fall within the scope of 'manifest arbitrariness' if it does not contain the reasons on which it is based, it is patently not founded on reason or fact, it is based on unreasonable discretion, prejudice or personal preference, or it is taken in wilful disregard of due process and proper procedure.

Being cautious of the cases associating investors' legitimate expectations with the FET standard, it is expressly stated in CETA that the CETA tribunal may take into account whether a party made a *specific*, and as the Draft Decision might add 'unambiguous' and 'written', representation *to an* investor to induce a covered investment, as opposed to a statement to the general

[77] It could have been omitted. See, eg, UNCTAD, 'Investment Policy Framework for Sustainable Development' (UNCTAD/DIAE/PCB/2012/5) (1 August 2012), 43–45 (including omission among policy options).

[78] On the relationship between FET and the international minimum standard, see Radi (n 47) 71ff.

[79] See Draft Decision of the CETA Joint Committee, Decision No X/2022 of the CETA Joint Committee on the interpretation of certain terms in Article 8.10, Annex 8-A and Article 8.39, following the Statement/22/5223, Statement from the Commission on clarifications discussed with Germany regarding investment protection in the context of the CETA agreement, STATEMENT/22/5223 (29 August 2022). This Draft Decision needs to be adopted by the CETA Joint Committee, after discussions in the remaining EU Member States and Canada.

[80] Article 8.10(4) CETA.

[81] See Statement/22/5223 (n 79).

public or a provision in national law[82] that created a legitimate expectation, and upon which the investor relied when deciding to make or maintain the covered investment.[83] Moreover, such representations generating potentially legitimate expectations would be made by the competent authority of the host state. The CETA tribunal 'shall notably consider whether a prudent and informed investor could have reasonably formed a legitimate and justifiable expectation on the basis of such representations'.[84]

Moving on to the FPS standard, EU IIAs deal with it quite restrictively. In arbitral case law, it is commonly accepted that it does not reach the level of strict liability.[85] It covers harm caused by both the host state[86] and private actors.[87] Despite FPS's differences with FET,[88] in some cases the boundaries between the two are blurred, with some tribunals holding that FPS applies beyond physical security or physical violence. In similar terms, the failure to provide FPS against physical violence can lead to a breach of FET.[89] In EU international agreements, FPS is limited to its core notion and function, namely protection against the physical security of investments and investors.[90] Thus, any application beyond physical security is excluded.[91]

[82] This requirement for 'specific' commitments was set by arbitral tribunals. See, eg, *Masdar Solar & Wind Cooperatief UA v Kingdom of Spain*, ICSID Case No ARB/14/1, paras 489–91. Cf eg *Enron* (n 73) para 264.

[83] Article 8.10(4) CETA. See also Article 2.4(3) EU-Singapore IPA.

[84] Draft Decision (n 79) point 1(g).

[85] See, eg, *Rumeli Telekom AS and Telsim Mobil Telekomunikasyon Hizmetleri AS v Republic of Kazakhstan*, ICSID Case No ARB/05/16, Award (29 July 2008) para 668; *Tecmed* (n 57) para 177.

[86] The case law is limited. See, for instance, *Biwater* (n 62) where the arbitral tribunal found a violation of the FPS standard. The case concerned the removal of management from the investor's premises without use of force. Even so, it was held 'unnecessary and abusive' (paras 730–731). See also *Wena Hotels Ltd v Arab Republic of Egypt*, ICSID Case No ARB/98/4, Award (8 December 2000), where Egypt was held in breach of FPS for failure to act and protect the investor when employees of a state entity seized the hotel.

[87] See, eg, in that regard Helge Elisabeth Zeitler 'The Guarantee of "Full Protection and Security" in Investment Treaties Regarding Harm caused by Private Actors' (2005) 3 *Stockholm Int'l Arbitration Rev* 1. See also *Eastern Sugar BV (Netherlands) v The Czech Republic*, SCC Case No 088/2004, Partial Award (27 March 2007) para 203 ('obligation of the host state to protect the investor from *third parties* … engaged in physical violence against the investor in violation of the state monopoly of physical force').

[88] Ronald Kläger, *'Fair and Equitable Treatment' in International Investment Law* (CUP, 2011) 281–316.

[89] *Wena* (n 86) para 95. Another example in case law where arbitral tribunals equated the two standards, FPS and FET, is *American Manufacturing & Trading, Inc v Republic of Zaire*, ICSID Case No ARB/93/1, Award (21 February 1977) paras 6.05–6.11.

[90] Article 8.10(5) CETA. See generally for a concise account of the FPS standard, Helge Elisabeth Zeitler, 'Full protection and security' in Stephan W Schill, *International Investment Law and Comparative Public Law* (OUP, 2010) 183; Christoph Schreuer, 'Full Protection and Security' (2010) 1(1) *Journal of International Dispute Settlement* 354.

[91] See, indicatively, *Azurix* (n 61) para 408 and *Wena* (n 86) paras 84–95. In some cases, tribunals have moved beyond the scope of police protection and have held that part of the FPS standard is legal security. See, for instance, *CME Czech Republic BV v Czech Republic*, Partial Award (13 September 2001) para 613 ('The host State is obliged to ensure that neither by amendment of its laws nor by actions of its administrative bodies is the agreed and approved security and protection

Finally, MFN clauses are commonplace in investment law, having been in place since the international agreements of friendship, commerce and navigation – the predecessors of BITs.[92] Through an MFN clause, the host state is bound to treat foreign investors (and their investments) who are nationals of its contracting party in the IIA at least as favourably as it would treat other foreign investors (and their investments) who are nationals of a third state (that is a non-party to that IIA). One of the heavily debated issues in international investment law is whether MFN clauses extend to ISDS.[93] Not all EU IIAs include an MFN clause. One example is the EUSFTA, which does not.[94] Contrariwise, the CETA does include one,[95] and the text of the provision offers an excellent example of how a change in wording can put an end to jurisprudential debates. The drafters expressly excluded from the scope of treatment procedures for the resolution of investor-state disputes.[96]

14.3.2. The States' Right to Regulate

The redefinition of investment protection standards in EU IIAs is coupled with the further balancing of investment protection with the 'basic underlying principle' of the right to regulate.[97] The Commission was of the view that the need to strike a balance between investment protection and safeguarding the regulatory powers of states 'was not sufficiently highlighted in the past'.[98]

of the foreign investor's investment withdrawn or devalued') for physical security only, see eg, *Enron* (n 73) para 286.

[92] See, on MFN clauses, UNCTAD, 'Most-favoured-nation treatment', UNCTAD Series on Issues in International Investment Agreements II (United Nations, New York, 2010).

[93] See, eg, Zachary Douglas, 'The MFN Clause in Investment Arbitration: Treaty Interpretation Off the Rails' (2011) 2 *Journal of International Dispute Settlement* 97; Stephan Schill, 'Allocating Adjudicatory Authority: Most-Favoured-Nation Clauses as a basis of Jurisdiction – A Reply to Zachary Douglas' (2011) 2 *Journal of International Dispute Settlement* 353. See also *RosInvest v Russia*, Award on Jurisdiction, Case No V079/2005, October 2007, paras 131–132 (noting that, 'if this is generally accepted in the context of substantive protection, the Tribunal sees no reason not to accept it in the context of procedural clauses such as arbitration clauses'); *Maffezini* (n 73) paras 54–55; *Garanti Koza LLP v Turkmenistan*, ICSID Case No ARB/11/20, Award (3 July 2013). Cf indicatively *ICS Inspection and Control Services Limited v Argentina*, PCA/UNCITRAL Case No 2010-9, Award (10 February 2012), para 296.

[94] Outside of the EU agreements, other 'new generation' BITs also opt for no MFN clause. See, for example, the 2016 Canada-Ukraine FTA and the 2015 Indian Model BIT.

[95] Article 8.7 CETA. See also Article 28.7(6) CETA providing for exceptions of advantages accorded by a Party pursuant to a tax convention.

[96] Article 8.7(4) CETA. This exclusion seems to start becoming a trend, see eg to this effect UNCTAD, Taking Stock of IIA Reforms: IIA Issues Note 1 (March 2016), where multiple examples of ISDS carve-outs from MFN clauses are listed.

[97] European Commission, Staff Working Document Report, 'Online public consultation on investment protection and investor-to-state dispute settlement (ISDS) in the Transatlantic Trade and Investment Partnership Agreement (TTIP)' SWD(2015) 3 final (13 January 2015), p 72.

[98] European Commission, 'Trade for all …' (n 8) para 4.1.2, p 21. European Commission, Inception Impact Report (n 37) 2.

Under public international law, only the states themselves can limit their sovereign prerogative. The assumption of obligations under IIAs amounts to such a limitation. In the context of investment law, a longstanding criticism has been that investors enjoy excessive protection under IIAs, to the detriment of states' regulatory powers in the public interest.[99] New EU international agreements attempt to remedy this imbalance, including references to the right to regulate, both in the preambles and the text of the agreements.[100] This reference comes with an indicative list of objectives that amount to the right to regulate. In CETA, for instance, an explicit reference to the right to regulate is made in its preamble,[101] while Article 8.9 CETA, entitled '[i]nvestment and regulatory measures', also provides a general protection clause concerning states' right to regulate, 'to achieve legitimate policy objectives', followed by an indicative enumeration of such objectives.[102] A shorter and simpler provision was adopted in the more recent EU-Mexico Agreement,[103] in which the same indicative enumeration of legitimate policy objectives is provided.

14.4. THE EU CONSTITUTIONAL FRAMEWORK CHALLENGE: RENDERING REGULATORY AUTONOMY PART OF THE COMPATIBILITY TEST

The EU's actions in the investment field have been shaped by its constitutional framework and the challenges stemming from it. The constitutional challenge that EU investment policy has been facing has two main strands. The first relates to the scope of the EU competence, which determines the number of actors involved in shaping its investment policy. The second relates to the compatibility of EU international agreements with the principle of autonomy of the EU legal order. Each of these two sides of the coin has had its day at the CJEU,

[99] See, eg, Alec Stone Sweet, Michael Yunsuck Chung and Adam Saltzman, 'Arbitral Lawmaking and State Power: An Empirical Analysis of Investor–State Arbitration' (2017) 8 *JIDS* 579–609.

[100] Of course, this is not a unique feature of EU agreements. Similar provisions with explicit references to the right to regulate can be found in other non-EU new generation bilateral investment treaties (BITs). See, eg, the 2015 Norway Draft Model BIT (Article 12) or the 2014 Georgia-Switzerland BIT (Article 9), as well as the FTA between Canada and Chile (CCFTA), and the 2016 Argentina-Qatar BIT (Article 10).

[101] The preamble reads as follows: 'the provisions of this Agreement preserve the right of the Parties to regulate within their territories and the Parties' flexibility to achieve legitimate policy objectives, such as public health, safety, environment, public morals and the promotion and protection of cultural diversity'. See also emphasis put by the European Commission in this express reference in the preamble of CETA in its TTIP Concept Paper (n 18) 2; and Joint Interpretative Instrument on the Comprehensive Economic and Trade Agreement (CETA) between Canada and the European Union and Its Member States [2017] OJ L11/3, pp 3–22.

[102] Article 8.9(1)–(4) CETA. The first paragraph aims to provide a general protection clause for states' regulatory powers in more general terms than in other treaties. Cf Article 1101(4) NAFTA.

[103] EU-Mexico IA, April 2018, Article 1 ('The parties affirm the right to regulate within their territories to achieve legitimate policy objectives, such as the protection of public health, social services, public education, safety, environment or public morals, social or consumer protection, privacy and data protection, the promotion and protection of cultural diversity, or competition.').

in the form of two significant (and widely discussed) Opinions: *Opinion 2/15 (EU-Singapore FTA)*[104] and *Opinion 1/17 (EU-Canada CETA)*.[105]

Other chapters in this volume have extensively dealt with *Opinion 2/15 (EU-Singapore FTA)*. In a nutshell, the CJEU was asked to opine on the scope of EU competence. Without prejudice to the compatibility question, the CJEU unequivocally confirmed that the EU has exclusive competence in relation to FDI,[106] but not in relation to ISDS, which was shared competence. This was a signal that the Commission should reconsider its approach to negotiate 'all inclusive' deals. Alternatively, trade and investment agreements including an ISDS chapter would have to be concluded as mixed agreements, leading to enhanced complexity.[107]

In *Opinion 1/17 (EU-Canada CETA)*, Belgium asked the CJEU to consider the compatibility of the ISDS mechanism provided for in CETA, namely, the ICS, with EU law, and notably with the principle of autonomy,[108] as this principle has been construed by the CJEU, notably in other judgments relating to external judicial bodies. Inevitably, the *Achmea* judgment was of relevance to the CJEU's reasoning.[109] In *Opinion 1/17 (EU-Canada CETA)*, the CJEU explicitly acknowledged the 'need to maintain the powers of the Union in international relations',[110] and found that the ICS may be compatible with EU law if it has no adverse effect on the autonomy of the EU legal order. One should not be fooled, however, by this green light to the ICS. Rather, a closer examination of the CJEU's findings and reasoning is needed to grasp the constitutional challenge construed therein. This compatibility challenge was embedded in the two-prong test introduced by the CJEU to examine the compatibility of the ICS in CETA with the principle of autonomy of the EU legal order. It is worthwhile briefly recalling this test.

Under the first limb of the autonomy test, for a judicial body that is outside the EU judicial system to be compatible with the autonomy of EU law, it should not have the power to apply and interpret EU law. The CJEU scrutinised the applicable law clause, Article 8.31 CETA, and concluded that the possibility that

[104] *Opinion 2/15* ECLI:EU:C:2017:376 (*EU-Singapore FTA*).

[105] *Opinion 1/17* ECLI:EU:C:2019:341 (*EU-Canada CETA*). See also Fanou (n 31), on which this section draws.

[106] *Opinion 2/15*, ECLI:EU:C:2017:376 (*EU-Singapore FTA*), para 87. See Christine Kaddous, 'The EU Competence to Conclude the New Generation of Free Trade Agreements: Opinion 2/15 (EU–Singapore FTA)' in Graham Butler and Ramses A Wessel (eds), *EU External Relations Law: The Cases in Context* (Oxford, Hart Publishing, 2022) 891–906.

[107] The history of ratification of CETA is the best illustration of the related complexities. Until late summer 2022, the ratification was pending in 11 EU Member States, including, inter alia, Belgium, France, Germany and Ireland.

[108] Other grounds of potential incompatibilities were raised, namely the principle of equal treatment, the requirement of effectiveness of EU law (discrimination and effectiveness concerns), and the right of access to an independent and impartial tribunal (independence concerns).

[109] Case C-284/16 *Achmea* ECLI:EU:C:2018:158.

[110] *Opinion 1/17* ECLI:EU:C:2019:341 (*EU-Canada CETA*), para 117.

the ICS, an external judicial body, will apply or interpret EU law is excluded.[111] Even if indeed the jurisdiction of the ICS is confined to the provisions of CETA, and thus there is not even a mere possibility that the ICS under CETA applies and interprets EU law, this is not the end of the compatibility inquiry.

According to the second limb of the test, compatibility depends on whether the jurisdiction of the ICS is determined in such a way that the awards it will issue may not have *the effect* of preventing the EU institutions from operating in accordance with the EU constitutional framework. Even if, as the CJEU observed, the ICS can only grant compensation and does not have the power to request a change to the regulatory framework,[112] this threat is still present as it could result in the forced lowering of the level of protection.[113]

The CJEU was concerned that despite the lack of direct effect of CETA, and all the reassurances it considered in the first limb, the case before the ICS might still require an 'examination' of a contested measure that relates to EU laws and regulations.[114] The CETA tribunal may need to decide on an EU law measure, treated as a fact, and whether it constitutes a breach of a substantive standard under CETA, such as, for example, the FET standard, as discussed above. In this event, it must be ensured, according to the CJEU, that the ICS, and any similar future investment court, does not 'call into question the level of protection of a public interest that led to the introduction of' the relevant EU legal framework.[115] Or, put differently, the second limb of the test requires that the ICS under CETA does not present a threat to EU regulatory autonomy. Of course, the question arises as to how EU regulatory autonomy is not under threat.

The answer offered by the CJEU mainly relied on the substantive provisions of CETA, and the inclusion of the right to regulate in EU international investment agreements.[116] In more detail, the CJEU relied on three reassurances. First, the explicit clause included in CETA on the right to regulate.[117] Second, the

[111] It goes beyond the scope of this contribution to get into the details of the CJEU's reasoning in relation to the applicable law clause. Briefly, the CJEU relied on the express provision that the CETA tribunal would (i) interpret CETA in accordance with the VCLT and other applicable rules of international law; (ii) would not have jurisdiction to rule upon the legality of domestic law measures; (iii) would consider any domestic measures as facts following the prevailing interpretation accorded to them by domestic courts/authorities; and (iv) in any event any meaning given to domestic law of the CETA Contracting Parties would not be binding upon the courts/authorities of the Parties. On this, see Fanou (n 31) 121–25. See also Kieran Bradley, 'Investor–State Dispute Tribunals Established under EU International Agreements: Opinion 1/17 (EU-Canada CETA)' in Graham Butler and Ramses A Wessel (eds), *EU External Relations Law: The Cases in Context* (Oxford, Hart Publishing, 2022) 959–70.

[112] *Opinion 1/17* ECLI:EU:C:2019:341 (*EU-Canada CETA*), para 144. See for the remedies provided under Article 8.39(1), (4) CETA (monetary damages, excluding punitive damages).

[113] *Opinion 1/17* (n 112) para 149.

[114] ibid para 131.

[115] ibid para 148.

[116] See above section 14.3 of this chapter.

[117] *Opinion 1/17* (n 112) para 154. See also Article 8.9(1)–(2) CETA.

commitment contained in a political statement, the CETA Joint Interpretative Statement, according to which the standards and regulations of each party will not be lowered.[118] Third, the restrictive manner in which the *substantive standards* contained in CETA are drafted. The CJEU took particular note of the clarification of the notion of indirect expropriation[119] and the exhaustive enumeration of situations in which a breach of FET may be found.[120]

Although, strictly speaking, nothing in the language of *Opinion 1/17 (EU-Canada CETA)* indicates that the enumeration of these reassurances is cumulative, it is difficult to envisage how any future international agreement could pass the *Opinion 1/17 (EU-Canada CETA)* test without, at least, the first and third reassurances being met. Without entering into the discussion about the perplexing way in which the CJEU interpreted the jurisdiction of an international tribunal and, implicitly, set the ground for future EU objections to the jurisdiction of the ICS,[121] it is apparent that the CJEU linked the substantive protections and the preservation of the right to regulate to the compatibility of an investment court with EU law. This inevitably means that the EU has a floor in relation to substantive provisions of future investment agreements, which will have to meet the high threshold set by the CJEU. Including regulatory autonomy and substantive standards in the compatibility test also raises the question of compatibility of procedure-only instruments, such as the envisaged convention establishing a MIC, which is the grand plan of the Commission.

14.5. CONCLUSION

EU IIAs with third states are examples of modern practice in international investment agreements that aim to address concerns about the states' right to regulate and recalibrate substantive protections. The EU's approach to investment standards, with its pros and cons, is a step in the right direction, and the key novelty of the EU investment policy, although the emphasis has been placed on EU actions vis-à-vis reforming investor-state dispute settlement. This focus has become part of the compatibility test that the CJEU introduced in *Opinion 1/17 (EU-Canada CETA)*. Therefore, in the future, and in relation to the ambitious grand plan of the Commission for a MIC, the EU will have to take account of the CJEU's construction of autonomy and compatibility requirements as set forth in *Opinion 1/17 (EU-Canada CETA)*.

[118] *Opinion 1/17* (n 112) para 155. See also CETA Joint Interpretative Instrument (n 101), Point 1(d).
[119] *Opinion 1/17* (n 112) para 157. See also CETA, Annex 8-A (Point 3, incorporating police power doctrine).
[120] *Opinion 1/17* (n 112) para 158. See also Article 8.10(2) CETA.
[121] Fanou (n 31) 127–28.

15

Towards a Multilateral Investment Court

COLIN M BROWN

15.1. INTRODUCTION[1]

THIS CHAPTER SEEKS to set out the logic behind the EU's effort to establish a Multilateral Investment Court (MIC). It posits that establishing such a MIC can be considered as enhancing the international rule of law in the field of investment protection, and hence, more generally, contributing to the international rule of law. This is both an end in itself, but also key to addressing the problems which beset the international investment protection regime. This contribution will first examine how the notion of the rule of law, which is traditionally understood and applied in a national or regional context, can be understood at an international level. It will then set out an understanding of the current system of investment protection. It finally will turn to examine in more detail the efforts of the EU to establish a MIC.

15.2. THE INTERNATIONAL RULE OF LAW

As noted by leading international lawyer Arthur Watts, '[t]he rule of law is more easily invoked than understood'.[2] The rule of law as a concept has been developed in a domestic context, applicable within states and largely focused on the vertical relationship between states and their citizens. It has been applied at a regional level, to entities such as the EU. It cannot be transposed, unthinkingly, to the international plane. This is because, as a general matter, the subjects of international law are principally states rather than

[1] The views expressed herein are personal to the author.
[2] See Arthur Watts, 'The International Rule of Law', *German Yearbook of International Law* (Berlin, Duncker & Humblot, 1993) 15.

individuals, although investment protection is one area where individuals are important actors. There is no single, unified set of institutions that cover significant areas of international law activity in the manner in which states or regional organisations have legislative institutions and courts that have complete, or close to complete jurisdiction. Indeed, the starting point of general international law is that international judicial bodies only exist when voluntarily created, and when states give consent.

Nevertheless, it cannot be said that a notion of the rule of law does not exist on the international plane. Watts enumerated the key principles, which can be summarised as follows:

(1) a certain degree of certainty, in the sense that the application of the law is largely predictable.[3] That is not to imply that the law can be mechanically applied, but that in any given situation the application of the rules is relatively predictable;
(2) equality before the law. This implies that states be treated equally before the law, but also be given an equal role in the formulation of the law;
(3) the absence of arbitrary actions, in the sense that states should not act in a manner which can be considered to be arbitrary;
(4) the effective application of the law. As noted, the international legal system does not have the compulsory jurisdiction of domestic legal systems. However, Watts describes this aspect as implying (a) that states can have recourse to impartial and independent tribunals to determine the law and settle disputes; (b) enforcement of the law and or legal remedies; and (c) the application or acceptance of rulings by states.[4]

Watts summarises this as follows: '… the primary requirements for an international rule of law are that a complete and certain system of international law, which treats all States as equal in the eyes of the law and which excludes arbitrary power, should be effectively applied and enforced.'[5]

That summary is already more than 30 years old. A more recent effort at a definition of the international rule of law takes into account the increased role of the individual at the international level, but contains essentially similar features. McCorquodale posits it thus:

> … the definition of the international rule of law comprises legal order and stability, equality of application of the law, the protection of human rights through access to justice, and the settlement of disputes before an independent legal body. The international rule of law is not defined by reference to the national institutional arrangements of some democratic, industrialized states, and it is broad

[3] ibid 28.
[4] ibid 36–41.
[5] ibid.

enough to include all the participants in the international system within its scope, and not just states.[6]

The United Nations (UN) has recognised the significance of the international rule of law. One of the specific targets of Goal 16 of the Sustainable Development Goals (SDG) – to promote just, peaceful and inclusive societies – is to '[p]romote the rule of law at the national and international levels and ensure equal access to justice for all'.[7]

The MIC will enhance the international rule of law in the field of protection of investment. It is debatable that the current form of dispute settlement for investment ensures that the international rule of law is respected in this field of international law. The broader question whether the protection of investment is, as such, a feature of the international rule of law is not examined here. There is a rich debate on this issue in the literature around investment law that is beyond the scope of the current contribution.[8]

15.3. THE INTERNATIONAL SYSTEM OF INVESTMENT PROTECTION

The modern law of international investment has grown out of the early international law on the protection of aliens.[9] The modern system grew particularly as of the end of World War II. It is characterised by two related sets of international agreements.

One is the bilateral investment treaty. The first such treaty was agreed between Germany and Pakistan in 1959. Despite some efforts at creating a multilateral code for the protection of investments, the bilateral investment treaty became the standard format. UNCTAD counts 2,850 such treaties, of which 2,221 are in force.[10] These treaties exhibit a high degree of similarity, being based on models developed conjointly by European states in the 1950s and 1960s. These have tended to be stand-alone agreements, but there has also been a practice of the same standard provisions of such agreements being incorporated into free trade agreements, the most prominent examples being the now defunct North

[6] Robert McCorquodale, 'Defining the International Rule of Law: Defying Gravity' (2016) 65 *Int'l & Comp LQ* 277 at 296.

[7] 'Transforming our world: the 2030 Agenda for Sustainable Development', United Nations General Assembly, A/RES/70/1 (21 October 2015) at p 25.

[8] See for a discussion, Stephan W Schill, 'International Investment Law and the Rule of Law' in Jeffrey Lowell, J Christopher Thomas and Jan van Zyl Smit (eds), *Rule of Law Symposium 2014: The Importance of the Rule of Law in Promoting Development* (Singapore, Academy Publishing, 2015) 81–102, Amsterdam Law School Research Paper No 2017-18, Amsterdam Centre for International Law No 2017-15, and S Puig and G Shaffer, 'Imperfect Alternatives: Institutional Choice and the Reform of Investment Law' (2018) 112(3) American Journal of International Law 361–409.

[9] See Kate Miles, *The Origins of International Investment Law: Empire, Environment and the Safeguarding of Capital* (Cambridge University Press, 2013).

[10] United Nations Conference on Trade and Development (UNCTAD), International Investment Agreement Navigator.

American Free Trade Agreement (NAFTA), and the Comprehensive Economic and Trade Agreement (CETA) between Canada and the European Union and its Member States.[11] EU Member States are party to 1,400 such agreements, the very large majority being bilateral investment treaties, since EU Member States do not, themselves, conclude FTAs.[12]

These contain substantive rules which are intended to protect the investment. It has been argued that these substantive rules were developed (or should be read) with the idea in mind that they be substantively equivalent to the protections which would have applied should the investment have instead been made in the home state of the investor.[13] This was certainly the logic behind the creation of the regime: that the investment in the third state should be encouraged, but should be protected because the investment is sunk – it cannot be easily redirected to another market in the case that a government takes measures which impact the investment.[14]

The most common, and what can be considered standard substantive rules, are also commonly found in other systems, whether these be other international regimes, EU law, the European Convention of Human Rights (ECHR), or national constitutions or legal systems. These are protection against discrimination, protection against uncompensated expropriation, fair and equitable treatment (FET), and the ability to repatriate capital.

Taking them in turn, the protection against discrimination is found in the World Trade Organization (WTO), with Article I of the General Agreement on Trade in Tariffs (GATT) in 1994 providing for most favoured nation treatment (that all third state's goods be treated no less favourably than each other), and Article III provides for national treatment (that there is no discrimination between imported and domestic goods). Similar norms are found in EU law. Article 34 TFEU prohibits quantitative restrictions and measures with equivalent effect between Member States (including, but going further than mere

[11] Comprehensive Economic and Trade Agreement (CETA) between Canada, of the one part, and the European Union and its Member States, of the other part [2017] OJ L11/23. See, in general, A Von Walter and ML Andrisani, 'Resolution of Investment Disputes' in Makane Moïse Mbengue and Stefanie Schacherer (eds), *Foreign Investment under the Comprehensive Economic and Trade Agreement (CETA)* (Springer, 2019) 189.

[12] See List of the bilateral investment agreements referred to in Article 4(1) of Regulation (EU) No 1219/2012 of the European Parliament and of the Council establishing transitional arrangements for bilateral investment agreements between Member States and third countries [2020] OJ C179. Note that this list includes agreements maintained by the United Kingdom and does not include agreements between the EU Member States, which the Court of Justice has ruled are unlawful in Case C-284/16 *Achmea* ECLI:EU:C:2018:158.

[13] Kleinhiesterkamp argues that 'the limitations on the exercise of sovereignty by the host state resulting from a bilateral investment treaty should be understood as being "capped" at the level at which the investor's home state affirms its own exercise of sovereignty in balancing private and public interests'. See Jan Kleinheisterkamp, 'Investment Treaty Law and the Fear for Sovereignty' (2015) 78 *MLR* 793–825, 796.

[14] See J Bonnitcha, LN Skovgaard Poulsen and M Waibel, *The Political Economy of the Investment Treaty Regime* (Oxford University Press, 2017), in particular ch 5.

discrimination, and capturing 'restrictions' more generally). Similarly, and more directly analogous, Article 49 TFEU provides that there should be freedom of establishment between EU Member States, allowing operators from one Member State to invest ('establish' in EU legal terminology[15]) in another, and protecting such establishment against discrimination (indeed, going further, including capturing restrictions).

Protection against uncompensated expropriation is also a feature of many other legal systems. It is found in national constitutional systems, in Article 1 of Protocol 1 of the ECHR, and Article 17 of the Charter of Fundamental Rights of the European Union.[16] FET, as a standard, has less direct one-to-one parallels in other systems, but many have general principles which can be broadly equated with the notion of fair and equitable treatment. To illustrate this, Article 8.10 CETA enumerates various actions which are intended to provide a complete list of governmental actions which would breach the FET standard. It is submitted that all of these could also be considered a breach of general principles of domestic (or the EU) legal systems if they were to occur. In the language of CETA, a 'denial of justice in criminal, civil or administrative proceedings; fundamental breach of due process, including a fundamental breach of transparency in judicial and administrative proceedings; manifest arbitrariness; targeted discrimination on manifestly wrongful grounds, such as gender, race or religious belief; abusive treatment of investors, such as coercion, duress or harassment'. Finally, the ability to repatriate capital falls in EU law terms under the free movement of capital provided for in Article 63 TFEU.

It is important to note that there is a high degree of homogeneity in such bilateral investment treaties. They essentially have the same core obligations of most favoured nation treatment, national treatment, protection against uncompensated expropriation, and FET. It has been noted that, '[a]bove all with respect to the standards of treatment of foreign investment, investment treaties display considerable convergence in their structure, object and purpose, and content'.[17] Whilst it is true that recent treaty practice has led to greater heterogeneity as different approaches to reform have been taken up, it remains the case that the core standards are the same, and hence the interpretation given, for example, to the national treatment clause in one agreement, will likely be relevant and useful, if not necessarily determinant, in interpreting a national treatment clause in another agreement.

Bilateral investment treaties also contain dispute settlement provisions which allow an investor to initiate dispute settlement proceedings against the state to

[15] Establishment and foreign direct investment are similar. Both are based on the notion that an investment has been made with a view to maintain control over the object of the investment.

[16] Building on existing case law of the Court of Justice on the protection of property (see, for example, Case 4/73 *Nold v Commission* ECLI:EU:C:1974:51 at recital 14 et seq and the cases which build on it).

[17] Stephan W Schill, *The Multilateralization of International Investment Law* (Cambridge University Press, 2009) 88. See in particular ch 3.

recover compensation.[18] This is one of the striking features of these treaties, and often results in obscuring the fact that these treaties are between two sovereign states.[19] States have chosen to transfer their rights to ensure the protection of aliens of their own origin (which were, in the past, enforced via 'gunboat' diplomacy[20]) to the aliens, now repackaged as investors.

There are a number of reasons for this, most significantly the notion of depoliticising the decision to initiate a dispute.[21] This has the important effect that the investor does not need to persuade the state to initiate a claim, which is otherwise necessary for state to state dispute settlement, and does not require the state to decide whether to initiate the claim by considering whether its political interests and relations with a particular third state are furthered by the initiation of a dispute.[22] This depoliticisation is, of course, also present in the EU legal system, where it is individuals (whether natural or legal persons) which enforce EU law through its direct effect, and the existence of the reference for a preliminary ruling procedure between national courts and the Court of Justice of the European Union, rather than Member States litigating on their behalf.[23] It is not argued that the investment system, to take the words of the Court of Justice, 'constitutes a new legal order of international law for the benefit of which the states have limited their sovereign rights, albeit within limited fields, and the subjects of which comprise not only Member States but also their nationals. [... Union law] is also intended to confer upon them rights which become part of their legal heritage'.[24] However, the parallels are obvious, as is the observation, evidenced by the withdrawal of the United Kingdom (UK) from the EU, that these rights can be removed from the legal heritage of individuals by states withdrawing from (or renegotiating the content of) their international treaties.[25]

Thus, the second set of rules are the international instruments which create the system for dispute settlement. The most prominent and specialised of these is the International Centre for the Settlement of Investment Disputes (ICSID). The ICSID Convention entered into force on 14 October 1966 after 20 states had ratified it, and now has 158 contracting parties. It provides for a system of dispute settlement based on arbitration. That was a conscious decision.

[18] ie to not have the measure annulled.

[19] Anthea Roberts, 'Triangular Treaties: The Extent and Limits of Investment Treaty Rights' (2015) 56(2) *Harvard International Law Journal*.

[20] See the remarkable study of the transformation of international law: Oona Hathaway and Scott Shapiro, *The Internationalists: And Their Plan to Outlaw War* (Penguin, 2017).

[21] See Ibrahim FI Shihata, 'Towards a Greater Depoliticization of Investment Disputes: The Roles of ICSID and MIGA (Spring 1986) 1(1) *ICSID Review – Foreign Investment Law Journal* 1–25.

[22] To be clear, this does not imply that a dispute may never be politically sensitive. Rather it implies that there are not political decisions which need to be taken as regards the initiation of disputes.

[23] The use of Article 259 TFEU permitting one Member State to initiate a case against another is rare, but has occurred. See Graham Butler, 'The Court of Justice as an inter-state court' (2017) 36 *Yearbook of European Law* 179.

[24] Case 26/62 *Van Gend en Loos* ECLI:EU:C:1963:1.

[25] See, for example, Case C-673/20 *Préfet du Gers* ECLI:EU:C:2022:449.

There are three routes by which ISCID may have jurisdiction. These are:

(1) where consent is given to ICSID dispute settlement in an investment contract or concession;
(2) a domestic investment law; or
(3) an international treaty (the bilateral investment treaties).

When the ICSID Convention was prepared, the extent of the growth of bilateral investment treaties was not something which could have been predicted.[26] There were only 63 bilateral investment treaties in place in 1970, and there would have been considerably fewer in the first years of the 1960s when the ICSID Convention was drafted. At the time, it was argued that most investment disputes would be based on either investment contracts or domestic investment laws, and the importance of treaty-based consent was either misunderstood or downplayed.[27] Indeed, it was not until 1990 that a bilateral investment treaty was found to provide 'standing consent', hence modifying the prevailing understanding that consent was required for each individual dispute, meaning that a state could decline to enter into dispute settlement despite a request from an investor.[28] In any event, up to 1 July 2022, only 23% of ICSID cases were, in fact, based on investment contracts or the investment law of the host state.[29]

This approach clearly enjoyed a certain logic at the time, but it was not preordained. Other ideas for dispute settlement were in the air, such as the creation of an international court for investments. However, when the ICSID Convention was negotiated, it was assumed that the advantages of arbitration outweighed the advantages linked to the creation of a court.[30] Those thinking of the appropriate dispute settlement mechanisms, at the time, did not have the advantage of being able to see into the future to identify the rise of investment treaty arbitration as the predominant form of investment dispute settlement.

[26] The definitive history of this period is provided by Taylor St John, *The Rise of Investor-State Arbitration: Politics, Law, and Unintended Consequences* (Oxford University Press, 2018).

[27] See J Christopher Thomas and Harpreet Kaur Dhillon, 'The Foundations of Investment Treaty Arbitration: The ICSID Convention, Investment Treaties and the Review of Arbitration Awards (Fall 2017) 32(3) *ICSID Review – Foreign Investment Law Journal* 459–502, contra St John (n 26) 151.

[28] See *Asian Agricultural Products Ltd (AAPL) v Democratic Socialist Republic of Sri Lanka*, ICISD Case No ARB/87/3, Award (27 June 1990) and Jan Paulsson, 'Arbitration Without Privity' (Fall 1995) 10(2) *ICSID Review – Foreign Investment Law Journal* 232–57. See Joost Pauwelyn, 'At the Edge of Chaos? Foreign Investment Law as a Complex Adaptive System, How It Emerged and How It Can Be Reformed' (2014) 29(2) *ICSID Review* 372-418, in particular at 401–02 quoting Professor Lowenfeld (a member of the US Delegation negotiating ICSID) who wrote: 'None of the discussions at the consultative meetings [in preparation of the ICSID Convention], or so far as I know in the contemporary writing and legislative consideration, addressed the possibility that a host state in a bilateral treaty could give its consent to arbitrate with investors from the other state without reference to a particular investment agreement or dispute. I know that I did not mention that possibility in my testimony before the US Congress, and neither did anyone else.'

[29] See ICSID Caseload – Statistics (Issue 2022-2), p 11.

[30] For a discussion, see Taylor St John and Yulia Chernykh, 'Déjà vu? Investment Court Proposals from 1960 and Today' (*EJIL Talk*, 15 May 2018).

The systems of arbitration used in the ICSID Convention, or under the United Nations Commission on International Trade Law (UNCITRAL) Arbitration Rules, are largely classical arbitration rules. Arbitrators are appointed for a specific case, one by each of the disputing parties, and the chair either by agreement between the disputing parties or the already appointed arbitrators, or by the ICSID Secretariat, or another appointing authority. The decision of an arbitral tribunal is final. There is no appeal. Awards can only be reviewed if there is an allegation of procedural incorrectness.[31]

The persons appointed to tribunals often have multiple roles ('double hatting'). Some will act as arbitrators in other cases, others will act both as counsel and arbitrators, or as experts.[32] Arbitrators have an economic interest in being reappointed. It has been argued that this affects their behaviour and the substantive outcome of cases.[33] To take a simplistic example, an arbitrator appointed by a respondent (a state) may concede on a point of law they may find debatable in order to ensure that a final award of damages is lower than might otherwise be the case.

Law firms are, of course, the gatekeepers to arbitral appointments, since they will be acting for investors, or for the states as respondents, and play an influential role in appointments.[34] In choosing arbitrators, law firms are looking for persons who will maximise their chances of obtaining a successful outcome for their client. To quote one person involved in arbitration: '[w]hen I am representing a client in an arbitration, what I am really looking for in a party-nominated arbitrator is someone with the maximum predisposition towards my client, but with the minimum appearance of bias'.[35]

In making appointments, there is a tendency to base appointments on prior experience, because that is the only tool available to justify choices that may later be questioned by hierarchical superiors, which in turn perpetuates the longevity of those who have already been frequently appointed and the importance of

[31] Article 52 of the ICSID Convention provides that the grounds for annulment are: (a) that the Tribunal was not properly constituted; (b) that the Tribunal has manifestly exceeded its powers; (c) that there was corruption on the part of a member of the Tribunal; (d) that there has been a serious departure from a fundamental rule of procedure; or (e) that the award has failed to state the reasons on which it is based. Similar rules apply when set-aside is sought under domestic arbitration laws. Similarly, Article V of the New York Convention on the Recognition and Enforcement of Foreign Arbitral Awards (1958) is narrowly drawn and does not permit a review (in this case decentralised) of the award on grounds of correctness. Similar narrow grounds are also typically found in domestic arbitration laws based, for example, on Article 36 of the UNCITRAL Model Law on International Commercial Arbitration.

[32] See Malcolm Langford, Daniel Behn and Runar Hilleren Lie, 'The Revolving Door in International Investment Arbitration (June 2017) 20(2) *Journal of International Economic Law* 301–32.

[33] See Todd N Tucker, *Judge Knot: Politics and Development in International Investment Law* (Anthem Press, 2018) (in particular ch 4).

[34] Very few states maintain in-house expertise to litigate. Canada, the United States, Argentina, and latterly the EU (in the *Nordstream* 2 case) are the main examples.

[35] M Hunter, 'Ethics of the International Arbitrator' (1987) 53(4) *Arbitration* 219–24.

gatekeepers.[36] This a powerful explainer of the fact that there are few frequently appointed women arbitrators, but also few non-Western European or non-North American arbitrators who are frequently appointed, despite the massive international network of treaties.

This system also can lead to significant costs for the disputing parties, and indeed accentuate the costs. Far from being the cheap alternative to a permanent tribunal as originally touted, arbitration in its modern form has developed into an expensive exercise, with costs for a case frequently running into multiple millions of euros. Philippe Sands has argued that the nature of the system, with the law firms acting as gatekeepers to appointment, leads to over-lengthy proceedings, more than would be tolerated in most standing courts.[37] The fact that arbitrators have to be appointed to each individual case, and are often subject to challenge, adds to the length of time and costs of investment dispute settlement.

Having described the system, it is appropriate to think about whether it is adequately constituted to satisfy the requirements of the international rule of law. It is evidently not the case that arbitration is, *per se*, inconsistent with the international rule of law. There will be circumstances when it is perfectly appropriate for states or other actors to have recourse to arbitration for disputes under international law. Not only is it one of the most historic forms of international law dispute settlement, including in investment disputes,[38] but evidently there will be cases when using arbitration is unobjectionable and entirely consistent with the international rule of law. However, it is submitted that when one views the structure of investment treaty as a system as it has developed, maintaining dispute settlement through a system of arbitration fails to ensure respect for the international rule of law in this area. In particular, returning to Watts' and McCorquodale's definition, the issue of predictability and stability and of independence of dispute settlement mechanisms is in need of further consideration.

15.4. CHARACTERISING THE INVESTMENT REGIME

The starting point for thinking about the application of the international rule of law in the field of investment arbitration is the framework one takes for analysing the adjudication of investment treaty disputes. Are they public law matters where the state has both a specific interest in a particular dispute and a longer-term interest in the treaties as providing a framework for future action by the

[36] See Taylor St John, Daniel Behn, Malcolm Langford and Runar Lie, 'Glass Ceilings and Arbitral Dealings: Explaining the Gender Gap in International Investment Arbitration' (2017).

[37] Philippe Sands, 'What I have Learned – Ten Years as an Investor-State Arbitrator', presentation, Columbia Law School, New York, United States (15 October 2018).

[38] See Jason W Yackee, 'The First Investor-State Arbitration' (15 March 2015), Univ of Wisconsin Legal Studies Research Paper No 1375, on the dispute between the Suez Canal Company and Egypt, arbitrated by a commission appointed by Napoleon III.

state, its treaty partners and its stakeholders, by analogy to national constitutions, which seek to balance the rights of states and the individuals subject to their jurisdiction? Or rather should disputes be considered as one-off events, where issues of consistency, predictability and correctness are less important, because they do not have long-term effects?

Whilst not seeking to capture the richness of debates that take place around this issue, nor summarise its breadth,[39] it is however submitted that, nevertheless, investment treaty adjudication is essentially a public law determination. Investment tribunals conduct reviews broadly similar to those which the Court of Justice of the European Union does when reviewing Member States' legislation for consistency with the EU Treaties, or which WTO panels do when reviewing WTO Members' laws for consistency with the WTO Agreements, or even when national courts undertake judicial or constitutional review. Like these examples, investment adjudication is public law in the dual sense, in that investment treaties are products of public international law, and also that the relationship which is being judged is a vertical one between the state and an individual, ie between the state and the foreign investor.

At the core of investor-state dispute adjudication is the allegation that a public authority has acted inconsistently with certain, specified obligations, deliberately drafted in a relatively open manner.[40] Public authorities are vested with powers to pursue the public interest, and investment treaties provide a legal framework for such action.[41] Disputes may range from relatively politically insignificant contractual obligations, to potentially very sensitive public interest regulation. The most typical remedy is the payment of compensation, which is, of course, likely to come from the public budget. This is a repeat action, given that the treaties are in place permanently, and any investor meeting the nationality requirements can bring a claim. Given that, be they investors, government agencies or the general public, stakeholders develop expectations as to how investment treaties will be understood and applied.

[39] For a discussion, see Anthea Roberts 'Clash of Paradigms: Actors and Analogies Shaping the Investment Treaty System' (2013) 107 *American Journal of International Law* 45; Andreas Kulick, *Global Public Interest in International Investment Law* (Cambridge University Press, 2012); Gus Van Harten and Martin Loughlin, 'Investment Treaty Arbitration as a Species of Global Administrative Law' (2006) 17 *European Journal of International Law* 121; Gus Van Harten, *Investment Treaty Arbitration and Public Law* (Oxford University Press, 2008); David Schneiderman, *Constitutionalizing Economic Globalization: Investment Rules and Democracy's Promise* (Cambridge University Press, 2008); Stephan W Schill, 'International Investment Law and Comparative Public Law – An Introduction' in Stephan W Schill (ed), *International Investment Law and Comparative Public Law* (Oxford University Press, 2010) 3; Santiago Montt, 'State Liability in Investment Treaty Arbitration: Global Constitutional and Administrative Law in the BIT Generation' (2011) 14(3) *Journal of International Economic Law* 715.

[40] It is noted that national constitutions, human rights conventions, the EU Treaties, the WTO Agreements and other trade agreements are drafted in an equally open manner.

[41] One of many, together with domestic constitutions and public law rules, international treaties protecting human rights, international trade law treaties, etc.

In its submissions to the UN process that is examining reform of the investor-state dispute settlement system, the EU enumerated the following features as being relevant for thinking about the system:

(a) a constitutional/administrative law component: the obligations set down in the investment treaties are intended to protect investors from certain (limited) state conduct. Hence applying the obligations implies striking a balance between the right to exercise sovereign authority and the duty to protect individuals, typical of constitutional/administrative law determinations;
(b) a uni-directional system: the investor initiates the case against the state because the investor accepts the standing offer to arbitrate provided in the treaties;
(c) a vertical relationship: disputes predominantly concern foreign investors bringing cases against host states that arise from the vertical, regulatory relationship between those actors due to the fact that the investor enters into the host state territory and its economic and legal order;
(d) a repeat function: the treaties in question potentially will give rise to multiple disputes over a potentially extended period of time. This is to be distinguished from legal instruments establishing one-off contractual arrangements;
(e) a determinacy component: the substantive obligations are indeterminate in the sense that they set down general, high level standards intended to apply in multiple different fact patterns, much like constitutional law provisions; and,
(f) a predictability/consistency function: given the general formulation of investment protection standards and conscious of the repeat function, stakeholders (governments, investors, civil society) look at precedents in order to understand how obligations in the treaties are being or should be interpreted. This occurs both within the same treaty and across treaties, given the relatively high degree of homogeneity of the treaties. This means the adjudicative role is key in elaborating and further refining the precise meaning of the substantive obligations.[42]

It is submitted that these features are such that predictability and stability take on a significant importance. It is vital for stakeholders to be able, with some degree of certainty, to determine how that legal framework will be interpreted in various situations. Given the high degree of similarity across treaties, it is highly likely that an interpretation developed under one treaty will be relevant for other treaties. This is important for government entities as they decide whether and how to act (ie whether a particular policy might lead them into conflict with international obligations); for investors, who need to take decisions as to

[42] 'Possible reform of investor-State dispute settlement (ISDS)', Submission from the European Union, 12 December 2017, A/CN.9/WG.III/WP.14.

whether to pursue a potential claim against the government; and for other stakeholders, who need to understand the environment in which the government in question is acting.

This is not an issue for commercial arbitration, for which the rules on arbitration have been originally developed. In a commercial relationship between two individual actors, the outcome of a dispute is not likely to have legal consequences for other actors.[43] However, these are problems in the investment treaty system because it involves judging the conduct of states acting in their public capacity against their public international law obligations, and there is a systemic interest in consistency and predictability in the interpretation of specific investment norms.

Lawyers acting with due diligence will properly exploit every possibility to bring an argument which might be of aid to their clients. The existing system creates incentives to run these arguments, since one never knows which interpretation will be preferred in any particular case due to the tendency, as noted, of the system to lead to fact-specific outcomes. The current system is replete with inconsistent interpretations of certain key provisions. For example, there is ongoing uncertainty as to the scope of the most favoured nation (MFN) clause, on the extent of the security exceptions in investment agreements and on the nature of the so-called 'umbrella clause'.

Consistency and predictability are important in another sense in the investment system. The dense network of investment treaties, considered together with the often-complex structures of international companies, are such that disputes can arise under different investment treaties. There is evidently a need to ensure that there is consistency in substantive outcome between different disputes, but there is also a need to ensure that a single dispute does not give rise to a state paying out more than the appropriate level of damages. This is particularly complex in the event that there are various companies and associated minority shareholders.

The poster child example of this is the well-known CME and Lauder cases against the Czech Republic, where related entities brought cases arising out of the same facts against the Czech Republic under the Netherlands-Czech Republic Bilateral Investment Treaty (BIT) and the comparable treaty between the United States and the Czech Republic.[44] The two tribunals reached different conclusions as to the law and its application to the facts. Whilst this is an extreme example, it is of course the case that investors and states decide their conduct in the 'shadow of the law', ie one of the issues which a state has to contend with is the lack of predictability which arises from the possibility that cases may be initiated under different treaties by different related parties.

[43] Setting aside, of course, potential issues of contract law which may arise.

[44] *CME Czech Republic BV (The Netherlands) v The Czech Republic*, Award (13 September 2001), and *Ronald S Lauder v The Czech Republic*, Award (3 September 2001).

A similar issue arises with respect to domestic litigation. It may be the case that there is also domestic litigation arising out of an investment dispute. It is important that these different elements of a dispute be coordinated, again, in order to ensure that there is no overlap in terms of compensation that may be provided.[45]

Correctness has been an issue in the investment regime. In *CMS v Argentina*, for example, the Annulment Committee stated:

> Throughout its consideration of the Award, the Committee has identified a series of errors and defects. The Award contained manifest errors of law. It suffered from lacunae and elisions. All this has been identified and underlined by the Committee. However the Committee is conscious that it exercises its jurisdiction under a narrow and limited mandate conferred by Article 52 of the ICSID Convention. The scope of this mandate allows annulment as an option only when certain specific conditions exist. As stated already (paragraph 136 above), in these circumstances the Committee cannot simply substitute its own view of the law and its own appreciation of the facts for those of the Tribunal.[46]

Consistency and predictability do not as such require the availability of appeal. However, to the extent that there is not a single central source of authority, then it is difficult to establish what is the authoritative understanding of a particular legal problem for the consistency and predictability to develop. As Justice Robert Jackson famously said of the US Supreme Court, 'we are not final because we are infallible, but we are infallible only because we are final'.[47]

One can see the effect of the creation of a single central authority playing out with the Appellate Body in the World Trade Organization (WTO AB). Before the creation of the WTO in 1995, and very much like the investment system, various panels developed understandings of the key GATT obligations, many of which had to establish a balance between trade and non-trade societal interests. Before 1995, one could never be sure what was the prevailing interpretation of the relevant norms. This changed with the gradual development of case law on the part of the WTO AB over the years. It settled and decided on interpretations which were final, dispositive, absent a decision of the WTO members to amend the WTO Agreements, or issue an interpretation of the relevant norms. Hence, it gradually became clear how a particular provision should be interpreted, and because, in the case of an appeal, the WTO AB would in principle follow its previous decision, this resulted in consistency and predictability being gradually ensured for all stakeholders.

One can therefore question whether a system designed for the resolution of private disputes is in fact best suited to the resolution of public international

[45] See J Arato, 'The Private Law Critique of International Investment Law' (2019) 113(1) *American Journal of International Law* 1–53.

[46] *CMS Gas Transmission Company v Argentine Republic*, ICSID Case No ARB/01/8, Annulment Decision, para 158.

[47] *Brown v Allen*, 344 US 443 (1953) at 540 (Jackson J concurring).

law and public law disputes. Instead, if one looks at how dispute resolution is managed in other public international law areas that regulate public law actions, it is striking that parties typically adopt a court-like solution that adheres to certain key public law principles such as independence, impartiality, and correctness, amongst others.

One can posit that systems of public adjudication have a number of features. They place a significant importance on the manner in which disputes are decided. At the core of that structure is a high degree of independence of the decision-makers, which needs to be both real and perceived. Typically, this is achieved through ensuring both that they are free from other financial pressures (ie that the activity of adjudicating is their quasi-exclusive occupation), and that they cannot be pressured into taking decisions on particular matters through their employment not being continued (typically through tenure). Another important feature of public adjudication is a pursuit of predictability through the development of consistent approaches to comparable situations. This works through permanency, where the adjudicators have an institutional interest in developing coherent approaches to the interpretative questions which they face.

Permanent bodies bring advantages in the way they operate in multiple and overlapping ways. Permanent bodies, by their very permanency, deliver predictability and consistency, and manage the fact that multiple disputes may arise, since they can elaborate and refine the understanding of a particular set of norms over time, as well as ensure their effective and consistent application. This is particularly relevant when the norms are relatively indeterminate.

States also have a longer-term approach. Their interests are split. They have an interest that public actions can be taken without being successfully challenged, and, at the same time, individual interests protected; and they know that the balance between these interests needs to be nurtured. In the EU, Member States know that their citizens (both individual and legal persons) benefit from the EU Treaties and secondary legislation, even if they accept that they will, from time to time, be found to have acted inconsistently with their obligations under the EU Treaties, or consider them to constrain possible public action. Permanent bodies with full-time adjudicators also free the adjudicators from the need to be remunerated from other sources, and typically provide some form of tenure. This prevents the adjudicators from coming under pressure to take short-term considerations into account.

It can be observed, both on the international and domestic level, that disputes in other regimes involving the characteristics enumerated above for the investment regime are normally settled before standing bodies. At the international level, the leading examples are the ECHR with the European Court of Human Rights (ECtHR), and the Inter-American Convention on Human Rights (IACHR) with the Inter-American Court of Human Rights (IACtHR). The Court of Justice of the European Union is another obvious example. The legal regimes applied by these courts are, in many aspects, very similar to the investment regime, since they involve balancing public action against international legal obligations.

At the domestic level, legal regimes with similar characteristics to the investment regime are also typically provided with permanent bodies for adjudication. It is a recognisable feature in domestic legal systems throughout the world that public or administrative law disputes are dealt with by standing permanent courts with independent judges, that are often positioned within a hierarchy that permits appellate review. This is not a new invention. Bentham, Hamilton and Voltaire argued that the move to a permanent, publicly funded judiciary was necessary.[48]

One striking feature of these permanent bodies is their independence. This is noted by McCorquodale as one of the features of the international rule of law. This entails independence from influences as to the outcome of disputes. As already noted, there are various questions which can be raised as to the current functioning of the investment system. Whereas the administration of justice is considered a public good in most domestic and international judicial systems, and, hence, financed from the public purse, the disputing parties themselves pay the remuneration of the adjudicators in the current ISDS system. This raises concerns about the risk that financial incentives may have an impact on the decision-making processes. In addition to the risks that flow from these elements, there is the risk that arbitrators have a vested interest, again, real or perceived, because they have a financial interest in either assuming jurisdiction, or failing to dismiss unmeritorious claims in order to generate more work. These elements further undermine the notion of neutrality. A system of remuneration on a case-by-case basis also creates risks of conflicts of interest that may result from other professional activities that, by necessity, are pursued in parallel by the adjudicators ('double hatting').

This amplifies a perception that the system lacks neutrality, or at least lacks the neutrality associated with other systems judging similar matters. Arbitrators often have the reputation of being either pro-investor or pro-state. This runs counter to the expectations of neutrality for persons undertaking the sensitive balancing act to be performed when looking at limitations to the regulatory autonomy of states. This risk to neutrality may be exacerbated by the background of many of the individuals. Relatively few have a background in public international law, or have experience in public law disputes in domestic law. Many have backgrounds in commercial arbitration, meaning that they have had little or no exposure to the complex issues which often arise when assessing the regulatory autonomy of states when their actions are being judged against public international law standards. Rather, they are more accustomed to the world of international contracts, where respect of the contract is obviously a key attribute.

[48] See 'OECD Economic considerations in dispute settlement: Adjudicator compensation systems' (DAF/INV/WD(2017)3), 10 February 2017.

It is submitted therefore that when the international investment system is conceived of as a network of largely identical public international law treaties, where adjudicators are undertaking a balancing between public interests and the protection of investment, it can be questioned whether the current system of arbitration for dispute settlement generates sufficient consistency and predictability on the one hand, and independence on the other, to ensure respect for the international rule of law.

15.5. ESTABLISHING THE INTERNATIONAL RULE OF LAW IN THE FIELD OF INVESTMENT

As will be evident from the preceding analysis, it is argued that the establishment of a permanent body to handle investment disputes would contribute to a more effective approach to respecting the international rule of law in the field of international investment protection. The EU embarked on a project to create a MIC in 2015.[49] The issue has been taken up in the UN system since 2017, when UNCITRAL established a mandate for one if its Working Groups to examine the need for reform of the dispute settlement system for investor-state disputes, and to develop reforms. The Working Group has concluded that there are problems with the current ISDS regime, and has concluded that reform is necessary. The Working Group is now working on developing reforms, which is the third stage of its mandate. Once it has completed its work, the outcomes will be adopted first by the UNCITRAL Commission, and thereafter by the United Nations General Assembly (UNGA).

The EU has argued that creating a permanent mechanism can address, in a systemic manner, the concerns which have been identified by UNCITRAL. These relate to the consistency and predictability of the system, the costs of the system, and the independence of the adjudicators. The EU has argued that these concerns are interrelated, and that addressing them in a piecemeal manner will not help leave certain concerns unaddressed.[50] It has also argued that the creation of a MIC, which could cover multiple investment treaties, and could establish a standing relationship with domestic courts could also address the issues of consistency and predictability. Responding to these key concerns can increase the degree of determinacy of the rules to the benefit of states' investors and other stakeholders.

The MIC project of the EU is not new or innovative as such. As already noted, the idea of a court to deal with investment claims was mooted in the 1950s and 1960s and reappeared in the academic literature in the 2000s.[51]

[49] Negotiating authorisation was granted and negotiating directives issued in 2018. See 12981/17ADD 1 of 1 March 2018.

[50] 'Possible reform of investor-State dispute settlement (ISDS)' (n 42).

[51] See Van Harten, *Investment Treaty Arbitration and Public Law* (n 39).

The international community has now a great deal of experience in the construction of international courts. Indeed, to the extent that the history of legal institutions is one of borrowing, adaptation and gradual development, there is plenty for the negotiators in the UNCITRAL Working Group to borrow and adapt. In particular, the last 20 to 30 years have brought a great deal of experience and of analysis of how best to ensure the effectiveness of international courts. Indeed, the UNCITRAL Working Group is accompanied by an Academic Forum, which has the objective to distil and disseminate the knowledge now available of how international courts function.

The EU has set out in a detailed concept paper how a permanent MIC could function.[52] The key features, as the EU envisages, would be as follows:

- a permanent court would be established, functioning at two levels, with a first instance, which would be the main locus for resolving a dispute, and an appeal function;
- adjudicators would be appointed on a full-time basis. They would not have any other activities outside of their appointment (other than with the permission of the President of the court – for example, academic activities);
- independence would be ensured through long, non-renewable terms;
- expertise would be required in public international law, and experience in judicial or dispute settlement functions sought;
- adjudicators would be appointed by a qualified majority of contracting parties, after being subject to a screening mechanism to check their suitability. The screening mechanism would be modelled on the Article 255 committee for appointments to the Court of Justice of the European Union and other international bodies, such as the International Criminal Court (ICC);[53]
- requirements would be built into the system to ensure that gender and regional diversity is respected in the appointment of adjudicators;
- there would be an opt-in mechanism to permit coverage of the large number of existing treaties. This technique implies that the existing treaties are amended through a single international instrument which will operate for a particular treaty between state A and B when both state A and B ratify the convention, and agree that it should cover their bilateral treaty. This is an established technique in international law which has been used for both the Multilateral Convention to Implement Tax Treaty Related Measures to Prevent Base Erosion and Profit Shifting, which deals

[52] See A/CN.9/WG.III/WP.159/Add.1 of 24 January 2019.

[53] See the submission by the EU to this effect, 'Annotated comments from the European Union and its Member States to the UNCITRAL Secretariat' on the issue of selection of 19 October 2020. See also the Decision of the Commission establishing a comparable mechanism for appointments by the European Union (Commission Decision of 16 December 2020 setting up a panel to assist the Commission in the selection of candidates to perform the duties of members of international investment courts and tribunals (C(2020)8905)).

with a similar situation with around 2,000 double taxation treaties, and the United Nations Convention on Transparency in Treaty-based Investor-State Arbitration (New York, 2014) (the Mauritius Convention on Transparency), which applies the same principle to the same category of investment treaties that would be covered by a multilateral investment court. This has the massive advantage of avoiding the problem of having to individually amend around 3,000 treaties;

- as more treaties are covered, then the permanent body would be more able to manage multiple proceedings; and
- enforcement of decisions would take place via a system providing for enforcement in the convention establishing the permanent MIC, and, as far as possible, via existing systems.

15.6. CONCLUSION

The notion of the international rule of law is distinct from the notion of domestic rule of law. However, it is increasingly possible to identify the main characteristics of the international rule of law. Examining the existing international investment regime against those characteristics suggests that improvements can be made. In particular, the decentralised and ad hoc nature of the dispute settlement system, designed for an international investment regime that turned out to be different from the one which has actually grown up, makes it incapable of generating the consistency and predictability which is a requirement for the international rule of law. Stakeholders, be they government, investors, or other actors, cannot reasonably predict how a particular case will be decided. Added to this are the concerns over independence generated by the perceptions created by the existing system, where the disputing parties appoint adjudicators for each case and where the fact that adjudicators by definition seek reappointment raises concerns as to the legitimacy of the system.

The EU has initiated a project to create a MIC. It precisely seeks to establish a permanent body, which would gradually create consistency and predictability in the system and which would establish independence of the adjudicators by employing them permanently. In so doing, it is argued, the EU would contribute to renovating the international rule of law in the field of investment protection.

Index

www.ingramcontent.com/pod-product-compliance
Ingram Content Group UK Ltd.
Pitfield, Milton Keynes, MK11 3LW, UK
UKHW021904150926
475560UK00004B/341

9 781509 965854